NEW BRUNSWICK
in
HISTORY

~ ~ ~

William H. Benedict

HERITAGE BOOKS
2011

HERITAGE BOOKS
AN IMPRINT OF HERITAGE BOOKS, INC.

Books, CDs, and more—Worldwide

For our listing of thousands of titles see our website
at
www.HeritageBooks.com

A Facsimile Reprint
Published 2011 by
HERITAGE BOOKS, INC.
Publishing Division
100 Railroad Ave. #104
Westminster, Maryland 21157

Copyright © 1925 William H. Benedict

— Publisher's Notice —
In reprints such as this, it is often not possible to remove blemishes from the original. We feel the contents of this book warrant its reissue despite these blemishes and hope you will agree and read it with pleasure.

International Standard Book Numbers
Paperbound: 978-0-7884-1709-2
Clothbound: 978-0-7884-8627-2

Introductory

IN SEARCHING FOR material relating to the early history of New Jersey and especially to the locality of New Brunswick, the brief mention of facts in any one work is apparent; yet very considerable data can be accumulated from various sources. To consolidate in this volume what has appeared in many books, newspapers and published documents, and to add thereto my own gleanings from unpublished records, is my main purpose in this publication.

While the printed authorities referred to are not given on each page, as that always detracts from the readability of a book, a list of works examined is given at the conclusion of the last Chapter, and this will enable anyone to go to an original source if desired. In addition much history is taken from deeds and public records, such as Road books, Court minutes, Wills, Marriage records, Chosen Freeholders' minutes, etc., both in the Middlesex county offices and in the records of Somerset; records of the Secretary of State's office in Trenton and the Proprietors' office in Perth Amboy; files of newspapers; minute books of Queens College, of the New Brunswick School Board, of the City Council, of the New Brunswick Toll Bridge Company, of Christ church and the Presbyterian church in New Brunswick; the Archives of the New Brunswick Historical Club and of the State Historical Society, and private manuscripts of friends, some of the latter going back four generations.

The frontispiece map, showing early land titles and occupancies (explanation of which appears at the end of the Appendix), is made from deeds and gives a fair idea of the changes from five or six original tracts to the divisions, large and small, as these tracts were cut up and sold. The Fortifications' map is also explained in the Appendix.

With these brief statements I offer the book to such as may be interested in its details.

WILLIAM H. BENEDICT.

New Brunswick, New Jersey, Nov. 1st, 1924.

Errata

Owner of this book should make following corrections:

Page 22, line 25. For "Greenfield's" read "Greenland's."
Page 30, line 17. For "Church St." read "Market."
Page 30, 7th line from bottom. For "Mile Run" read "Mine Run."
Page 43, line 9. For "Southland" read "Sourland."
Page 52, line 9. For "Philip French, 1st" read "Philip French, 3rd."
Page 62, line 9. For "1729" read "1778."
Page 164, 7th line from bottom. Omit word "by."
Page 178, line 20. Should read "and Isaac Lawrence. With three boats competition became."
Page 206, in line 14 from bottom, read: "The Bayard, the Colored School," etc.
Page 223, in 3rd line from bottom, for "Drs. Deare" read "Mrs. Deare."
Page 340, in line 20, for "in 1750" read "in 1720."

Contents

ILLUSTRATIONS

CHAPTER I

New Jersey Beginnings, Particularly in Middlesex and Somerset Counties—The Early Settlements—The Twenty-four Proprietors—Early Lines of New Brunswick—The City Streets Prior to 1800—The Early Courts—Some of the First Settlers............ 9

CHAPTER II

Early Cities and New Brunswick as an Example—The First Charter—Early Ordinances—The First Mayor and Family Connections—The Landing Accepting the Inevitable—The First City Freeholders—The Second Charter—Other Mayors...................... 26

CHAPTER III

The Successor to Mayor Ouke—Early Schools—The First Dutch Church—Hendrick Fisher and the Frelinghuysen Circuit—The Presbyterian Church—Church of England's Church—Lotteries for Churches—Members of the City Government—Various Vestrymen of the Episcopal Church—The Methodist and Baptist Congregations 40

CHAPTER IV

The Early Ferry—The Albany Street Bridge, 1790—Travel and Tavern Hand-in-Hand—Franklin's Trip to Philadelphia—Stages and Water Routes—Turnpikes and Steamboats—The Growth of Postal Facilities 55

CHAPTER V

The "Jersey Blues"—The "Sons of Liberty"—What Led to their Organization and Origin of the Name—Beginnings of the Revolution—Some New Brunswick Loyalists—Battle of Princeton and Subsequent Events 91

CONTENTS

CHAPTER VI

Capt. Adam Hyler and Other Noted Privateers—House and Park of Buccleuch—Its Successive Owners—New Brunswick as a College Town—Some Early College Commencements 127

CHAPTER VII

The Third Charter of the City—Various Events, 1784-1841—Value of Money—The Fourth Charter and Various Mayors—The Movement Culminating in the Court House of 1841 143

CHAPTER VIII

Council Minutes 1796 to 1832—Visit of General Lafayette in 1824—The Trenton and New Brunswick Turnpike—The "Hardenbergh Bank"—Colonial and Continental Money—National Bank of New Brunswick—Other Succeeding and Competing Banks—Steamboat Ventures—Various Organizations and Societies—Tribute to a Remarkable Woman, Mrs. James Neilson 156

CHAPTER IX

The Parker Family of Woodbridge, Perth Amboy and New Brunswick—James Parker, the Printer—The French Minister, de Neuville—The "Boom" in the Thirties—Early Finances of the City—Issuance of Paper Money—City Population in 1829—Town Meeting Minutes—The Increase of Taxes After the Legislature Began to Tax 186

CHAPTER X

School History in New Brunswick—Growth of the Buildings and Their Cost—The Public Library Facilities Beginning in 1796—Data Concerning Proposed Canals, and the One Finally Completed, Its Beginnings, Progress, Cost, Etc.—The Camden and Amboy Monopoly 203

CHAPTER XI

The Great Tornado of 1835—The Destruction It Caused in New Brunswick, Piscataway and a Few Nearby Places—Full Accounts from a Local Newspaper of the Time and from Professor Lewis C. Beck—Great Business Period of a New Sort—The Mayors from 1840 to the Civil War 223

CHAPTER XII

Some Prominent Visitors to and Citizens of New Brunswick in Early Days—Danker, the Earliest Traveler to New Brunswick—Dr. Henry Greenland—Cornelius Van Langvelt and His Son, Cornelius Longfield—Thomas Lawrence, the Baker—John Inian—The Two Tennent Ministers—Thomas Farmar, First Mayor—Capt. Christopher Billop—James Hude, Second Mayor—Governor Belcher—William Ouke, Third Mayor—The Bayard, Heermans and Kemble Families—Philip French—The Schuylers—Dr. John Cochrane, Etc. 241

CHAPTER XIII

Continuation as to Other Prominent Citizens of and Visitors to New Brunswick—Governor William Paterson—Col. Anthony Walton White—Mary Ellis—Gen. Charles Lee—Rev. Abraham Beach—Dr. Samuel Auchmuty—Bernardus Le Grange—Dr. William Farquhar—The Morris Family—General Washington's Visits—President John Adams—Baron de Neuville—Louis Andre Pichon—Gen. Lafayette's Visit—The Lyle Family—The Livingstons—Rev. John Croes—The Neilson Family 259

CHAPTER XIV

New Jersey As It Appeared to Early Observers and Travelers—Notices of and Extracts from Journals—Denton, Fox, Edmundson, Fenwick, Budd, Danker, Sluyter, Scot, Potter, Thomas, Brainerd, Hamilton, Kalm, Bernaby, Berkenhonts, Schoept 288

APPENDIX

I. Bibliography of Works, Etc., Consulted 307
II. The City Charters 313
III. Lotteries from 1723 to 1779 314
IV. First Revolutionary Movements 315
V. Prisoners' Bounds in New Brunswick, 1803 320
VI. Articles of Agreement with the Delaware and Raritan Canal Co., in 1832 321
VII. Some Expenses for Soldiers in the Civil War 324
VIII. Growth of School Buildings in New Brunswick and their Cost 325

CONTENTS

IX. Notes on Various Family Lines 332
    Bayard—Bennet—Billop—Ditmars—Drake — Farmar—French—Hardenbergh—Livingston — Low — Hude — Lawrence, Longfield, Inian, Greenland, Brinson and Cox—Livingston — Parker— Runyon — Schureman—Schuyler—Scott—Taylor—Van Wickle, Beach, Wells Voorhees, Williamson.
X. Map of Hessian Fortifications 354
XI. Index to Map of New Brunswick Lands, 1681-1800 354

INDEX

New Brunswick in History

CHAPTER I

New Jersey Beginnings, Particularly in Middlesex and Somerset Counties—The Early Settlements—The Twenty-Four Proprietors—Early Lines of New Brunswick—The City Streets Prior to 1800—The Early Courts—Some of the First Settlers.

THE history of every country begins with the coming of its inhabitants, or a collection of the traditions of the inhabitants already discovered there. In this sketch it is not proposed to take up the history of the native Indians, but to begin with the first efforts of the white man to make a settlement. The settlements both to the north and also to the south of this State were made much earlier. The first attempt in New Jersey came under the Dutch. Augustine Hermans, in 1651. purchased of the Indian sachems a tract of land bounded roughly by the Kills on the easterly side, the Raritan on the southerly, the Passaic on the northerly. It was about seventeen miles in width and extended up into the country about twice as far (description quite indefinite). Hermans did not succeed in peopling his tract. Certain English Long Islanders had been in negotiation with the Dutch Governor at New York with a view to establish a colony in New Jersey, but the terms were not acceptable to the Long Islanders, the right to self-government being the question they could not agree upon. When the Dutch surrendered to Governor Nicoll, Monday, August 29, 1664, the Long Islanders at once renewed their efforts and petitioned that Governor, September 29, 1664, and, obtaining his sanction, they purchased of the Indian sachems, October 28, 1664, the same tract that they had previously sold to Hermans, he having taken no steps to occupy his purchase and the Dutch government having been superceded by the English. The Indians, thrifty bodies, considered it a good thing to again sell this tract. This purchase Governor Nicoll confirmed December 1, 1664, and a settlement was made on Elizabethtown Point. That the Indians were not so stupid and unbusiness-like as we have been led to suppose was shown when the purchasers attempted to fix their westerly boundary, which was assumed to extend to the Raritan; this the Indians stoutly disputed, and a second purchase was necessary before they could get the boundaries they desired —the Raritan up to Bound Brook as the westerly boundary.

While Governor Nicoll, representing the Crown, was confirming land to settlers on the spot, King Charles II, the owner by virtue of discovery and conquest, was disposing of it by the wholesale on the other side of the ocean by making a present of the whole of New Jersey to the Duke of York, who, in turn, as a method of settling his debts, divided it between his friends, Lords Berkeley and Carteret; Berkeley getting the southwesterly half on the Delaware, and Carteret getting the northeasterly half on the Hudson. It was many years before the dividing line was finally agreed upon and established. Sir George Carteret sent his kinsman, Philip Carteret, to his new possessions as Governor, while Berkeley was represented by Governor Coxe. Since no determination of boundaries between New York and New Jersey, or between East and West Jersey, had yet been made, a conflict of authority began at once, and the slow communication between the mother country and the Colony resulted in transactions that conflicted, going on at the same time, Gov. Nicoll assuming to govern the whole broad territory, with hazy notions of limits. This was not conducive to the prosperity of the Colony, yet, in spite of it all, the growth was very considerable. Governor Philip Carteret at first recognized the rights confirmed by Governor Nicoll to the Elizabethtown Point Associates, to the extent of joining with their representatives, Luke Watson and John Ogden, in making a sale of the southern portion of their purchase to Joshua Pierce and associates, December 11, 1666. This sale afterwards became the settlements of Woodbridge, Perth Amboy and Piscataway. The associates mentioned were: John Pike, John Bishop, Henry Jacques, Hugh Marsh, Stephen Kent, Robert Dennis and John Smith. The date, Dec. 3rd, 1667, is also given; this being probably the date of the arrival of the forty families who came to take possession of this purchase. The date of the Woodbridge charter is given as June 1, 1669, and was for six miles square. In the meantime a second subdivision was made and Piscataway was set off by sale to Daniel Pierce and associates, the date being Dec. 18, 1667, and the associates named were: John Martin, Charles Gilman, Hugh Dunn, Hopewell Dunn, Robert Dennis, John Smith, John Gillman, Benjamin Hull. (John Smith and Robert Dennis are mentioned and were interested in both purchases).

The 250th Anniversary of the settlement of Elizabeth was celebrated Oct. 26th, 1914. About all that we positively know, beyond the dates of the petition, Sept. 26, 1664, and the purchase, Oct. 28, 1664, and the confirmation Dec. 1, 1664, is from the Elizabethtown Bill in Chancery, (probably one of the most famous lawsuits in this country), which says: "When Governor Philip Carteret arrived there on his own ship 'Philip,' Aug., 1665, there were but four houses there, and if the place had a name or not we do not know." Governor Carteret proceeded to name it "Elizabeth" after Sir George Carteret's wife. The first settlement was on the Point on the north side of the mouth of the Elizabeth river.

Newark was settled by thirty families in 1666. While the settlement of this large tract was going on under the rights confirmed by Gov. Nicoll of New York, Governor Philip Carteret began to contest these rights in every way possible, as he saw very soon that the rights obtained from Gov. Nicoll would make a large hole in his territory. John Reid came from London to map the territory and his map, dated 1684 to 1686, shows the pretended bounds of Elizabethtown; pretended bounds of Woodbridge; pretended bounds of Piscataway, with other interesting localities.

Sir George Carteret realized little from his grant before his death, making few sales. Lady Elizabeth Carteret, his executrix, made some sales and then, in 1682, disposed of the entire tract for £3,400 to Twelve Proprietors—William Penn, William West, Thomas Rudyard, Samuel Groom, Thomas Hart, Richard Mew, Thomas Wilcox, Ambrose Riggs, John Haywood, Hugh Hartshorn, Clement Plumstead and Thomas

Cooper. These twelve associated with themselves an additional twelve—Robert Barclay, Edward Billing, Robert Turner, James Braine, Arent Sonmans, William Gibson, Gawen Lawrie, Thomas Barker, Thomas Warne, James (Earl of Perth), Robert Gordon, and John Drummond, who were afterwards known as the Twenty-four Proprietors. When they came into possession of their purchase they were alarmed and chagrined to find so large a portion already claimed by parties under Dutch rights, under grants by Governor Nicoll, under sales by Sir George Carteret, and under sales by Lady Elizabeth, the executor. A contest at once began, disputing all claims, or, at least, restricting them to land actually in occupation. This contest was so bitter and so long fought that in 1744 the defendants petitioned the King, George II, for relief, saying they were being ruined by litigation and persecution on the part of the Proprietors. We can only touch very briefly on this quarrel.

In addition to the Elizabethtown grant there was a tract on the south and west side of the Raritan extending from the mouth of South river to the mouth of Bound Brook (called Sacunk by the Indians), and extending back about two miles; that was also covered by deeds from Sir George and Lady Elizabeth, before the sale to the Proprietors. Thomas Lawrence first purchased 1,300 acres of good land exclusive of "barrens" (barrens was the term used to designate poor, sandy lands along the ocean, or land that required to be drained), extending from the mouth of South river to a north and south line, now part of Clifton Ave., at the end of George St., in New Brunswick. Cornelius Longfield, an Indian trader and Lawrence's step-son, bought from the Lawrence tract to a line now the south side of Livingston Ave. (Our new High School is on Longfield's tract). Next, John Inian and associates purchased twelve lots, each lot one-half mile front and two miles deep, and known as the Inian lots. John Inian had the first two next to Longfield. Richard Jones, George Foreman, Joseph Snelling, Andrew Gibb, Andrew Bowne, Gresham Bowne, Jeremiah Tothill, Joseph Benbridge, Thomas Mathers and Edward Gibbon make the other ten of the twelve lot owners. These lots were called "Ahandewamock" by the Indians, and on Inian's lots there was (the tradition is) an Indian burying-ground. The Proprietors divided the land as to quality into Good Rights, Pine Rights and Barrens. The struggle between the Proprietors, mostly non-resident landowners, and the actual settlers, who claimed by grant, original purchase, Indian purchase, subsequent re-purchase or no purchase, and who had hewed for themselves a home out of the virgin forest, was long and bitter, and resulted as elsewhere in two parties; that of the Crown, and rights obtained from the Crown; and that of the Commons, who steadily, uniformly and persistently opposed those rights.

The first dividend declared by the Proprietors was made Nov. 13, 1684, of 10,000 acres each; and the map made by John Reid, already referred to, shows some of these allotments. There was an early traffic in proprieties, the 24 original shares being cut up into fractions and sold. Any fraction less than one-quarter had no vote in the management, but got its proportionate share in the dividends. These dividends were in some cases located on lands already claimed, and from the overlapping of the claims the troubles began. This fight, lasting for sixty years, we cannot enter into, but right seems generally to have prevailed. When settlers had genuine prior rights they were eventually sustained, and, when not genuine, the Proprietors prevailed. One great difficulty with the Proprietors was that they did not trust each other, and for this they had good reason. The first resolution put upon their minute book was directed against one of their own number. Arent Sonmans, a wealthy Hollander, with an English wife, Frances Hancock, seemed able to command large sums of money, and immediately proceeded to buy up the shares of other Proprietors He bought Edward Billings' 24th, Thomas Hart's 24th, David Barclay's 24th, ¼ of Robert Barclay's 24th, Hugh Hartshorne's 24th, Gawen Lawrie's 24th—altogether 5 and ¼ proprieties in addition to his own; and he was on a journey from London to Scotland, where a number of the Proprietors lived, probably for the purpose of picking up some more shares, when he was killed by a highwayman. The Proprietors, for the purpose of defeating Sonmans' attempt to gain control, passed a resolution that each ¼ of a 24th should have one vote—four votes to a 24th—and that no one should vote more than 2/24ths, as owner, though an additional 24th could be put in the name of a trustee for the benefit of their children, and could be voted by proxy. This resolution seems to have been a dead letter, as Peter Sonmans, Arent's son, who came over to look after the interests of his father's estate, returned to England, obtained power of attorney from eight of the twenty-four Proprietors and, with the 5 and ¼ (having sold one) that he controlled of the estate, had 13 and ¼ of the twenty-four Proprieties, and therefore a majority. The share sold was to William Dockwra, who kept the seal and the records of the corporation in London. He paid £520 for it. He was under no bonds, and he and Sonman seem to have managed the corporation about as they liked. Peter Sonmans' right to represent the absent Proprietors was recognized by Lord Cornbury, then Governor, and from 1702 till 1727 there was no regular meeting of the Proprietors. George Willocks complained that he had to bribe Dockwra to get his business accomplished. He made such grave charges that Dockwra was removed.

The rules governing dividends provided that lots should not be laid out in less than 2,100 acres, or not more than 21,000 acres, excepting in towns, where 1/7 was reserved for the Proprietors and the remainder divided to the actual settlers. Feb. 21, 1698, the second dividend of 5,000 acres is noted, and Dec. 2, 1702, an addition to the second dividend of 2,500 acres was made.

Sonmans was undoubtedly the most conspicuous of all of the Proprietors. His wife was Sarah Nevill, a sister of Samuel Nevill and John Nevill. His sister, Rachel, married John Ormiston, and another sister, Johanna, married Joseph Wright. Peter Sonmans died March 29, 1734, aged sixty-seven, and left a daughter, Bathsheba, who married George Glentworth. Peter left his estate to his wife, and she to her brother, Samuel Nevill, who admitted "one Peter Sonmans" to an equal share with him. This Peter Sonmans, presumably Peter Sonmans' son, was a practicing physician in Philadelphia.

In 1740 the Proprietors made another dividend of 19,500 acres of Good Rights, 4,000 acres of Pine Rights and 1,200 acres of barrens. These dividends aggregated 1,000,000 acres of land.

This disposition of land, distributed through dividends and purchases, resulted in a general settling up of the country and consequently in the formation of counties, townships and towns, as well as judicial and military divisions. The first centers of settlement we know were Elizabethtown (1664), Woodbridge (1666), Newark (1666), Piscataway (1667)—all before the sale to the Proprietors. Amboy was a venture of the Proprietors and dates from 1686. Just the date when these settlements were given charters is uncertain. Woodbridge charter was given in 1669, June 1. In 1682 an Act was passed setting off the counties of Bergen, Middlesex, Essex and Monmouth; the Townships of Woodbridge and Piscataway are mentioned that year; and Piscataway *town* is mentioned in 1683. In 1692 (Oct. 4) the inhabitants at county meetings were authorized to fix township lines. That this Act did not produce the desired results is evident, as in 1693 the following townships were set off, and defined by an Act: In Bergen County, two townships—Hackensack and Bergen; in Essex, four townships—Acquickanick, New Barbadoes, Newark and Elizabeth; in Monmouth, three townships—Middletown, Shrewsbury and Freehold; in Middlesex, three townships—Woodbridge, Piscataway and PerthAmboy, which then included South Amboy; and in Somerset (which had been made a county out of Middlesex in 1688), the township of Somerset. Piscataway was originally an immense tract, taking in all of Middlesex across the Raritan as well as Piscataway proper on the east side, and for some time a large part of Somerset was originally Piscataway, as far northwest as Bound Brook certainly. Somerset did not attain its present dimensions till 1709, when it took a large slice out of Piscataway and Middlesex Its lines were changed again in 1713, 1741, 1776, 1790 and 1850—seven changes in all.[1]

---

[1]Somerset County was made out of Middlesex with three boundaries, North, East and South. The last began at the mouth of a brook, 70 chains South of the mouth of Bound Brook, and remained so from 1688 to 1709-'10, twenty-one years.

Samuel Moor was the first Sheriff of Middlesex, and John Inians was the Treasurer of Somerset in 1688. In 1683 the population of Woodbridge was given as 600, and Piscataway 400 in the same year.

A description of Piscataway in two pieces is as follows: the first piece, east of the Raritan and extending from Woodbridge to Cedar brook, along Cedar brook to Bound Brook, along Bound Brook to Raritan, and down Raritan to Woodbridge and the beginning. The second was all the land from South river to Somerset county and from Raritan to the Partition Line, or the line between East and West Jersey, just the other side of Princeton. Without an understanding of the boundaries of Piscataway many early deeds and early references would be very confusing. The date of the formation of the Township of New Brunswick is not certain.

Piscataway had a military organization as early as 1675,

The South line was changed to the mouth of Lawrence's Brook; remained so from 1709-'10 till 1713-'14—four years.

The South line was again changed to Inians' ferry, thence along the road by Jedediah Higgins to East and West Jersey line (his house was 17 chains east of Kingston), and remained so 1713-'14 till 1741—twenty-seven years. Then was along the old road, apparently a confirmation of the preceding, 1741 till 1766—twenty-five years. The line of the "old road" is very dubious, by reason of persons altering the road. At this period the Freeholders and Justices were:

	Freeholders	Justices
John Coombs	Geo. Wetherill	James Neilson
Joseph Rae, Jr.	William Ouke	John Barclay
John Schenck	Hendrick van Deursen	Theo. Walker
Jeremiah Field	John Reed	N. Everson
Micajah Dunn	James Olden	

This line was run June 24, 1765, and the map and field notes were recorded May 10, 1766, in Book A, "Records of Deeds, Conveyances and Roads of Middlesex and Somerset Counties," by John Smyth, Clerk. This line did not follow the road strictly, but ran north of all the houses and stables on Albany St., and remained so, 1766 till 1790 —twenty-four years.

Line was then changed to follow the middle of road, and to the line of Hunterdon Co., 1790 till 1850—sixty years.

Line in New Brunswick was next moved to Mile Run. Before 1850 conveyances north of French or Albany streets were recorded in Somerville; after that at New Brunswick.

Bridgewater Township in Somerset county created in 1794, began at the mouth of Bound Brook, ran along same to Green Brook, to Second Mountain, along the North Branch of the Raritan and back to the beginning.

when Francis Drake was elected its first Captain, but declined, and Henry Greenland was elected in his place, with Samuel Doughtie, Lieutenant, and John Martin, Ensign. But in 1721, July 4, a commission was issued to Enoch Vreeland as Captain, Conrad Barcalow as Lieutenant, and Dollius "Heggemin" [Hegemen] as Ensign, of a Company of Militia to form part of Col. John Parker's Regiment, and it was to be raised "within the following bounds;" and these bounds are the first mention we find of the lines of New Brunswick Township, or town. While the name of the Township, or town, is not mentioned, the lines are as follows: Beginning at Inion's [Inians] ferry on the south side of the road [the north side of the road being Somerset Co.]; thence down Raritan river to Lawrence brook; thence up said brook to a place called the windfalls; thence directly to a brook called Heathcoat's brook; thence down said brook to the Millstone river, and along the river to the road that divides the county of Middlesex from Somerset; thence along said road to the place where it began, being on the west side of Raritan. These lines are approximately those given to the city of New Brunswick in its charter of 1730; the charter going down to South river and then West.

In 1724 we find the first use of the name "Brunswick" in this locality. In that year the sloop "Brunswick" enters inwards at Amboy from Barbadoes, Gibb, Master. This sloop we have reason to believe was on its return to its home-port, Brunswick, where Capt. Richard Gibb lived and owned a dock. In 1716 we find mention of a road through this military designation on which four houses are mentioned by the owners' names, all located where is now New Brunswick City, viz., John Inians', Benjamin Pridmore's, Leandert Smock's and Cornelius Longfield's. In 1723 three additional roads or streets are mentioned; one Burnet; one a short alley to the river from Burnet, and one either Peace or Church. It may be as well here to give dates as to some of the early streets prior to 1800:

Apr. 12, 1716. The post road to Cranberry brook, referred to in Book I, Court Records, 1686. John Inians opened it up and improved the Indian trails. He was the first road-builder in Middlesex county, and his roadmaking was inspected and approved.

1716. Mention of road two rods wide, beginning over against John Inian's house; thence southerly over the brook where Neversink road formerly (for above 40 years) ran by Benjamin Pridmore's, within 2 or 3 rods of Leandert Smock's, and through Cornelius Longfield to his mill. (Starts along Burnet from the ferry).

1723. Beginning at George's road 3 chains from the river; thence to the north-east corner of Jacob Oakey's house, along Lawrence Williamson's house, to Freeland's north-west corner; thence along all the houses to the front of Court Van "Vores" and there to end. Road 1½ rods wide. (From Albany through Little Burnet and from Burnet to New, or Lyle's brook).

1723. Another street along Lawrence Williamson's house to low water, 1 rod wide; half the land Williamson's and half John Van ——'s (?). From Burnet to river alongside Paterson block. (Ross coal road is the remains of it).

1723. Another, beginning at Samuel C. Mulford's, along Deldine's and Abram LeForge's into the Broad street leading to Court Van Voorhees—1 rod wide. (This looks like Peace from the foot of Church into Burnet, as Samuel Mulford's was at the foot of Church).

1726. From Court Van Voorhees along William Cox's east side, and by Mrs. Peacock's (supposed to be the same as Pridmore's in 1716) west side, 2 rods distant to John Voorhees' brook (College Farm brook) thence to Capt. Vreeland's (Smock's in 1716) mill dam, and to Longfield's mills.

1733. From Dirck Van Arsdalen's to the Burlington road. (New St.)

1734. From house of Abram Heyer, lately Samuel Mulford's, and along the east side of John Van Orden to main road (Church street), and from ferry to Delaware (French St.)—2 rods wide.

1741. Beginning near the house of Nicholas Van Dyck; thence along Van Cleave's and Garret DeGraw's, and from thence to French St.; called Peace St. (See Minutes Council, May 20, 1741).

1775. Dutch Church street; 87°W. 8 ch., 76 links to Queen, 56 links wide.

1785. Drift, Queen, George, Prince, Barrack, Church, Church Alley, Richmond (formerly Court), all continued as streets in 1785.

1792. White St. (heretofore called Church St., now White).

In 1724-'5 the first record of the name, New Brunswick, is found. Then Simon Brinly, of Piscataway, bequeaths "my plantation lying in *New Brunswick.*" (March 22, 1724-'5; see Book A, folio 348, of Deeds, Secretary of State's office, Trenton). Enoch Vreeland, as Captain of the military company "of the town of New Brunswick" deeds land to David Drake, situate, lying and being in the town "of New Brunswick aforesaid." (See Book K. (large) 256, of Deeds, Trenton). In 1726 the surveyors of Piscataway and New Brunswick lay out a road, and again in 1726 the township of New Brunswick is referred to without connection with Piscataway, and now the use of the name begins to multiply. I believe the military division made in 1721 omitted to mention the name. The City Charter of 1730 was of sufficient interest to reproduce, and it has been published by Dr. Austin Scott of New Brunswick.

Settling any new country, transfer of houses and lands, building of roads, military appointments as well as civil, must be by authority, and this was first in the Governor. Gov. Philip Carteret and his Council met first at Elizabeth in 1668-1675, his home town, and, in 1676, the second Wednesday in November was appointed New Jersey's first Thanksgiving Day. Three meetings of the Governor and Council, called Assemblies, were held next in Woodbridge in 1676, in Elizabeth 1677, in Middletown 1679, in New Piscataqua 1679, again in Elizabeth 1681, in "Amboy Perth" 1686, in Perth Amboy 1688, and, after 1688, continuously at Amboy. We observe, therefore, that Amboy was of importance enough for the Governor and Council to meet there in 1686, though it is to be recalled that it was not until 1693 that Amboy was officially recognized as a township.

In early history dates are usually confirmatory of something that may have been recognized for some years before, as existing. The Assemblies at an early date created Courts. In 1670 we find mention of the Court of Woodbridge and Bergen; in 1673 of a Court of Oyer and Terminer in Woodbridge; in 1674 of a General Court, the gentlemen of the Council being the magistracy. There was one County Court for Woodbridge and Piscataway; one County Court for Bergen; one for two towns of Nevesink; one for Elizabeth and Newark—four County Courts in all, while a Provincial Court was to be held at Woodbridge, a Monthly Court in Piscataway, a Court of Small Causes in Piscataway (probably the same as the Monthly Court). At this latter Court Henry Greenland, I. Gillman and E. Slaughter were overseers. There was also a Court of Chancery and one of Common Rights. Of a Court of 1683 there is a book of interesting minutes preserved, Daniel Dennis being Judge. In 1694 a semi-annual Court for Middlesex and Somerset was to be held at Amboy in March, at Piscataway in September, at Woodbridge in March, and at Amboy in September, and so on a continuous round. In 1699 the Proprietors attempted to establish Courts in Piscataway, Newark and Elizabeth; this resulted in riots and the inhabitants forcibly ejected the Proprietor's appointees, as the Court minutes of 1699 show. In 1673 Francis Drake[2] was licensed to keep an inn or tavern, and in 1685 he was constable. In 1686 George Drake, a brother, was Deputy to the Assembly from Piscataway, and again in 1692. In 1673, while the Dutch were in power, 43 Freeholders of Piscataway took the Dutch oath. In 1693 John Inians was member of Council and John Drake represented Piscataway. In 1693 an Act was passed providing for schools.

In 1695 Cornelius Longfield and Jedediah Higgins were Deputies for Piscataway; the latter lived half-way between the Ferry and Princeton, and the former at the Ferry; neither in Piscataway village. In 1700 the Court of Middlesex and Piscataway is referred to. In 1695-1698 John Inians was in Hamilton's Council, and again in Council in 1703. In 1708 we find this comment: If "vacancies in the Council" could be "filled up with honest, well-meaning men, such as . . . Cornelius

---

[2]See Appendix as to Drakes.

Longfield," etc. In 1710 we find Longfield in Gov. Hunter's Council. In 1713 there was a protest against the election of Thomas Farmar and Adam Hude. These names, above referred to, were all historical figures. The Drakes were preachers as well as civil office-holders. John Inian was progressive and public spirited; he established the ferry at New Brunswick; he opened the first roads of record to the Delaware.[3] He was a large landowner and he lived in New Brunswick. His home stood either where the Parkway Hotel is, or very close to it, as it was opposite the end of Little Burnet St. in 1716. Longfield and his step-father, Lawrence (for whom Lawrence Brook was named), owned all the way from South River to Livingston Ave. in New Brunswick, and Longfield himself lived on Cromelin creek at the end of what is known as Teunison's Lane. He was an Indian trader, a great friend of John and Mary Inians, and a son-in-law of Henry Greenland, who lived where Johnson's place, called "Bellevue," is now located.

Henry Greenland, the first innkeeper at the Ferry; Captain of the Piscataway military company; a doctor, and a man of note, though of a very turbulent disposition, and Inians and Longfield, were without doubt the first three settlers on the Raritan at the Ferry and should be honored as our first settlers.

In the charter of New Brunswick (1730) we find provision for a Mayor's and Recorder's Court of General Quarter Sessions of the Peace on the first Monday in November, February, May and August, with authority to build a court house, and it was built on the corner of Burnet and Court Streets, now Richmond St. In 1738 an Act was passed to rebuild the court house and jail in Somerset county. In 1710 we find at the Court

---

[3]See Book I, Court Minutes and Early Records. In 1686 the Inian's road, between his house and Claswick's Bridge, then the best road to Burlington, was approved by the highway commissioners, as was the road made by him to Piscataway. In 1723 this road was referred to as "George's Road." When or how it got the name, like Burnet St. in New Brunswick, has not yet been determined, though both still retain these names. The first care of these roads was by the innkeepers. This was unsatisfactory, and a tax of £10 was laid annually for the care of the Burlington and Inians ferry road, and George Drake was made responsible for its care.

at Amboy, Peter Sonmans, Judge, and Cornelius Longfield and John Tunnison Assistants; and in 1711, in the same Court, Thomas Farmar and Adam Hude.

These brief notes give a fair idea of the early Assemblies and Courts, and some of their members.[4]

Having followed the Courts in New Jersey as a whole, let us now take up more particularly details relating to our city and county. As our county and Piscataway township reached out west to the division line between East and West Jersey, and as this line was long in dispute, much uncertainty in early land titles resulted, but, as the south side of the Raritan was bought very early and held by a few men, after the Proprietors failed in an effort to dispossess Longfield and the owners of the Inians' lots, the title along the south side of the Raritan was clearly good, including deeds from the Indians, and from Sir George Carteret, and from Lady Elizabeth Carteret, before the sales made to the Proprietors. It never belonged to the Proprietors and has the distinction of antedating the Proprietors, who are usually looked to as the origin of all land titles in New Jersey.

Thomas Lawrence, whose purchase in 1678 we have already referred to, does not appear as a settler. His step-son, Cornelius Longfield, seems to have disposed of all his stepfather's land as well as his own, and, having married Dr. Henry Greenland's daughter Mary, inheriting some of Greenfield's lands on the opposite side of the river, and being executor for John Inians' wife Mary, who inherited from her husband (they had no children), he disposed of much of the land along this side of the Raritan. To follow all of the steps in the land ownership would become tedious, but a few of the principal ones may be mentioned, as follows:

Longfield sold a farm on the south side of Livingston Ave., which, after one or two transfers, was bought by Enoch Vrieland. Vrieland sold a number of lots on the river end of this

---

[4]The first Court House built in Somerset was in 1716, at Six-Mile Run, now Franklin Park, which was burned in 1737 and rebuilt at Hillsboro, now Millstone. This again was burned by Simcoe, Oct. 25, 1779 and rebuilt at Raritan, now Somerville, 1784.

farm, and then sold the remainder of the farm to John Van Nuys. This farm bounds on Livingston Ave. on one side, and on Remsen Ave. on the other. The next farm from Remsen Ave. to Commercial Ave. went to his son-in-law, William Cox. The third farm from Commercial Ave. to Nichol Ave. was bought by John Voorhees, as was also the next, from Nichol Ave. to Clifton Ave., at the end of George; Clifton Ave. being one of those peculiar streets which runs in nearly every direction, as it begins in Burnet St. and ends in Burnet St., after making a long detour around the head of several ravines or gullies; and a portion of it, viz., from Mr. James Neilson's east carriage drive entrance to a lane on the east of Mr. Phelp's place, is the same as the old Minnisink Indian path, which came from Minnisink Island in the Delaware to the river at New Brunswick, crossing at the ford, or falls, and continuing to the Highlands of Navesink. Much of this old highway of the Indians is still in use. I have ridden over a portion of it in Middletown, and both the towns of Middletown and Shrewsbury were on this path.

Following now Longfield's division of lands: Next to John Voorhees he opened a lane, which we call Ryder's Lane, and on this lane he sold lots on both sides as well as both sides of Clifton Ave. to James Neilson's old entrance already referred to, and on one side, the east, to the river. Next to these lots he sold Anthony White the Cold Spring farm of 300 acres, and beyond that came the Mary Nevill, or the Evans' place, and two or three farms on Teunison's, or Wilcox's lane, running from Weston's Mills pond down through the point of land made by the river and Cromelins' creek (which, by the way, is the portion of Lawrence's brook below the dam, getting its name from the purchaser of a farm along the creek side of the land). It was at the extreme, or river, end of this lane that Longfield lived, with a mill at Weston's pond.

The first historian that we are indebted to for mention of this locality was Danker, who crossed New Jersey to the Delaware in 1679; his guide was a son of the Hermans who bought of the Indians in 1651, and he stayed over night with Longfield at the mouth of Lawrence's brook, called by the Indians Piscopeek creek. It would be impossible to locate Longfield by Danker's description as he has his water courses badly mixed up in his "Journal," but from other information combined with his we can follow him very well. He stayed with Henry Greenland going, and with Longfield coming back, taking two different routes from a point now near Princeton.

The next traveler through this section was a Capt. Nicholas, who, in 1680, is quoted in "Scot's Model" (a treatise for immigrants). Nicholas says there are few plantations on the south side of the Raritan, but mentions Thomas Lawrence, a baker of New York and his wife's son, i. e., Cornelius Longfield, and also locates the falls as two miles above Longfield's, which would bring it about where the preponderance of evidence places it, viz., between Henry Greenland's, or Johnson's pond outlet on the east side, and Cannon's Point, where the old rubber factory stood on the west; or, roughly just about the foot of Hamilton St. Below the falls, or ford, John Inians established his ferry which crossed from a little above Raritan Ave. in Highland Park to the foot of Albany St., in New Brunswick. This ferry, established in 1686, and granted for life in 1697, was operated continuously till the bridge was built in 1791-'3. The falls, or ford, was made use of by the Indians, and, in addition to the Minnisink path already described, there was also another path that crossed here leading from New York via Elizabethport and Piscataway, and, after crossing here, proceeded to the falls of the Delaware at what is now Trenton; crossing there it continued to Philadelphia, and was a more important path to the white man than the other, as it connected New York and Philadelphia and the New England and Southern Colonies.

John Inians first undertook to open and improve this path for regular travel and also improved a path known as the lower road, and later as George's road, which went to the Delaware at Burlington. It was on these two paths that New Brunswick began to build its first houses and the town.

Kalm, a Swedish traveler, in 1748, describes the city as of one street lengthwise (the Minnisink path) and one street crosswise (the path to the Delaware). The first was called

Burnet, and the second French St. While Enoch Vreeland and John Van Nuys were selling lots on Burnet St. and later cutting up the land immediately south of Livingston Ave., or Inians' Line as it was then known, Philip French acquired much of Inians' two lots. A very interesting book of leases, still preserved, shows how the land on French, Albany, Drift, Water, Peace and Church streets was disposed of by him. The growth of the city for the first 100 years was mainly on Longfield's and Inians' adjoining lots, while the Dutch and Presbyterian churches and the Court House and market were located on the Vreeland-Van Nuys and William Cox tracts, and a two-acre burying-ground was donated by Van Nuys. French gave the Church of England and the Dutch handsome church sites with ample graveyards, and also a site for the Colonial Barracks, which were built in New Brunswick under an Act passed Apr. 17, 1758. On June 18, 1773, the latter was made the legal Court House and jail for Middlesex county.

CHAPTER II

Early Cities and New Brunswick as an Example—The First Charter—
Early Ordinances—The First Mayor and Family Connections—The
Landing Accepting the Inevitable—The First City Freeholders—
The Second Charter—Other Mayors.

NEWARK, Elizabeth, Woodbridge, Piscataway and New Brunswick were original centres of settlement which grew with the surrounding country, prospered as it prospered. But Amboy was a town laid out by the Proprietors in which they retained an interest, and that was promoted and pushed for the profits of its owners; hence it is not strange that it was first to get a charter. Elizabeth dates from 1664, Newark 1666, Piscataway 1667, Woodbridge 1669, while the scheme to lay out Amboy is dated July 9, 1680, and in 1683 it was yet to be built. On Aug. 4, 1718, it got its charter. New Brunswick's charter is dated Dec. 30, 1730; Burlington's, May 7, 1773; Elizabeth's, Feb. 8, 1739-'40; Trenton's, Sept. 6, 1746; Newark, settled in May, 1666, by Robert Treat and 30 families and called Milford, (the 17th was accepted as Founders Day at the 250th celebration in 1916), the name changed to Newark two years later, had a charter of the township granted to ten trustees by Queen Anne, Apr. 12, 1714, and got its city charter in 1736. Dr. Austin Scott says that Middlesex was the only county in America then with two cities. As showing the relative importance of these early cities, Gov. Robert Hunter wrote James Alexander in 1730 of his desire to purchase 600 or 700 acres in New Brunswick, if the land could be bought reasonably. Alexander replied that lots in New Brunswick were nearly as high as a lot in the heart of New York. Either Alexander was misinformed, or lots in New York were not dear, as Enoch Vreeland sold John Van Nuys 100 acres, now within the city limits of New Brunswick, for £800 in 1727, or £8 per acre; and, in 1750, 321 acres in the city limits were valued, in adjusting an estate, at £1,800, including farm buildings and house; say £5.12 per acre. As city lot prices these certainly were not high.

The charter of New Brunswick sets forth "that the said town is standing near the head of a fine navigable river, being the most convenient place for shipping off the produce of a large and plentiful country lying on the back thereof. Is a place of very considerable trade and commerce and confirmed to these petitioners by name—Thomas Farmar, Jacob Oake, James Hude, Dolin Hagerman, Lawrence Williamson, Duncan Hutchinson, Derrick Schuyler, William Oaky, Paul Miller, William Williamson, Abraham Bennet, Cort Voorhees, James Neilson, John Balding and the rest of the Freeholders and Inhabitants of said New Brunswick and land adjoining," with boundaries beginning at the boundary line of Perth Amboy, at the mouth of South river, thence via the Post Road from Perth Amboy to Burlington, to the Millstone river, down the same to the county (line) road, from Trenton to Inians' ferry, along this road to the Mile Run, down it to its mouth, crossing the river to high water mark, and down the river to bounds of Perth Amboy, and along same to beginning. The city officers were to be a Mayor, Recorder and six Aldermen, a Town Clerk, six assistants, a Sheriff, a Chamberlain, or Treasurer, a Coroner, a Marshall, or Serjeant-at-Mace, three Constables, and two Overseers of the Poor.

The city was to have seals engraven, on the dexter with a sheaf of wheat and a pair of balances, or scales, weighing a barrel of flour, and over it the words "Alma sed Aequa;" and on the sinister with a boat riding at anchor in a river before a town, and under it "Læta Revertor." The first officers (appointed by the charter) were: Thomas Farmar, Mayor and Clerk of the market, to remain and continue until another fit person be assigned, nominated, appointed and sworn into said offices; James Hude, Recorder; William Cox, Jacob Oakey (Ouke—three spellings in the copy of the charter—Oake, Oaky and Oakey— and neither correct), Dally [Dollius] Hageman, William Cheesman, Josiah Davison and Lawrence Williamson as the six Aldermen; James Neilson, Clerk; Evan Drummond, Sheriff and Water Bailiff; John Thomson, Cort Voorhees, Minne Voorhees, Henry Longfield, William Williamson, and John Van Dyck, Assistants; Alexander Moore, Chamberlain or Treasurer; Thomas Marshall, Coroner; John Dally, Marshall, or Serjeant-at-Mace (the magistrate being privileged to have a mace borne before him); John Van Nuys and Daniel Fitch, Overseers of the Poor; John Stevens, David Lee and Michael Moore, Constables. The Mayor, Recorder, Aldermen, and Assistants were to be called the Common Council with votes therein; the Mayor and four Aldermen to be a quorum to appoint a place and hold meetings of the Common Council, and to make laws, ordinances and constitutions.

The charter provided for the future appointment of a Mayor, Recorder and Sheriff by the Governor, and for the election of the Aldermen and Assistants annually on the second Tuesday in March, as well as the other officers named by the charter. The charter further provides for a Court of Quarter Sessions, of which James Neilson should be clerk. Finally, for all of these offices, powers, privileges, etc., there must be paid annually, if legally demanded, "one sheaf of wheat at the dwelling house of the Mayor." This charter was signed by "John Montgomeree, Gov."

The first thirteen ordinances passed by the Council, (of which the first four are missing), though referred to by title and number in 1733, were, briefly stated, the following:

1. Admitting of strangers to be made free of the city.
2. The law of the Lord's Day.
3. Children or servants not to play on the Lord's Day.
4. Law relating to public houses (shall not sell on the Lord's Day).
5. Negro, Indian or Mulatto slaves not allowed on streets after ten.
6. Three shillings penalty for failure to be present to hold Court.
7. All meat, fruit and vegetables must be exposed for sale at market.
8. Hucksters must wait two hours before buying at market.
9. Fire ordinances, appointing chimney and hearth viewers.
10. Hay not to be within 16 ft., 6 in., of any chimney.
11. Strangers not free to city; to be reported every month by constable.
12. Roads and bridges worked by inhabitants on summons, or fined.

13. Regulating weights and measures.
14. A law for levying £20 to defraying the charge of the poor. Three years later, Feb. 11, 1734, the next ordinance was passed, viz.:
15. For paving streets in the city of New Brunswick, applied to Little Burnet.

Two years later bills for building the Court House came up for payment.

16. Forbids the firing of guns, squibbs or fire crackers in the streets, with three shillings fine.

[The Council had been meeting at Mrs. Baulding's, the first public house mentioned in New Brunswick].

17. Provides for the furnishing of a good leather bucket by each householder, who shall have a fireplace. If two fireplaces, then two buckets for public use at time of fires.

The Council met at the Court House Oct. 18, 1737, and the 18th Ordinance for the recovery of fines, penalties, etc., was passed, and Nicholas Lake appointed poundkeeper. The 19th Ordinance provides that Council shall meet four times a year, on the third Monday of January, April, July and October at two o'clock, with penalty of six shillings for failing to attend. Garret DeGraw was appointed sealer of weights and measures. Reuben Runyon and Aaron Van Cleave were appointed chimney-viewers. Ordinance 5 was amended with a gaol penalty. Jan. 16, 1737-'8 the first Coroner's fee is noted, of £1.14.9, on the body of John Perkins, and the same on the body of Elizabeth Williams, and the first tax levy of £20 is noted, according to the discretion of the assessors on March 1, payable on or before May 1. Ordinance 5 regulating slaves or negroes on the street at night is reconsidered and made more strict and exacting.

Up to this date the only expenses of the city noted are the bridges on Burnet St., the Court House, the poor and the Coroner. The revenue from the market seems to have taken care of that item. In 1739 the playing of the children on the Lord's Day required a new ordinance, and William Ouke and Dirck Schuyler were directed to prepare it; and an ordinance was passed that the bell of the Court House should be rung for the Dutch congregation till they are provided with a bell of their own. In January, 1739, the price of paving in Burnet

St. is given as 2s. 6d. a foot front. On Oct. 20, 1740, a street from Jeseynthes Van Norden's corner to Nicholas Van Dycke's was ordered to be made. This was from French's line, or the foot of Church St., to Burnet; and on May 20, 1741, it was opened through into French St. and "cald Peace St."

The next tax was levied for £35 to repair the Court House, and it was further ordered that no person shall be assessed less than one shilling, nor any above seven in the tax. In September, 1742, it appears that the city was the owner of a fire engine (bought by subscription, I presume, as this is the first reference to it in the minutes). It was at Jacobus Turck's in New York for repairs. In 1743 the Court House bell was to be rung for "both" the congregations. "Both" at this date evidently referred to the Dutch and Presbyterian Churches, as the Episcopal was not built till two years later. They still worshipped at Piscataway. Having secured a market lot of Lawrence Williamson, deeded Feb. 6, 1742, a church was built by subscription, and was on a lot between Burnet and Peace (now Commerce Square). It was to be 30 ft. in length and 14 ft. in breadth, on a stone foundation, the roof to be supported by brick pillars and to project 2 ft. over on every side.

The price of bread was fixed as follows: With wheat at 3s. per bushel, the price of a 3 lb. loaf of bread was to be 4d; of a 1 lb., 8 oz. loaf 2d; of a 12 oz. loaf 1d. Fine "carnell," which was a second-quality loaf (carnell being defined as shapeless), apparently an irregular, rough loaf, not much care taken as to its appearance, must weigh 3 lb., 5 oz., at 4d., while the wheaten loaf with the bran out (what we would call whole wheat bread) was to be 4 lbs. for 4d. This ordinance was passed Apr. 16, 1744.

In November, 1745, the street from Wm. Ouke's shop to the bridge (over Mile Run) near John Cannon's Point, was accepted and ordered worked as the other streets; this was Water St., from French to Mine Run, about where the upper lock now is.

On Jan. 9, 1747, Mayor Farmar conducted Council for the last time, having served nearly seventeen years. He was born in 1674 and died in 1747, at the age of 73. He married Ann, daughter of Capt. Christopher Billop, of Billop Manor, Staten

Island. Who Capt. Billop's first wife, the mother of his two daughters, was, we do not know; but he again married, between 1685-'9, Katherine, the widow of Jasper Farmer of Philadelphia, and Jasper's son, Thomas, married, in 1705, Capt. Billop's daughter Ann, and so became his son-in-law. Thomas Farmer was sheriff of Philadelphia; then, coming to New Jersey, was Collector of the port of Perth Amboy, a Member of the Assembly and of the Governor's Council, Justice of the Supreme Court and Mayor of New Brunswick. His house, referred to in Council minutes, has not been located. His children were: Jasper, Christopher, Thomas, Brooke, Edward, Robert, Samuel, William, John, Mary, Elizabeth and Ann—twelve. Jasper, William, Robert and John were Army officers. Thomas Farmar, Jr., took the name of Billop to inherit his grandfather Billop's manor. Brooke was a tavern-keeper, not then considered an occupation beneath a gentleman. His home in New Brunswick was burned during the British occupation, on Jan. 10, 1777, and he went to Princeton. His widow married John Hodge of Princeton. Brooke Farmar's mother had one sister, who married a missionary named John Brooke, sent out by the Society for the Propagation of the Gospel in Foreign Parts, a Society which supplied all missionaries and clergymen of the Church of England to America. Brooke found it necessary to return to England and on the trip he was lost at sea. His widow married Rev. William Skinner, of Perth Amboy, by some said to have been a Chief of the McGregor Clan. Samuel Farmar, a merchant in New York City, married Christina, daughter of Benjamin and Hannah Peck. Samuel and his father-in-law had lots next to Peck's slip. Edward was unmarried. Christopher died young, otherwise he would have obtained Billop Manor for his name. Of the daughters, Mary married Paul Miller, a tavern keeper and owner, and Judge in Somerset Co. Elizabeth married William Farquhar, M. D., of New Brunswick and afterwards of New York; he married, second, Jane Colden and so became connected with the Antill family and the Auchmuty's (Dr. Auchmuty of Trinity Church, N. Y.) and Richard Nicholls. Ann married Philip French, who married twice, his first wife having been Susannah, daughter of Gov. Anthony Brockholst.

Philip French was the son of Philip French of Kelshall, Suffolk Co., England, who was in New York before 1680, returning to England that year. He had serious trouble with Leisler; was Speaker of the Assembly under Gov. Bellomont, and again under Lieut. Gov. Nanfan. He was Mayor of New York in October, 1702. Philipse, his father-in-law with the powers and privileges of a Lord of the Manor, made a will in 1702 and mentions Philip French's son Philip. Philip French, Sr., did not long outlive his father-in-law, as his will is dated May 20, 1706, and proved June 3, 1707. That he still had interests in England is shown by his leaving land in Suffolk Co. to his son. His brother-in-law, Adolph Philipse, his wife and Col. Lewis Morris were his executors. His wife outlived him by forty years. He left land to his three daughters in East Jersey. Philip (the son) soon acquired large interests there himself. He purchased the Ferry rights in New Brunswick in 1732; had a fine house in New Brunswick in 1735 and large holdings of land. His plan was to dispose of it on long leases, much like the groundrent sales to-day. Like many large landowners he became bankrupt just before the Revolution, and the sheriff was offering his lands, negroes, furniture, etc., in April, 1776. In addition to these troubles he was also a Tory, and the Commissioners for Forfeited Estates joined with the sheriff in attachments of his property in 1778; so that between the two his heirs fared badly.

Captain Christopher Billop, owner of Bentley Manor, Staten Island, and father-in-law of Mayor Thomas Farmar, had a brother Joseph, who died intestate in 1720 and a (sup.) son, Lieut. Christopher Billop, of Major Andros Co., N. Y. State Troops in 1674. Mary, the oldest daughter of Capt. Christopher, married (1st), about 1705, Rev. John Brooke, a Missionary of the Society for Propagating the Gospel in Foreign Parts, who was lost at sea while on a return trip to England, in 1707; she married (2nd) about 1715 Rev. William Skinner of Perth Amboy, who came to New Jersey in 1705. Ann, the youngest daughter of Capt. Christopher, married, as

NEW BRUNSWICK IN HISTORY 33

before stated, Mayor Thomas Farmar about 1706; he was born 1674.

In the absence of male issue, Bentley Manor was left to Thomas Farmar's son, Christopher; in case of his death, to go to his son Thomas, on condition he take the name Billop. As Christopher died in childhood Thomas inherited under the will.

There were some other Billops on Staten Island: Jacobus, who married Ann Stilwell in 1675; John Billop, who made an inventory of "Mih" Crochran in 1701; Joseph Billop, who was Escheater-General in 1711 and who inventoried Fred Walmsey's estate in 1703. This Joseph was the same as above mentioned (brother of Christopher) and when he died intestate in 1710 his estate was administered on by Thomas Farmar.[1]

James Hude, who had been Recorder since 1730, was now made Mayor, and presided on Monday, 17th of August. 1747, when the bill for entertaining Gov. Jonathan Belcher at Paul Miller's was ordered paid. The Governor probably came to install the new Mayor. Just about this time "The Landing," at the head of navigation on the Raritan, and which at one time threatened to become the *City* on the Raritan, had given place to New Brunswick, which had deep water at both high and low tides. The increase in the shipping business had made it necessary to be independent of the tide. Before The Landing accepted the inevitable, the residents in that vicinity made a great effort at what we would, to-day, call a "boom." Johannis Tenbroeck made up a lottery with three grand prizes, each a lot with a dwelling, or a store house, on it; 2,000 tickets, 14s. each. Peter Bodine also got up a lottery with 195 lots from 63 x150 up to half an acre in size, as prizes; 930 tickets at 28s. each. Both seem to have gone through successfully. Christ Church had a lottery in 1758 to finish the church. Queens College had several lotteries. Lotteries are found from 1727 to 1779, or during about 50 years.[2] They became such a nuisance, however, that laws were passed prohibiting the drawings, and

---

[1] For some additional genealogical notes concerning the Farmar, French and Billop Families, see the Appendix.
[2] For a list of Lotteries for these years, see Appendix.

these were evaded for awhile by having the drawings take place at Biles' Island in the Delaware river. The City Minutes, covering a period of 20 years, from 1730 to 1750, give a most interesting glimpse of the life of a small city, its officers and ordinances, its moderation and simplicity. The Court House, market, bridges, fire engine, paving, poor, with an occasional coroner's or doctor's fee, seem about the only expenses. The poor seem to have been a considerable charge; paving was directly assessed on the property; every man had to turn out and help do road mending; public improvements seem to have been provided for by subscription, the market house being an example.

New Brunswick was not settled at once, with a colony all coming together, as was Woodbridge, or Elizabeth, or Newark; or built, as was Amboy, by a powerful association like the Proprietors, but its members dropped in one by one. It is true that quite a number came from Flatlands and that neighborhood on Long Island, as Court, Lucas, Minne, and others of the Van Voorhees family; Jacob and William Ouke; Lawrence and William Williamson; Jeremiah Vanderbilt, Dirck Schuyler, Abram Schuyler, Adriense Quackenbos, Jacobus Schuyler, from Albany. (Just who constituted the large party who came from Albany and changed the name of French St. to Albany in honor, I have never been able to discover). Then Philip French, Peter Kemble, Gerardus DePeyster, John Cholwell, Samuel Bayard, William Farquhar, Anthony White, Edward Antil, etc., from New York. New Brunswick was eminently cosmopolitan. Among the aldermen were: Henry Longfield, son of the first settler; William Cox, a son-in-law; Court, Minne and Lucas Voorhees; Jacob and Wm. Ouke; Lawrence and William Williamson; Jeremiah Vanderbelt, Gerardus De Peyster, Peter Kemble, Philip French, Dirck Schuyler, James Neilson (who came from Ireland via Amboy), James Hude, Judiah Higgins (who lived near Franklin Park), Paul Miller, etc.

At the time Mayor James Hude took office New Brunswick was credited with ninety-one Freeholders, the names following being taken from the City Charter and Ordinances and Philip

NEW BRUNSWICK IN HISTORY 35

French's Lease Book, being of "Our Town of New Brunswick and land thereunto adjoining:"

Ashley, Thomas
Alleson, James
Authors, Thomas
Aten (Auton), Thomas
Bennet, Abraham
Baulding, John and Anne
Belknap, Samuel
Breaser, Francis
Binge, Jacob
Blane, William
Bogert, Jacob
Bilson, William
Beveridge, John
Cox, William (ald.)
Cheasman, Wm. (ald.)
Chambers, David (chim. viewer)
Coyle, Cornelius
Callehan, John
Cannon, John
Cochrane, John
Cochrane, Peter
Cook, Matthew
Drummond, Evan (sheriff)
Dally, John (marshall)
Davidson, Josiah (ald.)
DePeyster, Gerardus (asst.)
Deldine, Francis
DeGraw, Garret
DeGraw, John
Dela-Montagne, Tunis
French, Philip (asst. & ald.)
Fitch, Daniel (overseer poor)
Farmar, Thomas (mayor)
Farquhar, Dr. William
Farmar, Brooke
Fushee, Margaret
Forenekes, Mrs.
Giddiman, John
Gibbs, Capt. Richard
Groosbeek, Nicholas
Godfrie, John

Hutchinson, Duncan
Heegerman, Dallis (ald.)
Higgins, Judiah (ald.)
Hude, James (mayor)
Heyer, Abraham
Hoagland, Hendrick
Harding, Thomas
Henry, Alexander
Harrison, William
Hickels, Mrs.
Johnson, Isaac
Johnson, Gerard
Kemble, Peter (asst.)
Kemper, Isaac
Lake, Nicholas
Laforge, David
Longfield, Henry (asst.)
Lee, David (constable)
Lyne, James (asst.)
Lyel, John
Lambson, Ebenezer
Moore, Alex. (treas.)
Moore, Michael (constable)
Marshal, Thomas (coroner)
Mollet, Theo. (poundkeeper, ald.)
Miller, Paul (poundkeeper asst.)
Murphy, William
Market, Peter
Manson, Elizabeth
Neilson, James (clerk, ald.)
Norwood, Andrew
Ouke, Jacob (ald.)
Ouke, Wm. (ald., recorder)
Ouke, Abraham
Ogden, Nathaniel
Pridmore, John
Price, Benjamin
Pitt, Samuel
Perkins, John
Pittenger, Elizabeth

Reynolds, John (ald.)
Runyon, Reuben
Reed, James
Reason, William
Royce, John
Riley, John
Rezeau (Reseau), Mrs. Mary
Quackenboss, Adrianne
Schuyler, Dirck (ald.)
Schuyler, Abraham
Schuyler, Jacobus
Sleght, Peter (chimney-viewer)
Sollom, Tise
Sollom, Mort
Sollom, Cornelius
South, Daniel
Symonds, William
Stryker, Peter
Tingle, John
Tomson, John
Thomson, Archibald
Stevens, John (constable)
Vredenburg, Peter
Van Arsdalen, Dirck (ald.)
Van Beuren, John
Van Allen, Dirck

Van Cleave, Aaron
Van Cleave, Benjamin
Van Corlear, Arent
Van Derbilt, Jeremiah
Van Derbelt, Hendrick
Van Dyck, John (asst.)
Van Dyck, Nicholas
Van Dyck, Francis
Van Duersen, Hendrick (ald.)
Van Norden, Jeseynthes
Van Norden, John, Jr.
Van Norden, Peter
Van Vechten, Dirck (asst.)
Van Nuys, John (overseer poor)
Van Voorhees, Minne (asst.)
Voorhees, Court (asst.)
Voorhees, Lucas (asst.)
Van Nuys, Jacobus
Wetherill, John (ald.)
Williamson, Lawrence (ald.)
Williamson, Wm. (asst.)
Walmsay, Wm.
Wright, Thomas
Wyser, Jacob
Wylee, John
Williams, Elizabeth

There were two New Brunswicks—one that outlined in the charter and of imposing dimensions; another recognized in administering city affairs, which was the "line of the houses." These 91 Freeholders must, I think, have referred to the latter, as certainly New Brunswick in its city limits must have contained many more.

Taxing was eminently fair. In 1747 a tax laid of £25 was to be assessed "from Thomas Authors' to Reuben Runyon and Lucas (Voorhees) upon the hill, Jacobus Van Nuys and Mr. French inclusive." Authors was at one end of the street and Voorhees at the other, while Van Nuys and French had built outside of the line of houses.

We must pass briefly over James Hude's mayoralty as we have no official records to which to refer (the Minutes of Council are missing till Apr. 5, 1796). He served till his death in

NEW BRUNSWICK IN HISTORY 37

1762, fifteen years, which, added to seventeen years as Recorder, makes a total of 32 years; a long service even in those days of long terms of office. Hude was a merchant, served also as Judge and a member of Gov. Francis Bernard's Council in 1758. He was a son of Adam and Marion Hude, and his wife was Mary Johnson.

New Brunswick obtained a second charter dated Feb. 12, 1763. This second charter was obtained under Gov. Josiah Hardy, and is much a repetition of the first, with a few peculiar and important variations. It stated that inhabitants had obtained ground and erected a Court House and market house, which, together with other matters relating to the Corporation, were "in a declining state." It established wards in the city; the north ward comprising the real city of New Brunswick and the south ward comprising a great stretch of country west and southwest of the north ward, with separate power, separate taxation and separate care of the poor, and with two freeholders, four aldermen, four councilmen, one assessor, one collector, two constables. One overseer should reside in the north ward and two aldermen, two councilmen, and the same number of others in the south, thus fastening upon the city the ward system that has taken 150 years to even partially get rid of. It appointed William Ouke, Mayor. The Charter also conferred the powers and privileges enjoyed by "any other precinct or township" in the province—broad but unknown rights. The wards divided at Nicholas Johnson's plantation on the county line road, near Nine-mile Run; thence on a line to George's Road, where Rocky Brook crosses it, and down Rocky Brook to Lawrence Brook. The Aldermen for the city were to be Philip French, Henry Guest, David Gano and Azariah Dunham; and, in the south ward, Isaac Van Dyck and Arie Bennet. Other officers were: James Hude, Clerk (son of the former Mayor); William Ouke and Hendrick Van Deursen, freeholders in the north ward, and John Terheune and George Wetherill in south ward; James Neilson, Recorder. Free citizens were to be made by the Mayor, under seal fee, £5, or less, and only such could follow an art, trade, mystery or occupation in the city. Punishments were not to exceed loss of life or limb. Council could fill offices under certain conditions. Election to be second Tuesday in March. The charter was approved by Cortlandt Skinner, Attorney General.

William Ouke,[3] the third Mayor, probably took office at once, as Hude died in November, and Council met once in three months.

Again we have a Governor in New Brunswick, William Franklin this time, who was probably here to install William Ouke in office. The Middlesex Troop of Horse escorted him from New Brunswick to Amboy. Ouke was a petitioner for the charter; an alderman in 1737; took Hude's place as recorder in 1747, and, naturally becoming Mayor on Hude's death in 1763, was probably acting Mayor in the brief interim. He is believed to have filled the office till his death in 1779, serving about 42 years in the three offices of alderman, recorder and Mayor. Here we must again lament the lack of an official record. That Ouke was a progressive and excellent Mayor we have abundant evidence, for, if the direct minutes are lacking, we find his efforts for better education shown by his being one of six gentlemen who started a preparatory school in New Brunswick in 1768 while waiting for Queens College to get started. During his mayoralty the New Jersey Medical Society was formed, in 1766. John Cochrane, M. D., of New Brunswick, was one of the founders of that Society and its President in 1769. The Middlesex and Somerset County line was surveyed and re-established in 1765; the charter to Queens College was obtained in 1766. An Act to build a new Court House and jail was obtained in 1763, with consid-

---

[3]It is said that the Ouke (later spelled Oake) and Van Nuys families are of common origin; that William Ouke was the son of Auke Janse, grandson of Jan Aukerse, sometimes called Van Nuys; hence that Jacob and William Ouke and John Van Nuys were brothers. Both Jacob and William Ouke came to New Brunswick as early as 1718 (Jacob was in New York city in 1718 but also became a Deacon in the Dutch Ref. Church of the River and Lawrence's Brook in 1718, and bought land in 1725), and were petitioners for the Charter in 1730. John Van Nuys bought a farm in 1727 on the south side of Livingston Ave. William Ouke was baptised 1708 and died 1779. Mary Ouke married Abraham Hyer, whose home was at the foot of Church St. on Peace, east side. There was also Abraham Ouke, a brother of William and Jacob, or a son of one of them; the records as to them are not clear.

erable opposition from Amboy. The County bridge at the landing was built in 1772, by John Duyckinck and Charles Suydam. The counties raised £450 under the Act which did not quite build the bridge.

From these sidelights I think we are warranted in saying Mayor Ouke was a progressive Mayor during a progressive period; like many other prominent men of the day he owned a tavern on Little Burnet St. He must have had an exciting time during the Revolution. Whether he continued to exercise his office during the British occupation, December, 1776, till June, 1777, I do not know. He was probably too old to take an active part in Revolutionary affairs, as we do not find his name on the Committees. He probably welcomed Washington here in his brief visits.

New Brunswick was a garrison town for some years and there was a most friendly relation between troops and citizens. The 26th Regiment, Col. John Scott, called Cameronians, was in Barracks here for three years from 1767 till 1770, and the 29th took its place, and was here till 1771. We find them assisting to put out fires. General Gage reviewed them here June 23rd, 1769.

CHAPTER III

The Successor to Mayor Ouke—Early Schools—The First Dutch Church—Hendrick Fisher and the Frelinghuysen Circuit—The Presbyterian Church—Church of England's Church—Lotteries for Churches—Members of the City Government—Various Vestrymen of the Episcopal Church—The Methodist and Baptist Congregations.

WHEN Mayor Ouke died in 1777 the office of Mayor became vacant. The last Provincial Governor was William Franklin. His last Council met in Burlington, Nov. 16, 1775. The Journal of Council ends Nov. 24, 1775, although they continued in session till Dec. 6, 1775, then terminating the Provincial Legislature of New Jersey. Governor Franklin was sent to Connecticut June 20, 1776, under guard, where he remained till November, 1778, when he was exchanged. In the meantime, on July 19, 1776, the State of New Jersey was formed, and at Princeton, Aug. 31, 1776, William Livingston was chosen Governor. Richard Stockton was the opposing candidate, the first ballot being a tie. Livingston was reëlected in 1778 by 31 votes against Gen. Dickinson's seven.

We have absolutely nothing more reliable than tradition as to Mayor Ouke's successor, who is given as William Harrison. Harrison was chimney-viewer in 1745; member of the Engine Company in 1747; lived in William Cox's house, next to James Neilson's, in 1754; one of Christ Church vestry in 1759, and, on Apr. 7, 1779, was chairman of a meeting in the north ward of New Brunswick, i. e., New Brunswick proper, to consider the destruction of property lines in that ward by the British occupation in 1776-1777. Fortifications and earthworks had obliterated old landmarks, and there had been a failure to record deeds in addition, so that it was proposed to relieve the situation and pass an Act that, in certain cases, made *use* or *possession* sufficient title.

Harrison, by tradition, was the Mayor from William Ouke's death till 1784, when Azariah Dunham took office as fifth Mayor and under a new and third charter.

Before taking up the next period, we will briefly note a few of the happenings under the old charters, and the first four Mayors. Since the city was the outgrowth of the grain production of the surrounding country, mills were obviously the first necessity. Greenland's and Drake's were on opposite sides of Johnson's pond, and date from 1694; Longfield's was on his stepfather's, Lawrence's, brook, 1716; Enoch Vreeland on College Farm pond, 1717; Gerardus De Peyster on Mile Run, 1739; Puklehammer and French on the same Run, 1754. Miller's Run, the gully next to Commercial Ave. from the name, must have had a mill on it. In fact, almost every little stream that could turn a wheel had its mill, while brew houses and tanneries were located on smaller streams. Lyles brook had a brewery on Brewer St., now John. Barrack Spring brook, the one between Albany and Church, had a tannery. Still House Run, at steamboat dock, had a brewery, and this Run also furnished water for boats at the steamboat dock, and the water right was at one period valuable. In time these small streams, not proving adequate, a dam of the Raritan at the Landing was sought, and an Act was passed, Aug. 5, 1779, authorizing it. It was built later by Hassert Freeman and Disbro.

While business was pushed education was not neglected. New Brunswick had its schoolmaster, Jacobus Schureman, 1719, and John Cholwell in 1724. His home was next to Enoch Vreeland and, in 1741, he was still there, as we find he then received a legacy from his sister, Elizabeth Cholwell, of New York. In 1760 Edward Cooper had a school, and in 1768 Caleb Cooper, A. B., of King's College, New York, opened the school already referred to as started under Mayor Ouke's administration. During the Revolution schools were not overlooked, as a teacher with fifteen scholars was exempt from military duty, so the school should not be broken up.

The Dutch Church, first built about 1½ miles beyond the *present* city limits (though within the *first* city limits) on the Six-Mile Run, or Franklin Park road, served three different neighborhoods—The River, Six-Mile Run, and Ten-Mile Run. It was built by Abraham Bennet at Three-Mile Run. In an old Dutch document, preserved by the First Dutch Church, it was agreed, Apr. 12, 1717, "in view of differences," the Six-Mile Run and Ten-Mile Run communities shall build where they may agree, and the Three-Mile Run Church shall belong to the congregation of "Lawrence's Brook by the River."

Evidently the three neighborhoods had previously to this date worshipped as one congregation, and in fact Dr. Steele in his "Historical Discourse" refers to a subscription paper dated 1703 for a fund to bring over a clergyman. The earliest church, built by Abram Bennet, was not in New Brunswick; was without doubt the Three-Mile Run church, as the records show that members met in New Brunswick from time to time in private houses for Church meetings and for the purpose of receiving members into their communion, and that on one occasion they met in the College Hall. This College Hall I take it was at Princeton. But in 1735 they had built a church, and a set of rules for the renting of pews and to provide means for maintaining a clergyman and paying for the church, accompanied by a pew plan of the church, with the names of the occupants written in, is entered in the records.

This Association, or church family, is first spoken of as "The People of Lawrence's Brook by the River," then "The Church of Lawrence's Brook and the River," and again "Lawrence's Brook and George's Road."

The church building of 1735 is, without doubt, the Burnet Street church, although before the name Burnet Street was in use. It stood on the street from the Dutch church to the Market and a street along its south side was called Dutch Church Street and afterwards Schureman Street.

Under date of 1718, there are entered the names of the Elders and Deacons as follows:

Elders—Roelof Sebring, Ian Atan (John Auten), Laurens Willimse.

Deacons—Hendrick Bries, Roelof Lucas, Jacob Auke.

Dr. Davidson, in his "History of the Presbyterian Church," says the above congregation had 78 members in 1717. In 1790 the church availed itself of permission by an Act of the Legislature and gave up the cumbersome title of "Ministers, Elders and Deacons of the Dutch Reformed Church of Raritan, North Branch, New Brunswick, Six-Mile Run and Millstone, in the Counties of Somerset, Hunterdon and Middlesex," and took the simpler title it now bears.

Hendrick Fisher, living between New Brunswick and Bound Brook, was made a lay preacher in 1736 to assist the pastor (with his large circuit) in the New Brunswick Church just built. This circuit was Raritan (now Somerville), New Brunswick, Six-Mile Run, Three-Mile Run, North Branch, Southland, and occasionally North and South Hampton, Pa. The pastor, Rev. Theodorus Jacobus Frelinghuysen, was the first Reformed minister in central New Jersey, including all the churches in Middlesex and Somerset counties. Jan Van Nuys, about 1729, gave the Dutch church a burial-ground, afterwards cut through by the opening of Liberty Street. This burial plot, of about two acres, was not built on by the Dutch congregation, and probably for the very good reason that they did not have a good title to it, as we find that, in 1773, Dennis and Ida Van Liew, for 5s., give the Dutch church a deed to this lot, confirming their right to use it as a burying ground, and stating that it was designed and always had been used for this purpose. We know that the Indians had a burial-place at New Brunswick and it seems as if this might have been that old Indian burial-place. Be that as it may, this was the burying-ground until the church was moved from Burnet Street to Queen Street, per Philip French's gift. Here a new graveyard was established and the old one fell into disuse, went to decay, and is now built over.

The Presbyterian church first established itself at Bound Brook about 1700. Just when the New Brunswick congregation was formed is uncertain. Rev. Gilbert Tennent took charge in 1726; whether they had a building then does not appear. Whitefield preached in "Mr. Tennent's Meeting House" on the evening of Nov. 13, 1730. The church in New Brunswick was built on Burnet St., about two blocks south of the Dutch Church, on a lot of 54 ft. front, on the westerly side of the street, obtained of William Cox. In 1743 the Common Council allowed the Court house bell to be rung for the English congregation, the same permission having been granted to the Dutch congregation. There is a note that the church was struck by lightning in July, 1752, and badly shattered.

Rev. Thomas Arthur, 1748, was the second pastor, and Rev. Israel Reed, in 1768, supplied both churches, Bound Brook and New Brunswick. The British so nearly destroyed the New Brunswick building that it was never used again; so in 1787 a new building was built by subscription on Barrack St. The deed (of 1784, Book 6, pp. 649 of Deeds) calls the streets "George and Barrack," now Paterson St.

The Committee appointed to build the church (on Jan. 25, 1784), was John Neilson, treasurer; John Taylor, secretary; Wm. Paterson, Moses Scott, M. D., and James Richmond. The pews were sold Nov. 1, 1787, and were purchased by the following 33 persons:

John Neilson	Dr. Lewis Dunham	Thomas Talmage
Wm. Paterson	James Richmond	John Henry
James Cole	Thomas Egbert	Elijah Philips
Wm. Tenbrooke	John Meyers	Shelly Arnett
Wm. French	Gabriel Silcocks	Ellitt Crecy
Thomas Grant	Joshua Kershon	Andrew Gibb
John Paul	James Hortwick	Jacob Voorhees
Ephraim Lorree	John Taylor	John Van Emburgh
Dr. Robt. Harris	Dr. Moses Scott	John Lyle, Jr.
George Hance	John Plum	John Pool
William Letson	Wm. Applegate	James Drake

and pews were rented by 27 others:

John Dennis	Azariah Dunham	John Priestly
Peter Dumondt	Jonathan Combs	Henry Guest, Sr.
J. Van Norden, Jr.	Jonathan Dean	John Smith, Jr.
William Ryder	John Hartwick	John Bray
John DeGraw	Abraham Ouke	Wm. Richmond
John Guest	And. Kirkpatrick	John Lyle
James Hude	John Hendrickson	Henry Lupp
Joseph Robinson	Mary Meyers	John Baker
Moses Lyle	William Young	John Lyle, 2nd

The Church of England, by its missionaries, sent out by the "Society for the Propagation of the Gospel in Foreign Parts" (and all Episcopal missionaries or clergymen before the Revolution were supplied by this Society) occupied Piscataway in 1704. The missionary circuit (John Brooks' circuit) included Elizabeth, Amboy, Chesequakes, Freehold, Rocky Hill and Piscataway—about fifty miles and New Brunswick Episcopalians attended at Piscataway till 1745. In 1742 a movement to build in New Brunswick was under way and a deed from Philip French to a lot on which the building was going up, dated Dec. 4, 1745, speaks of the building as "in great forwardness." This deed was to Peter Kemble, Francis Costigan, James Lyne and John Kearney, and was for a lot 150 ft. square. This church had a lottery in 1758 and obtained a charter in 1759. Its first permanent rector was Rev. William Wood, 1747. Its lottery was managed by Edward Antill, Bernardus Lagrange, Wm. Mercer, M. D., John Berrian, Samuel Kemble, William Harrison and Peter Kemble.

To the foregoing brief paragraph on the Episcopal church of Piscataway and New Brunswick, the names of its early officers, with a few words as to who they were, and what their standing was in the community, so far as our imperfect sources of information will permit, may be of interest.

The deed to the church, made by Philip French in 1745, was to James Lyne, John Kearney, Peter Kemble, and Francis Costigan.

But little is known of James Lyne; in fact, this statement will apply to many of the names connected with this church. We know of his marriage to Helena Williamson, Aug. 6, 1744; that he was one of the Executors of Alexander Henry of New Brunswick, Apr. 5, 1745; one of the managers of Christ Church Lottery, 1748. He was an attorney-at-law in active practice, as Court records show, from 1741 to 1748. He was "Assistant" in Council in 1748 and in January 1749-'50, when the minutes end. Then he disappears. There is an uncalled-for letter for him in the N. Y. Post Office in 1751. He was made a "freeman" of New York City, Sept. 2, 1735.

Of John Kearney, though of a well-known and large family, we have but a single item, from the "New York Post Boy" of Sept. 15, 1746: "Ann Kearney, widow and executor of John Kearney, late of New Brunswick."

To Peter Kemble the reader will find extended references, in other parts of this volume.

Francis Costigan was an attorney-at-law. He appeared before Gov. Lewis Morris and the Council May 16, 1740, as counsel for Aaron Dean. His house in New Brunswick is advertised for sale in the "New York Gazette," May 19, 1740, and is described as "over against the Court House" in said city, which would be on the river side of Burnet St., at the foot of Richmond St. Application to be made to Benjamin Price, attorney, or Mr. John Taylor, a brasier in New York. No sale was made and he continued in New Brunswick. In 1741 he offered 20s. reward for a lost horse, and in 1743 40s. for an Irish servant lad, Daniel Brien, 18 years old. He records a mortgage on 365 acres of land of Francis Hollingshead, and was a manager of the Christ Church Lottery in 1751. His son, Francis Costigan, Jr., of Trenton, married Jean Carr, Mar. 2, 1769, and, on July 8, 1773, a notice appeared that "on Thursday last Francis Costigan, attorney-at-law" died at New Brunswick.

The next move in connection with the church was the lottery to build a church and parsonage, dated Aug. 4, 1748. The drawing was held March 30 to April 30, 1749. Two new names appear as managers, John Berrien and John Boughton. This was an effort to gain outside assistance. John Berrien was one of the most noted men of his day. Born in 1711, he married Margaret daughter of Thomas Eaton of Eatontown, lived at Rocky Hill, was a Trustee of Princeton, 1763, Justice of the Supreme Court and Member of Assembly. Washington wrote his Farewell to the army at his house in Rocky Hill. He died Apr. 22, 1772.

John Boughton, of Raritan (Somerville), was evidently added to sell tickets and stir up interest in that rich and growing community.

A second lottery to complete the church, Dec. 4, 1758, ten years later, drawing on July 17, 1759, brings us a new set of names—Edward Antill, Bernardus Legrange, William Mercer, Samuel Kemble, William Harrison, Francis Brasier.

NEW BRUNSWICK IN HISTORY 47

Edward Antill is probably one of the best-known men connected with Christ Church, and is referred to elsewhere.

Bernardus Lagrange was a lawyer of New Brunswick. Johannes De La Grange, a Huguenot from La Rochelle, France, settled in New Amsterdam about 1656 and left four sons: Johannes, Omy, Isaac and Jacobus. Omy came to Albany in 1665, and one of his sons was Jacobus, baptized Apr. 23, 1692; it is his son, baptized March 11, 1721, that is the Bernardus of New Brunswick. He was a lawyer in practice until the Revolution, and has been listed as a Loyalist, but with his French Huguenot and Dutch ancestry (they were intermarried with the Croessell, De Vries, Van Loon, Van Schaick, etc., families), his only excuse for being a Tory lies in the fact that he married Frances Brasier, whose father was vestryman in St. Peter's, Amboy; two of his daughters married officers in the British Army; the third married an officer in a Tory Regiment. These connections seem to have been his undoing, as he is listed by the Commissioner for Forfeited Estates, and finally had to ask for a passage to England. He probably had transferred his property to England, for he lived in Westminster and, at his death, had a 28-year lease still to run on his house.

William Mercer, M. D., was a physician of New Brunswick, who lived over the river from 1745 to his death in 1768. He was connected with the old Piscataway Church, and was a close friend of Edward Antill.

Samuel Kemble has been already noticed in other connections. He married Catharine French, and was a brother of Peter Kemble.

William Harrison, the supposed fourth Mayor of New Brunswick, has been referred to.

Francis Brasier, father-in-law of Bernardus Lagrange, was, as stated, a vestryman at Amboy, and was probably added for the sake of enlisting outside support in Amboy, or to dispose of tickets there.

A third lottery for the purpose of building the steeple was held in 1772; the drawing was Jan. 6, 1773. Certain new names again appear—Walter Livingston, John Dennis, James Hude,

Derrick Van Vechten, Hendrick Van Duersen, and Philip French.

Walter Livingston, of the Manor line of the Livingston family, came to New Brunswick for a wife, and married Cornelia Schuyler, step-daughter of Dr. John Cochrane, of New Brunswick, who married her mother, Cornelia Van Cortlandt, widow of Col. John Schuyler. Walter's brother, Robert Cambridge, also came here for a wife, and married Mary Hude, daughter of New Brunswick's second Mayor, James Hude. Another sister, Susan Hude, married William Neilson of New York, a branch of the well-known New Brunswick Neilson family.

John Dennis, of the Piscataway Dennis family, became a large landowner in New Brunswick and, when he died in 1806, was noted as one of the oldest inhabitants; he was 83. His son, John Dennis, has descendants in the west.

Van Vechten and Van Duersen were members of the city government, and I presume were added to give confidence in the lottery. Hendrick Van Duersen died about 1776, and his executor was the Dutch minister, Johannes Van Harlingen, and I think it quite evident he was not a "Churchman."

Christ Church Charter obtained in 1761 adds a few additional names—Brook Farmar, Anthony White, Paul Miller, Joseph Vickers and Patrick Riley.

Brook Farmar, son of Thomas Farmar, first Mayor of New Brunswick and one of New Jersey's prominent men, was named for his uncle, the missionary of the S. P. G. F. P., before 1707, Rev. John Brooks. Brook is one of the least known and least prominent of Thomas Farmar's sons. He married but had no family. His widow married John Hodge of Princeton. He kept a tavern in New Brunswick, the "Sign of the Red Lion," and took the sign with him when he moved. He was postmaster in New Brunswick 1764, but the War seemed to have driven him out of New Brunswick, and in 1779 he was keeping a tavern in Princeton.

Paul Miller married Brook Farmer's sister, Mary. He was prominent in the city under its first charter. Governor Belcher was entertained at his house in 1747. His home in New Bruns-

NEW BRUNSWICK IN HISTORY 49

wick was in Somerset county, on the north side of Albany street, between Water and Peace Sts., He was Judge in Somerset County.

Anthony White married a daughter of Governor Lewis Morris and built in New Brunswick about 1740. He filled many positions of public office. His house stands in Buccleuch Park.

Joseph Vickers married Sarah Walker, of Piscataway. Henry Lupp married his sister, Mary Vickers. Joseph was a member of the law firm of Van Emburgh, Vickers & Taylor.

Patrick Riley we cannot trace.

From these 21 men must be formed the Vestrymen of Christ Church from 1745 till the Minutes, preserved by the Church, begin, and which, from 1790 on, give the names of the Vestrymen. On these Minutes, from 1790 to 1800, there are found:

Henry Guest, 1790
Dr. C. A. Howard, 1790-1
John D. Alvey, 1790-1
Levinus Clarkson, 1790-1
Matthew Egerton, 1790
John Bowers, 1790-3
Thomas L. Vickers, 1790-4
Jonathan Deare, 1790-4
Robert Morris, 1791-1808
John Parker, 1791
Simon Hillyer, 1791
Peter Keenon, 1791
James Duyckinck, 1791-8
Joseph Vickers, 1794

William Leupp, 1794
Robert Boggs, 1794-1814
Philip French, 1794
Willett Warne, 1796-1800
Nehemiah Vernon, 1796-1804
George Farmar, 1796
Willis Reed, 1797-8
John Auten, 1797-8
Joseph Sutton, 1798-9
William Leslie, 1798
William Peacock, 1798-1807
John Dennis, 1793-1806
Nathaniel Fitz, 1794-6
John Garnett, 1799-1809

Here we have 28 names in ten years against a probable 21 names in forty-five years. Rotation in office did not obtain in our early civic life, and probably did not in the ecclesiastical; office was held for life or good behavior. On the other hand, without minutes or records, it is possible there were other names of which we have no record.

Of the above 28 men we can give a descriptive word or so for some of them:

Levinus Clarkson's grandfather, Mathew Clarkson, was Secretary of the Province in 1698 His father, David Clarkson, married Anna Margaretta Freeman and had four sons—David, who married Elizabeth French of New Brunswick; Matthew, who married Elizabeth DePeyster of New York; Freeman, who did not marry; and Levinus (born 1740, died 1798), who married Mary Van Horn David owned a large tract at Mapletown near Princeton. Levinus built the house (now torn down) where the Y. M. C. A. building stands, and was active in New Brunswick.

Matthew Egerton was a cabinet-maker, and made much old fine mahogany for New Brunswick. He married Maria Bergen, whose father built the houses, 82, 84, 86 Carroll Place. No. 86 was long the residence of Bishop Croes. He was a Warden in Christ Church and died at 63, in 1802.

Henry Guest applied for the second City Charter of 1763 and was an alderman; a tanner by trade. He built the house on the corner of Livingston Avenue and New St., the southwest corner. He married Ruth Bong Dec. 19, 1748. He proposed to the New York Society of Arts that leather, treated by a special process of his own, be used instead of copper for roofs. He died on Jan. 24, 1805, aged 89.

Dr. Charles Abraham Howard lived over the river in the house built by Edward Antill and called "Ross Hall." He married Sarah Farmar (a daughter of Thomas Farmar and widow of Dr. Alexander Ross), who died Feb. 27, 1776. Dr. Howard was a pupil of Dr. Ross. Mrs. Ross outlived both her husbands and died, in 1796, at Shrewsbury.

Thomas Leonard Vickers, a son of Joseph Vickers according to an advertisement of his executors in 1793, died before that date. He left two daughters—Sarah and Mary.

Jonathan Deare was sheriff of Middlesex county in 1788. His wife's name was Frances ———. He appears to have died in 1794, when in office.

I have been unsuccessful in finding a record of John D. Alvey. In 1794 I find Moses Scott advertising a house in Queen St., "lately occupied by Mrs. Alvey," which would indicate the earlier death of John D. Alvey.

John Bowers was drawn for jury duty, July term, 1792, and had a suit against Henry Lane for debt in 1794. In a deed in

1801 he describes himself as the son of John and Susannah Bowers, late of Burlington, and his mother joins him in the deed. This completes the list of Vestrymen of 1790.

Robert Morris was a son of Robert Hunter Morris who died at a dance in 1764, and a grandson of Gov. Lewis Morris; also a nephew of Mrs. Edward Antill and Mrs. Anthony White. He was born in New Brunswick 1745, died June 22, 1815. Was Chief Justice, a large land owner, for a time owning most of the city lying between Livingston and Nicholl Avenues.

There was a John Parker of Somerset (the city north of French or Albany was then in Somerset), who, in his will, 175c, mentions his wife Elizabeth, and children James, John, Elender, and Janet. This son John was probably the vestryman. In 1792-'3-'4 he is actively practicing as an attorney in the Courts in Middlesex. At the Fourth of July Celebration in 1795 he gave as a toast, "The Sons of Columbus," and in 1798 he offers 3,000 acres of Proprietary Rights in East New Jersey.

Captain Simon Hillyer has a Revolutionary record. He died Dec. 24, 1802, and was buried in the Episcopal churchyard with military and Masonic honors.

Col. Peter Keenon, another Revolutionary soldier, kept a tavern after the War on Queen St., at the foot of Bayard. He was Captain of the New Brunswick Light Infantry and postmaster. He got into some trouble with the church, as the Rector, wardens and vestry sue him and John Baker jointly for a debt of £1,500 and obtained judgment for $943.92. At the same time they brought a similar suit against John Parker and Abraham Blauvelt, which was settled out of Court. It is to be noticed that these two vestrymen are only listed for one year, 1791. Peter Keenon had great losses by death in his family; his daughter, Mary, wife of John Williamson, died in 1812 at the age of 33; Peggy died in 1814 at the age of 25; Catharine, wife of James B. Low, died in 1815 at the age of 28, and Keenon himself died in 1814 at the age of 69.

James Duyckinck married Mary Taylor in 1772. The Landing Bridge was completed in 1775 by John Duyckinck and Charles Suydam. John's house was in Burnet St. in 1795. I presume they were brothers. These were the 1791 Vestrymen.

There are no noted vestrymen in 1792, and but one in 1793, John Dennis, who, as stated already, died in office.

Joseph Vickers is the same one who petitioned for the charter, and has been noted already.

The Leupp family are still with us and need no mention.

Philip French, of 1794, is not the Philip French who gave the church lot; he died in 1782 and it is his son, Philip French 3rd, who became vestryman. The "Guardian" announced the death of Philip French 1st, a native and among the oldest inhabitants, Dec. 26, 1803, and that he was interred in his family burying-ground, afterwards the site of the Baptist church, corner George and Somerset Streets.

Robert Boggs was a practicing attorney. On July 22, 1795, he married Miss Polly Morris. The Boggs' family connection with Christ Church is well known.

Nathaniel Fitz was a saddle and harness maker from Burlington. His shop was on Burnet St., a few doors above Col. Neilson's (see advertisement in "Guardian," 1795).

These were the Vestrymen of 1794. There were none for 1795. For 1796 we have—

George Farmar, a great-grandson of Thomas Farmar, first Mayor of New Brunswick, through Jasper, Peter, to George. He married Gertrude Coejeman, whose father was a cousin of Col. Neilson. George lived at Bellevue (formerly the residence of Dr. William Mercer), Highland Park.

Nehemiah Vernon kept the celebrated White Hall Tavern 1793 to 1804. His widow married John Keyworth, and they kept the Steamboat Hotel next to Vanderbilt's. These two hotels are closely connected with our early steamboat days.

Willet Warne married Alletta Johnson in 1794, and Marinus Willet Warne was married to Elizabeth Brush by Rev. Mr. Croes in 1803. Willet Warne kept an ironmongery (hardware store) at the "Black Padlock," corner of Albany and Queen Sts. Ironware, saddles, tools, nails, paints, etc., imported by himself and at New York prices, were advertised in the "Guardian" in 1795, 1796, 1797.

The vestrymen for 1797 are: John Auten, who was master of the sloop "Susannah," running from New Brunswick to

Albany. In 1798 he advertises his house on the bank of the river which he was occupying then, and which he says has six fireplaces, and that there is also a good wharf.

Thomas Auten was master of the schooner "Cornelia" for Savannah, and Nicholas Auten sailed a boat to Albany. In 1800 John, Thomas and widow Anna Auten lived on the south west corner of George and Church Sts., being 100 ft .front on George and 105 ft. on Church. This corner was next owned by John Van Harlingen and then by A. R. Taylor in 1812. John Auten died before 1813 and his estate was being settled then.

Willis Reed advertises in the "Guardian" in 1795 as a hair dresser, with shop on Albany St.

The vestrymen for 1798 were:

Joseph Sutton, who married, according to the will of Sarah (Langstaff) Bunn, Priscilla Langstaff, and his children were Sarah, Priscilla, Henry and Jacob. His wife's uncle was Samuel Potter, Piscataway people. He was executor for Samuel Walker in Piscataway in 1802, and probably kept a tavern.

Of William Peacock, I can only say that a William Peacock owned in 1732 where Ross's coal yard now is; he was probably the father of the vestryman.

Of William Leslie nothing is to be found.

John Garnett long owned, and lived in, the house now called Buccleuch. He was one of the prominent men in New Brunswick, was instrumental in getting Dr. Adrain for the College, and Garnet Adrain was named for him by his friend, Dr. Adrain.

The Methodist Episcopal Church, organized in 1803, had as their trustees, John Bray, Joseph Williams, Michael Pool and John Henry, who purchased a lot on which they agree to erect a house and place of worship. This was on the east side of King St., 49 feet front and 116 feet deep, next north of John Bray's house. (See Book C of Deeds, Somerville, folio 561).

The Baptists bought and built at the corner of George and Somerset. This lot was originally Philip French's family burying-ground, where afterwards the railroad depot stood. Book J of Deeds, Somerville, folio 704, reads: "on the north side of Somerset and east side of George 178 feet along Somerset to

16 feet Alley; N. 200 feet to lot Rev. John Croes; west 167 feet to George; south along George 200 feet to beginning." While this church in New Brunswick is later than some other denominations, the Baptists probably have the honor of being the oldest religious association in this county for the church of Piscataway, or Stelton, dates from 1683, of which John Drake and Hugh Dunn were lay preachers.

The Catholics held their first mass by Dr. Powers of New York here in 1825. The first church was built on Bayard St. about opposite the Bayard St. Public School, in 1830, while the first resident priest came in 1838.

It is very interesting to note that in an early note on church buildings of the religious denominations in New Jersey there are no Catholic and no Methodist—the two largest bodies today. In 1767 a list of the "Houses of Worship of the Various Denominations in New Jersey" is given as:

    46 Presbyterian Meeting Houses
    38 Quaker
    21 Episcopalian
    21 Dutch (Calvin)
    19 Baptist
     7 Dutch (Lutheran)
     2 Seven Day Baptist
     1 Moravian

Total 155

CHAPTER IV

The Early Ferry—The Albany Street Bridge, 1790—Travel and Tavern Hand-in-Hand—Franklin's Trip to Philadelphia—Stages and Water Routes—Turnpikes and Steamboats—The Growth of Postal Facilities.

NO doubt it has been already noted how frequently the "Ferry" at New Brunswick is referred to. In fact the only designation it had for some time was "The Ferry." John Inian established it as early as 1686, though he did not receive the exclusive rights to operate it until 1697. After Inian's death we find the Ferry in the hands of Thomas Farmar, who was the son-in-law of Christopher Billop, to whom Inian had mortgaged most of his land. As the legal right to the Ferry was only Inian's and his wife's for their lifetime, Farmar petitioned Council, May, 1720, for the ferry rights, and in 1732 he deeded these rights to Philip French. Capt. Samuel Leonard, in 1749, obtained a patent for these ferry rights; this resulted in a disagreeable family squabble, as Thomas Farmar's son, Thomas Farmar Billop (heir of his grandfather, Christopher Billop), had married Sarah Leonard, daughter of Capt. Samuel Leonard. I do not find, however, that Capt. Leonard ever exercised the rights under his patent; perhaps French bought him out, or, by owning the landings, kept him out. At all events, James Drake is next mentioned as keeping the Ferry in connection with the Indian Queen Tavern in 1778, and in 1784 French's ferry rights, with the Ferry house and 194 acres in Highland Park were sold (as per Deed in Book I of Deeds, p. 10, Middlesex Co.) by Abraham Schuyler, Sheriff, and bought by Ann Van Horne. Philip French's sister, Elizabeth, married Cornelius Van Horne, so perhaps Ann was a niece and heir protecting her interests. In 1772 a bridge was built at the Landing, referred to under Mayor Ouke's administration, but it was a two-mile detour to use it and avoid the Ferry, so it probably was not a very strong competitor.

The courage and enterprise of our early capitalists in venturing into an unknown field is clearly seen in the building of the Albany Street bridge, its vicissitudes, disappointments and final triumph; it did away with the ford and ferry of one hundred years. But, unfortunately, the renumeration was not such as the enterprise deserved. Nov. 24, 1790, an Act was passed for a lottery to raise £27,000 to be used in building a road to Newark, for a bridge at New Brunswick and for buildings for the Legislature. There is no record of any movement to carry out this Act, at least as far as the bridge at New Brunswick is concerned. This was followed by an Act to build a toll bridge at New Brunswick. In pursuance of this Act commissioners met at James Drake's Indian Queen Tavern on Nov. 28, 1791, to open a road on the east side of the river, six rods wide, and to be opposite the end of the street called French, or Albany. A record of this road will be found in Book 1 of Deeds, folio 541. Stockholders met at the White Hall Tavern. They were: William Paterson, who subscribed for five shares; John Bayard, 8 shares; Moses Scott, 10 shares, five shares of the ten being for Dr. John Woodhull of Monmouth; J. R. Hardenbergh, 7 shares; John Dennis, Jr., 12 shares, 5 shares of which for John C. Shaw and five shares for Leroy and Bayard; John Dennis, Sr., 28 shares, 20 shares of which were for Thomas Marsten, of New York; Leroy and Bayard 30 shares—a total of 100 shares. The shares were assessed £65, payable, Feb. 12, 1793, £5; May 2, £15; Nov. 3, £15; Jan. 4, 1794, £15; Apr. 5, £5; June 6, £5; Aug., £5.

At the June 6th meeting it was voted that £6,500, proc., additional be raised and on Feb. 11, 1795, that an assessment of £7,000 be made, and it was briefly mentioned that the bridge so far as built, was obliged to be taken down, and as the date of completion of the bridge in the Act was fixed for Nov. 1, 1795, it was resolved to apply to the Legislature for an extension of time. A draft of the bridge by Mr. Newton was unanimously approved and adopted June 6, 1794. The piers were to be 14x12, and five of the piers were to be built on a foundation of pine logs. June 28, 1795, a temporary work and foot bridge was carried away by a flood, but the piers, which were finished, were not injured and stood firm. The Bridge Co.

ledger puts the final cost of the bridge at $86,695.41. Total cost per share, $866.95. There is no explanation given as to why the bridge had to be taken down and rebuilt, but from some of the notes it can be seen that the workers were inexperienced. The iron work was furnished by John Plumb, for 7d. specie per pound, though James Dunham's price was 6¾d; Mr. Randolph would furnish the lumber, but not to be over 16s. per 100 feet. Mr. John Dennis, Sr., attempted to act as superintendent at $1.25 per day. Stelle Randolph furnished stone. After one month John Dennis resigned as superintendent and recommended that "some proper person be employed." In Dec., 1793, the timber of two spans was ordered removed to some secure place and the New York stockholders were requested to procure two skillful persons, masons by profession, experienced in the laying of stone, to view the mason work of the bridge, and that a skillful person be procured to undertake the completion of the bridge. In June, 1794, Mr. Gosman and Mr. Russel of New York, masons, were appointed to superintend and conduct the building of the bridge as to the masonwork and Mr. Newton as to the carpenter work. Oct. 28, 1795, a toll gatherer, John Vandeventer, was engaged at $150 per year and use of toll house.

The toll sheet gives us a list of the vehicles then in use: "A single horse and chaise, or sulkey, 1s., 1d. A two horse wagon or sleigh, 1s., 6d.; if covered, 1s., 10½d. Two horses and chaise, coach or chariot, 1s., 10½d. Two horse phaeton, 1s., 10½d. Four-horse coach, chariot or post chaise, 2s., 9d. Phæton the same. Four-horse wagon, or sleigh, covered, 2s., 9d. One-horse cart, 1s., man 2d., and man and wheelbarrow, 3d. Hogs and sheep, 1d. Cattle, 2½d. Man and horse, 5d."

The bridge was opened Nov. 2, 1795. The first three months' dividend from tolls was declared Jan. 30, 1796, and the "New Jersey Chronicle," Nov. 16, 1795, notes that "we feel a pleasure in announcing that the bridge is so far completed as to render it possible for carriages, and we congratulate our fellow-citizens that this useful and arduous undertaking has been accomplished with such expedition and without any distressing accident occurring to the workmen. The length of this structure is about three hundred and thirty yards; its width sufficient for carriages to pass each other exclusive of a convenient footwalk. The woodwork of this lofty structure rests upon thirteen large and lofty pillars, including two abutments, which for strength and elegance we are warranted in claiming far exceeds anything of its kind in America. A draw is placed over the deepest water for permitting vessels to pass and repass. It is to be regretted that the burden of this great public convenience should be bourne by a few individuals, as there is reason to believe that a suitable rate per cent. will not be realized for the great advances, pains and trouble to which the proprietors have been subjected."

That this prediction was warranted is proved by the dividends. The first ten years the return average three per cent.; for the next ten years 4.6 per cent., and for the next ten years, to 1826, it averaged but 2.58 per cent.; a disappointing result, due to the errors and mistakes in building and a corresponding excessive cost of $86,695.41, as a later bridge, on the same site, cost below $25,000 or less than a third as much, and at that figure the return would have been about ten per cent. on the investment.

In 1829 the stock was increased to 1,000 shares and the cost per share thereby reduced to $86.69. The next ten years brought some radical changes. The Canal Company in 1832 bought out a conflict of rights which did not seem to be adjustable, and in 1835 a suit was contemplated; and now a new menace appeared. The New Jersey Railroad Co., which had built to the river, began to build a bridge, which in 1836 was approaching completion, and as the Bridge Company charter forbade building another bridge between the Landing bridge and the mouth of Lawrence's Brook, and as the railroad bridge had a lower story, wagon and foot bridge, an injunction was decided upon. A settlement of both the canal and railroad questions was brought about by the Railroad Co. buying 600 of the 1,000 shares of the Bridge Co.

At a meeting, held Sept. 6, 1836, at the City Hotel, in the evening. Dr. Charles Smith, Littleton Kirkpatrick, and Joseph W. Scott present, the minutes recite that Herman LeRoy, having sold his stock, resigned as President and director. The Ocean Insurance Co., by Abram Ogden, having sold, resigned; and John P. Jackson and George P. Mollison were appointed in their place and took seats. Littleton Kirkpatrick, executor, W. B. Paterson, Joseph W. Scott, Executor, Moses Scott, having sold and resigned as directors, F. R. Smith and George L Schuyler were appointed directors in their place; Dr. Charles Smith having sold and resigned, John Worthington was appointed in his place. Then George P. Mollison was appointed President and John Worthington secretary and treasurer. These new directors met May 4, 1838 (no record of meeting), at De Graw's Mansion House and took the following action:

"Whereas the bridge of this Company is in a condition to require frequent repairs and cause great interruption to the travelling public, and the lower story of the railroad's viaduct will afford a convenient means of crossing, therefore the Bridge Co. can use and collect the same tolls as on the Albany Street bridge, and in return shall tend the draw and keep the lower story of the bridge in repair."

The minutes and accounts cease here, and resume May 26, 1851. But it is evident that this scheme did not meet public approval, as the public newspapers show. In June 29, 1838, and Jan. 9, 1839, public meetings were held "to protest the condition of the Albany Street bridge, which is owned by the New Jersey Railroad and Transportation Co., which have erected a viaduct for their cars in combination with a toll bridge and are allowing the old bridge to fall into decay." In 1846 it is reported in a dilapidated condition. In 1847 a petition was made that it be reconstructed, as it was anything but a credit. In 1849 it was proposed to apply to the Legislature for permission to lease to the city the charter of the bridge, the bridge having gone to decay. In April, 1849, the bridge material was left at the foot of Albany street, and all but the piers was removed.

In May, 1851, there seems to have been nothing left of the old bridge except the piers and abutments, and a new move to rebuild was brought forward. Eight men met at B. D. Stell's house: F. R. Smith, R. J. Livingston, Samuel V. Hoffman,

James Bishop, L. Kirkpatrick, and, representing the Railroad, J. Phillips Phenix, President, John P. Jackson and John Acken. They formed a new Company. The first five names were to have 97 shares each, and the Railroad to have 485 shares. Each share of stock was assessed twelve dollars. The piers and abutments were valued at $11,000, and the capitalization of the new Company was not to be over $25,000. Plans for the bridge were made by Daniel Stone of Philadelphia. The stock of the old Bridge Company, now owned by the N. J. R. R. & Trans. Co., was to be surrendered. Each holder of 97 shares would have free passage for himself and family and teams over the bridge, and the railroad had the right to lay track and pass cars, passengers and freight, if necessary. It was rebuilt on the plan of Daniel Stone, and by him as contractor, for $8,500. Neilson and Miller furnished the timber; Doty and Ford the plank; Harra and Wesner to be the blacksmiths; John B. Outcalt to furnish iron at 14½d; Isaiah Rolfe and Letson & Strong the hardware; Peter N. Wyckoff to repair the piers; H. Richmond to furnish pale brick at $4.00 a thousand. Mason's wages were to be $1.75. Newark Lime & Cement Co. would supply coal at $4.75; painting was to be $1.75. J. H. Newell graded the road up the hill.

In April, 1853, the bridge was completed and paid 6½ per cent. dividend the first year. The dividends gradually increased from year to year, till in 1871 they were $400 to the 97 shares, or about 30 per cent. What became of the minority stockholders when the Railroad got control in 1836, or when the old stock was surrendered in 1851, does not appear.

But the history of the bridge now draws to a close. The County Board of Freeholders, by an Act of the Legislature, were authorized to have a free bridge at New Brunswick, and the Bridge Co. offered them the bridge at $75,000. The matter dragged along for several years. The Freeholders then had the bridge condemned, and, Sept. 7, 1875, paid $58,000 for the bridge. In consequence of the delay the Bridge Co. received $15,000 in dividends in the four years and so got pretty nearly what they asked.

In 1893 the bridge was removed, piers and all, and a new

arch bridge, with a paved roadway, took the place of the old wooden bridge, just a hundred years after the original. There was almost as much trouble over this bridge as over the original, and part of it was taken down and rebuilt. The Freeholders had no engineer on the job, which was looked after by the city engineer, whose opinion was that the faulty work was the result of removing the false work too soon. Three arches being built, the false work was wanted for the next three.

The bridge has stood for thirty years now, and is apparently good for many years more. The present trouble is that it barely accommodates the travel using it, owing to intercity and interstate auto truck lines. At present (1924) the bridge is being widened 14 feet on the south side.

Before the building of the bridge of 1793 there was a movement made toward a bridge by James Parker and others in the city of New Brunswick, and by Peter Probasco, owner of Livingston Manor, opposite thereto. Again by the inhabitants of the City of New Brunswick and Middlesex and Somerset Counties. John Bayard, John Neilson, Andrew Kirkpatrick, Dr. Lewis Dunham and J. R. Hardenbergh were also a committee to build a bridge in 1791. An Act of 1831 named John Neilson, among others, as a committee to build a bridge at New Brunswick. None of these movements materialized.

Local affairs did not entirely monopolize our early men of affairs. In 1791, when the site for a great cotton manufacturing industry was selected, and called Paterson after Governor William Paterson (a New Brunswick man), John Bayard, John Neilson, More Furman and Elisha Boudinot, all Brunswickers and Jerseymen, are found on the Board. With so noted a ferry and its growing shipping business, the tavern early became an absolute necessity. In fact, travel and the tavern went hand-in-hand. In 1728 we find Capt. John Balding sailing the sloop "Two Brothers," and in 1730 the sloop "Phœbe." In 1734 a Council meeting was held at the house of Ann Balding, while awaiting the building of the Court House, and, in fact, Council evidently preferred her hospitality to that of the empty, and, from all accounts, cheerless Court House, as we find that, after meeting at the Court House they would adjourn to Ann Balding's. In 1734 she is called "the widow Baldwin," Balding having probably been a careless spelling. Henry Greenland and John Inian both kept taverns, or, more probably, made the traveler welcome, rather conferring a favor than looking for custom.

New Brunswick had two decidedly noted taverns, the "White Hart," afterwards called the White Hall, and the "Indian Queen." The first dates from 1761 and is still a hotel under the same name; the second dates from 1729, perhaps earlier, and has been a hotel continuously ever since, though with a change of name, first to "Bell Hotel," about 1817, and recently as the "Parkway." Most of the early entertainment of people of note was at one or the other of these hotels. President John Adams, with "Lady and Suit," stayed at the Indian Queen in November, 1797, and were entertained at dinner at the White Hall.

A later-day tavern was, in 1838, DeGraw's "Mansion House," once the Bank of New Brunswick, and afterwards Miss Hoyt's School, cor. George and Paterson streets, northwest corner. DeGraw had just given up the "Bell" and opened it, but it did not live very long, as Miss Hoyt bought it and moved her school into it in 1847.

While horseback, chair and chaise by land, and sailboat by water, had been the only reliance of travelers, it soon became evident that a regular means of travel was needed, and the stage-wagon and stage-coach, on regular days, appeared.

The early traveller who crossed New Jersey in the first fifty years of its history either walked or rode horseback and arranged for his own transportation, sometimes buying a horse for his journey; and it is not until 1723 that we find a proposal to transport passengers and goods on a definite day and over a particular route.

The three first roads across New Jersey were: the "Upper Road," starting at Elizabethtown and going by Brunswick, Princeton and Trenton to the Delaware; the "Lower Road," which branched off from the Upper west of the Raritan and went by Cranberry and Crosswicks to Burlington and the Delaware; while the "Road from Pearth Town," which was opened in 1684 and ran to Burlington, started from Redford's Ferry (now South Amboy). A man named Dellaman was given the exclusive right by Governor Hamilton to haul freight over this latter road and that caused great dissatisfaction. In 1707 Governor Cornbury was petitioned that this exclusive right was contrary to the statute respecting monopolies and should be withdrawn. The Governor replied, saying, that "by this arrangement everybody was sure once a fortnight of an opportunity to send goods, and that the wagon, instead of a grievance or a monopoly, was the means, and no other, by which trade had been carried on between New York, Amboy, Burlington and Philadelphia, which was never known before." This privilege was abrogated later (1710).

The notice of 1723 referred to above is exceedingly modest and reads: "If any person or persons have occasion to pass or repass, or convey goods from Philadelphia to Trenton and backward, their goods may be secured at the house of John Wolland at Trenton. In order for further conveyance, such persons may inquire or repair to the house of the said John Wolland in Trenton, or at the mill there, or at the Crooked Billet Wharf in Philadelphia." (Benjamin Franklin stopped on first going to Philadelphia at the Crooked Billet Tavern.

It is to be noted that John Wolland does not say in the above notice that he conveys by land or water, wagon or boat. However, he goes on to say in his notice; "Passengers may come and goods may be conveyed from Trenton every Monday or Tuesday, and from Philadelphia every Thursday or Friday. This adventure hinges upon whether there shall be any demand for the service and will be furnished once a week, and upon one of two days, as the demand may warrant." Doubtless this was boat service, from the Crooked Billet Wharf to the mill in Trenton.

We have in Benjamin Franklin's trip to Philadelphia this same year, 1723, a specimen of how the man who could not afford to buy a horse travelled. Franklin was going to Philadelphia to work in a printing office. There was a ferry boat between New York and Amboy on which he took passage. It was a boisterous day on the water, and, finally, when night came on, to prevent being blown on the Long Island shore, they cast anchor and tossed about there all night, getting to Amboy the next day. The following morning (the third day) he crossed Redford's Ferry to what is now South Amboy, and set out a-foot for Burlington. At noon he arrived at a "poor Inn," where he stayed till next day; then (the fourth day) walked to Dr. Brown's Inn where he spent the night. The next, and fifth day, he walked into Burlington and found that the Saturday boat had sailed and that the next would not go until Tuesday. While strolling along the river bank he found a row boat and some men intending to row to Philadelphia. He joined them. They rowed until midnight when some, thinking they had passed Philadelphia, would row no more, and pulled into a small creek, where they lay till morning, when they found they were not far from Philadelphia; and they got in between 8 and 9 o'clock Sunday morning (the sixth day).

Franklin says he "had one silver Dutch dollar and a shilling in copper, which latter he paid for his ride in the boat, although he rowed as much as the others."

Lee, in his "New Jersey as a Colony and a State," mentions the three ferries of Inians, at New Brunswick, Billops and Redford's. We shall have occasion in this sketch to go via Cooper's, at Philadelphia; Ramsey's, at Trenton; Coryell's, about five miles above Trenton, now Lambertville; the New Blazing Star on the Kil von Kull to Staten Island; go back again to Bergen Point by John Beck; take the ferry over the Passaic and also over the Hackensack, and finally the Powles Hook Ferry to New York.

In addition we have the ferries, or rather water portions of the earliest routes, viz., Philadelphia to Trenton, to Burlington or to Bordentown—three routes; and from Amboy, Woodbridge, Blazing Star and Elizabethtown Point to New York—four other routes; all of which will appear in the various advertisements of stage-boats and stage-wagons in the following sixty years.

It is six years to the next advertisement, 1729, when, in the "Mercury" of Feb. 18-25, 1728-'29, we see that—

"The Plantation called Redford's Ferry, over against Amboy, is to be let, with a good dwelling house, kitchen and stables, scow and carrier. Any person that has a mind to hire it may apply himself to Gabrielle Stelle who lives at said place and agree at reasonable terms.—N. B. There is also a Stage Wagon kept at said Ferry for transporting of passengers and goods from thence to Burlington, and doth attend whenever freight presents."

This is the first definite mention of a stage-wagon, but not yet with a schedule of days; it only goes "when business presents."

An item in the "Pennsylvania Gazette" of Sept. 13-'20, 1729, gives an idea of the roads:

"We hear from Gloucester Co. in the Jerseys that on Saturday last one John Matson was riding in his cart; the wheel passing over a stump overturned the cart and killed him on the spot."

The water journey was not without its excitements also, as the "Mercury," of April 16-'23, 1730, notes:

"On Tuesday last at Amboy we had a sudden storm of wind and rain in which a canoe that was going over the ferry here was overset and three persons drowned."

The stage-wagon waiting at the Amboy ferry for such travel as might present itself in 1728 is improved upon, in 1733, by the establishing of a regular wagon, once a week, from Burlington to Amboy Ferry. The "Mercury," of March 13-'20, 1732-'33, says:

"This is to give notice unto Gentlemen, Merchants, Tradesmen, Travellers and others that Solomon Smith and James Moon of Burlington keepeth two Stage Waggons intending to go from Burlington to Amboy and back from Amboy to Burlington again, once every week, or offt'er if that Business presents. They have also a very good Store House, very commodious for the storing of any sort of merchant's goods, free from any charges, where good care will be taken of all sorts of goods by Solomon Smith and James Moon."

Now we have a definite proposal, but still contingent on the demand. This New York-Amboy-Burlington-Philadelphia route is in opposition to the Philadelphia-Trenton route, and from now on added attractions by one route are met by similar efforts on the other. In 1738 a stage-wagon to connect up the water sections at each end is advertised in the "Mercury" (Jan. 31-Feb. 7):

"To accommodate the Public—There will be a Stage Waggon set out from Trenton to Brunswick Twice a week and back again during next summer. It will be fitted up with benches and covered over so that passengers may sit easy and dry, and care will be taken to deliver goods and messages safe. Note: The Waggon will set out for the first time from Wm. Atlees and Thomas Hootons in Trenton" [Thomas Hooton lived at Trenton Ferry] "on Monday, the 27th March next, and continue going every Monday and Thursday, and return from Brunswick every Tuesday and Friday."

The water ride to Trenton, stage to Brunswick, and water again to New York, is now made by two complete opposition routes from New York to Philadelphia. Water accidents were not rare. For example, Nov. 26, 1729, a Perth Amboy notice says:

"Last Saturday our Ferry Boat coming over from the other side with seven men and seven horses; a gust of wind arose and overset the Boat by means whereof Two Horses and two men were drowned. The rest were saved."

Again, Philadelphia, Oct. 21, 1731:

"On Tuesday last one Samuel Crosteyn, a Baker, going from this city to Burlington in a passage boat, fell overboard near Pennypack and was drowned. His body is not yet found."

And again, Philadelphia, March 12:

"Three persons were drowned by the upsetting of a wherry from Burlington hither; five other persons in it were saved."

The stage-wagon of 1738, Trenton to Brunswick, was not a success and was discontinued in 1739, as appears from a notice in 1740. William Atlee had associated himself with Joseph Yeates and gives notice:

"Whereas there was a Stage Waggon went twice a week from Trenton to Brunswick and back again in the summer of 1738, the convenience of which from its certainty and cheapness, and the inconveniences people labored under from being detained and paying extravagant rates, has induced several people to apply to the owners promising them their assistance and encouragement: This is to give notice that the Stage Waggon will be continued and go twice a week certain, from Trenton Ferry every Monday and Thursday and from Brunswick back again every Tuesday and Friday during the summer. The waggon will be covered over so that passengers may sit easy and dry and care will be taken to deliver goods and messages safe. To encourage People to travel and send goods by the said Waggon the following low prices are fixed: Every passenger 2s., 6d., proc. Merchant goods, 2s. per C. Household goods, boxes, etc., at the cheapest rates. Performed by William Atlee and Joseph Yeates. Note: The Waggon will set out Monday, the 21st of this instant April from the Ferry at Trenton." ("Penn. Gazette," Apr. 10, 1740).

The Amboy Ferry and Burlington route of 1733, by Smith and Moon, is not again mentioned, but Joseph Borden, the energetic promoter of Borden's Town in 1740, gives notice that 'on the first day of May next, there will be ready and well-fixed a stage wagon to carry passengers and goods between Perth Amboy and Borden's Town, which will attend at Amboy Ferry on every Tuesday and Borden's Town every Thursday, on which days all persons intending to transport themselves or goods may be carried from either of said places to the other for four shillings a passenger, and all goods at reasonable rates. Security is given by the wagoner for the safe conveying all goods delivered into his charge. All persons having goods to transport, as aforesaid, may send them to Joseph Borden at Borden's Town or Pontius Stelle at Amboy who will take proper care that they shall be sent according to order.' Joseph Borden also established stage-boats to Philadelphia from Borden's Town to head off his growing rival at Trenton.

The next year (June, 1741) William Meghee advertises a Stage by the Amboy-Borden's Town route, probably a weak opposition. He gives notice that he will attend on Monday and will go twice a week "when there is occasion," if the passengers "will pay what is reasonable" in that case. We hear no more of Meghee. Borden and Stelle had a supplementary notice in 1740 to get the Burlington trade also, viz., that 'their Stage Wagon will attend at Perth Amboy Ferry every Tuesday and Burlington every Thursday, they being the two most convenient places for a speedy transportation of any yet projected from New York to Philadelphia. Said Wagon will go the old post road from Amboy as far as Crosswicks Bridge and, if lading presents, will go with it to Burlington, or it may be carried at small expense from Borden's Town to Burlington or Philadelphia by water in a few hours' time. Passengers will be carried for four shillings.' This advertisement was also printed in Dutch.

The next notice, June 7, 1744, is of the Trenton-Brunswick route, hitherto run from the Trenton end by Atlee-Hooten and Atlee-Yeates. Now it is a Brunswick man, William Willson, who heads the venture and the start is from Brunswick. It is to go certainly 'twice a week on the following days: from Brunswick Monday and Thursday, and from Trenton every Tuesday and Friday, when passengers can be carried safe and dry. All persons sending goods from Philadelphia are desired to direct to the care of Thomas Hutton, who will attend in Trenton, and those in New York to William Willson in New Brunswick, where care will be taken to forward them speedily and in good order.' This is the first notice by this route that considers through business between New York and Philadelphia.

The water portions of both routes were still subject to accidents. On April 29, 1742, we read: "A boat with passengers from New York to Brunswick was overset and the daughter of one Solemn was drowned. The rest of the passengers were taken up by another boat then in company." And the next year: "A boat between Philadelphia and Burlington, a shallop, in which were seven passengers, was overset by a violent gale of wind; four of them were drowned before assistance could come." Feb. 29, 1743-'44. And on Aug. 19, 1745: "A boat from New York to Brunswick, Mr. Brooks boatman, took in seventeen passengers. Three women and three children were drowned by being overset."

The next notice of 1750 is of the Bordentown and Amboy route in the "New York Gazette and Weekly Post Boy," Oct. 15, 1750:

"This is to give notice to all Gentlemen and Ladies that have occasion to transport either themselves, goods, wares or merchandizes from New York to Philadelphia, that by the subscriber there is now a Stage-Boat well fitted for that purpose kept, and if wind and weather permit shall attend at the late Col. Moore's wharf in New York every Wednesday in every week (and at other times if occasion), and to proceed to the Ferry at Amboy on Thursday, where on Friday morning a Stage Waggon, well fitted, will be ready to receive them and immediately proceed to Borden's Town, where there is another Stage-Boat ready to receive them and proceed directly to Philadelphia. All people may depend on the best usage and all passengers and merchandise shall be transported at the same rates as are customary from New Brunswick to Trenton. And as the passages by water are much shorter and easier perform'd than the Brunswick-way, and the roads generally drier, it is hoped this way will be found the most deserving of encouragement. "DANIEL O'BRIEN."

Here we have the first distinct recognition of the two routes and a strong bid for patronage by the Amboy one; and the claims are all well made, for the water route to New Brunswick must pass right by the Amboy Ferry and then come all the way up the river to New Brunswick, while the water route from Trenton is a little longer than from Bordentown. We also have here the first notice of an effort to connect up the various links of the route and to convey the passengers all the way through under one management.

A notice, in the "Pennsylvania Gazette," May 14, 1752, is that by Joseph Borden, Jr.:

"There is a Stage-Boat, well fitted and kept for that purpose, and if wind and weather permit, will attend at the Crooked Billet Wharff in Philadelphia every Tuesday and proceed up to Bordentown on Wednesday, and on Thursday morning a Stage-Wagon with a good arning [awning] kept by Joseph Richards will be ready to receive them and proceed directly to

John Cluck's [the old Redford Ferry of 1684] opposite the City of Perth Amboy, who keeps a house of good entertainment; and on Friday morning a Stage-Boat, well fitted and kept by Daniel Obryant, will proceed directly to New York and give her attendance at the White-hall slip, near the Half-moon battery. If people be ready at the stage days and places 'tis believed they may pass the quickest 30 or 40 hours, the cheapest and safest way that has yet been made use of. . . . All passengers or goods, that shall come to Bordentown on Sunday or Monday by any Trenton shallop, White-hall shallop, or Bordentown shallops or boats, or in any other whatsoever, whose waggon hire shall amount to 16s. or upwards, shall upon first notice have a waggon, and be transported to the above John Cluck's, opposite Amboy, where if the Stage-Boat is not ready to receive them (but 'tis intended she shall) it must be allowed they have the greatest chance for despatch of any other place whatsoever, for all the Brunswick, the place above Brunswick called the Landing; and all the river boats must pass that place in whom people may have passage.

"JOSEPH RICHARDS.

"N. B. Attendance will be also at the Crooked Billet Wharff, in Philadelphia, every Friday and Saturday and proceed to Bordentown on Sunday, and on Monday the Stage-waggon will set out for Amboy, passengers or not."

The 30 or 40 hours above evidently refers to actual time of travel and does not include the layovers at the taverns, as the time of arrival and departure covers three days, seventy-two hours.

They seem to have taken turns in advertising, O'Brien (sometimes spelled "Obryant") the New York end, Richards the stage section, and next, Jan. 2, 1753, Joseph Borden, Jr., Nicholas George, Master, the Philadelphia end, when it says that "it is the quickest by 24 hours than any other way as the land carriage is 10 miles shorter than by Burlington and our waggon does not fail to go through in a day." Signed by "Joseph Borden, Jr., Joseph Richards and Daniel Obryant," with an "N. B." stating that the "shallop, Charles Vandike, Master, will also be at Philadelphia every Friday and Saturday in every week. Enquire for him at the Queen's Head. He proceeds to Bordentown on Sunday and the Stage-Waggon proceeds to Amboy every Monday."

In June, 1753, we have another step forward. Abraham Webb, 'being provided with a boat exceedingly well fitted with a very handsome cabin and all necessary accommodations, proposes to give his attendance at the White Hall Slip every Monday and Thursday, and the same day, wind and weather permitting, to proceed from Amboy Ferry to John Cluck's, where John Richards will be ready to proceed, load or no load, to Bordentown where a Stage-Boat will carry them to Philadelphia.'

After a nine years' silence we hear again from the Trenton and Brunswick route. Andrew Ramsey, an Innholder of New York, received a lease, Sept. 26, 1750, of the Brooklyn Ferry for the term of two years and six months for £455. He was bound to keep one or more scows and one or more boats for the transportation of cattle, one of which was to be always in readiness on the New York side of the river at Wall St. His lease having expired in 1753 he gives notice to all travellers between New York and Philadelphia "that the Trenton Ferry is now revived by Andrew Ramsay, late of Long Island Ferry, where all travellers who are pleased to put up at his house may depend on having good entertainment for themselves and horses. Said Ramsay is providing a Stage-Waggon to go from Brunswick to Trenton and a Stage-Boat from Philadelphia to Trenton. N. B. Notice will be given what days in the week the boat and waggon will proceed from stage to stage—per me, Andrew Ramsay."

With the revival of the Trenton route the Burlington route is also revived and with, now, two competitors, the rivalry becomes active. In 1753 James Wells and John Weggery 'with a commodious Stage-Boat will attend at the Crooked Billet wharff twice a week and Wednesday and Saturday proceed to the house of Jonathan Thomas in Burlington, who keeps a good Stage-Waggon ready, which, on Thursday morning, will proceed to Perth Amboy Ferry, where a house of good entertainment is kept by Daniel O'Bryant, master and a commodious Stage-Boat will, on Friday morning, proceed directly to New York at the Whitehall slip at the house of Scotch John, returning Saturday.' Monday, the Stage kept by John Prigmore would set out for Burlington, so that Wells and Weggery would complete the trip to Philadelphia on Monday. The advertisement then goes on to say:

"Although the owners of the Bordentown stage have been pleased, by way of hyperbole, to advertise that their stage can perform the aforesaid passage sooner by 24 hours than any other stages, but have omitted to inform the public that their stage-boat from Philadelphia to Borden's Town is frequently three tides upon the water, or the greatest part thereof, viz., two tides of flood and one of ebb, during which time the Burlington stage is capable of landing her passengers at Perth Amboy, and, upon cases of emergency, is capable of performing the whole stage from Philadelphia to New York in 24 hours; and as an undertaking of this kind tends to the general good of mankind in increasing and facilitating trade and commerce between the two places, besides many other advantages to the subject, we hope that those gentlemen who have occasion to transport themselves or goods from either of the places aforesaid to the other will encourage so public a good. . . . The public's humble servants, Jonathan Thomas, John Prigmore, James Wells, John Weggery, Daniel O'Bryant."

There seems to be room for more stage-boats, and, on Aug. 30, 1753, 'Patrick Cowan, Master of two commodious Stage Boats, attends at the Crooked Billet Wharf and connects with Jonathan Thomas at Burlington.' And, Sept. 24, 1753, John "Predmore" and Daniel "O'Brian" give notice that the stage from Perth Amboy will change horses and drivers at the house of John Predmore in Cranberry and proceed to Burlington the same day. Here we get the first mention of a relay of horses. On April 11, 1754, the Bordentown Line retorts:

"Our adversaries have been pleased to advertise that they can give people greater dispatch than we can, so that we appeal to fact. As we were the promoters of this scheme, as yet of no advantage to any but the publick, and as we take pay for 13 miles less land carriage than the Burlington people do, we hope all well-minded people will lay their commands upon their humble servants, Joseph Borden, Jr., Joseph Richards, James Wells."

It took the Burlington people a year to reply, but on April 17, 1755, they say:

"The owners of the Bordentown stage in their last advertisement unkindly call us their adversaries, and in a manner, too, that seems as if they were angry, but for no other reason that we know of than a dislike to the increase of our business. In return, without calling names (a practise unbecoming brother adventurers, pro bona publica) we assure them we intend to improve the natural advantages of our situation to such general satisfaction as neither to be thought adversaries ourselves nor to harbour such an ill opinion of our neighbors; so we remain the publick's friends, JONATHAN THOMAS, JOSEPH HANCOCK.

"N. B. The master of the Bordentown Stage has been pleased to inform the publick that he takes pay for 13 miles less land carriage than we do, but has not been kind enough to inform them that he takes pay for 10 miles more water carriage, and that they lie one tide more of the water than we do."

These advertisements are curiosities, but we hear little further from these two routes; new and more expeditious routes apparently crowded them out. That the roads were still rough and the water routes still dangerous the next few notices show:

Aug. 12, 1751. "We hear from Elizabeth that two women have been killed within these few weeks past near that place by falling out of riding chairs" [high, two-wheeled vehicles, much like that used to-day for tandem driving].

Jan. 19. 1753. "On Christmas Day 3 persons attempted to cross Raritan in a canoe. They were overset by the ice and two of them drowned."

June 10, 1754. "A Brunswick boat in coming across New York Bay was overset by a squall and five of her 18 passengers were drowned in the cabin, entirely owing to the obstinacy or rather unskilfulness of the boatman."

We now come to a new stage line and route. Hitherto the stages have started from Trenton, Burlington and Bordentown, but in 1756 notice appears that John Butler, at the sign of the Death of the Fox in Strawberry Alley, Philadelphia, would begin on Tuesday, the 9th of Nov., and proceed with his "waggon" to the house of Nathaniel Parker at Trenton; from thence over the ferry to the house kept by George Moschel, where Francis Holman would meet John Butler and exchange passengers and then proceed on Wednesday through Princetown and New Brunswick to the house of Obadiah Airies in Perth Amboy, where would be a good boat with all conveniences kept by John Thomson and William Waller, who would proceed on Thursday morning without delay for New York and there land at Whitehall and give attention at the house of Abraham Bockeys until Monday morning and then return. It was signed by John Butler, Francis Holman, John Thomson and William Waller.

The above route extended the land route to Perth Amboy. The Bordentown line, to meet this, gives notice, Jan. 31, 1757, as follows:

"Whereas the subscriber hath been instrumental of propagating a stage between Philadelphia and New York, and by experience finding some difficulty, sometimes, to pass by water from Amboy Ferry to New York; Notice is hereby given That a Stage-Waggon is erected, to proceed from Mr. Isaac Dole's, opposite to Perth Amboy, on Monday, the 17th instant, January, and to pass through Staten-Island, load or no load, to Mr. John Watson's, [Elizabethtown Point Ferry], Mrs. Ducket's, and Mr. Vantile's [Bergen Point Ferry], and on Tuesday proceed back to the aforesaid Dole's, and so in like manner every day in the week; where due attendance will be given . . . by me, "JOSEPH RICHARDS.

"N. B. To hinder disputes or resentments that may arise hereafter I have thought fit to inform the public of my price and custom. Each passenger to pay 3s., before they proceed on their journey and in proportion for other things (except letters, which are to be carried gratis)."

This stage was to go to a New York and Staten Island Ferry,[1] evidently at Vantile's, though the notice fails to state that fact.

---

[1] Staten Island abounded in ferries; its geographical position made it a desirable link in the New York-Philadelphia stage route, saving a considerable detour, if the Newark route is considered, and the routes across the Island were many. One could cross at Amboy to Isaac Dole's [Doly's] as per the advertisement just read, stopping at the Blazing Star and at the Elizabethtown Point ferries (two each) to pick up passengers and continue to the Bergen Point ferry, or, still further, to the New Brighton ferries (again two). The stages crossed at the Blazing Star or Elizabethtown Point ferries and crossed back again at Bergen Point ferry. If we begin at the southwest end of the Island,

The result of the Bordentown notice was that John Butler promptly meets the change by a re-arrangement of his own route, and Francis Holman, instead of proceeding Wednesday to Amboy, was to proceed to Brunswick only, where Isaac Fitz Randolph would meet him and take his passengers to the New Blazing Star and to Jacob Fitz Randolph's, where Reuben Fitz Randolph, with a boat well-fitted, would receive and take them to New York that night, cutting about ten miles out of the water carriage and avoiding the Lower Bay, the night ride saving a day.

That goods sometimes got astray appears in a notice of Oct. 30, 1758, that 'a small trunk that came from Philadelphia in the Stage-Boat about the first of August is now in the possession of John Thompson, Jr., of Amboy; 'tis 2 feet long, 13 inches broad and pretty ponderous; the owner paying charges may have said trunk.'

Now appears a new stage line through an entirely different

opposite Amboy, for the first or Billop's ferry, then came the Old Blazing Star ferry at Seawarren; next, the New Blazing Star ferry, now Linoleumville, kept by Jacob Fitz Randolph in 1757 and by Joshua Mersereau in 1774. The two Elizabethtown Point ferries were John Watson's noted ferry, 1764, and that of William Douglas in 1769. About 400 yards below was Simonson's, 1769; then Jesse Johnson's. Then, coming to Joseph Corson, 1753 (probably the *first New York Ferry*, as Booth in his "History" says the first ferry to Staten Island was in 1754, while the "Memorial History of New York" says 1755—certainly not the first to Staten Island as Billop's and the Old Blazing Star must have been older), John Beck in 1764 operating it, though owned and offered for sale in that year by Abraham Vantile and John Mersereau. This was the Bergen Point and sixth ferry. Then John Ryer's ferry in 1769, not certainly located, to New York from what is now, I believe, New Brighton, and, adjoining it, Hilliken's ferry. These were oppositions, Ryer charging 25 cents and Hilliken 18 cents per ferriage. David Mersereau bought out and combined them. He is the third Mersereau to own and operate ferries. As they were sons of Joshua and Maria Corson Mersereau, and Joseph Corson has the first ferry on record, they nearly controlled the ferries on the Island. Isaac Decker, in 1774, maintained his ferry was but one to two hours from New York and ten or twelve miles shorter to Philadelphia than by Powles Hook. He was operating in opposition to Mersereau and to the Powles Hook and Bergen Point route. Otto Van Tuyl offers what seems to be this ferry for sale in 1774, noting that, "It has long been a ferry," and refers to Van Tuyl & Varrick, New York. One more ferry was that at the Narrows to Brooklyn. Among the early ferrymen was Cornelius Vanderbilt, but later than the period we are considering; about 1810 he sailed his periaugers and does not belong in this early stage-and-ferry transport age.

territory, more for the convenience of Mount Holly, Middletown and Shrewsbury than for passengers from Philadelphia to New York, as a notice is given to the public that 'the subscribers have erected a stage wagon to transport passengers, etc., from Mr. Daniel Cooper's ferry opposite the City of Philadelphia to Mount Holly, from there through the county of Monmouth to Middletown, where a stage will connect for Shrewsbury, thence to the Bay near Sandy Hook,[2] where a boat will attend to carry passengers, etc., to the City of New York. The Stage will attend at the ferry on the second Tuesday in Oct., 1761, at seven in the morning and the boat will attend at the City of New York on the second Monday.' This was probably a five or six day trip.

The Coopers were a ferrying family and "Cooper's Ferry" to Philadelphia was maintained for many years. A Daniel Cooper, when a boy, said he and his sister rowed passengers over the ferry at Brunswick about 1720, claiming to be of the first settlers. This was reported by him in 1816.

On Oct. 14, 1762, Joseph Borden, Jr., gives notice that 'the Magistrates of Philadelphia, having forbidden my boats sailing upon the Sabbath, puts me under the necessity of changing my stage days, and hereafter they will sail Monday and Thursday.' Here we have an instance of the enforcement of the "Blue laws" in Pennsylvania.

In 1762 the Burlington Stage line was running as usual, the last we hear of it for ten years.

On Aug. 18, 1763, Jonathan Biles, probably of Biles Island, where it was the custom to hold lottery drawings, living in 3rd Street a few doors above Race, Philadelphia, announces that he has provided a stage wagon to go to Trenton Ferry on Monday, Tuesday, Thursday and Friday, 'where other stage waggons will carry to Brunswick and from there to Elizabethtown or Amboy, as passengers may choose.' He seems to have succeeded John Butler, who, by the next notice, has joined with John Buckingham, who, June, 1764, gives notice that he will

---

[2]Probably at Middletown Point or Middletown Harbour, where there used to be a ferry to Long Island. William Edmondson, the Quaker preacher, crossed New Jersey about this route in 1672.

drive a stage to Bordentown from 3rd and Race streets and proceed to Dunk's Ferry (a new ferry on the Delaware), where John Butler will meet and exchange loads and proceed to Bordentown every Wednesday and Saturday. This cuts out the boat ride to Bordentown. Biles soon tired of his venture and, June, 1764, sold his stages to John Barnhill, who continues the line, but from his house, the Golden Ball, in Elm Street, between 2nd and 3rd, near Vine.

Oct. 1, 1764. Now we may vary the monotony of these notices by an entirely new route. Sovereign Sybrandt will set out from Philadelphia Monday and run thence to Trenton; from Trenton to New Brunswick and from Brunswick to Sybrandt's House, known by the Sign of the Roebuck, two miles and a-half of Elizabethtown; and from there by the new and established post road ("on Bergen, which is now generally resorted to by the populace who prefer a passage by said place before the danger of crossing the Bay") to Powles Hook, opposite to New York where it discharges its passengers, from which last place it returns on Wednesday and is in Philadelphia the Friday following. Each single passenger at the rate of 2 pence half-penny a mile from Powles Hook to Sybrant's House, "as it's the longest stage and obliged to return back the same day;" and at the rate of 2 pence for every mile after. We now have an all land route, excepting for the ferries, in three days.

There had been, without doubt, a road from Newark to Bergen and to Powles Hook from an early date, but not such a road as would accommodate stage travel. But on the completion of the Post Road and the establishment of the ferry at Powles Hook in 1764 (opened June 18 by Abraham Mesier from the New York side, foot of Grand St., also foot of Thomas St. and foot of Cortlandt St., as I find by different authorities, probably at different dates at each of them), it seems Michael Cornelisse built a Tavern on Powles Hook and operated the ferry at that end under a lease from Cornelius Van Vorst, who owned all of Powles Hook and continued to do so until 1800, when conditions changed. Van Vorst improved the road from the ferry to Bergen Point ferry (corduroy for the swampy portions), and so opened a new route across Staten Island, and by the Blazing Star Ferry near Woodbridge back to the main land. And John Mercereau was not slow in taking advantage of it, for, early in 1765, he gives notice that his wagon sets off from Powles Hook every Wednesday and Saturday between seven and eight in the morning (as the boat did not get over that early it was necessary to come over the night before and stay at Cornelisse's Tavern) and is met at the Blazing Star at 12 the same day by William Richard's wagon, which proceeds immediately to New Brunswick. John Downey's wagon then proceeds to Trenton on every Monday and Thursday between seven and eight, and from Trenton John Barnhill's wagon proceeds on Tuesday and Friday to Philadelphia. This trip is made in three days at the farthest. Fare 4s. per stage, or 12s. New York to Philadelphia.

There were five ferries on the route via Trenton, Brunswick, Blazing Star, Bergen Point and Powles Hook, and five on the new post road route, viz., Trenton, Brunswick, Passaic, Hackensack and Powles Hook, which latter route, now that the delays and dangers of the water portions have been eliminated, are referred to as an unmitigated nuisance. Sybrandt had to ferry his wagon over all four ferries, while by Mercereau's route and wagon from ferry to ferry he only transfers the passengers at Blazing Star, Brunswick and Trenton; much simpler than taking over the horses and stage.

The water danger was still to be reckoned with, notwithstanding that John Beck, ferryman at Bergen Point ferry in 1764, gives notice that there was a fine road to Powles Hook, so that a short, safe and convenient way is fixed by means of these two ferries for all travelers passing from New York to any of the southern governments. We have a news article regarding this ferry in 1767. The stage, in which some of the passengers had remained seated while crossing in the scow, was overturned into the water and Mrs. Morris and her maid were drowned. Mrs. Morris was an actress and her husband was then playing King Henry in "Richard the Third" in the old playhouse in John St., New York.

NEW BRUNSWICK IN HISTORY

We still find records of stage accidents from time to time. A New York newspaper of Aug. 15, 1765, says:

"On Tuesday, the week before last one of the Borden Town stage waggoners, named Bliss, on returning home from Amboy Ferry, endeavored to get before one of the other waggons, and, turning out of the road for that purpose, ran against a small stump, by which he was flung out of the waggon and the wheel, going over his head, crushed it, and instantly killed him, without his speaking a word."

The next effort is to shorten the journey to two days, and, on Feb. 13, 1766, John Barnhill and John "Masherew" give notice to the public that a stage-waggon, kept by John Barnhill in Elm St., Philadelphia and John Masherew at the Blazing Star, New York, "intend to perform the journey from Philadelphia to New York in two days," commencing the 14th of April, and to continue for seven months (and over those roads that Franklin says were seldom passable without danger and difficulty). This was after 37 years of staging, to meet the requirements of rapid driving. "The waggon seats to be set on springs." They would "set out from Philadelphia and New York on Mondays and Thursdays, as they now do, punctually at sunrise, and change their passengers at Prince Town, and return to Philadelphia and New York the following days." Prices, 10s. to Princeton and 10s. to Powles Hook opposite New York, with ferriage free, and 3d. each mile any distance between. This brings Princeton into prominence as the halfway house. The stages in one of their advertisements are designated "flying machines."

The "New York Post Boy" of May 9, 1768, calls attention to the fact that with two waggons and four sets of horses persons may now go from New York to Philadelphia and back in five days and remain two nights and one day in Philadelphia. The stage waggon puts up at the Hudibras Tavern in Princeton, kept by Jacob Hyer; and the "Post Boy," June 20, 1768, gives further notice that there is a ferry now at Hackensack River on the Powles Hook route, which would indicate that it had been discontinued since Sybrant used it in 1764, the stages going by Bergen Point.

We have still another new route begun, in an effort to reduce the number of ferries. It is from Philadelphia to New York on the old York Road, which I find to be defined in 1756 as via Lambertville, Flemington, Somerville, Bound Brook, Plainfield, Springfield, Elizabeth, starting from the Sign of the Bunch of Grapes in 3rd Street, at sunrise Tuesday, going by Coryell's Ferry (now Lambertville), Bound Brook, Elizabeth, Newark and Powles Hook, exchanging passengers at Obadiah Taylor's at South Branch of the Raritan on Wednesday morning. The notice is of Sept. 25, 1769, and says: "That part of the country is very pleasant, the roads not inferior to any from Philadelphia to New York, and there is but one ferry to Newark." It is signed by Joseph Crane and Josiah F. Davenport. (The notice omits to say that there are three more ferries between Newark and New York).

By a notice of April 21, 1770, we learn that the Burlington and Amboy Stage has been dropped for some time past, but Joseph Haight revives it for the convenience of people who want to go that route. It is, however, a three-day trip against two by the all-land route, and with the uncertainties of the water sections.

May 28, 1770, Abraham Skillman gives notice that he will take passengers through to Philadelphia via Newark, Elizabeth Town, Woodbridge, Brunswick, Princetown, Trenton and Bristol in two days for 20s; "keeps two setts of horses, but drives all the way himself," (so passengers are not so likely to leave things behind as when there is a change of wagons). He limits his load to eight passengers.

Jan. 14, 1771 John Mercereau and John Barnhill remind the public that they continue to run their stages. Now competition really becomes keen. Abraham Skillman, though only one year in the business, now dubs his stage a "Flying Machine," and gives notice that it will leave Powles Hook Tuesday morning and be in Philadelphia Wednesday at 12 noon, starting at 5.00 A. M., and making the trip in one day and a-half.

John Mercereau, Aug. 23, 1771, follows Skillman and gives notice that his "Flying Machine" will perform the journey in a day and a-half, and make three trips a week in summer and

NEW BRUNSWICK IN HISTORY

two trips a week in winter. This is the quickest time made as yet, and will not be equalled for many years to come.

According to a notice by Joseph Hart, July 23, 1772, the Philadelphia Stage Coach, from Indian Queen, by way of Bristol, Trenton, Brunswick, Elizabeth and Newark, fare 30s, leaves Friday and goes through in two days—four good horses—and accommodates eight passengers. Here we have the use of the word "coach" for the first time; it has been stage-waggon, stage, flying machine, and now "coach," and this is a revival of the Newark and Post Road route. The Bordentown and Burlington stage to South Amboy is continued and advertised by Joseph Borden and Joseph Folwell, Dec. 2, 1772. (These two old competitors seem to have combined). The fare is 5s. from Amboy to Bordentown and 6s. to Burlington. They were still running in 1773, as there is a note of stages passing through Cranbury that year. The Philadelphia and New York Stage Coaches from Indian Queen began, Apr. 13, 1773, to exchange at Princeton, making the trip in two days; fare $4.00, but instead of Joseph Hart they were now operated by Charles Bessnot & Co. In Jan., 1774, Joseph Hart is again operating this line on the same schedule, baggage now limited to 14 lbs. In June, 1774, John Mercereau has dropped back to two days, starting now from The Cross Keys, Philadelphia, and exchanging at Princeton. The day and a-half was too much for him. But Abraham Skillman continues the day and a-half schedule, leaving Arch and Second Sts., and going by Newark (as per a notice of August, 1774).

In Sept., 1774, the Philadelphia and New York Stage-wagon from Cross Keys, Philadelphia, exchanges at Princeton; fare 20s.; trips two days. It is so advertised by Charles Bessonett. Apparently "Bessonett & Co." was composed of Bessonett and Hart.

In 1775 a change of stages at the Hackensack Ferry was made to save the delay in ferrying.

We are now at the end of the pre-Revolutionary Stage-Coach days. The War is upon us. There is but one more notice of a through stage:

'July 9, 1776.—The Bordentown Stage-Boat will leave Sunday only and passengers will be conveyed to Powles Hook, the usual route being interrupted by the enemy's fleet.' ("Philadelphia Evening Post").

In March 31, 1777, there is a notice of a ferry between New York and Amboy, under the auspices of the British:

'The Subscriber, having permission from their Excellencies the Commanders-in-Chief to establish a stage boat from New York to Perth Amboy, will sail every Monday and Thursday.—WM. DeMAYNE.'

That there was an effort to keep communications and a semblance of transportation open the following notices indicate (all being abridged):

Dec., 1778. The Bordentown Stage from Crooked Billet Wharf on Saturday or Sunday; wagon to Brunswick Monday; to Elizabeth Tuesday and return to Brunswick same day.—Joseph Borden. He repeats this notice in 1780.

Feb. 15, 1779.—From Burlington to Brunswick; from Crooked Billet Wharf in Philadelphia Wednesday; stage Thursday to Brunswick.—John Willis. (Back to boat and stage once more).

June 6, 1780.—A Stage-Wagon to go from New Brunswick; ferry to Elizabeth; every Tuesday.—Wm. Rider.

Sept. 6, 1780.—A Stage-Wagon by John DeGrove, innholder and ferry keeper, on his side Raritan River in New Brunswick, to go to Elizabeth every Tuesday. Also horses, or a horse and chair can be hired.

Sept. 27, 1780.—Philadelphia to Trenton. Stage-Wagon from Cross Keys Tavern, 3rd and Chestnut Sts., on Tuesdays and return Wednesdays.—Jonathan Scholfield. (The through route again broken up into stages).

Oct. 20, 1780.—Elizabethtown Stage from Cross Keys, Philadelphia, Wednesday and Saturday at 10; to proceed to Princeton and meet the stages from Elizabethtown engaged to be there on Thursday at noon. The route is from Cross Keys to Four Lanes End, Wednesday; Thursday to Trenton, to house of J. G. Bergen for breakfast; thence to Princeton, to Col. Jacob Hyer's and return to Trenton same evening; Friday by Four Lanes End (now Langhorne, Pa.) to Philadelphia; fare two silver dollars.—Gershom Johnson.

Jan. 27, 1781.—Extended to Elizabethtown.

Apr. 30, 1781.—The Elizabethtown Stage-Wagon, with four horses, change every 20 miles, Monday and Thursday; breakfast at Four Lanes End and shift horses; cross new ferry at Trenton and drive to Bergen's at Princeton; shift horses and lodge in Brunswick; next day to Elizabethtown at 10 A. M., at Dr. Winant's Tavern.—George Johnson and James Drake. (Here we have an attempt to revive the regular and scheduled routes of pre-war days, making Philadelphia to Elizabeth in less than a day and a half).

May, 1781.—The so-called Trenton and Elizabeth Stage by Young and Grummond was really a Philadelphia and New York line, operated as far as the War would permit.

August, 1781.—Johnson and Twinning will take the Philadelphia end to Princeton, and Grummond & Drake the Elizabeth end; a two-day run.

April, 1782.—Johnson & Grummond now run this line via Bristol, dine at Princeton; Brunswick that night; Elizabethtown next day; fare 35s.

1783.—"Through travel to New York" resumed by Aaron Longstreet & Co. by the Communipaw Ferry, who made it known that a boat was in constant attendance at the ferry stairs to bring passengers to Communipaw, where the Newark Stage would be ready to carry them to Newark, and there, "by the excellent New York and Philadelphia *running machine,*" in one day to Philadelphia.

1786. This route superceded by the Powles Hook Ferry route, as Messer's widow was getting the ferry stairs in New York repaired.

In 1793 Charles William Jansen made the trip from New York to Philadelphia, crossing at Paulus Hook Ferry to Powles Hook, "a miserable place;" then the stages had the horses hitched to them and were all ready to leave, the stage being literally a kind of light wagon holding 12, 3 on a seat; only the rear seat with anything to rest the back against; arrived at Trenton, 66 miles, late in the day and left at six next morning, arriving in Philadelphia at 2 in the afternoon.

There is a dearth of information in books of history and travel as to means of travel between New York and Philadelphia after 1786. We know that stages called at the Indian Queen Tavern at New Brunswick in 1797, and there were one or more stages running from Newark to Powles Hook in 1799 and 1800. Tuttle's Newark and Powles Hook Federal Stage began Monday, July 21, 1799, at 7.00 A. M., leaving New York at 4 and, by returning passengers by coach to Philadelphia, arrived the fourth day. Aaron Munn, Jan. 13, 1800, had the same route.

The enterprises and rivalry that brought about the day-and-a-half trip disappeared, but with the new century came in a great impetus and improvement in travel. First the *turnpikes*: Trenton to New Brunswick in 1804; Jersey City to Hackensack in 1804; New Brunswick to Newark in 1806; to Bordentown and Burlington in 1806; followed closely by the *steamboats*, the "Phoenix" to New Brunswick in 1807, and that only a little ahead of the Railroad.

Powles Hook, or Jersey, as it was afterward called, deserves a few words. By 1804 upwards of 20 stages a day arrived at and departed from there, and the future of the place began to be seen. In 1805 the rent of the ferry to Major David Hunt, who operated it, was $1,500 annually, and Anthony Dey, acting for his associates, Mr. Varick and Mr. Radcliff, purchased the Hook from Van Vorst for an annuity of $6,000 (Spanish milled dollars), the title being first passed upon by Alexander Hamilton and Josiah Ogden Hoffman, eminent lawyers, whose fee was $100. The amount of land upon the Hook was 117 acres. The Act of incorporation designated the purchasers as the Jersey Company, the place being then called "Jersey," and a charter was asked for the "City of Jersey" to balance the name of the City of New York on the other side of the river. The inhabitants in 1802 consisted of Major Hunt's family, John Murphy and wife, Joseph Bryant and employés, 13 or 15 persons in all. The charter of Jan. 23, 1829, was entitled "An Act to Incorporate the *City of Jersey*," while in the body of the Act it was unwittingly written *Jersey City*, and Jersey City it has remained.

The Jersey Company of 1804 offered Robert Fulton special terms to locate his shipyard there, and he acquired one block for $1,000, payable in five years without interest.

To return to our stage travel: John Voorhees ran a Coach to Elizabeth in 1805, three times a week; fare 6½ cents a mile. In 1805 the ferry to New York from Elizabethtown Point

Ferry consisted of six boats, and they made two trips in the forenoon and two in the afternoon, every day.

In 1806 there were stages from the City Hotel to Powles Hook three times a week. In 1809 Joseph Letson ran a stage from New Brunswick, and Stevens' steamboat, "Phoenix," ran for a while to New Brunswick. Her trial trip to New Brunswick was made in nine hours and thirty-two minutes, and her return in nine hours and twenty minutes. Fulton's "Raritan" succeeded her in 1809, but from 1811 to 1815 there were no steamboats to New Brunswick. In 1810 Samuel Brush made the trip from Philadelphia to New York; drove to Trenton the first day and slept there; dined next day at Brunswick and slept at Elizabeth, arriving at New York before noon next day.

In 1816 the "Raritan," second of that name, gives notice of travel from city to city (25 miles by land); fare $4.50; to go Monday, Wednesday and Friday, from north side of the Battery at 9.00 A. M.; passengers would lodge at Trenton and reach Philadelphia next day at 11.00 A. M. Here, with a steamboat at both ends (the "Phoenix" was on the Delaware), the time has about got back to Skillman's day-and-a-half in 1771, forty-five years before.

In 1818, the "Mouse" and the "Mountain" and "Bellona," Captain Vanderbilt, and the "Olive Branch," the Livingston-Stevens boat, with William Gibbons' stages, occupied the field with other steamboats until the railroad carried us another stride forward.

In "Niles' Register," 1839, appeared an article entitled "Travel as It Was and Is," or New York to New Orleans in 1800 and in 1839, the gist of which is;

'April 3, 1800. Left New York on Ferry Boat for Jersey City; thence by a two-horse Coach to Philadelphia, arriving on fourth day at 4 P. M. Left Philadelphia next morning in one-horse shay, with mail-bag behind, for Lancaster, where arrived the third day. Bought a horse and in 9 days reached Pittsburgh. Bought a flat boat for $18 and, with some others, left for New Orleans, floating with the current. After divers adventures and escapes from great peril by land and by water reached Natches, the fifty-seventh day after leaving Pittsburgh, and arrived at New Orleans 13 days thereafter; all told 84 days, which friends in New Orleans said was expeditious. Personal cost was £27.11.4¼.

'In 1839 had occasion to make the journey again. Left New York Jan. 21, at 6.00 A. M.; took train at Jersey City and arrived in Philadelphia ten minutes past 12—time 6 hrs., 10 min.; cost $4. Ot 2.00 P. M. left by railroad for Baltimore and arrived at 8.00 P. M.; time 6 hrs.; cost $4. Left Baltimore next P. M. at 4.00 in Mail Chariot for Wheeling; arrived five minutes before 12 Saturday noon; time 43 hrs. 50 min.; cost $23.00. Left Wheeling next morning in stage for Cincinnati; arrived in 59 hours., 30 min.; cost $24.50. Left Cincinnati 10 next morning on Steamboat Pike and reached Louisville at 10 P. M.; time 12 hrs.; cost $4. Left Louisville next morning at 11 in steamboat "Diana" and reached Natchez the sixth day, 149 hrs.; cost $35.00. Left Natchez the same day and reached New Orleans next evening; time 30 hrs.; cost $10. Expenses at Philadelphia, Baltimore and Cincinnati and Louisville, $10. Total, 306 hrs. 30 min., or 12 days, 18 hrs., 30 min., and cost $114.50. Difference in time about 71 days, and difference in expense $25.00 in favor of 1839. This was a Winter journey, a Summer trip could be made for $80 and in less time.'

At present the through best running railroad time from New York to New Orleans is about 40 hours; total cost including Pullman and meals about $75; gain in time 11 days, 2½ hours; cost about the same as the summer trip in 1839.

When we look at our wonderful postal facilities of to-day—not only as to letters, papers, periodicals, but also the special delivery, registered mail, insurance and parcels post—and then turn back 231 years to the beginning in 1693, one cannot help being astonished at the contrast. The following shows the progress of the postal system:

1639. Massachusetts enacted legislation looking to postal facilities, and Richard Fairbanks' house in Boston was designated as a postoffice.

1657. Virginia now took similar steps. The Directors of the West India Company, in 1652, wrote Peter Stuyvesant that they, "for the accommodation of private parties, had put up a box at the new warehouse for the collection of all mail, which will be sent by the first ship sailing, and inform you thereof so you may do the same." Stuyvesant did not act upon this suggestion, which was repeated in 1654 and 1655.

1672. On the completion of the new road from New York to Harlem under Governor Francis Lovelace in 1672, a monthly mail to Boston was inaugurated (January 1, 1673), and a locked box was put up in the office of the Colonial Secretary in New York, where the mail could accumulate until the next monthly post started out. The incoming mail, postage being paid, was left on a table in the Coffee House until called for, thus carrying out the suggestion made to Peter Stuyvesant in 1652, twenty years earlier. This arrangement, and a post, is mentioned as the greatest act of Gov. Lovelace's administration.

1683. William Penn established a postoffice in Philadelphia and granted Henry Waldy authority to hold one.

1687. William Bradford was deputy-postmaster. The office was sought by printers, who then sent their own newspapers by the post-riders and excluded all rival papers.

1691. A patent was issued to Thomas Neale with authority to establish postoffices in the chief seaports in the Colonies. Neale does not seem to have availed himself of this privilege.

1692. Gov. Andrew Hamilton was appointed Postmaster-General of America under a patent that made the mails his personal perquisite.

1693. Gov. Fletcher, of New Jersey, advised a grant of £50 to provide postal facilities in the Province, which the Council voted as desired. All the efforts hitherto had been detached and local, but this year service began under Hamilton's patent, with a weekly post from Portsmouth, New Hampshire, to Boston, Saybrook, New York, Philadelphia, Maryland and Virginia. Five riders covered each of the five stages twice a week in Summer and fortnightly in Winter. Just what comprised the five stages is not clear, but we know that Henry Pratt rode the post from Philadelphia to Newport, Virginia, and took twenty-four days to make the round trip. What New Jersey received in the way of service from the New York-to-Philadelphia route is not given at this time. The £50 voted Gov. Fletcher would indicate something; probably a mail left at Amboy.

Massachusetts established a general letter office and rates

of postage ranging from two pence to two shillings, in 1693, in addition to the earlier move in 1639. 1693 was quite a stirring year in postal matters; the provinces seem to have tried to co-operate with Gov. Hamilton.

1703. Gov. Hamilton died and his son Col. John Hamilton succeeded him under the patent, and the service continued.

1704. It is noted that post-riders went as far north as Boston and as far south as Charleston.

1707. The Crown purchased the good will of the American post-routes from Hamilton, but continued him as Postmaster-General, now under the control of the General Post Office in London. (Incidentally New York is reported to have numbered 1,000 houses in 1708).

1709. In April, Gov. John Lovelace, of New Jersey, a grandson of Gov. Francis Lovelace of New York, procured the passage of a bill settling a postoffice in the Province, the first positive knowledge we have of a New Jersey postoffice. He seems to have followed in the footsteps of his grandfather, who put up the mail box in New York thirty-six years before.

1710. An Act of Parliament passed for reorganizing the postal system of Great Britain and establishing posts under authority common to all colonies; a general post in the Queen's dominions.

1711. A postoffice evidently had been established in New York. The "Boston News Letter," Jan. 28 to Feb. 4, 1711-'12, has an advertisement of the Philadelphia-Burlington-Amboy and New York route, with the rates of postage, which gives the route across New Jersey and mentions two postoffices.

1716. A statute of Queen Anne placed the postoffice department under the Crown, pursuant to the purchase of 1707.

1720. It would appear that the post towns were still confined to seaports, and they were given as Philadelphia, Baltimore, Amboy and New York; although, in 1717, there was a weekly post between New York and Williamsburgh, Virginia.

1731. Col. John Hamilton seems to have been succeeded by Col. Alexander Spotswood in 1731 (although the date is uncertain), but on or about 1731 there was a change in the postal route across New Jersey, said to have been made by Col. Spotswood. The route, via Burlington and Amboy, was abandoned, and a new route established, via Bristol, where mail for Burlington was left. Trenton was a distributing centre for at least forty-eight surrounding points, which sent there for mail; Brunswick for some twenty-two surrounding points; Woodbridge, where the mail for Amboy was left; and Elizabethtown Point, where the mail left by water for New York. This change is given in detail in a letter by Benjamin Franklin, who had received a letter complaining of the change because Governor Boone's residence at Amboy and his seat of government at Burlington had been left off the route. We are also indebted to this letter for a number of facts and dates connected with the early post routes. Franklin says the change was made on an application to Col. Spotswood "about thirty years ago." His letter was written in 1761; this gives us the date of the change as about 1731. Franklin, though only Deputy-Postmaster from 1753, had been Postmaster of Philadelphia from 1737, and he says: "Have been concerned in the management of the postoffices between Philadelphia and New York for twenty-four years, or since 1737." He gives a sketch of the old and new routes, and says that the old route crossed from Bristol by a long ferry about one and one-half miles to Burlington, another long ferry near two miles at Redford's, and ferries again to Staten Island, to Long Island, about three miles, and New York—five in all. I do not find this route described anywhere else. Then he speaks of the new route, "with a short ferry at Trenton and at Raritan, and a good ferry from Elizabethport to New York, with postoffices on the new route at Bristol (where the mail is left conveniently to Burlington), Trenton, Brunswick, Woodbridge (where the mail for Amboy is left);" and he "don't see that either place suffers. But if it is the wish of the authorities in London that the mail shall go by the Governor's house (though unfortunately the Governors have selected in turn different places of residence)" he "will be governed accordingly." In corroboration we have two items.

1733. Letters were left at the house of James Neilson in New Brunswick.

1734. It is noted that "there is now a post office settled in

Trenton in the house of Joseph Read, and his son Andrew is appointed postmaster." From the word "settled" I infer that there had been an earlier temporary arrangement.

1745. William Bradford had been postmaster in Philadelphia from 1732-1737 and was succeeded by Franklin, as already stated. In 1745 John Dally, Surveyor of the State of New Jersey, made a survey of a road from Trenton to Amboy and set up marks every two miles; heretofore the road had been from Burlington to Amboy. How much of this was a new road and how much followed the old road is not clear, nor does it seem to have had any connection with the mails, though it is so intimated.

1750, 1751. There is reason to believe that the postoffices in the old towns of Burlington and Amboy were retained, as we have a note that Jonathan Thomas was postmaster in Burlington in 1750 and John Fox was postmaster in Amboy in 1751, long after the change of route.

1752. There was only one mail in two weeks through the winter from New York to Philadelphia. Col. Spotswood died in 1740 and Col. Hamilton in 1746.

1753. There are thirteen years between the death of Spotswood and the appointment of Franklin and William Hunter as Deputy Postmaster-Generals in 1753. Without note as to who had been Deputy Postmaster-General, great activity in postal matters began. Postoffices were established; the advertising of uncalled-for letters by the postoffice was introduced; every postoffice in the Colonies, except Charleston, was visited and put upon an improved footing.

1754. In Woodbridge, in 1754, the Postmaster was James Parker, the printer. Brook Farmar was postmaster in New Brunswick in 1764, and Michael Duffy in 1767, both innkeepers. It is from the advertising by Trenton and Brunswick of uncalled-for letters, Sept. 23rd and Sept. 28th, 1754, that we get the names of the surrounding places dependent on these two for their mail; also showing that the new law was promptly put into effect.

1774. Franklin was removed in 1774, but reinstated in 1775. He was followed by Richard Bache in 1776, and by Samuel Osgood 1779 to 1791.

CHAPTER V

The "Jersey Blues"—The "Sons of Liberty"—What Led to their Organization and Origin of the Name—Beginnings of the Revolution—Some New Brunswick Loyalists—Battle of Princeton and Subsequent Events.

"JERSEY Blues" is a name that has been applied to New Jersey Troops from time to time and has been claimed by some writers to have originated during the Revolution. But it is very much older than that, and was first applied in 1747; by whom, or for what reason, and on what occasion I cannot positively say.

When New Jersey was called on to assist in protecting our border from the French and Indians, who had become an alarming menace, Gov. John Hamilton, on the recommendation of his Council, Robert H. Morris, Edward Antill, James Hude and John Coxe, appointed and commissioned Col. Peter Schuyler to command the Regiment of Troops, the first ever raised for service outside of the State in other Colonies, excepting troops sent to the West Indies in 1739-'40. Leaving early in September, 1746, via New York and the Hudson river to Albany, they were thirteen months in the neighborhood of Albany, going first to the relief of Saratoga, where they were for four months. In October, 1747, they returned home, and it was in that year they were given the title of "Jersey Blues."

There are two origins of the name given by different writers; one is that the name came from their blue uniform, and the other that it came from the Blue Mountains. The men, we are told, were supplied with one hat, one pair of stockings and one pair of shoes, and were expected to furnish their own arms. Nothing was said about a uniform and it is most likely that they had none. It is not until 1760, their third campaign, that we are told (Aug. 9, 1760) that the uniform was blue, faced with scarlet, but they received the name in 1747, thirteen years before.

In 1755 Col. Peter Schuyler again raised his Regiment, and it is recorded that, while 500 men were asked for, 1,000 offered I think the 1,000 were accepted, although the records are not clear on this point. The Colony voted £15,000 for the support of the troops. This campaign was most disastrous. July 19, 1755, Gen. Braddock was killed and his army defeated, while a large part of Col. Schuyler's Regiment was captured at Oswego, where Col. Mercer and Col. Schuyler, with 1,400 men, were attacked by 5,000 French and Indians under Montcalm. About 350 escaped under Capt. Parker, the ranking Captain. The captured officers, excepting Col. Schuyler, were sent to France, among them Capt. William Skinner and Lieut. John Skinner, his brother, of Amboy, who, upon being exchanged, entered the regular British service and, later, came with Cornwallis to fight their old neighbors in the Revolution, though they were on a rather different footing from their brother, Cortlandt Skinner, who later was in command of a Tory Regiment of Jerseymen.

Col. Peter Schuyler was held in Canada (I do not think the French wanted him exchanged), but, Oct. 29, 1757, he was permitted to make a visit to his home on parole, and, if not exchanged, he was to return, which he did in July, 1758, and was held until November, 1758, when he was released by the capitulation of Fort Frontenac.

In the meantime the fragment of the Regiment under Capt. Parker, on July 8, 1758, (about the time that Col. Schuyler was returning to Canada), was ambushed at Sabbath Day Point near Ticonderoga, where he lost all but about eighty of the men who had escaped with him at Oswego. Truly a most unfortunate campaign.

Owing to these reverses the Indians on the frontier became more troublesome, and it was necessary to call out the militia— that of Morris county under Col. Joseph Tuttle; of Hunterdon county under Col. Joseph Stout; of Bergen county under Col. John Schuyler (brother of Peter); of Essex county under Col. John Low; of Middlesex county under Col. Johnson; and of Somerset county under Col. Philip Van Horne—and send against them.

In 1759 the Jersey Blues, 1,000 strong, again arrived in Albany (May 27), Col. Peter Schuyler again in command, and in August, at Niagara, they were completely successful, and the campaign ended in 1760 with the capture of Quebec. Gen. Shirley, who succeeded Gen. Braddock, said of Col. Schuyler that he was greatly indebted to him, and that he would be an honor to the service in any corps. The Jersey Blues were affectionately called the "Old Blues" in this campaign.

John Wetherill, of New Brunswick, was the paymaster of the Blues till 1756; after that John Stevens (who married Elizabeth Alexander, sister of Lord Stirling), whose brother, Capt. Campbell Stevens, was one of Col. Peter Schuyler's officers. John Stevens lived at that time in Amboy, but in 1761 bought No. 7 Broadway, New York, then in the most fashionable part of New York City. He was quite a man, trading with the West Indies, sailing his own vessels, interested in a copper mine at Rocky Hill, a Trustee of Queen's College and member of a Convention held in New Brunswick May 13-14, 1744, for the purpose of forming a union of all the Episcopal Churches in America.

In 1764 the Jersey Blues were again under arms and, on Dec. 6, a party of officers and men of that Regiment were in New York on their way back from Albany. In the ensuing ten years the Barracks at Trenton, Amboy, Elizabeth and New Brunswick were almost constantly occupied with troops.

In November, 1767, Gen. Gage went to Burlington to get Gov. Franklin to review with him the troops at New Brunswick. In 1768 they gave great assistance in fighting an alarming fire on Burnet street. In 1769 the Cameronians, or 26th, were reviewed by Gen. Gage. In 1770 the 29th replaced the 26th until Nov. 7, 1771, when they were sent to St. Augustine. Fla. The citizens gave the officers a dinner at the White Hall before they left. Part of the 47th, Gen. Guy Carleton, were in New Brunswick in 1773. So New Brunswick was really a garrison town all these years.

Not having made much of a case in tracing the Jersey Blues' name to their uniforms, how about the "mountains?" In "Glimpses of Colonial Society," by W. J. Mills, Class of 1763, Princeton, we find an ode to the Jersey Blues. The song was among a manuscript of songs (sung at Princeton in the Eighteenth century) of William Paterson, who was also of the Class of 1763, and is as follows:

> "To arms once more our Heroines!
> Sedition lives and order dies
> To Peace and Ease; then bid adieu
> And dash to the mountains, Jersey Blue!
>
> CHORUS
> Jersey Blue, Jersey Blue,
> And dash to the mountains, Jersey Blue!
>
> "Since proud ambition rears its head
> And murderous rage and discord spread
> To save from spoil the virtuous few,
> Dash to the mountains, Jersey Blue! CHORUS.
>
> "Roused at the call with magic sound
> The drums and trumpets circle round,
> And soon the corps their route pursue,
> So dash to the mountains, Jersey Blue! CHORUS.

Here, it seems to me, is clearly a recognition of the "mountains;" but let us go a little further.

In the "N. J. Historical Proceedings," Ser. I, Vol. III, folio 191, in a Journal by Maj. William Gould of the Expedition to Pennsylvania in 1794, we find a Jersey Blue poem of six verses. These are the same as the above, excepting that the "Heroines" in the first verse is changed to "Hero cries," and a note says that Washington is referred to. This is attributed to Gov. Howell as the author. It is, apparently, an adaptation of the earlier poem to suit the Revolutionary conditions, and, as Washington's weaker force was obliged to run for the mountains whenever Howe or Cornwallis gave chase, it very well depicts the situation, though the martial ring of the verses and the chorus do not agree so well. The added verses are:

> "Unstained with crimes, unused to fear,
> In deep array our youth appear
> And fly to crush the rebel crew,
> Or die in the mountains, Jersey Blue. CHORUS.

"Tho' tears bedew the maiden's cheek
And storms hang round the mountains bleak,
'Tis glory calls, to love adieu,
Then dash to the mountains, Jersey Blue! CHORUS.

"Should foul misrule and party rage
With law and liberty engage,
Push home your steel, you'll soon review
Your native plains, brave Jersey Blue. CHORUS."

Gov. Howell (Mayor Howell, of Trenton, as he was then) did write an "Ode to Washington" in 1789, to be sung when Washington passed through Trenton on his way to his Inauguration as President at New York. Gov. Howell died May 5, 1802, aged 48 and was, therefore, born in 1754.

HOWELL'S ODE TO WASHINGTON

"Welcome Mighty Chief, once more
Welcome to this grateful shore;
Now no mercenary foe
Aims again the fatal blow
Aims at thee *the* fatal blow.
Virgins fair and matrons grave,
These thy conquering arms did save,
Build for thee triumphant bowers
Strew, ye fair, his way with flowers,
Strew your Hero's way with flowers."

Some time since in the "New York Evening Post" David Lawrence Pierson wrote rather fancifully of the Jersey Blues, and made the assertion that the origin of the name was by "legal enactment," quoting Sec. 18 of an Act of Apr. 4, 1758, in proof. This Act was for equipment and does provide a blue uniform for the Jersey Blues, but it is a case of the uniform following the name and not of the name being bestowed with the uniform, this being the 3rd campaign of the Jersey Blues, while the name was bestowed during their first campaign of 1746-'7. Authorities admit that the origin of the name is obscure—but several agree on 1747.

"New Jersey Past and Present," p. 166, says the name originated between 1745 and 1748. Urquhart's "Hist. of Newark," p. 228, gives it as 1747. Probably the best authority is Thomas

Mante, who in his London "History of Late Wars in America," London, 1772, pp. 29-30, says: "It was resolved that Gen. Shirley should conduct the operation against Niagara with his own Regiment, Sir Wm. Pepperel's the Jersey Blue, commanded by Col. Schuyler, and a detachment of Royal Artillery." In the middle of July the Jersey Blues began the March, 1755 (the second) campaign of the Jersey Blues, which makes Mr. Pierson's statement that they obtained it in 1758 certainly wrong by three years. My own opinion is that the name was conferred for their fighting ability and was perhaps *True Blue.*

Perhaps one of the first guns fired in the Revolutionary movement was when Patrick Henry, elected to the House of Burgesses in Virginia from Louisa Co., in May, 1763, startled the house with a warning flash from History as he exclaimed: "Tarquin and Caesar had each a Brutus, Charles the First his Cromwell, and George the Third"—and paused, when the Speaker cried "Treason!" and the word was repeated on the floor. Henry, with his eyes fixed on the Chair, closed the sentence, "may profit by their example." Some authorities add these words: "If that be treason make the most of it." This was the greater surprise since Henry was a new member, a man who had failed as a merchant and struggled manfully with poverty, and after a short course of study became a lawyer. He was of ungainly figure, wore coarse clothes, loved music, dancing and pleasantry, and among his boon companions lapsed into the vernacular or would talk of the "yearth," and of "men's naiteral parts being improved by larnin' ".

The Stamp Act, passed by the Commons and receiving the Royal assent on March 22, 1765, was the means of welding the masses into organized opposition.

In the debate in the Commons Charles Townshend, leader of the Commons and first Lord of Trade, speaking in favor of the Stamp duty bill, said:

"These children of our own planting, nourished by our indulgence until they are grown to a good degree of strength and opulence, and protected by our arms, will they grudge to contribute their mite to relieve us from the heavy load of national expense which we lie under?"

Mr. Barre arose and said in reply:

"Children planted by *your* care. No! Your oppression planted them in America; they fled from your tyranny into a then uncultivated land, where they were exposed to almost all the hardships to which human nature is liable, and, among others, to the cruelty of the enemy of the country, a people of the most subtle, and, I take it upon me to say, the most truly terrible of any people that ever inhabited any part of God's earth; and yet, actuated by principles of true English liberty, they met all these hardships with pleasure compared with those they suffered in their own country from the hands of those that should have been their friends.

"They nourished by your indulgence! They grew by your neglect of them. As soon as you began to care about them, that care was exercised in sending persons to rule over them in one department or another, who were perhaps deputies of deputies to some members of this House, sent to spy out their liberty; to misrepresent their actions and to prey upon them. Men whose behaviour on many occasions have caused the blood of the Sons of Liberty to recoil within them; men promoted to the highest seats of justice; some, to my knowledge were glad, by going to foreign countries, to escape being brought to the bar of justice in their own.

"They protected by your arms! They have notably taken up arms in your defense, have exerted their valor amidst their constant and laborious industry for the defense of a country whose frontiers, while drenched in blood, its interior parts have yielded all its little savings to your enlargement, and believe me—remember I this day told you so—that the same spirit which actuated that people at first will continue with them still; but prudence forbids me to explain myself any further. God knows I do not at this time speak from motives of party heat. What I declare are the genuine sentiments of my heart. However superior to me in general knowledge and experience the respectable body of this House may be, yet I claim to know more of America than most of you, having seen and been conversant in that country. The people there are truly loyal, I believe, as any subject the King has, but a people jealous of their liberties, and who will vindicate them if they should be violated. But the subject is too delicate, I will say no more."

There are upwards of thirty variations of this speech; this is from one sent by Jared Ingersoll and printed in the "Boston

Post Boy and Advertiser," May 27, 1765. After its publication Barre's designation "Sons of Liberty" was adopted by the opposition, the two parties being known as Whigs and Patriots; "Sons of Liberty" on the one hand, and "Loyalists," "Tories" and "Friends of Government" on the other. The "Boston Gazette" of Aug. 12, 1765, says that in the town of Providence the Sons of Liberty were to convene again.

The history of the Sons of Liberty is obscure. The organization was long kept secret, so that Loyalists said there was a private union among a certain sect, from one end of the continent to the other. As they increased in numbers they grew in boldness and publicity, announcing in the newspapers their committees and interchanging solemn pledges of support. The "Virginia Resolves," circulated in the press, strengthened the purpose of this association. Their organization from the first meant business of the most determined character.

Freedom of the Press had been established in 1735. John Peter Zenger, when 13, was apprenticed for four years to William Bradford, printer, Oct. 23, 1710, and in 1714 was taken in as a partner. In 1725 the members of the Dutch Reformed Church of Raritan had complained of Theodorus J. Frelinghuysen, and the complaint was printed by Bradford and Zenger. In 1735 Zenger was tried for the method of conducting his paper, "The New York Weekly Journal," the organ of the popular party. Zenger had been imprisoned and the names of his counsel arbitrarily erased from the rolls of the church, when Andrew Hamilton of Philadelphia volunteered to defend him and would take no fee for doing so. It was this suit that established the Freedom of the Press. Zenger was acquitted, and in September the Common Council of New York City voted Hamilton the freedom of the city and the city seal was to be enclosed in a $5\frac{1}{2}$ ounce gold box, which, with the freedom, was conveyed to him in Philadelphia by Alderman Stephen Bayard.

The "New York Gazette and Weekly Post Boy," issued on Thursdays by John Holt, was the principal organ of the Sons of Liberty in 1765. A great elm in Boston at the corner of the present Washington and Essex streets, under which the opponents of the Stamp Act were accustomed to assemble, soon became famous as Liberty Tree. Persons supposed to be favorable to the ministry were hung in effigy on the branches of it. A great concourse gathered under this elm, marched through the streets and the words "Liberty, Property, and No Stamps!" passed from mouth to mouth; in some cases the unhappy Stamp distributors were forced to stand high before the people and shout the same slogan. The dates of these popular uprisings as noted in the press were: Boston, Aug. 14; Norwich, Aug. 21; New London, Aug. 22; Providence, Aug. 24; Lebanon, Aug. 26; Newport, Aug. 27; Windham, Aug. 27; Annapolis, Aug. 29; Elk Ridge, Aug. 30; New Haven, Sept. 6; Portsmouth, Sept. 12; Dover, Sept. 13; Philadelphia, Oct. 5; New York, Nov. 1; Woodbridge, Sept. 28. The "Constitutional Courant" was originated for the occasion. The device on its title page was a snake cut in two, with the motto "Join or Die," believed to have been printed secretly in Woodbridge by James Parker, though ostensibly it was printed by Andrew Marvel at the Sign of "The Bribe Refused" on Constitution Hill, North America." In trying to trace the paper, one of the readers said it came from Peter Hassenclever's Iron Works.

A Congress of the Sons of Liberty met in New York Sept. 30, 1765. Maryland and New Jersey had not chosen delegates, but on Tuesday, Oct. 1, an express arrived saying delegates would be chosen from Maryland, and on the next day another, stating that the New Jersey Assembly would choose. That the delay in Maryland was not from any lack of sympathy is shown by the fact that the Sons of Liberty in Maryland had so frightened the Stamp Distributor for that province, Zacharias Hood, that he had fled to New York, and not feeling safe in the inn moved into the fort for safety. The Congress met at the City Hall in New York. In no place were the Sons of Liberty more determined or their opponents more influential. It was the headquarters of the British forces and General Gage wielded the powers of a viceroy. The fort within the city was heavily mounted with cannon; ships of war were moored near the wharves. The Executive, Governor Colden, was resolved to execute the law. When the Massachusetts delegates called on him he remarked that the proposed Congress would be unconstitutional and unprecedented and he should give it no countenance ("Boston Post Boy," Oct. 14, 1765). This Congress consisted of 26 delegates from 9 colonies; four, though sympathizing with the movement, not choosing delegates—Virginia, New Hampshire, Georgia and North Carolina. Massachusetts sent James Otis, Oliver Partridge and Timothy Ruggles, chosen June 8 by General Assembly and their commission was signed by Samuel White, Speaker. South Carolina sent Thomas Lynch, Christopher Gadsen and John Rutledge, chosen Aug. 2 by the Assembly and they bore the Journal of the votes of the election, signed by Edward Rawlins, Speaker. Pennsylvania sent John Dickinson, John Morton and George Bryan, chosen Sept. 11 by the Assembly and their instructions were signed by Charles Moore, Clerk. Rhode Island sent Metcalf Bowles and Henry Ward, chosen by the Assembly and bearing commissions signed by Samuel Ward, Governor. Connecticut sent Eliphalet Dyer, David Rowland and William S. Johnson, chosen Sept. 19 by the Assembly, and bearing a copy of the vote appointing them and instructions signed by Thomas Fitch, Governor. Delaware sent Thomas McKean and Cæsar Rodney, who were designated informally by fifteen of the eighteen members of the Assembly and bore instruments dated Sept. 13, 17 and 20, signed by members from the counties of New Castle, Kent and Sussex. Maryland sent William Murdock, Edward Tilghman and Thomas Ringold, chosen by the Assembly in October, and bore a commission signed by Robert Lloyd, Speaker. New Jersey sent Robert Ogden, Hendrick Fisher and Joseph Borden, designated by a large number of the Representatives on Oct. 3, and bore a certificate signed by John Lawrence. New York sent Robert R. Livingston, John Cruger, Philip Livingston, William Bayard and Leonard Lespinard, who bore a certified copy of the vote of the Journals dated Apr. 4, 1759, Dec. 9, 1762, and Oct. 18, 1764, which constituted the members from the City of New York and Robert R. Livingston as a Committee of Correspondence. The Journal of the Proceedings of the Convention contains a letter from Georgia, of Sept. 6, signed by Alexander Wylly in behalf of sixteen of the twenty-five representatives, warmly sympathizing with the cause and stating that the Governor would not call them together, but promising a concurrence with their action. The foregoing statements are from the Journal of the Proceedings in Niles' "Principles and Acts of the Revolution," p. 451.

James Otis stood in this body as the foremost speaker. The pens of the brothers Robert and Philip Livingston were summoned to service in a wider field. John Dickinson of Pennsylvania was soon to be known by "The Farmer's Letters." Thomas McKean and Cæsar Rodney were pillars of the cause in Delaware. Edward Tilghman was an honored name in Maryland. South Carolina, in addition to the intrepid Gadsen, had in Thomas Lynch and John Rutledge two patriots who appear prominently in the subsequent career of that Colony. Thus this body was graced by ability, genius, learning and common sense.

This Congress, while conceived by James Otis, to be formed by committees from the Assemblies, was brought to a reality by the pressure from the Sons of Liberty, and though the Tory element elected Timothy Ruggles Chairman by one vote majority, on the second day it took up for consideration the rights, privileges and grievances of the British-American colonists, and, after eleven days' debate, each Colony having one vote, agreed upon a declaration of rights and grievances, and ordered it to be inserted in the Journal. It consisted of a preamble and fourteen resolves. ("Niles' Register," July 25, 1812, contains the whole proceedings from a MSS. copy attested by the Secretary, John Cotton, and found among the papers of Cæsar Rodney). The resolves and petitions elicited long debates. Christopher Gadsen said: "There should be no New Englandman and no New Yorker on the continent, but all of us Americans." When signing was discussed, some members objected. Ruggles said it was against his conscience to sign. McKean rang the changes on the word "conscience" so loud that Ruggles gave him a challenge before all the members. The challenge was accepted promptly by McKean, who said Ruggles left early next morning without an adieu to any of the brethren.

The delegates from six of the colonies, except Ruggles and Ogden, signed. (Ogden was afterward burned in effigy by the people of New Jersey). Those from New York, Connecticut and South Carolina were not authorized to sign. On the 25th Congress adjourned. The Massachusetts Assembly, Feb. 12, voted that Brigadier Ruggles, with respect to his conduct at the New York Congress, 'has been guilty of neglect of duty, and that he be reprimanded by the Speaker.' This was done the next day. Connecticut Assembly ordered their Committee to sign and forward the petitions. South Carolina concurred Dec. 2, New York approved Nov. 20. Virginia is understood to have concurred. These actions, though stated a little out of their order, complete the report of the Convention.

On Oct. 22 the ship "Edward," nine weeks from London, Davis Commander, having ten packages of the Stamps, came to anchor under the guns of the fort, the shipping in port flying their flags at half mast. That night there was posted on office doors and street corners this notice:

"PRO PATRIA.
"The first man who either distributes or makes use of Stamps and paper let him take care of his house, person and effects.
"VOX POPULI."

The Sons of Liberty published that, on the 1st of November, when the Act was to take effect, they would rise against the Government and bury Major James alive, he having said he would cram the stamps down their throats with his sword. And two hundred merchants made a non-importation agreement—to cancel orders placed; not to sell goods on the way and to arrive; and to place no more orders till the Stamp Act was repealed. Philadelphia followed in this agreement Nov. 14 and Boston Dec. 9.

Some of the Stamp Distributors were Oliver for Massachusetts, Jared Ingersoll for Connecticut, James McEvers for New York (lived at 50 Wall St.), Zacharias Hood for Maryland, and William Coxe, of Philadelphia, for New Jersey. The 1st day of November, the day appointed for the Stamp Act to go into operation, came and went, but not a stamp was anywhere to be seen. Two companies of rioters paraded that evening in the streets of New York demanding the delivery of the stamps, which Gov. Colden, on the resignation of the Stamp Distributor and his refusal to receive them, had taken into the fort. Gov. Colden was burned in effigy and his carriage was seized and burned under the muzzle of the guns of the fort. Committees of the Sons of Liberty guided all of these movements in New York. They were: John Morris Scott, William Smith, Jr., and William Livingston, who led the theoretical opposition; and Alexander McDougall, Isaac Sears, John Lamb, Marinus Willett, and Gershom Mott, who led the practical opposition.

Tuesday, Nov. 5, 1765, a meeting was called in the fields, to which citizens were requested to appear armed for the purpose of storming the fort. The City Arms Tavern was now the Headquarters of the Sons of Liberty and the movements were guided from there. The Governor then informed the Mayor and Aldermen that if they would attend at the fort gate, the stamped papers would be delivered to them. This was done and tranquility was restored to the city.

On Saturday, Dec. 28, 1765, the Sons of Liberty of Woodbridge had a meeting and debated and instructed two of their number to wait upon William Coxe, appointed Distributor of Stamps for the Province of New Jersey; said instructions read as follows:

"First, we command and strictly enjoin it upon you, upon pain of our high displeasure, that you do immediately, with the greatest expedition possible, repair to the house of William Coxe, our Stamp Distributor in Philadelphia, or elsewhere, and into his hand deliver our letter, praying his resignation, according to the tenor of said letter, etc., which, if he comply with, you are to bear the same to us, and in the name of every Son of Liberty in the Province of New Jersey return him your thanks thereupon. Second, upon said Mr. Coxe's refusal we command you to return immediately and make report to us of the same. Third, we command and strictly enjoin it upon you that whether said Mr. Coxe resign his commission, etc., or not, you do treat him with complaisance and decorum becoming a gentleman of honor."

The following is the copy of the letter to Mr. Coxe:

"SIR: Whereas you have been appointed to the most odious and detestable office of Distributor of Stamps for the government of New Jersey, and whereas the former resignation (said to be yours) is no way satisfactory to the inhabitants of the same; We, the Sons of Liberty in said Government, hereby desire your resignation in as simple form as possible; expressing and solemnly declaring upon the veracity of a gentleman and man of honor that you will never directly or indirectly, yourself, or by deputies under you, ever distribute said stamps, or be anyways accessory in putting said stamps in force in the government aforesaid; whereby you will not only endear yourself to the inhabitants but prevent such methods as may be taken through necessity to oblige you to the same; and whereas it is publicly reported and generally believed that you have already nominated and appointed deputies under you to distribute stamped papers in said government, whereby we are and shall continue to be in the utmost danger, by reason of said declared enemies to their country, notwithstanding your said resignation, now, Sir, we desire and insist that you, without reserve, acquaint us of all such deputies (if any there be) that they may be dealt with in proper manner. It is expected that you do in the presence of our deputies comply with every of our aforesaid requests and deliver the same (signed by yourself) to them, to be brought to us. If, Sir, you refuse our very reasonable request, it will put us to the trouble of waiting upon you, in such a way and manner as perhaps will be disagreeable both to yourself and us, which we hereby notify you we shall do on Saturday the 4th of January next, and it is expected you will be there ready to answer us.

"SONS OF LIBERTY IN EAST JERSEY."

On Tuesday, Dec. 31, the deputies returned and reported that they had waited upon Mr. Coxe at his house in Philadelphia and delivered him the letter aforesaid; that, after reading it and being informed of their business, they were treated with the utmost civility and respect both by him and his lady, and he delivered them in writing the following copy of his "genteel and ample resignation," viz.:

"I do hereby resign into the hands of the right honorable, the Lord Commissioners of His Majesty's Treasury, the office of Distributor of Stamps for the Province of New Jersey.

"Witness my hand and seal this third day of Sept., in the Year of our Lord 1765.   WILLIAM COXE.
"Sealed and delivered in the presence of
    "WILLIAM HUMPHRIES,
    "EDWARD TILGHMAN."

This was followed on Dec. 30, 1765, by this declaration:

"Having received information that my resignation of the office of Distributor of Stamps for the Province of New Jersey not having been fully inserted in the public papers is a matter of uneasiness to the minds of the good people of that Province, I do hereby certify and declare upon my honor and veracity the above to be a true copy of my resignation of that office, which I sent to England on the 3rd of Sept. last. I do hereby further declare that on receiving the commission of the said office of Distributor of Stamps for New Jersey, on or about the first of this instant, December, I returned the same commission to England the seventh instant. I do further declare upon my honor that I have not appointed any officer or officers for the distribution of stamps in the said Province, nor done any other acts towards carrying the Stamp Act into execution, and I do upon my honor assure the gentlemen of New Jersey that they may depend I never will accept of any office whatsoever under the Stamp Act, nor will I directly or indirectly be accessory to carrying the same into execution.
                              "WILLIAM COXE."

The deputies being entirely satisfied by these papers and Mr. Coxe's declaration, addressed him as follows:

"SIR: We, being appointed to wait upon you by the Sons of Liberty of New Jersey for a more satisfactory resignation of your office of Distributor of Stamps in said Province, are fully satisfied of your early resignation by the copy which you have favored us with, as also your present cheerfulness in further satisfying us. We do in the name of every Son of Liberty of New Jersey return you our hearty thanks, hoping your example may influence those to do the like who yet hold that detestable office."

The deputies further reported that on their return home they were met by the gentlemen of New Brunswick, who gave them their hearty thanks, which also was given them in Piscataway and Woodbridge, where long life and prosperity were drunk to his Majesty and also to Mr. Coxe, and 'confusion to every

American Stamp Master unless he resigned his abhorred and detestable office.'

At a meeting of the Sons of Liberty of Woodbridge, Feb. 26, 1766, called to pass resolutions regarding the Stamp Tax Act, there were six resolutions passed, the fourth reading: "That a Committee of five persons be immediately chosen to act in conjunction with the several Committees of our neighboring townships in the county of Middlesex in order that the respective Committees of the several townships may form a Committee out of their own body to act in conjunction with the several Committees of the neighboring counties in the Province of New Jersey that we may be in actual readiness on any emergency." There was a "P. S." to this, viz: "We have taken the above measure in consequence of a letter from a Committee of the Sons of Liberty of the City of New York recommending such a step as a necessary precaution against the Stamp Act."

On March 11, 1766, at a meeting of the Sons of Liberty of the township of Piscataway, the second of the resolutions passed reads: "That we will oppose all attempts to deprive us of our rights and privileges as Englishmen, and therefore will at all events oppose the operation of that detestable thing called the Stamp Act in this Colony."

On March 18, 1766, the Sons of Liberty of Hunterdon county met at John Ringo's at Amwell and the third resolution was: "We will likewise endeavor to support all persons that proceed in business as usual without paying any regard to said detestable Act."

At a meeting of nearly 1,000 Sons of Liberty of Sussex county at the Court House, April 1, 1766, the third resolution reads: "That the Stamp Act is unconstitutional and arbitrary and deemed by us destructive of our civil liberties, and as such will oppose same to the utmost of our power."

At a meeting of the Sons of Liberty of the Township of Freehold the second day of April, 1766, the fourth resolution reads: "That we will with all our might join with the several towns and counties in this and the several neighboring Provinces, and all others, who are the true Sons of Liberty, to uphold and ever maintain that near and dear friend, Liberty, as far as our might, influence and power extend."

At a meeting of the Sons of Liberty of the township of Upper Freehold, assembled at Imlaystown April 28, 1766, they said: "We mutually and solemnly plight our faith and honor that we will at any risque whatever, when called upon, unite ourselves, truly and faithfully to assist this and the neighboring Provinces in opposing all attempts that hath arisen or may arise to deprive us of our rights and privileges as by charter have been handed down to us, and will at all events oppose the oppression of that most unreasonable, most unconstitutional, most horrid and detestable thing called the Stamp Act, within this and the neighboring colonies."

June 4, 1766, being the birthday of George III, the Sons of Liberty assembled at the Liberty Oak on the square in Woodbridge, a company of many hundreds, to celebrate the same and to testify their joy at the repeal of the Stamp Act. A large ox was roasted whole and liquors of different kinds in great plenty provided for the company. The Liberty Oak was handsomely decorated. The ladies, likewise genteelly dressed, graced the entertainments of the day, dined principally upon plum pudding in honor of the Queen, and afterwards regaled themselves with plum cake, tea, etc. In the evening the town was illuminated and a large bonfire made as near the Liberty Oak as the safety of that ancient tree would admit, while eighteen toasts were drunk, among which these: "The Sons of Liberty in America"; "The Noble Asserters of Liberty"; "No St. Christopher and Nevis"; "All those who distinguished themselves to obtain a Repeal of the Stamp Act"; "Pitt and Freedom."

A large gallows was erected in Elizabethtown during February, with a rope ready fixed thereto, and the inhabitants there "vowed and declared that the first person that either distributes or takes out a stamped paper, shall be hung thereon without Judge or jury."

The Boston Sons of Liberty proposed, the same February (1766) to the brotherhood at Norwich a Continental Union, which Norwich greatly approved. The New York Sons of Liberty sent circular letters as far as South Carolina urging a Continental Union. Gadsen expressed the Americanism of the hour as he wrote: "Nothing will save us but acting together. The Province that endeavors to act separately must fall with the rest, and be branded with everlasting infamy."

The Stamp Act was repealed 28th March, 1766, by a majority of 108, the vote being 275 to 167 in the House of Commons. The Sons of Liberty meantime kept up the agitation, holding meetings, demanding and compelling the resignations of the Stamp Distributors. Herein we may discern signs of the movement destined to culminate within ten years in the assertion of total independence of the Mother Country. The merchants of London demanded the repeal of the Stamp Act to save their American trade, and there was a grim feeling in America and a realization of the indomitable power of the united American people.

According to an admirable though brief summary of the situation in the Preface to Vol. XXV of the "N. J. Archives," the first book of Blackstone's "Commentaries," issued in November, 1765, was a new inspiration to thoughtful men of the civil rights of British subjects. An able reply in the "London Chronicle" to an article asserting the dependence of the colonies to the Mother Country, was ascribed to Richard Stockton, then in England or in Scotland. The excited and inflammable condition of the public mind after the Stamp Act episode was shown by the apprehension aroused by the untimely sermon of the Bishop of Landaff, deploring the heathenism of the Americans, and urging the appointment of American Bishops to supervise their assumed spiritual needs. William Livingston, of New York, and the Rev. Dr. Charles Channing, of Boston, leaped to the defense of America and attacked the Bishop, whose suggestion was looked upon as a most insidious design on the liberties of the people. Rev. Dr. Thomas Bradbury Chandler, of Elizabethtown, replied with his appeal on behalf of the Church of England in the newspapers of Nov. 23, 1767, which increased the popular alarm. A curious view the English had of America in that year is given in a London newspaper, which describes the colonies as occupying a low and narrow strip of unfertile land stretching a short distance from the ocean to the Allegheny Mountains, beyond which was a still more unattractive region, inhabited only by hostile savages.

The continued activity of the Sons of Liberty appears when the New York Assembly, Sept., 1769, gave great offense by yielding over the "Quarternary Act," with which two previous Assemblies had refused to comply, and Alexander McDougall, a chief leader among the Sons of Liberty and a merchant, called a public meeting of the citizens to take the proceedings of the Assembly into consideration. The Assembly committed McDougall to prison, where he was visited by crowds of sympathizers.

Again, in 1770 the "Liberty Boys," as then called, and the soldiers were having constant collisions, and after several failures the soldiers cut down the Liberty Pole on the Commons (called "The Park," by Henry B. Dawson in his pamphlet, entitled, "The Sons of Liberty," published in 1859), and piled it in front of Montanyes, the Headquarters of the Sons of Liberty.

The 16th Regiment, quartered in New York, put up a scurrilous hand-bill aimed at the Sons of Liberty, Jan. 18, 1770; the latter captured some of the soldiers engaged in posting them up. They, in turn, were attacked by a squad of soldiers. Both sides were reinforced and the "Battle of Gold Hill" (on John Street, between Cliff Street and Burling Slip), claimed as the first conflict of the American Revolution, was fought. The trouble was renewed the next day, but less vigorously.

Again, March 6, 1770, the Sons of Liberty collected in great numbers, and Faneuil Hall, Boston, was crowded, the conflict between soldiers and ropemakers the day before being the occasion of this meeting.

Nov. 3, 1773, we hear of them once more in connection with a shipment of tea then expected. It would appear that the organization was kept alive until the actual conflict of war and the formation of Militia and Continentals obliterated the earlier organization. As late as July 14, 1774, the Sons of Liberty assembled at Fondee's Tavern, at Savannah, Ga.

In New York the Sons of Liberty, or the "Liberty Boys," seem to have drifted into the Sons of St. Tammany or the

Columbian Order, and finally became the organization still known as Tammany. (See Meyer's "History of Tammany Hall"). And the force who opposed the Federalists, i. e., the Anti-Federal Party, was in greater part the old organization known as Liberty Boys, and formed the opposition from 1783 to 1787, while the Liberty Boys of the Revolutionary Period were the majority of the working and middle classes and governed New York City politics.

It has probably never occurred to many what a powerful weapon those who were promoting the Revolution had in the Committee of Correspondence and Safety, and of Observation and Inspection? These Committees could make life intolerable and could practically drive out of the community any one they disapproved of, or suspected. They passed along the news of any movement of the enemy from Committee to Committee. They would call for troops to enforce their orders; impose fines for asking a higher price in Continental money than in hard money, or than fixed by law; cited the families of men who had gone over to the enemy before them; made full use of the boycott, though the name had not then been coined and adopted; in fact, would to-day have been considered a *terror*.

That all of New Jersey was not a unit in sentiment is shown by the fact that on Jan. 17, 1775, Shrewsbury declined to appoint a Committee of Inspection. Staten Island refused, as did Jamaica, Long Island, by 91 citizens; one was Teunis Bergen. Now, what was the result? Woodbridge promptly refused to supply Staten Island with lumber, plank, iron, etc., and ordered a suspension of all trade and intercourse. Thomas Leonard, of Freehold, was ostracised; Silas Newcomb, of Cumberland Co., was published for drinking tea, whereupon he recanted. To have the courage of one's convictions at that time was by no means an empty or high-sounding phrase.

Middlesex took an early part in this movement. On July 15, 1774, John Dennis and Reune Runyon were made the Committee of Correspondence and Observation, and, July 21, the County Committees met in New Brunswick, 72 members being present, and five delegates were appointed to the Continental Congress to be held in Philadelphia on Sept. 1. They were

James Kinsey, William Livingston, John DeHart, Stephen Crane, Richard Smith. On Jan. 16, 1775, two Committees, one of Observation (Azariah Dunham, James Schureman, John Dennis, John Lyle, Abraham Schuyler, Geo. Hance, Jacobus Van Nuys, John Sleight, and John Voorhees), and one of Correspondence (James Neilson, William Ouke, Azariah Dunham, John Dennis, who was Clerk).

At the Second Continental Congress Middlesex was represented by John Wetherill and Hendrick Fisher, and was held Feb., 1775, when Middlesex and Somerset were called upon to raise two regiments of militia. For the Continentals, two companies were raised in New Brunswick, Captain John Conway and Captain John Polhemus, while Capt. Daniel Piatt raised one at Raritan Landing.[1] And when the Barracks[2] at New Brunswick were wanted for these troops it was found that they were full of refugees from New York City. Gen. Stirling ordered Capt. Conway to march his men five hours a day, by way of drill and discipline. Capt. John Taylor, First Lieut. John Mersural, Second Lieut. James Schureman and Ensign John Voorhees received their certificates of commission from the New Brunswick Committee of Safety, this being another of the powers of these Committees.

The first use made of the New Jersey Troops was to awe and disarm the Tories of Long Island; crossing over Friday, Jan.

---

[1] I have come to the conclusion that the term "Raritan Landing" did not always apply to the point where the Landing Bridge now stands, having reason to believe that a landing on the river where Martin's dock is located was largely used by the people of Piscataway, and also called Raritan Landing. In this case it seems more than likely that Daniel Piatt's Company was drawn from Piscataway to the latter landing rather than from the surrounding farms at the Landing Bridge.

[2] April 17, 1758, an Act, was passed to erect barracks in New Jersey. Philip French furnished the lot in New Brunswick. In 1766 Commissioners to furnish and rent it when not needed for soldiers were appointed. British troops occupied them from 1767 to 1771. In 1775 they came into use for Continentals or State militia. Hendrick Fisher and John Schureman were appointed Barrack Masters at New Brunswick March 1, 1776. The barracks was used again during the British occupation, Dec., '76 to June, '77. In 1783 it was made the legal Court House and jail, and was so used till it burned down in 1794. The stones of the barracks were afterward used to build a jail, and the stones of the jail were used in the Bayard Street School.

19, 1776, and collecting 500 arms and 4 standards of colors; evidently a successful and apparently a bloodless campaign, if a peculiar one. The first prize ship fell to New Jersey Troops, another unusual adventure for infantry. Lord Stirling, with small boats filled with infantry, captured the transport "The Blue Mountain Valley" in New York Bay, first taking it to Amboy and then through the Kill to Elizabethtown Point and the Elizabeth river. She was loaded mainly with potatoes, which nearly all rotted before it was decided to whom the prize belonged.

Dr. Moses Scott, of New Brunswick, was appointed surgeon Feb. 14, 1776, to the 2nd Regiment of Middlesex Co. Foot Militia. On Feb. 23, 1776, Capt. John Voorhees, father of Ensign Voorhees, with his sloop "Brunswick," loaded with bread, flour and butter for New York, was stopped by the British ships "Asia" and "Dutchess" and his cargo appropriated. They gave in payment an order on Abraham Lott, Treasurer of the Colony of New York, who was charged with provisioning the British ships. When Washington arrived and took command at New York he ordered this stopped. On July 20, 1776, the militia were permitted to go home to harvest their crops, having been strung along from Amboy to Powles Hook (Jersey City) watching the British movements. But on Aug. 12 one-half were called back to do duty one month, and the other half the next. On Nov. 17 Lord Stirling and eight regiments were at or within a few miles of New Brunswick.

In connection with Washington and his army's visit to New Brunswick, July 4, 1778, it is of interest that Gen. Lee's court-martial was held here, or rather begun here. It was ordered to meet at 8 o'clock at the house of Mr. Voorhees in "the town of New Brunswick" and on the 4th at the same time and place, and continued on the 5th and 6th. This was, without doubt, the same Myndert Voorhees who entertained the Provincial Congress in 1776 and presumably at the White Hall.

The reading of the Declaration of Independence in New Brunswick has been a matter of some controversy. Force's "Archives" notes that it was read publicly in the State House in Philadelphia on the 8th, at Trenton the same day, at Nassau

Hall, Princeton, on the evening of the 9th, and in New York City on the 18th, as it was not signed by the New York delegates until the 16th. At Bridgeton it was read Aug. 7th, but there is no mention of New Brunswick.

From other sources we learn that it was read by Col. John Neilson in New Brunswick from the top of a table brought out of Dr. Moses Scott's house and placed in the street. Dr. Moses Scott's house was on the north side of Albany and west side of Neilson on the corner. Col. Neilson and Dr. Scott were both army men. The date, however, is lacking. As the militia were allowed to go home July 20 and called out again Aug. 12th, I think that very soon after they returned would be the time.

The Provincial Congress met Jan. 31 to March 2, 1776, and again July 22 to Aug. 21 at New Brunswick. On Monday, Aug. 1, it ordered that John Neilson, who had been Colonel of a Middlesex Battalion of Minute Men, be Colonel of the 2nd Battalion Foot Militia, County of Middlesex. On Aug. 17th it ordered that proclamation money of New Jersey be taken at 7s.6d. the dollar.

The Commissioners of Forfeited Estates, during the latter part of the Revolution, were nearly as formidable as the earlier Committees. They dealt with persons (to quote from the deeds they gave for these confiscated properties) who "had offended against the form of his allegiance." In just what this consisted seems to have been a matter for the decision of the Courts. The Commissioners for Middlesex were John Lloyd and William Scudder with seven cases, William Manning and Ebenezer Ford with thirteen cases, and David Olden with a few cases. Of these cases but three were in New Brunswick, viz., of William Burton, owner of what is now "Buccleuch Park," a British officer; Bernardus Lagrange, a lawyer, and one of Christ Church Vestry, who owned the stone house on Albany street, where Simcoe was confined, and other tracts, and whose two daughters had married British officers of the 26th and 29th Regiments when they were stationed in New Brunswick; and John Dumont, who owned the brewery lot on Brewer, now John street, on Lyle's brook. The largest number of confiscations were made in Amboy, and the next largest were in Woodbridge.

Philip French was the largest owner of confiscated lands in New Brunswick, but he had gone into bankruptcy just prior to the Revolution, most of his lands had been sold on 50-year leases, and the equity in these properties was mostly bought in by the occupants under the leases. The sheriff seems to have taken precedence over the Commissioners in this case. Some people do not seem to have been disturbed at all. Stephen Kemble, a life-long British naval officer, born in New Brunswick, returned here afterwards and died in the house in which he was born on Albany street. Rev. Abraham Beach,[3] Rector of Christ Church, and quite naturally a Loyalist, and who lived on the Lawrence Wells' place on the Easton Pike, kept his property. In 1777 it was stated of Beach that "from his prudent and good conduct he had been permitted to stay at home," but "was not free from insults and was in a state of constant apprehension."

New Brunswick was the home of a number of Loyalists of the more distinguished class. In addition to Gen. William Burton, Bernardus Legrange, the distinguished lawyer, Stephen Kemble, whose "Diary," kept during the War has been published by the New York Historical Society, and Rev. Abraham Beach, already referred to, there were others bound together by the relations of blood or marriage, the church or the army; as William Farquhar, M.D., whose first wife was Elizabeth Farmar, daughter of Thomas Farmar, Mayor, and whose second wife was Jane Colden; Rev. Dr. Samuel Auchmuty, Rector of Trinity, N. Y., whose daughter Isabella married Gen. Burton.

Dr. Auchmuty's family were much in New Brunswick, coming here when the Continentals occupied New York. After the British occupied New York he asked permission to return there. He practically filled the office of Bishop in America, excepting as to ordination and confirmation. He was the business head of the Episcopal Church. It was while he was in

---

[3]Referred to in the Appendix under the head of The Van Wickle-Beach-Wells Families.

New Brunswick that the fire causing so great a loss to Trinity occurred. He placed his own loss at $12,000, and Trinity's loss at £22,200, exclusive of the rents from buildings on 246 lots belonging to Trinity. Sir Samuel, his oldest son, was in the British army and was presented by Parliament with a service of plate. His second son, Robert, was also in the British army. His third son, Richard, was likewise in the British army and surrendered with Cornwallis at Yorktown. Rev. Samuel had a brother, a Judge in Boston, whose house in Roxbury was confiscated and afterwards became the home of Governor Increase Sumner. In the "Mischianza" (a tribute to Gen. Howe given in Philadelphia on the eve of his return to England), a tilt and tournament, first on the list is Miss Auchmuty, whose Knight was Lord Cathcart, who was chief of six Knights. There were seven Knights of the Blended Rose, and seven of the Burning Mountain.

Edward Antill, who built Ross Hall, had one son in each army. Stephen Kemble in his "Diary" says: 'Saw his old schoolmate, Antill, among the prisoners.' He was on one of the prison ships. John and Lewis Antill married Margaret and Alice Colden, the same family with which Dr. Farquhar and Dr. Auchmuty were connected. Mrs. Antill, her child and her sister, Miss Colden, obtained permission from the Continental Congress in Philadelphia to proceed from New Brunswick to New York, after taking an oath to carry no information to the enemy. So here we notice a group of distinguished Tories—Loyalists I prefer to call them—as so many were British army officers. After the War this class of citizens was lost to New Brunswick. Some returned to England, others removed to Canada. Their property losses must have been very heavy.

On June 23, 1775, Gen. Washington and military escort left Philadelphia and were in New Brunswick the 24th and in Newark, Powles Hook and New York on the 25th, a three-day journey, and he was presumably in haste, as he was on his way to take command of the army. The bill of expenses of this trip, if itemized, would be exceedingly interesting, but, unfortunately, it was made out and paid in bulk. Gov. William Franklin was entertained at the White Hall, March 1st to 2nd,

1763, and I think it quite likely Washington and his party stayed there June 24 and 25, 1775. In 1776 the bill for entertaining the Provincial Congress was paid to Myndert Voorhees; unfortunately the hotel is not named, but the widow Voorhees had been keeping the White Hall from 1771 to 1779, and I take it that Myndert was her son.[4]

As there is always considerable interest connected with Washington's stay and possible Headquarters, and in view of claims of a Headquarters in New Brunswick, I will run over his various stops in New Brunswick.

His second visit was when his army was in retreat through New Jersey, just ahead of the British. David Rittenhouse, of Philadelphia, says, Nov. 24, 1776: "General Howe, having reduced Fort Washington and obtained possession of Fort Lee, is now directing his operations against New Jersey." Washington, as early as Nov. 7th, had anticipated this movement and inquired of Governor Livingston as to the state of the Barracks in New Jersey at Amboy, Elizabeth, Brunswick, etc. On Nov. 9th, he wrote: "Gen. Howe still has in view an expedition into New Jersey, and is preparing for it with great industry." This was dated from White Plains, N. Y. On the 12th he writes Congress "that the enemy were landing on the Jersey shore." This seems to have been a false alarm. On the 14th Washington informed Congress 'that this army was now south of the Hudson, and it was his intention to quarter the troops at Newark, Elizabeth, Amboy, and Brunswick.' Clement Biddle writes from Brunswick Nov. 17th: "Lord Stirling and eight regiments are here and within a few miles; Gen. Stephens' Brigade at Amboy." The four Regiments in New Brunswick amounted to about 1900, with Col. Hand's Brigade of 1,200 between Elizabeth and Woodbridge. On the 18th Lord Stirling reports to Congress a command of "eight regiments; three at Rahway and five at New Brunswick." The

---

[4]The Provincial Congress met at New Brunswick July, 1774; again Aug. 5, 1774; then Jan. 31 to March 2, 1776; April 1 to May 4; July 22 to Aug. 21. It dissolved Monday, May 4, 1776, and met at Burlington June, 1776. (Force's "Archives," Vol. IV, f. 1626). Myndert Voorhees' bill for firewood, candles and large room for £15 was ordered paid when the Congress left New Brunswick.

Congress in Philadelphia was beginning to feel very nervous at the approach of the enemy.

At this same date (Nov. 18) Washington, with 5,410 troops, was at Hackensack retreating towards New Brunswick. The Board of War notified Washington, Nov. 28, that the prisoners for exchange were being sent to Brunswick, and on the same date Washington wrote Congress from Newark giving a list of his troops and said of Gen. Beall's Brigade of 1,200 men and Gen. Heard's Brigade of 800 that the term of enlistment expired Dec. 1, and urged the necessity of sending troops to replace them. Washington was still at Newark on the 27th.

On the 28th a private letter from Woodbridge says: "The enemy appeared at Second River four miles from Newark [Belleville] this morning, and about 7.00 A. M. the retreat began from Newark, and, after a very tedious march, we arrived at Woodbridge at sunset, and we march for New Brunswick to-morrow," and it gives the strength of the enemy as 17 Regiments and 36 pieces of artillery. On the same date Gen. Scott reports the enemy as advancing from Hackensack, crossing the Passaic at a ford above the Acquackanonck bridge, that another body has landed at Amboy 8,000 strong, and says: "I am constantly keeping horsemen riding down towards the enemy to procure me intelligence." Gen. Washington, writing from Brunswick, Saturday, Nov. 30th, says: "We left Newark on Thursday and arrived here Friday with the troops that were there. The enemy's advance entered Newark as our rear got out. If those go whose service expire to-day our force will be reduced to a mere handful. Intelligence received this morning reports: 'One division of the enemy was advanced last night as far as Elizabethtown.' Other accounts report: 'A division of Hessians are on the road through Springfield.' I am moving my stores from this place towards Philadelphia."

Sir William Howe, describing his movements in a letter says: "The troops crossed from King's Bridge on the night of the 17th and landed about seven miles above Fort Lee, which was hurriedly abandoned and fell into our hands. Thence to the New Bridge upon the Hackensack, and on the 22nd as far as the Passaic, taking Newark on the 28th and now following them towards Brunswick."

Sunday, Dec. 1st, Washington writes several letters from Brunswick. In one to Congress he says: "Dec. 1. Half after 1.00 P. M. The enemy are fast advancing, some of 'em are now in sight. All the men of the Jersey Flying Camp have refused to continue longer in service." To Gov. Livingston he declares that he has not more than 4,000 men, 1,000 of which are Gen. Williamson's militia, having been reduced by the departure of the Maryland Flying Camp men. "Dec. 1, half after 7.00 P. M.," he writes to Congress: "A little after I wrote you this evening, the enemy appeared in several parties on the heights opposite Brunswick, and were advancing in a large body towards the crossing place. We had a smart cannonade whilst we were parading our men, but without any or but little loss on either side. It being impossible to oppose them with our present force with the least prospect of success, we shall retreat to the west side of the Delaware and have advanced about eight miles."

Dec. 2, Princeton, Washington to Congress: "Arrived here this morning between 8.00 and 9.00. An officer writing from New York Dec. 2nd gives the British side thus: Gen. Cornwallis, after driving the rebels from Fort Lee, or Constitution, proceeded from Hackensack to Newark, and Newark to Elizabeth, where they captured 20 tons of musket balls. Lord Cornwallis plunged into the Raritan river and seized the town. Congress paper currency sells at 30 silver dollars the hundred, and salt is $8.00 the bushel. Gen. Howe joins the army tomorrow morning (the 3rd) in the Jerseys, whither I shall accompany him."

Dec. 3, Trenton, Washington to Congress: "Arrived here yesterday morning with the main body of the army, having left Lord Stirling at Princeton. I am informed that they had not entered Brunswick yesterday morning at 9:00 A. M. (Dec. 2). A countryman who was in Brunswick said every house was full of Redcoats, and on the 8th the New York Committee of Safety reported Gen. Howe in New Brunswick with 10,000 men, and General Washington at Trenton with 6,000,

NEW BRUNSWICK IN HISTORY

and General Cornwallis was with the troops that occupied Brunswick."

Dec. 4 Washington writes from Trenton that the enemy were in Brunswick, and their advance parties 2 miles this side. Two Brigades, the Jersey and the Maryland, left Washington while he was in Brunswick, notwithstanding the enemy were within two hours' march and coming on. The loss of these troops necessitated a retreat. When Washington left Brunswick he had not 3,000 men. Gen. Nathaniel Greene, Dec. 7th, says the enemy were advancing on Princeton. Washington crossed the river at Trenton, Saturday night, Dec. 8; on Sunday the enemy appeared at Trenton and a cannonade ensued. Washington was at Trenton Falls Dec. 10, 11, 12, 13, and Generals Howe, Cornwallis and Vaughn at Pennytown [Pennington], Trenton and down toward Burlington with 12,000 men. Washington's Headquarters from the 14th to the 24th inclusive were in Bucks Co., Pa., at Keith's, and while here Washington says: "The conduct of the Jerseys has been most infamous."

Sir William Howe, writing Dec. 20, says: "Prevented the passage of the Raritan by breaking a part of the Brunswick bridge. On the 6th I joined Lord Cornwallis with the 4th Brigade." On the 7th Lord Cornwallis advanced to Princeton and from there to Trenton and Pennytown, and on the 21st is reported as having been in Brunswick, Princeton, Pennytown, Trenton, Bordentown, Burlington, Morristown, Mt. Holly and Haddonfield.

Dec. 22nd it was reported that there were 600 or 800 men in Brunswick and in Headquarters at Princeton, where troops were in the College, meeting-house and other places. At Burlington eight to fifteen were quartered in a house. 24th, Washington reports still in camp above Trenton Falls.

But on the night of the 25th, Christmas, Washington at the head of 2,500 men passed over the Delaware, at 3 A. M. was on the march by two routes for Trenton, and at daybreak was two miles from Trenton, where, with almost no defense, 1,500 Hessians were routed, and three standards, six brass cannon, about 1,000 stand of arms, 23 officers and 886 men were captured. Washington's loss was 4 killed and 8 wounded. Washington returned the same day to Pennsylvania.

The British occupied New Brunswick Dec. 1, 1776, marching in as our troops marched out, and remained till June 22, 1777, when they in turn evacuated it. Stephen Kemble, the British officer before referred to, born in New Brunswick, says in his "Diary" under date of June 25, 1777, that Washington was reported in New Brunswick; probably a brief visit on the heels of the retiring British.

The next and last date was July 4, 1778. Washington's army camped on the river just above Brunswick to celebrate the Fourth and also the Battle of Monmouth, just fought. At none of these four brief visits is there any intimation that he established Headquarters in the city; in fact, the little information we have seems to argue against it, and to designate any building as his Headquarters on no better evidence seems unwarranted, however much we should like to make the claim.

The British on their first visit used James Neilson's house on Burnet street as Headquarters for the British officers (he was an uncle and father by adoption of Col. John Neilson, whose house it was after his uncle's death, March 4, 1783); and Jacob Van Nuis' house on Queen, north of Schureman and west side of Queen, was the Headquarters of the Hessian officers. Neither of these houses remain; the Howell Lumber Co. occupies the site of the first, and the Hinger Furniture Co. the site of the second. But when Gen. Howe brought, as was reported, 10,000 men into New Brunswick, it was said that every house was full of Red-coats.

When Washington reluctantly retreated and the British, following on his heels, occupied the city, for seven months it was a fortified garrison, but by no means a quiet or comfortable one.

Of the (about) ninety engagements, great and small, that occurred in New Jersey a goodly number of them took place around this city. The activities of those seven months surprise one, for while the greater number of the engagements were small, between patrols and foraging parties, or skirmishes with picket guards, they were kept up so constantly that there could have been little relaxation or rest in the beleaguered city. We know that the Rev. Abraham Beach complained bitterly of Washington's sharpshooters using his house as a convenient breast work to take "pot-shots" at the British when they ventured that way. Washington's army at Middlebrook and in the hills at Chimney Rock and Washington Rock kept a close watch on the town, and troops seldom left New Brunswick without some sort of engagement before they got back.

As I understand the somewhat confusing reports of this period the British had posts not only at Amboy and Brunswick but at Bonhamtown, The Landing, Bennet's Island, Quibbletown (New Market), Samptown (South Plainfield), Spanktown (Rahway), Elizabethtown and Woodbridge. To watch these places, Washington, according to a list dated May 14, 1777, had patrol guards as follows: 70 to watch Brunswick, 60 for lower Raritan, 60 for upper Raritan, 44 for Quibbletown, 23 for Somerset, and the main patrol of 39. It must have been upon these patrols that he depended for information as to the enemy's movements. There were one or two horsemen attached to each patrol. The audacity of many of the small engagements spoke well for our Jersey Militia. For example:

Only a few days after the fight at Princeton, about Jan. 6, 1776, Col. Spencer, with forty or fifty militia, surprised an equal number of Hessians near Springfield, (northwest of Elizabeth in present Union Co.) and killed or captured the whole party.

On Friday night, Jan. 17, a party of 200 attacked the piquet guard at Brunswick, but were beaten off, quite naturally, as there were about 5,000 troops here and behind fortifications; but it shows the spirit of our men.

Jan. 20 Gen. Dickinson, with 400 militia and 50 Pennsylvania troops, attacked 600 British at Millstone bridge. Not being able to carry the bridge, which was protected by artillery, they made a detour, fording the river and coming up in the rear, captured 43 wagons, 104 horses, 118 cattle, 60 or 70 sheep and 12 prisoners.

On Jan. 23 the Sixth Virginia (Col. Parker) attacked the

British three miles above New Brunswick; the latter was a foraging party up the Raritan, which lost 65 men, killed and wounded, and with Col. Preston killed.

On Feb. 18 Col. Neilson and Capt. Forman surprised the stockade on Bennet's Island and captured Major Richard V. Stockton and the Sixth Battalion N. J. Loyalists; of 63 men not one escaped. Stockton was called "the Land Pilot," and was sent to Philadelphia in irons, but when Washington heard of it he directed that he should be treated as a prisoner of war.

Feb. 23 a foraging party was attacked very near Amboy and 4 officers and 100 men were reported killed; this was between Amboy and Woodbridge.

Feb. 8 and 20 there were two small engagements at Quibbletown; in the first the Americans were surprised, in the second the Americans drove in the guard and captured a loaded wagon.

On March 1st a party of 3,000 came out of Brunswick to forage; 600 Americans under Col. Scott attacked them. We lost 3 officers and 12 men; the British loss was 36 killed and about 100 wounded.

On March 5, 500 attacked the piquet guard at Brunswick, drove in the guard and captured 11 cows, 2 horses and 15 loads of hay. They probably burned the hay. The British were shut up in Brunswick till late in March, and communication with Amboy was cut off except by water. The Americans placed a battery of 32-pounders on the heights overlooking the river, and when a fleet of boats with supplies came up the river they were attacked, four or five boats were sunk and the remainder returned to Amboy. There was quite an engagement at Punkhill near Amboy, with the Americans between Carman's Hill and Woodbridge, in favor of the Americans; and on the same day near Quibbletown or Squabbletown, we had three men wounded and the enemy expelled.

On the 16th Major General Vaughan marched from Amboy to Spanktown (Rahway) and the engagement resulted very favorably to the Americans.

On the 24th Major Butler had a brush with the enemy near

Samptown (South Plainfield), drove in the guard; 4 were slain and 7 of the enemy made prisoners.

April 4th there was another small engagement at Quibbletown; 5 British killed, and we had one rifleman wounded.

At Bound Brook Gen. Lincoln had quite a respectable force, which Cornwallis, with Generals Grant and Mathews, surprised Apr. 12th. They occupied his camp for an hour and a half, capturing 35 prisoners, 2 officers and two pieces of artillery and considerable stores. The surprise came near being complete on account of the carelessness of a piquet guard at the ford. The party of British and Hessians under Col. Donlop was estimated at 4,000.

General Stevens one evening drove in all the piquets at Bonhamtown, killed a captain and 7 privates and took 16 prisoners, capturing the whole guard.

On May 10th the Royal Highlanders, six companies, were attacked at Piscataway, two miles from Brunswick and two miles from Bonhamtown. The action continued an hour and a half. Gen. Maxwell was at the head of the attacking party. After twice compelling the British to give way, on account of the nearness of the British reserves at Brunswick, Amboy and The Landing, it was thought best to withdraw. The enemy had a Captain, Major and two Lieutenants wounded and 65 men killed or wounded.

On June 9th, 1777, there is noted by the British an event that I think has not had proper notice, and that was the hanging of one of Washington's spies. The British account says: "Abraham Patton,[5] a spy from the Rebel Army, was executed last Friday between 11 and 12 at Brunswick—two weeks before the British evacuated the town. He gave a grenadier 50 guineas to deliver four letters to Washington and Putnam, wherein it was proposed on a certain day to set fire to Brunswick in four places at once and blow up the magazine, and then set off a rocket as a signal for the Rebels to attack the town.

---

[5]James Paton, a Revolutionary soldier, died in New Brunswick Nov. 6, 1816, aged 58. Possibly of the same family. The one is spelled with two *t*'s and the other with one.

The said Patton lived in New Brunswick formerly and left a wife and four children at Baltimore, Md."

On June 7th Lieut. Martin, with 10 men of a scouting party, fell in with 15 light horsemen. At the first fire the Commander of the Lighthorse was killed, but they spurred up, our men gave way and the Lieutenant was surrounded and butchered though calling for quarter. He had seventeen wounds, any one of which would have been fatal; our loss was three or four killed and as many wounded.

The British becoming uneasy at Washington's movements about Brunswick made an advance to Somerset Court House (Millstone), burning the Dutch Reformed meeting-house in part and another church, in hopes of drawing Washington into a general engagement. Failing in this they retreated to Brunswick. Washington, planning to cut off their rear guard, was following them so closely that his troops were within a mile of the bridge at Brunswick when Gen. Howe's troops passed from the town, and Gen. Wayne pushed them so closely that they did not have time to form behind earthworks, previously prepared for that purpose, to cover the retreat. Our loss in this pursuit was but 3 or 4 killed and as many wounded. Morgan's Regiment of riflemen were actively harassing the enemy's rear, but as there were between 4,000 and 5,000 in the British column and the retreat was so rapid, a sufficient number of troops to attack in earnest could not be brought up in time.

The Americans occupied New Brunswick immediately on the departure of the British. The same day Washington moved his headquarters to Quibbletown (New Market) to the Vermeule house, and Stephen Kemble, a British officer in New York, though born and raised in New Brunswick, notes in his diary: "Washington reported in New Brunswick on the 25th." As it was but a short ride from Quibbletown he probably rode over to see the condition of the town after its six months occupancy by the enemy.

On June 26th Howe made a final attempt to surprise Washington's Army at Quibbletown, sending Gen. Knyphausen to get between them and the Blue Hills, advancing as far as Westfield. But the Continentals and the Jersey Blues checked them first at one bridge and then at another while Washington and his army had promptly retired to the Hills and Howe returned the next day to Amboy. From officers' letters from Morristown during this period we learn that some small clash of patrol or foragers, skirmishers and piquet guards occurred almost daily; evidently many more than are on record.

These small and large affairs around Brunswick give one a fair idea of what was going on and shows that the army behind their fortifications at Brunswick had anything but a quiet time and were kept on pretty short rations.

Express riders during the war were hard to get, as the work was both difficult and dangerous. Col. Frelinghuysen reports that he had induced John Bennet and John DeCamp to undertake the job between Trenton and Morristown at $2.00 per day. In Jan., 1778, "200 Rebels attacked a piquet guard at New Brunswick"—this would indicate that the British were again in New Brunswick at that time.

On Oct. 25, 1779, Simcoe, who commanded a Regiment of Horse, crossed from Staten Island at the Blazing Star Ferry in the night with 75 men; thence on to Woodbridge. His object was to surprise and capture Gov. Livingston. He was not discovered until he was seven miles north of New Brunswick at Quibbletown, from which place an express was sent to Col. John Neilson, at New Brunswick, who immediately ordered out the Regiment and it marched to the bridge at Raritan Landing. Col. Simcoe, meanwhile, had proceeded rapidly to Col. Philip Van Horne's house at Middlebrook and was much disappointed at not finding the Governor there (he being in New Brunswick); from there he went via Chimney Rock to Van Vechten's bridge on the Raritan river (near present Manville), fired some boats and forage and the Dutch meeting-house; then to Millstone, called Hillsborough, 8 miles north-west of New Brunswick and fired the Court House and jail.

Col. Neilson despatched Capt. Moses Guest and 35 men to intercept Simcoe if possible, which they did almost immediately and fired one volley into them as they dashed by. Col. Simcoe's horse was shot and fell on him, one soldier was killed, and several wounded. Simcoe's doctor and servant came back under a flag to attend to him, while the enemy continued to retreat under Maj. Stuart, a refugee who had piloted the party. Capt. Peter Voorhees, with a few militia horsemen, who had just returned with him from Gen. Sullivan's army, pursued so close on the enemy that they sent a detachment after him, which quickly overtook him and cut him with the broad swords in a most shocking manner. This occurred within a half-mile of New Brunswick on George's road; I think about where the street-car barn is located. The pursuit was abandoned at South River bridge. Guest wrote a poem on the sad death of Capt. Voorhees, and these lines are part of the poem:

> "The brave intrepid Voorhees now no more;
> He's gone! We grieve; the generous youth has fled,
> Untimely sent to number with the dead—
> Voorhees, brave Voorhees; yes, that is a name
> To patriots dear, and New Brunswick's boast."

He devotes another poem to Mina Voorhees, who fell 64 feet from the top of the Episcopal church steeple and yet lived to do his part as a soldier of the Revolution, and even lived to come home safely when the War was over.

Lieutenant-Col. Simcoe says in his Journal: "On the high grounds beyond the barracks" they rallied, and "Capt. Voorhees of the Jersey Continental troops was overtaken and killed."

CHAPTER VI

Capt. Adam Hyler and Other Noted Privateers—House and Park of Buccleuch—Its Successive Owners—New Brunswick as a College Town—Some Early College Commencements.

NEW BRUNSWICK acquired no little notoriety in 1780-'81 from the raids of the "Whale Boat Privateers," Capt. William Marriner and Capt. Adam Hyler. Capt. Marriner was active as early as Nov., 1778, then operating from Middletown Point or Harbor, about 6 miles from Middletown. His raid from there rather curiously followed the old route from New Jersey to Long Island (Geo. Fox crossing there in 1671, more than 100 years before). On this raid into Long Island he captured Simon and Jacques Cortelyou, and specie and goods of about $5,000 in value. The following June he captured Major Moncrief, Theopoles Bache and David Mathews. On May 18, 1780, he captured the brig "Black Snake," a privateer, and 20 men previously captured by the "Galatea," a British war vessel, and at the same time captured the schooner "Morning Star" and took both to Egg Harbour. This raid was made from Amboy.

In October, 1780, Capt. Hyler, with one gunboat, made an expedition to the Refugee town near Sandy Hook, "where the horse thieves congregated," but he did not find them there. In December he captured the sloop "Savannah." In August, 1781, he landed from an armed boat on Long Island, marched 3½ miles inland and captured Capt. Jeromus Lot, a Lieut.-Colonel of Militia, and John Hankins, and brought them to New Brunswick. In October, with one gunboat and two whale boats,[1] he attacked five vessels within a quarter of a mile of the guard ship at Sandy Hook, carried them off in fifteen minutes and burned four of them; a woman and four children on board saved the other. A week later, with the same three boats, he captured one sloop and two schooners, burned one,

---

[1]The question may suggest itself, how did New Brunswick happen to have whale boats? One answer is that Henry Guest was engaged in whaling from this place.

and one ran aground, was stripped and brought one to New Brunswick. In November he captured a ship and started to bring her to New Brunswick but she ran aground. The cargo was rum and pork. He got from it 20 hogshead of rum and 30 barrels of pork and was then obliged to burn the ship, which was called "Father's Desire." In April, 1781, with one gunboat and one barge, he captured the British cutter of six 18-pounders and 10 9-pounders and a crew of 50. After landing the crew he burned the ship. At the same time he captured a sloop that he ransomed for $400.

In June, with the armed privateer "Revenge," Hyler captured the cutter "Alert" and sold its 9 negro men. Being on the 25th of May in the "Shrewsbury," Capt. Shack with 25 men of the 57th British Regiment were sent to intercept him. Huyler landed 13 men and charged, killing and wounding four and capturing the Captain and eight men.

The British finally decided to break up, if possible, Capt. Hyler's raids, and on Jan. 10 it is noted that 'last Wednesday, (Jan. 4, 1782), a party came up the river at night, landed at the lower end of the town and took possession with very little difficulty. They captured the whale boats, which was the object of their raid, losing 4 killed and carrying off several wounded. Col. John Taylor reported for the American side 5 wounded and two houses pillaged.' This brought Capt. Hyler's activities to an end.[2]

William Marriner we find keeping tavern in New Brunswick and the surrender of Cornwallis was celebrated at his Inn by the gentlemen of the city, and some strangers, of whom were Sir James Jay and Richard Stevens. Mr. Kirkpatrick was Toastmaster and thirteen toasts were drunk. After the war Marriner lived in Harlem.

There was another privateer to be credited to New Brunswick. John White, of Philadelphia, Major Van Emburgh and Col. John Neilson fitted out the "Endeavor" as a privateer to cruise in the West Indies under a Capt. Brown. A fighting

---

[2] Adam Huyler married, in 1760, Ann Nefie, of New Brunswick. Capt. Hiram Marriner was his mate, or 1st officer. Capt. Huyler died Sept. 6, 1782, said to have been poisoned.

crew was difficult to obtain at £20 a month. While in harbor on the Jersey coast, and while Capt. Brown and three sailors were ashore, a storm drove her on the beach where she upset and the rest of the crew were lost. I have no record of the cruises of this vessel.

The house and park of Buccleuch have three distinct claims to our interest. First, the handsome gift to our city of its house and acres as a park for our people, a gift that is thoroughly appreciated. Second, the fact that the house is a well-preserved specimen of Colonial architecture and is being converted into an interesting Museum by our Jersey Blue Chapter of the D. A. R. Third, of chief general interest, perhaps, the occupation of the house has been distinctly military. The son of the builder of "Buccleuch" was a Colonel in the Revolution. The second owner was a British General. The interim between the second and third owner was divided between a Captain and a man who was so offensively active in the American cause that the British marked his home in New York City with a red letter "R" for Rebel, so he came here; 'discretion being the better part of valor.' But he was again forced to move on when a British Regiment made the house their headquarters. The third owner was again a Colonel on the Revolutionary side. The fourth owner so far ranks as a man of peace, while of the last family the purchaser was a Colonel of the War of 1812, and his father was not only a surgeon of the Revolution (was in several battles and near some distinguished officers when they fell), but he began life as a soldier under Braddock and fought his way up to a commission from the ranks.

Now let me review briefly these successive owners and occupants. With no written record to draw upon, I must build up a record from the known facts.

Anthony White, the father of the first owner and builder of the house, was a son of Leonard White of the Bermudas, who came to New York about 1715 and married, Jan. 26, 1717, Joanna Staats, who was born Jan. 31, 1694, and was, therefore, twenty-three years of age. Their son, baptized Nov. 6, 1717, was also named Anthony White. The father died on a trip to the Bermudas and his mother later, Sept. 26, 1726, married Admiral Norton Kelsall.

Young Anthony White was made freeman in New York when he became twenty-one in 1738. He married Elizabeth, daughter of Governor Lewis Morris, in 1739 or 1740. His wife's sister, Anne, married, June 10, 1739, Edward Antill, who immediately proceeded to build on a tract of 350 acres, acquired by his father fifty years earlier. The house we now call "Ross Hall," is not the name given by its builder, whose first child was born in the house in 1740; and we have every reason to believe that Anthony White was building his house at the same time on the other side of the river. This latter house is now called "Buccleuch" (again not the name given by the builder, for it was called for many years the "White House" or "White House Farm"), and his oldest child, Joanna, wife of Judge Bayard, has on her tombstone, "Died June 26, 1831, in her 91st year." She, too, seems to have been born in 1740. I think we are reasonably safe in giving the date of both houses as 1739.

The next child of record of the second Anthony White was Euphemia, born 1746, wife of Gov. William Paterson. She died Jan. 29, 1832, in her 86th year. There was another daughter, Isabella, unmarried, and then a son, the famous Gen. Anthony Walton White,[3] who was born July 7th, 1750. He married, in 1783, Margaret Vanderhorse Ellis of Charleston who was but 15. As Gen. White, then Colonel, was with the army of Lafayette before Savannah and Charleston in the winter of 1782-'3, it is easy to construct again the romance where the characters were the dashing officer and an impressionable girl of fifteen. They had one daughter who married Thomas Evans and had four children. Mrs. White's sister, Mary Ellis, followed her sister to New Brunswick and, though Gen. White ruined himself, first by a lavish use of his own means to equip his troops, expecting to be repaid later, and second by a speculation to recoup himself, which turned out unfortunately (he was going through bankruptcy proceedings at the time of

---

[3] A fine portrait and a life of Gen. Anthony W. White appeared in the "N. J. Hist. Soc. Proceedings" of 1882, Second Series, Vol. VII, p. 105.

his death, Feb. 10, 1803), the sister stood by them through life. Her home was theirs so completely that her house in Livingstone Ave., where the Y. M. C. A. now stands, was frequently referred to as "General White's house."

While the two sisters, Joanna and Euphemia, are buried side by side in the Presbyterian churchyard, Gen. White is buried in the Episcopal churchyard, and his tombstone bears a bronze memorial plate, placed there by the Jersey Blue Chapter of the D. A. R.

Mary Ellis was a shrewd business woman. The advertisement of her lots on Oppression St. (Schureman) is a curiosity, as is also a lengthy advertisement of half of the Cold Spring farm, a, farm of 300 acres that Gen. White deeded to her in hopes of saving it, but it was taken later and sold by the sheriff. She bought the Hill, called then Pine Tree Hill, which is now the site, in part, of our Woman's College, together with nine acres in the rear belonging to Mr. James Neilson and the late Mr. C. J. Carpenter. This was in 1799. She intended to build on it and present it to her sister, but, owing to a dispute with Judge Robert Morris over the ownership of the brook running to the east of the property, she employed Judge Andrew Kirkpatrick as her lawyer, and, not being able to get the boundaries she wished, took the place as she had agreed to but refused to build there. After the trouble over Schureman St. she moved to what we call the "Evans Place," where grew up Gen. White's granddaughters, the Misses Evans—among the belles of New Brunswick in their day.

Gen. White's wife is, I presume, buried in Miss Ellis' private burying-ground on the Evans' place.

Anthony White's children were evidently born in the Buccleuch house, but were neither married in nor buried from it, as he sold the place in 1774 (as nearly as I can determine) after an ownership of 35 years. The purchaser was the English army officer, Gen. William Burton. The notice of his wedding in the paper of March 3 reads: "On Tuesday last William Burton, Esq., to Isabella Auchmuty, second daughter of the Rector of Trinity Church, New York City." Burton was a nephew of Bartholomas Burton, late Governor of the

Bank of England. It would seem that he had bought the place of Anthony White to take his bride to it.

There is little to be said of this next owner. It is somewhere stated that Gen. William Burton went to England "with his family" May 29, 1766. Evidently he had been here in our Colonial wars and had returned with his family to England. What this family consisted of and what disposition he made of it I have no means of knowing. That he was here again very shortly, taking a second wife, and getting pleasantly settled only to be broken up by the Revolution, is the brief story. Of his war record there is one note, namely, that he was Commander in charge of naval prisoners in New York in 1779. The Commissioners of Forfeited Estates, Jacob Bergen, Frederick Frelinghuysen and Hendrick Wilson in 1783 say, in the notice of advertisement of a sale: "The famous house and lands late the property of William Burton, formerly in the occupancy of Anthony White."

Now the ownership becomes in the State, and the Commissioners—say from 1776 till 1783. Of this period we can account for only one year. George Janeway, son of Jacob Janeway and Sarah Hoagland and grandson of William Janeway and Agnes DeKay, and also father of Rev. Jacob, a Dutch Reformed minister and Vice-President of Rutgers, the father of the late Henry L. Janeway, upon the occupation of New York by the British, Sept. 15, 1776, being an ardent patriot and Captain of Company S, Second Regiment N. Y. Militia, had a red letter "R" painted on his front door, which he found so unpleasant that he came to New Brunswick and undoubtedly rented the Burton house from the Commissioners, only to have the British follow him up six weeks later and to find himself again within their lines. Here we have the curious situation of the Rebel compelled to leave his home in New York City occupying the house of the Tory who had abandoned his home in New Brunswick! So we again have the military occupant in Capt. Janeway.

There are a couple of anecdotes handed down from George's son Jacob to his son Henry L. Jacob, who was a small boy, had two vivid recollections of his stay in the "White House."

He fell into a cistern which supplied the house with water and was nearly drowned; and he saw a young farmer killed, who was in the habit of riding up as near as he could to the fort on Seminary Hill and taunting the soldiers. Trusting to the fast horse he rode to get away. Jacob's father had warned him that he would do that once too often, and so it turned out. One day his horse was tired and the British, sallying out, overtook him and cut him down.

According to Mr. Dey the Ennis Killen Dragoons, who got their name from the town in Ulster where the Regiment was raised, were quartered at the "White House," and many of their buttons were found there from time to time. This would explain the brief stay of the Janeways. George was baptized in the old Piscataway church, his father living on the river between New Brunswick and Bound Brook, and he did not go to New York until he was of age. Jacob bought the house already referred to as Mary Ellis's house in 1833. It remained in that family until recently purchased for the Y. M. C. A. building, which is now on the site.

In 1783 the Commissioners sold the White House to John Bergen, who immediately resold it to Col. Charles Stewart, the third resident owner.

Charles Stewart came to America in 1750. He married Mary, daughter of Judge Samuel Johnson, of Hunterdon county. He lived in the then Bethlehem Township, probably near present High Bridge, and was Colonel of the First Regiment of Minute Men in 1776, then Colonel of the Line, then Commissary-General on Washington's Staff till the end of the war. Mary, his wife, had the reputation of being "the best read woman in the Province." Johann David Schoepf, M. D., in a book of his travels in July, 1783, speaks of Col. Stewart's house on "a rising ground by the road" (he was going from New Brunswick to Bound Brook), which, "like so many in America is thinly built of wood but after a tasteful plan." After leaving Col. Stewart's he again crossed the Raritan over a wooden bridge and after a few miles reached Bound Brook. On Feb. 12, 1776, Stewart's daughter, Matty, was married to Robert Wilson at Kingwood (west of Flemington, on the Delaware). After an ownership of 15 years, Col. Stewart sold the place to John Garnett, and in 1798, having previously (how long before is unknown), returned to Hunterdon Co., where he died two years later (1800). Frederick Frelinghuysen at 21 was Major in Col. Stewart's Battalion of Minute Men.

John Garnett, the fourth resident owner, 1798-1820, was a native of England (his deed says "late from Europe"), probably coming almost directly to the "White House." In addition to the place we know as Buccleuch he bought adjoining lands until he had over 300 acres. Six years after his purchase we find in "The Guardian," of Jan. 1, 1804, a notice of the marriage of Anna Maria Garnett, oldest daughter of John Garnett, to Charles Henry Stone of New York. This is the first wedding on record from this house that I have found. The Rev. John Croes performed the marriage ceremony, and it was on Sunday, which was somewhat unusual. John Garnett was a vestryman in Christ Church in 1799, a year after buying here, and served for ten years.

In the "Fredonian," July 26, 1826, we find the obituary of Henry Garnett, "aged 42, son of the late John Garnett, well-known in the scientific world," who died in this city. Mary Garnett, wife and administrator of John Garnett, gives the children as Fanny, Julia, Harriet and Henry, placing the son last, from which fact I infer he was the youngest, which would make him fourteen when the family came to New Brunswick; so the family were all well-grown. And the Dorcas Society acknowledges a donation from the Misses Garnett in April, 1818.

After the statement in Henry Garnett's obituary that his father was "well known in the scientific world," while a search through the biographical lists amounted to nothing, in a volume in Rutgers' Library of Astronomical Tables, of about 150 pp., published Oct. 11, 1806, John Garnett, author, gave us his scientific bent, and in this work he is also credited with the editorship of the "American Nautical Almanac," 1803-1809. This "Almanac" is now published by the U. S. Government at Washington. The copy of Garnett's book, for which we are indebted for our first knowledge of his work, was presented to the Agricultural Society of New Brunswick by Mrs. Garnett. This Society was formed in February, or March, 1818. Its first business meeting, I find, was called to meet Nov. 25, 1818, at Abraham DeGraw's Bell Tavern. This Society shows how early we were interested in agriculture and was the feeble forerunner of the N. J. State Agricultural Experiment Station located here to-day.

That John Garnett had time for other things besides mathematics is proven by his taking a prize for the best boar exhibited before this Society in 1820, just before his death, and the presentation of a copy of his book to this Society is also a mark of his interest in the Society. His obituary in the "Fredonian" of May 18, 1820, is of an unusual length. I have condensed it considerably, as follows:

'Died suddenly of apoplexy on the 11th of May, at his late residence, the White House Farm, near this city, John Garnett, Esq., in the 72nd year of his age. He was a native of England and had resided in this state about twenty years. Strict probity, integrity and benevolent deportment commanded respect and attention from all with whom he had communication. He was an affectionate and respectful husband, a tender and instructive father, a highly respected and charitable neighbor; distinguished for profound mathematical research and application to practical purposes in the arts. Gentlemen of science and erudition cultivated his acquaintance and esteemed his friendship. His home was the resort of science, intelligence and letters. His scientific knowledge rendered him an ornament to the country which he had adopted. His mental abilities were not impaired. He contemplated visiting his native country in the approaching summer. He retired in good health and spirits, and, about midnight, his soul winged its way to that bourne from which no traveller returns.'

There is a notice in July, 1820, that his dwelling, windmill, 300 acres, stock farm, utensils, etc., are for sale. In August a sale for Oct. 10th is announced, almost immediately adjourned till Spring, and it is not until Spring, May 3rd, that it is again advertised for sale by permission of the Court. His stone has disappeared from Christ churchyard, but a diagram of the yard shows his grave as next to Mrs. Martha Croes, while the Church record says: "Died May 11, 1820, aged 69." The obituary is, I should say, more likely to be correct, although the obituary also says, "About twenty years a resident of this State," while his ownership of the "White House" was 22 years.

From the chief bibliographer in the Congressional Library at Washington I learn that John Garnett edited the "Nautical Almanac" and the "Astronomical Ephemeris" for the years 1804 to 1813 and published it in New Brunswick. Also that he was a member of the American Philosophical Society of Philadelphia. He also edited "Clark's Seamans' Desiderata, or Concise Practical Rules for Computing the Apparent Time at Sea, the Latitude from Double Solar Altitudes and the Longitude from Lunar Observations, with Addresses and Corrections." This was printed by Abraham Blauvelt in 1801.

We now come to the fifth resident-owner, another Colonel—Colonel Joseph Warren Scott—the very eminent and successful lawyer; one of the really great lawyers of New Jersey, who bought the place June 6, 1821, and at this time we get the present name "Buccleuch" rightfully, as that is the name he gave it. It is said to have been named for the family and estates of his Scotch ancestor. Mr. Richard Dey traces his genealogy to John Scott of Farras and Lough Doine, who left the land of his birth soon after the House of Hanover succeeded to the British Throne. With his bosom friend, the Earl of Bethaven, they had bid adieu to Mother Caledonia, and wandered four or five years without a resting place. Bethaven died and was buried on the shore of Lake Killarney. John Scott crossed the ocean, settled in Pennsylvania about 1724 (another authority makes it 1721). He was an elder in the Neshaminy Presbyterian Church in Bucks Co., Pa. His son, Moses Scott, born 1738, decided for a military career and at 17 was with Braddock on his disastrous campaign. At the capture of Fort DuQuesne, three years afterward, he had risen to be a commissioned officer, but the next year he resigned on account of the invidious distinction between the Royal and Colonial officers, and, by the advice of Dr. Ewing (Rev. Dr. John Ewing, Provost of the University of Philadelphia) and Mr. Beattie (Dr. Reading Beattie of Bucks Co.) betook himself to the study of medicine. When the War began he was appointed Surgeon-General of State forces, and was present at the Battles of Trenton, Princeton, Brandywine and Germantown, and not until the restoration of peace did he resume his profession in this city. He was a Trustee of the new Presbyterian Church, being very active in the movement to build it; and his oldest daughter, Hannah, organized the first Sunday School in this city in 1816 and was the superintendent.

Moses Scott married Anna Johnson and came to New Brunswick about 1774. He had two sons (one died in infancy), both named Joseph Warren after General Joseph Warren, who was killed at Bunker Hill and whom he greatly admired; and General Warren, in turn, named a son Moses Scott. He also had ten daughters: Hannah, who remained unmarried; Jane, who married Abraham Blauvelt; Anna Johnson, who married Dr. Fitzrandolph Smith; Mary Dickinson, who married Dr. Charles Smith; Eliza, who married Rev. Peter P. Rouse; two other unmarried daughters and two who died in infancy; and there was still another child.

The son Joseph Warren Scott was born Nov. 21, 1778, and died Apr. 21, 1871, in his 93rd year. He was a graduate of Princeton before he was seventeen (1795). He first studied medicine with his father, but abandoned it for the ministry. He soon withdrew from that, studied law with Gen. Frederick Frelinghuysen, and was licensed in 1801. He and William Ratoon were admitted Feb. 29, 1804, as counsellors-at-law. His practice was large and lucrative. He was a member of the Order of the Cincinnati, and its President in 1804; received the degree of LL.D. from Princeton in 1868. In early life he was on the Governor's Staff with the rank of Colonel. In the War of 1812-'15 he was Captain of Light Infantry in Gen. Colfax's Brigade from Sept. 5, 1814 until the Company was discharged, Dec. 2, 1814. He succeeded his father as trustee of the Presbyterian Church in 1822 and was for a time Secretary of the Union Library Company, successor to the New Brunswick Library Company formed in 1792. He married, in 1804 (aged 26), Jane Griffiths of New York and they had six children. She died Dec. 5, 1821. His father also died in December of that year, the same in which he bought Buccleuch. In 1818 Joseph Warren Scott bought of J. R. Hardenbergh and wife the old Bayard House on Albany street, and in a deed executed in 1818 he described himself as "of Somerset Co." (the Bayard House was in Somerset Co.). Before that he is noted as resident of the City of New Brunswick.

During the first fourteen years of his married life I find he owned these houses in New Brunswick: in 1804 one on the north side of George's Road, bought of John Hendricks; in 1806 one on the west side of Burnet St. (about at Oliver St.) and one on Little Burnet St. next Market House Square; in 1814 one on Livingston Ave. and Schureman, bought of William Bell Paterson; in 1818, on Albany St. the Col. John Bayard house, and in 1821 the White House Farm (Buccleuch) of Mary Garnett. He sold the Bayard House in 1866 to Martin Nevius and Buccleuch he sold in 1865 to Anthony Dey.

Anthony Dey in 1911 deeded Buccleuch to the Mayor and Council of New Brunswick as a memorial to Col. Joseph Warren Scott, in which deed Mary Laidlie Dey, Joseph W. Dey and Richard Varick Dey joined.

Joseph Warren Scott's six children were: Lavinia Agnes, who married Rev. Richard Varrick Dey; Anna Cornelia, who died in infancy; Joseph Griffiths, who married Eliza Duryee; Moses Warren, who married Julie Ann Cornell; Cornelia DeDiemar, who married Rev. John D. Ogilby; Charles Smith, unmarried.

Mrs. Dey on the death of her husband, Rev. Richard Varick Dey, in the Fall of 1837, went with her children to live with her father, Col. Joseph Warren Scott, at Buccleuch, and in 1843 she removed to New York City. Her son, Anthony, returned to Buccleuch, attended Rutgers Preparatory School, entered the College, Class 1850, and made Buccleuch his home. His mother and sister, Mary Laidlie Dey, made their home there again in 1865, remaining till 1874, when Mrs. Dey again made her home in New York City, where she died on March 31, 1886.

Charles Smith Scott, son of Col. Joseph Warren Scott, continued to make Buccleuch his home until he died Dec. 24, 1893.

NEW BRUNSWICK IN HISTORY 139

After that Anthony continued there alone until the gift to the City of New Brunswick in 1911.[4]

New Brunswick as a college town has a long and interesting record dating from 1766. The efforts to get organized and in operation run through 1767, 1768, 1769, 1770 and 1771. When a hotel, corner of French and King Streets, was purchased for a college building,[5] its first Board was composed of some of the most noted men in the colony—Col. Teunis Dey of Preakness, Bergen Co., Hendrick Fisher of Somerset Co.; Peter Hassenclever, the great iron master of that day; Hendrick Kuyper, another Bergen Co. man of note; Judge Peter Schenck of Somerset Co.; Jan Van Metern of Salem Co.; Peter Zabriskie, a Judge in Bergen Co. Forestalling the opening of the College, and as a necessary adjunct, the three Dutch domines, Leydt, Hardenbergh and Van Harlingen; the Rev. Abraham Beach, of the Church of England; Dr. John Cochrane, M.D., and William Ouke, Mayor of New Brunswick, opened the school already referred to as belonging to Mayor Ouke's progressive administration. Twenty years later, in 1786, the College felt the need of more commodious quarters, and, having obtained a fine site at the then south end of George St., they sold the original College on French St. and built the College Hall. There a second twenty-year period was passed, when the opening of Schureman, Liberty and George Streets through the College property, leaving College Hall standing right in the middle of George St., necessitated another move.

---

[4]The full dates of Colonel Scott's family not having hitherto been printed, they are placed in the Appendix, as obtained from various sources.

[5]In an old Book of Mortgages (Somerset County, Book A, folio 467), Philip French mortgaged for £200 to Mary Evan (in another mortgage she is styled Mary Price alias Evans) the same lot which had previously been leased to Alexander Henry, Dirck Van Veghte and *Trustees of Queens College.* It was located on French St. and King St., viz.: Beginning on French, at the corner of Abraham Ouke; west to King 128 ft.; thence northerly along King 150 ft.; thence easterly parallel to French 128 ft. and southerly down to French and to the beginning. The College probably left the site for these reasons: It was leased to the College; then mortgaged to Mary Price Evan, then was seized by the sheriff to satisfy judgments for £3240. All French's property was seized by Robert Stockton, Sheriff, in 1787, and finally confiscated by the Commissioners of Forfeited Estates, he being adjudged a Tory.

The following are College notes from the "Guardian; or New Brunswick's Advertiser," of Wednesday, September 25, 1793:

"Yesterday was the day appointed for the annual Commencement of Queens College, but the trustees have postponed it on account of the prevailing fever in Philadelphia.

"The Presbytery of New Brunswick, which met at Princeton on the 17th current, has appointed Friday next to be observed as a day of fasting and prayer and solemn humiliation before God on account of the abounding sins of the land; and that the judgments of Almighty God, to which we have justly exposed ourselves, may be averted.

"We are happy to inform our readers that this city is at present entirely clear of the contagious disorder raging in Philadelphia.

"Friday last was observed by the citizens of New York as a day of humiliation, fasting and prayer to Almighty God for the preservation of the city from the prevailing fever, and of other places not yet infected therewith, and for the comfort and support of their brethren in Philadelphia in this season of distress, for the sanctified use of their affliction, and from their deliverance therefrom in God's good time.

"At a meeting of the citizens of New York, at the Tontine Coffee House the 13th of September, 1793, among other resolutions adopted to prevent the introduction of infectious disorders into the city, they have agreed to the following:

"To check as much as possible the intercourse by the stages, and for this purpose to appoint a committee to acquaint the proprietors of the different southern stages that it is the earnest wish of the inhabitants of this city that their carriages and boats do not pass while the infection prevails in Philadelphia, to direct all ferry boats to land their passengers at their proper wharves only, and to have a prudent person at each to examine the passengers.

"By a Proclamation of the Governor of New York of the 13th inst. all vessels bound from Philadelphia to that city, are to perform quarantine."

The "Guardian" of Tuesday, September 30, 1794, says: "This day is to be held the annual commencement of Queens College," and the following is from the same newspaper of Tuesday, October 13, 1795:

"The Trustees of Queens College, in New Brunswick, having suspended all collegiate exercises, and determined to turn their whole attention to the Grammar School, for that purpose appointed a committee from their body of the following persons, viz., Rev. Ira Condict, Dr. Lewis Dunham, James Schureman, John Neilson and Jacob R. Hardenbergh, Esqrs., to whose immediate inspection the said school shall be subject. The public are hereby informed that the committee have employed the Rev. Benjamin Lindsey, as teacher, whose reputation and success as an instructor, separate from the particular circumstances of very advantageous terms, depending upon his own exertions, they flatter themselves will be a sufficient inducement for parents and guardians to put their children under his tuition.

"The committee pledge themselves to the public for the good government and faithful attention to instruction in said institution, which will commence on Monday, the 2nd day of Nov. next.

"By order of the Committee,
"IRA CONDICT, Chairman."

Again the College property was sold, and a third site (the present Queens Campus) was secured, and the building known as Old Queens was built, again in Somerset Co., where the first building was located. The second building was in Middlesex.

On this third site a long period of gradual growth has taken place. Grouped around the original Queens, and spreading out on the newer Neilson Campus on the north, an array of goodly buildings is adding both strength and fame as the equipment grows. The story of the College and its Preparatory School is one of many vicissitudes, and is a long and most interesting one by itself.

The following account of the Commencement exercises of 1811 is taken from the "Guardian" of Wednesday, Oct. 16, 1811:

"The annual Commencement in Queen's College in New Jersey, was held in this city on Tuesday, the 24th ult. The procession moved from the New College, down Albany Street, through Queen St. and up Paterson St. to the Presbyterian Church, preceded by Capt. James Neilson with his company of artillery and a band of music. After prayer, the following exercises drew the attention of a large and approving assembly:

"1. A Latin Salutatory Oration, De Origine Erroris, by J. H. Van Dike.

"2. An English Salutatory Oration on the influence of Religion on Civil Government, by A. D. Wilson.

"3. An Oration on Moral Science, by J. H. Carle.
"4. An Oration on Modern Improvements, by J. H. Stephenson, Jr.
"5. An Oration on the Right of Suffrage, by A. D. Wilson.
"6. A debate upon the question, Is the Chinese Policy preferable to that adopted by Commercial Nations? J. H. Carle, Affirm. J. H. Van Dike, Opp.

"After conferring the Degree of Bachelor of Arts upon J. H. Van Dike, A.D. Wilson, J. H. Carle, and J. H. Stephenson, Jr., the President addressed the young gentlemen, and the Valedictory Oration was pronounced by J. Stephenson, Jun.

"The Trustees of Queens College have on this occasion also conferred the degree of Doctor of Divinity upon the Rev. Solomon Froeligh, of Schralenburgh, State of New Jersey; the degree of Doctor of Laws upon the Hon. John Lansing, Jun., Esq., the Chancellor of the State of N. York; and the degree of Master of Arts upon the following Reverend Gentlemen: viz., James Spencer Cannon, Jeremiah Romaine, Charles Hardenbergh, Jacob Broadhead, Peter Labagh, Christian Borck, James Van Campen Romeyne, and Cornelius De Morest."

CHAPTER VII

The Third Charter of the City—Various Events, 1784-1841—Value of Money—The Fourth Charter and Various Mayors—The Movement Culminating in the Court House of 1841.

HAVING briefly run over some of the events connected with the first two charters and four Mayors, and given a chapter to the Revolutionary period, returning to our city, we come to a third charter; not a Royal charter, but a State charter obtained in 1784.[1]

From Paterson's Compilation of Laws we find that the third charter of New Brunswick, given by Act of Sept., 1784, was applied for by—

Azariah Dunham,	F. Frelinghuysen,	Henry Guest,
John Schureman,	John Neilson,	John Taylor,
Peter Dumont,	J. Van Emburgh,	John Bray,
W. Van Duersen,	James Douglass,	Lewis Dunham,
		and others.

The boundaries was stated to be: Beginning at Steep Gully, running south-west two miles, northwest two miles, north-east to Raritan, crossing same and down the river to opposite Steep Gully and so to beginning; much smaller than the earlier charter. Instead of Mayor, Recorder, Aldermen and Assistants, the officers were to be President, Registrar, Directors and Assistants. They were:

Azariah Dunham, President.

Directors	*Assistants*
John Taylor,	Peter Dumont,
John Neilson,	John Bray,
John Schureman,	John Van Emburgh,
Henry Guest,	James Douglass,
	Wm. Van Duersen,
	Lewis Dunham.

---

[1] Under the first charter, tax was laid by law, or ordinance (see City Minutes, No. 14, which provides for £20 for the Poor). By the second charter, tax was voted at town meeting.

Just why it was considered desirable to have a new charter I have never seen stated. Azariah Dunham came in with the new charter as our 5th Mayor. He held the office 6 years, dying in January 1790, and was succeded by Col. John Bayard,[2] who held the office for two years, till 1792. As there are no Council minutes preserved from 1750 until 1796 we have but little help as to the city's official doings.

After the close of the War New Brunswick was obliged to make very special efforts. The marching and counter-marching of troops through New Jersey; the alternate authority of the British military, the Provincial military, and the somewhat weak local authority backed up by the powerful Committees of Safety; the burning and destruction of buildings and property, churches, Court House, etc.—all required a great effort of all the people to repair the damage, restore the buildings, fences, stock, etc., build up the business, (which had so hard a struggle even to keep alive), and which had been left during the years of the War to the very old and the very young.

In 1784 the New Brunswick School Committee, William Paterson, John Neilson and James Richmond appearing as the active men, bought, Apr. 13th, a lot on the south side of church St., at or near Dennis, 49½ ft. front and 99 ft. deep, for a schoolhouse lot, for £30 proclamation money. On March 1, 1799, the schoolhouse and lot were transferred by the three men just mentioned to eight gentlemen. The stock was divided into 40 shares and issued as follows: to John Neilson 9, Moses Scott 9, John Bayard 6, James Cromelin 6, John Plum 4, John Poole 3, Joseph Clarke 2, Moses Guest 1. Moses Guest sold his one share a little later for $28, which would make the value of the investment, say $1120.

A Merchant's Association was formed in 1784, and the merchants of Elizabeth were invited to join the organization.

The movement to rebuild the Presbyterian Church, already referred to, was in 1784. The lot cost £148 proclamation money; the building cost £1,674, and Walter Monteith was secured as pastor.

---

[2] See Appendix for notes on Bayard family lines.

Proclamation money was the legal value fixed to the depreciated paper money of that day as compared with hard money, and whether it was reckoned in a pound of $5 or of $2.50.

After the Revolution Congress made the shilling of the Republic 12½c; that would make 20 shillings $2.50, while an English shilling was worth 25 cents, and 20 shillings would be equivalent to $5.00 or £1.

In 1704 Queen Anne issued a proclamation fixing the values of the various circulating mediums in the Colonies in stirling. While calculations were made in pounds, shillings and pence, there was no such money in circulation. The piece of 8 was valued at 4s. 6d.; the Spanish real at 72 pence. The Spanish peso, or dollar, was the basic money then, but the dollar of 100 cents was not established till 1792, and was not accepted till after the Revolution.

New York fixed the value of silver money at 8 shillings per ounce Troy weight, and hence the term New York money. So it made quite a difference in price according to the currency in which contracts were made. But this subject of the value of money will receive more attention on a succeeding page.

When the Council minutes are resumed in 1796 almost the first thing before the Council was the issue of paper money by New Brunswick City. A Committee of Council had charge of it and reported amounts taken in and cancelled, amounts issued and outstanding. In 1804 they reported that £42.4.7 that had been issued had returned into the treasury and that they had bills to the amount of £157 which could be put into circulation, and in 1814 a second issue of $5,000 was authorized. In 1817 they had condemned and burned $6,126.90 and had in circulaation $3,574.10. After some figuring, Council decided it did not pay to issue money and voted to discontinue it. This might be considered our first attempt at banking. New Brunswick had no bank at the time Council began the issue of paper money but had two before they dropped it. Council also held a small amount of U. S. 6 per cent. stock and a few shares of Trenton and New Brunswick Turnpike Co. stock, *and no bonded debt.*

Col. Bayard was succeeded in 1792 by James Schureman,

Mayor, (or President, as styled in the 1784, or 3rd Charter); in 1793 Lewis Dunham was President; in 1795 John Bayard (not in the list of Mayors as printed; he apparently came in before Abraham Schuyler[3] in 1796—this information gathered from newspaper items in the "Guardian)."

The first charter answered for 33 years, the second for 21, while the third was only in service 17 years. On Feb. 14, 1801, still another, a fourth, charter drawn by Mr. Boggs, a lawyer, in New Brunswick, was procured, and on Monday, May 18, 1801, this charter with James Schureman as Mayor became effective. He served till Nov. 12, 1813, when it is entered in the minutes, 'James Bennet appointed Mayor in place of James Schureman, resigned.' James Bennet died in office and was buried Jan. 30, 1821, and James Schureman was chosen to fill his place, though Augustus R. Taylor acted as Mayor from January till December when James Schureman took his seat again. The Mayor died in office and the funeral of James Schureman was held Wednesday, Jan. 23, 1824.

Augustus R. Taylor was acting Mayor till regularly appointed, when he took his seat Nov. 19, 1824. The two succeeding Mayors were: J. R. Hardenbergh, Nov. 4, 1829; C. L. Hardenbergh, Nov. 5, 1830..

The fourth charter of New Brunswick passed Feb. 23, 1801, and repealed the third charter of Sept., 1784. The boundaries by it were: Beginning at the mouth of Lawrence's Brook, up same to Cornell's Brook, up Cornell's Brook to George's Road, thence on a straight line to the westerly corner of the plantation of Hermanus Cortelyou on the road from Princeton to New Brunswick; then following the road east to the Mile-run, and down same to bridge near its mouth on the road from Bound Brook to New Brunswick [the bridge on Easton Ave.?]; thence along the road to Garnett's Gully, down the Gully to Raritan, crossing to high water mark; thence down the river on the east side to a point opposite the mouth of Lawrence's Brook, and so to the beginning. These bounds were amended in 1818, 1837, 1838 and 1844.

---

[3]See Appendix as to Schuyler family.

The first charter of 1730 provided for a Court House for the meetings of the city Mayor and Aldermen, and for the Mayor, Aldermen and Recorder's Court. In the first city records we find the Court House was begun in 1732, and there are items from time to time for repairs.

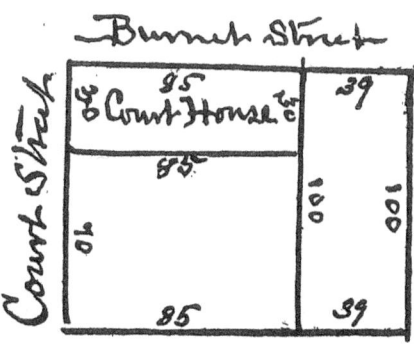

In 1739 it was ordered that the Court House bell should be rung for the Dutch meeting until they got a bell of their own; in 1746 it was rung for the English meeting and a sum fixed to be paid to John DeGraw for ringing it. This Court House was in use until the Revolution War, though there was an Act passed in 1793 to build a Court House and jail in New Brunswick on the ground that the one in use was so dilapidated; however, I do not note any action under this bill. This property was sold by Council in 1800-1802. The building seems to have disappeared during the War.

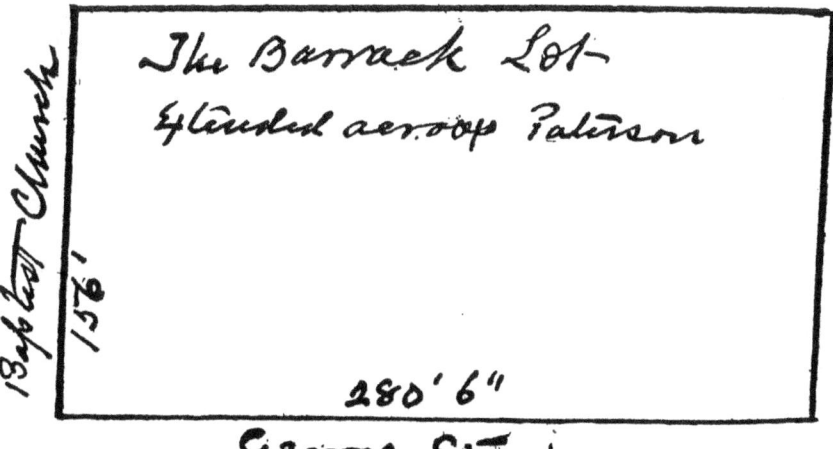

After the War the old Barracks were repaired and put in order and declared a legal Court House and jail (see Act of June 18, 1783), and Court was held there till it was burned in

1794, though it is indicated by Court notices that it was used at least in 1778, as a Court of Quarter Sessions was held in New Brunswick for Middlesex the 3rd Tuesday in Jan., 1778. The Barracks was quite clearly our second Court House.

The old Court House, corner of Burnet and Richmond, having been destroyed during the Revolution, a new one was necessary, and a committee was selected in 1787, consisting of John Schureman, Levinus Clarkson and John Neilson, to build one. But the Barracks, made the legal Court House in 1783 were in use, and it was not until that was burned, in 1794, that the committee really got busy. The Freeholders bought a lot of John Dennis, 40x40, for a jail site, now the site of the Bayard St. School, while a Court House lot, on the corner of Bayard and Neilson, was given by John Dennis (where now the First Dutch Church Consistory building stands). The new building was ready and the first meeting was held in it on Jan. 16, 1796. The old subscription list, still preserved by Mr. James Neilson, with the original and interesting signatures, was to raise £400, and it petitioned the Legislature that New Brunswick, in alternation with some place in the western part of the State, should be the seat of the Legislature and for the holding of the Supreme Court; it got the building but not the Legislature!

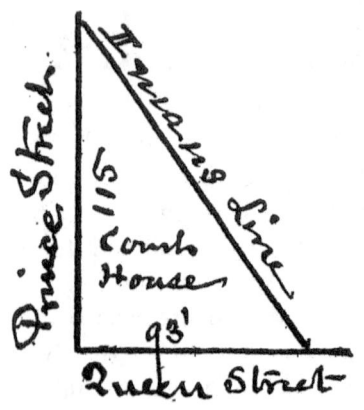

Knowing that a new Court House was contemplated on May 8, 1822, James Schureman and Staats Van Deursen, on the part of Queens College, made an overture to the Board of Freeholders offering the College building and lot in exchange for the present Court House and "gaol" (the Court House being on the northwest corner of Queen and Prince, and the "gaol" on the site now the Bayard Street School) with the ground thereto belonging. It was ordered that the proposition lie on the table.

The next proposition was Feb. 28, 1826, when James Crommelin was Director of the Board, and it was made by E. G. Mackay, G. H. Stout, James Ryno and John T. Duyckinck, who offered a certain lot of land for a new Court House and "gaol," which offer was laid over till next meeting, and it was voted that a committee of three be appointed to report then as to the expediency of erecting a new Court House and jail and the sum that may be obtained for the old Court House and jail. Those appointed were the Director, James Crommelin, James McChesney and Edward Stelle. At the May meeting this committee reported "that they believe that the Court House may be advantageously disposed of and a new Court House may be built for not exceeding $10,000, and now is the proper time to procure a proper site; that a Court House may be built with little additional tax; and your Committee thinks proper and just that the expenditure undertaken, for the benefit of many years to come, should not all be borne by a tax within a short period." This report was laid over till next meeting.

The lot, George and Prince, 140 on George and 200 on Prince, offered by Ephraim G. Mackay and others for $1,500, payable in two years without interest, was offered. The lot opposite, 100 on George and 150 deep on Prince, was offered by James Crommelin for $1,000. The lot on Prince, westward of the house of William P. Deare, dec'd, 495 feet front and 230 feet deep to Paterson, owned by Ephraim G. Mackay and others was offered for $1,800; it was the easterly part of 390 feet on Prince; terms payable in one year without interest. A motion to purchase the whole of the lot on Prince Street at a price not to exceed $1,600 was carried.

May 9, 1827, with Peter Spader Director, Mr. Parker reported the purchase of the lot at the price limited by the Board, but that, owing to the death of Mr. Mackay, in whom the title was vested, a contract was not signed, yet that the Legislature had authorized trustees to sell the lot and fulfill the contract which they reported as safe and advantageous to the County; that the lot was considered worth much more than the sum agreed to be paid. This report was accepted by ten ayes and six nays and the collector was authorized to pay $800 at once and give a note for the residue. Mr. McDowell offered a motion that the Board sell the lot. The vote was seven ayes and nine nays: East Windsor 1, West Windsor 2, South Amboy 2, South Brunswick 2; total 7 ayes. New Brunswick 2, East Windsor 1, Woodbridge 2, Perth Amboy 2, Piscataway 2; total 9 nays.

Feb. 4, 1828, C. L. Hardenbergh, on the part of the Bank of New Brunswick, offered the Banking House on George Street for $8,000; said the Bank would purchase the present Court House for $1,600, and gave an estimate of the cost of altering the Bank building as not over $1,000. The Board inspected the building and resolved that it was inexpedient to purchase.

Wednesday, May 11, 1831, Messrs. Parker, Lee and McDowell were made a committee to inquire for what sum a good and convenient Court House can be erected on the lot purchased for that purpose, and directed that the crop of grass thereon be sold.

May 9, 1832, Mr. Parker reported for the committee on the new Court House that they were not prepared to report. Here the movement seems to have died out.

August 14, 1832, James Bishop became Director.

May 14, 1834, the Director and Mr. Phillips were instructed to rent out the County lot.

Feb. 21, 1837, a special meeting was called by the Director, Dr. Frederick Richmond, at the request of a Committee appointed May 11, 1836 (Louis Golding, Edward T. Stelle and Henry Van Liew), as the result of the action by the Chief Justice in his charge to the Grand Inquest, at the June term, 1835, on the want of a suitable building as a public grievance. He had again, pointedly, animadverted upon matters in a charge to the grand jury, with the declaration that he would continue to notice the neglect of the representatives of the county and the absolute necessities of the people as long as he had the honor of presiding at the Middlesex Courts. This committee then reported that the Court House at Salem had been examined at the suggestion of the Chief Justice, and he had represented it as a well-adapted building. They had also examined the one at Burlington and others, and from ideas so obtained they had caused a draft to be drawn by Nicholas Wyckoff, a practical mechanic of the city, and now presented for the examination of the Board a plan, to include the clerk's and surrogate's offices. The cost as proposed would be about $15,000.

The title to the old Court House and jail conveyed by John Dennis and Mary, his wife, Aug. 20, 1794, was subject to the following conditions, viz.: that if at any time the County Courts should not be held in the Court House built on this lot but removed to some other part of the county, the county should pay to John Dennis or his legal representatives, £120 for the Court House lot, and £90 for the jail lot, and also the first cost of shingles and glass which he had given toward the building of the Court House.

A memorial was presented asking that the building of a new Court House be deferred till the question of its location, then pending before the Legislature, be determined.

A proposition by David Messereau and Oliver Sharlock was made to the Board, that if they would build the Court House on the plot which they own (lately of Jacob Richmond, dec'd), they would give and convey to them a lot two hundred feet square, bounded southerly by Hassert, easterly by John, northerly by Oliver, and westerly by the continuation of Neilson Street. And they would purchase the real estate owned by the County at the price of $18,000. This proposition was laid on the table, and it was—

"Resolved that the Director, Edward T. Stelle, and Henry Van Liew be a building committee authorized to borrow $5,000 to defray immediate necessary expenses; and resolved that the sum expended be limited to $20,000."

Friday, March 31, 1837. The Director was requested to call a new special meeting for the purpose of further considering the propriety of erecting a new Court House. The following resolutions were offered by McDowell and adopted as a by-law: "That in all future appropriations of money it shall require at least nine votes of members present." Also resolved: "That the action at the last special meeting respecting the erection of a Court House be reconsidered, and that the building committee with power to borrow be rescinded."

Here seems to have been the second failure to move in this matter. At the next meeting, April 20, 1837, the subject was not brought up. But on Aug. 16, 1838, a special meeting was called, because the Grand Inquest at the last term of Court had taken public notice of the insufficiency of the building in which the business of the County was transacted and had presented the matter as a public grievance, to which presentment the Chief Justice, then presiding, had responded, expressing great satisfaction that the Grand Jury had thus publicly and officially presented the subject to the view and consideration of the inhabitants of the county. The call was signed by Edward T. Stelle, Jacob Edmonds and Samuel F. Randolph. At this meeting the following resolutions were moved and adopted:

"By Mr. Cruser: Resolved, that it is expedient to make the necessary arrangements to build a new Court House in the City of New Brunswick.
"By Mr. McDowell: That a committee be appointed to employ an architect to make a draft and estimate of cost of erecting a new Court House, and to select and stake out the particular location, and to examine Court Houses in other counties in order to adopt the best model and report on Sept. 21, next. Messrs. Cruser, Stelle and Edmonds were appointed to the Committee."

On Sept. 21, 1838, the foregoing Committee reported that they had visited the Court Houses at Troy and Fundy, N. Y., and that they were superior to any in our own State; that they had also visited the Court Houses in Newark, Hackensack, Hudson and Albany. That at Newark was of stone, 100 feet square and cost $71,000, but was badly planned and located, and the people there much dissatisfied with it. That at Hackensack was small and much inferior to any other visited. That at Albany was large and connected with the City Hall, and not suited to the wants of our county. Those at Hudson, Fundy and Troy were the best visited by the Committee, and externally very similar to the plans of the previous Committee, which were recommended to the Board by that Committee three years before. That at Hudson had two wings, one of which was used for the jail. The center building, 50x60, was built of

Sing Sing marble, except the rear which was of limestone and cost $26,000. That at Troy was marble, 90x60, and cost $40,000. That at Fundy was of brick, 56x66, and cost $25,000, including the commissioner's fees of $1,500. There was nothing in the interior of their plans superior to the plan proposed theretofore, which the Committee respectfully recommended to the Board, and for these reasons:

"First, on the score of economy, the plan was contracted for two or three years since, to be built of good brick for $20,000. As labour and materials are much lower now than at the date of the contract, it is fair to presume that the same building can be erected now for proportionately less. In the next place, the exterior—being almost precisely similar to the houses at Troy and Fundy—will present quite as splendid an appearance as either of them, while the interior is decidedly superior. The basement is entirely fire proof. Should the whole of the upper part be destroyed, the offices with their contents would remain perfect and safe, an importance not secured in any other building visited by your Committee.

"Mr. LeFevre, the architect who prepared the draft and plan, very frankly stated that if called on to prepare another plan, he did not think it possible to suggest any improvement. The Committee has also staked out the spot on which the building should be located and the Board is requested to examine and decide if the duty has been judiciously performed."

The report was signed by Abram Cruser, Jacob Edmonds and Edward T. Stelle.

The Board visited and approved the site selected. The plan of the earlier committee was adopted; the building was to be of brick and brown freestone sills and lintels, and the Director, Mr. Cruser, and Mr. Edmonds were appointed a building committee, authorized to advertise for proposals by contract not to exceed $20,000. The Director, Mr. Edwards and Mr. Vail (the clerk of the Board) were to superintend the building of the Court House. Mr. Cruser asked to be excused on account of living so far from the building.

May 8, 1839. The building was under construction this year as items in the minutes show. The basement was to be flag instead of plank, and grey stone was substituted at the entrance,

Messrs. Cheeseman and Garrigues were paid for granite and setting.

May 13, 1840. Ordered that the Court House lot be filled up, graded, trees planted and fenced.

Feb. 11, 1841. The building committee submitted the following account:

Borrowed	$6,000
Received from Surplus Revenue	15,613 34
	21,613 34
Expended to date ....'......	20,654 82
Balance on hand	$958 52

Feb. 17, 1841. Ordered that the several Courts of the County be hereafter held in the new building.

May 12, 1841. P. P. Runyon was elected Director, and the final payments on account of the building were ordered made, viz.: To masons, $625. To carpenters, $789.20. Coal, chairs, tables, lamps, etc., $305.61. Interest, $66. Also $400 to each Commissioner, or $1,200. Total, $2,985.81. Total cost, $23,-640.63. The County Clerk and Surrogate were accommodated in the basement.

The "Fredonian" of March 10, 1841, had this notice of the opening of the new Court House:

"The new and beautiful Court House which Middlesex has, with a liberal and enlightened spirit, provided for the accommodation of her Courts of Justice, and the preservation of her important records, was opened for business on the ninth of March with prayer by the Rev. Dr. Milledoler, and an address by Judge Nevius. The Circuit and other Courts are in session. Chief Justice Hornblower is present. The trial of Robinson for murder and perhaps of the negro boy on a similar charge will impart great interest to the criminal side of the Court. In the Robinson case John Van Dyke, Esq., prosecutor of the pleas for Middlesex, conducts the prosecution on the part of the State, and Edward Wood, Esq., of this city, and David ———, of New York, will defend the prisoner."

Thus the movement to build a Court House in 1826, under James Crommelin as Director, and continued under Directors Peter Spader, James Bishop and Dr. Frederick Richmond, on the lot bought of Ephraim G. Mackay and with plans by Nicholas Wyckoff, a practical mechanic, and Mr. LeFevre, architect, resulted in a Court House ready for use on the ninth of March, 1841.

CHAPTER VIII

Council Minutes 1796 to 1832—Visit of General Lafayette in 1824—The Trenton and New Brunswick Turnpike—The "Hardenbergh Bank"—Colonial and Continental Money—National Bank of New Brunswick—Other Succeeding and Competing Banks—Steamboat Ventures—Various Organizations and Societies—Tribute to a Remarkable Woman, Mrs. James Neilson.

THE second volume of old minutes of Council of the city, from April 5, 1796, to May 7, 1832, is quite as interesting as the ones from 1730 to 1750, and I could quote at great length without exhausting the interest, but space will not allow extensive reference. They well exhibit the life of the city at that period, its simplicity and economy, its attention to small things, the very evident disposition of the officials to serve the city and to promote its welfare. The contrast to city governments of to-day is most striking. Deliberateness was a prominent feature.

Take the building of a new market house as an example. In 1796 Council decided to build one, but it was 1811 before it had decided on a site—fifteen years. In 1813 a contract was entered into with Low & Voorhees for $1,100, but the completed house cost $1,339.37. This market stood at the head of Hiram St., in the middle of the street, and is still well remembered.

May 6, 1809, John Stevens gave notice that his steamboat ("Phœnix") would leave on the Sabbath. Council at once notified him of both the City Ordinance and the State laws against his doing so; and the Mayor of Trenton asked the coöperation of the New Brunswick authorities in dealing with the stage lines that were disregarding the Sabbath laws.

Oct. 23, 1812, the city bought a lot on Schureman St., and also the old College building, which they moved from George St. to it, just below the corner of Schureman and George, to be used as a possible school. This is the first movement towards a free or public school in New Brunswick and from it we may date its public school system.

Another record was established March 29, 1813, when the city was authorized to borrow money at interest for the first time. James Schureman, Mayor a second term, and Council will have to stand responsible for that!

In 1823 the question of numbering the houses came up, complicated with uncertainty as to where the numbering should begin.

In 1824 Council sent a committee to invite General Lafayette to visit the city. He accepted, and a reception and dinner were given him. He left New York Sept. 23, crossed to Paulus Hook and arrived here Sept. 24th.

The Committee of Entertainment consisted of A. R. Taylor, Mayor; C. L. Hardenbergh and William Van Deursen. Lafayette was met near Bonhamtown with the 1st Squadron of Horse Artillery, commanded by Major Van Dyke. The Military Artillery made a salute by cannon when he reached the bridge, where he was met by about 8,000 people. Then the parade formed as follows:

> Gen. Lafayette in a coach, drawn by four white horses supplied by Capt. Vanderbilt of the Thistle.
> Governor of the State.
> Committee of Arrangements.
> Common Council.
> Officers and Soldiers of the Revolution.
> Officers of the Navy, Militia and Military; Clergy, Judiciary, Bar.
> Strangers, Citizens.
> Reception at Court House. Dinner at Follett's City Hotel at six P. M.

The Recorder made the speech of welcome; John Neilson presided, with the General on his right, the Governor on his left. This was followed by a reception of the ladies at Follett's at 9 in the evening.

The military consisted of the 1st Squadron Horse Artillery, Major Van Dyke, Com.; B. M. Voorhees, Adj.; New Brunswick Artillery Co., Joseph Dilke, Orderly; City Guards, Thos. H. Dunn, Orderly.

On Sunday Lafayette visited Joseph Bonaparte at his seat near Trenton.

In 1825 Council very cordially recommended that a dam with a lock be constructed across the river. This was evidently in response to proposals by the Canal Co., which made an active start that year, and whose first plan was a dam near Martin's Dock. In 1827 the village of Plainfield bought an old fire engine No. 3 from the city, and in 1837 Council discovered that for 31 years they had been meeting in taverns, when they had a right to use a room in the Court House; so they fitted up a room and met there after that date.

March 20, 1829, Council divided the city into six wards, it having had four for some years. When the change from three to four was made is not on record.[1] A Census had just been made, however, and showed a population of 4,993—just missing 5,000. There were 780 families and 654 dwellings, and there were still 184 slaves in the city, though manumission had been going on slowly for twenty-five or more years.

A map was ordered and the map of 1829 is, to-day, quite an interesting curiosity.

One of the things going on during this general period, not quoted from in Council Minutes, was the incorporation of the Fountain Company in 1801 to supply water from Barrack Spring, or Nathan Haviland's spring, as it was sometimes called, located on a lot on the north side of Church St., 46 ft. west of Spring St.; to be conveyed in wooden logs, bored as the old pump logs were bored. They were laid down Albany St. I do not think the spring can be found now.

The Trenton and New Brunswick Turnpike was, perhaps, the most beneficial of the movements of that day, chartered Nov. 14, 1804, with supplement Nov. 28, 1806. Capital, $200,-000. An advertisement of Nov. 29, 1804, says: "Subscrip-

---

[1] New Brunswick, as has been stated, was divided into wards by the Charter of 1763, the North Ward (the city) and the South Ward (the country). Later it was divided into three wards—North, Middle and South. This was probably at the time of the third Charter, 1784, when the city was reduced to two miles square. Still later came four wards, North, Middle, Market and South, probably at time of the fourth Charter, when the city was enlarged again. Just before the Census of 1829 it was made into six wards.

tions to the new pike were received Dec. 20, and for two succeeding days, signed by James Ewing, Joshua Wright, John Neilson, James Schureman (Mayor), and Thomas Hill." The stockholders met to organize Jan. 31, 1805. S. W. Johnson wrote an article for the papers, published in January, setting forth the great advantages that would accrue from the pike, and how those using it would have hours to spare over those who plodded through the old mud roads. He gave the proposed fare or toll at 12½ cents for a horseman, 25 cents for a chaise, and 50 cents for a carriage and pair. $64,000 was subscribed and the road was built. It started at Albany St. bridge, up Albany to George, along George to Livingston Ave., and so west. It became a great thoroughfare and continued in successful and profitable operation until 1833, when, it being proposed to convert the road into a railroad, the balance of the capital was subscribed and overtures were made by the Philadelphia and Trenton R. R. to unite with them, Dec. 15, 1832. But New Brunswick was noted for its deliberateness, and it was Sept. 7, 1833, before a profile was ordered made and the laying of timbers therein, longitudinally or otherwise, inquired into. The Board of Directors were: James Bishop, President; Fitz-Randolph Smith, Treasurer; Staats Van Deursen, James Reeside, Edward Curtis, Elisha Tibbets, John Savage and Samuel R. Hamilton. The Board had expressed an opinion that the application of steam power had not been sufficiently tested to justify them in incurring so large an expense. Eighteen months later, however, an engineer, Charles L. Schlatter, was appointed, and in May, 1835, profiles, grades and estimates were presented; so two and a-half years had slipped away. In June, Staats Van Deursen was made sole agent and Superintendent, with power to make contracts, and voted a salary of $1,250 per annum. Now the work started. Five miles of rails were laid, when an Act relative to the Delaware and Raritan Canal Co. and the Camden and Amboy R. R. & Transportation Co. made the further prosecution of the work under their Turnpike charter unsafe, and the work was stopped. With a little more hustle and with the Charter of 1804 broadened to include building a railroad, what a very different result might have been obtained!²

These growing ambitions made banks a necessity and in 1807 the Bank of New Brunswick, or "Hardenbergh's Bank," was incorporated, James Phelan, Cashier; and in 1812 the State Bank was formed, James J. Margerum, Cashier, and opened for business in 1812, but failed in 1873 and 1877.

A few words may be interesting at this point about the circulating medium, before further describing the banks. The first money was Indian wampum, called by the Hollanders *sewant*, and the Holland guilder, the latter valued at 42 cents. William Ouke, third Mayor (from 1763 to 1779) offered in 1768 bills of exchange on Amsterdam of 1,000 to 5,000 guilders and upwards. In the Council Minutes beginning with 1796 we find from time to time the report of a Committee which had charge of the money issued by the City of New Brunswick. They report having burned £42.4.7, and that there were 471 sheets of new bills unsigned, which could be put into circulation. Later, in 1814, they reported an authorized issue of $5,000 in small bills, and in 1817, after the banks had begun business, they reported $6,126.90 condemned, and burned $3,574.10 outstanding bills, stating they were unprofitable, whereupon any further issue was voted discontinued. I may add, incidentally, that at this date New Brunswick owned some United

---

²This movement for a railroad, started in New Brunswick in 1835, will show how very early the city was in the new venture. The first railroad in this country was from the granite quarries of Quincy, Mass., to tide water, and was built in 1826, but was only a horse and gravity-power road. The second was opened May 27, 1827, and was from Mauch Chunk to the Lehigh river. It was also a horse and gravity-power road. The first chartered passenger and freight railroad company began July 4, 1828, on what is now part of the Baltimore and Ohio R. R., using mule power.

The first locomotive was imported in 1829 and placed on the track of the Del. & Hudson Canal Co.'s R. R. The first locomotive built in America was constructed in Baltimore, and was used on the Charleston & Hamburgh R. R. to carry cotton to tidewater. That railroad was also the first to carry the mail, and was built through the enterprise of Horatio Allen. The Mohawk & Hudson, from Albany to Schenectady, claim the first steam train with imported engine, the John Bull, four tons, in 1831. George Stephenson built for R. L. Stevens an engine of ten tons, wheels, hubs and rims of iron and wooden spokes, which arrived Aug., 1831, called also the "John Bull." This engine was exhibited by the P. R. R. at both the Centennial and Chicago World's Fair.

States 6% stock, and some Trenton Turnpike shares and had no debt.

The Colonial money, Continental money, "Hard" and "Light," and "Proclamation," and the various shillings of the States made a most complex circulating medium. There was the New England shilling of which six equalled a dollar; the New York shilling of which eight equalled a dollar; the Pennsylvania and New Jersey shilling, of which seven and one-half shillings equalled a dollar. Hard money was mostly the Spanish peso, or dollar, weighing one ounce silver, but varying in shillings' value in different localities as above, and there were some Portugese gold coins. The paper money bills of the Colonies were printed in pounds, shillings and pence. Prices were generally shillings and dollars, and account books were kept in pounds, shillings and pence; later in dollars. Light money was clipped and worn silver, and Proclamation money was depreciated paper money and was of greatly varying value.

Dr. Witherspoon, writing in 1801 of the New Jersey currency, says that the statute currency of money was in the same proportion to sterling as in Pennsylvania; that is, 5 to 3; a Spanish milled dollar was of N. J. Proclamation money, 7s 6d. Johannes David Schoepf, a traveller in 1777, says: "A pound in Virginia equals 3¼ Spanish dollars; in New York it equals 2½ Spanish dollars, and in Pennsylvania 2⅓ Spanish dollars." There was a gradual descending variation of the pound from $4.444 to $2.50 in 1756, and it remained thereafter at that figure.

Andrew Burnaby, writing 1759-1760, says: "The New Jersey paper currency is about 70% discount, but in very good repute and preferred by Pennsylvania and New York to that of their own Province. In Rhode Island the paper money is as bad as possible, the difference in exchange being at least 2,500%, while that of New Hampshire is no better." New York fixed the value of silver money at 8 shillings per ounce; hence the term frequently met with of "York money." While the value of the silver in the peso, or Spanish piece of 8, is given at 72 cents, contracts were stipulated to be in certain money as Hard, Proclamation, York money, etc. In Philadelphia the *levie* was the unit of reckoning as goods were so priced, and did not begin again at the peso, or pound, after 8 or 9 levies; but, instead of $2.50 a yard, merchants would say "20 levies." (I am not sure whether the levie was 11 or 12½c). In Florida the "bit" was equivalent to a shilling of 12½c, and goods were priced in bits up to one dollar only.

Few people who use our notes in circulation to-day consider what a simple affair the circulating medium is. For though, until the Federal Reserve notes drove the others out of circulation, while we had a variety of notes—the old Civil War greenbacks, the gold notes, the silver notes, the silver bullion treasury notes, the National Bank notes—they were all U. S. Government notes practically, and few people gave any thought as to what stood behind them. Besides the government notes, as compared to the old bank note issue (when a "Peterson's Detector" was issued monthly to inform the business man of counterfeits, broken banks, etc., and a study of it was imperative), the present system is simplicity itself.

In early business dealings barter was much in use and debts were also settled in goods, and it was customary to accept payment in goods at double the invoice value of the goods.

In lost money advertisements we find mentioned £3 bills; £1.10 bills; 16s.3d., of Jersey; £2 of N. Y.; 2/3 of a dol.; Maryland bills; 30s.15s., 12s., 6s. and 3s. bills, besides many others.

The history of the Bank of New Jersey, will prove to be practically the history of banking in New Brunswick from the establishment of our first bank—that of the Bank of New Brunswick Dec. 4, 1807—and to, and through its successor, the Farmers' and Mechanics', incorporated Feb. 6, 1834, under a charter expiring in Jan., 1855, when the Bank of New Jersey was organized to take over and carry on the banking business of the Farmers' and Mechanics', thus making a continuing banking life of 116 years to date (July, 1923).

Before there was a regularly incorporated bank, the city conducted a limited banking business for profit. It issued paper money, as much as $5,000 authorized at one time, made invest-

NEW BRUNSWICK IN HISTORY   163

ments, and we find notes in the balance sheet of individuals as well as notes for circulation.

While the Bank of New Brunswick was not the first in the State, it was a close second. The Newark Banking and Insurance Co. was incorporated Feb. 18, 1804, with a branch at Powles Hook, incorporated Nov. 13, 1804, and was called The Jersey Bank, but it failed to pay the State Tax of ½ of 1% under the Act of Jan. 25, 1811. The Trenton Banking Co., incorporated Dec. 3, 1804, also preceded the Bank of New Brunswick by three years.

There are no minutes of the Bank of New Brunswick to be found, but one fact turned up here and another there give us a good general idea of its career. There was a bank on Queen Street (now Neilson Street) in 1810, in the brick house, now the Wieda Bakery. The Bank of New Brunswick was this bank, as there was no other in the city at that date, and they had opened for business in a rented house. The capital was fixed by the Act of Incorporation at one hundred thousand dollars and the Act was passed at the request of Andrew Kirkpatrick, Joseph W. Scott, Phineas Carmen, and J. R. Hardenbergh, who became the President, with James Phelan as Cashier. While the bank was officially the Bank of New Brunswick, it was familiarly spoken of as "Hardenbergh's Bank."

In 1811 the Bank of New Brunswick bought of Stephen Kemble the northerly one hundred feet of the old Barrack lot. This lot began on the north side of the Baptist church lot, and ran two hundred and eight feet six inches northerly on George and, crossing Paterson Street, was one hundred and fifty-six feet in depth. Paterson Street was opened through this purchase and in 1813 the bank bought thirty-two feet more on the north. Here the bank built a banking house.

The next item to affect the bank is found in the "Fredonian" of February 20, 1817, which says: "After to-day the banks will resume specie payments." This must have been quite an event, and one that affected the banks very considerably. 1817 was one of the panic years, and for the bank it was a notable year, for we find the bank securing a judgment for $40,000 against John Phelan. As James Phelan had been the Cashier of the bank ("The Times" notes, in 1816, that Edward Wood Dunham had been elected Cashier), it looks as if this was a suit against a bondsman, but all we know is just the bare fact and that the bank bought at the sheriff's sale a number of John Phelan's properties, one of the lots being the corner of Church and George Streets, fifty feet on Church and one hundred and twenty on George. This corner is where the People's Bank now stands.

We find still another remarkable banking event in this year. A resolution passed by six of the eleven directors allowed the borrowers of the bank to pay off their notes in the stock of the bank, and, as this stock was at a discount, so many availed themselves of the permission that $71,000 of notes were taken up with stock. Of course the capital of the bank was reduced that much, so, with $71,000 of stock on hand and John Phelan's debt of $40,000 transferred into real estate, the bank must have been put to it to do business; and this view is confirmed by its executing a mortgage in 1825 to the Mechanics' Bank of New York on the New Brunswick bank's real estate, to secure a loan of $11,000. (See Mortgage Book, 12 F, 570; Dec. 5, 1825). The six directors who were responsible for the exchange of notes for stock were: J. R. Hardenbergh, John Pool, Moses Scott, M. D., John N. Simpson (who became Cashier in 1821), Andrew Howell and Samuel Holcomb. The five who protested were: James Schureman, Lewis Dunham, James Richmond, John Dennis and James Neilson. This mortgage and the $11,000 tided the bank along for a while, but in 1829 we find the bank in difficulties and a reorganization was seen to be necessary. In 1827 the bank was removed from George St., to Burnet St., to the home of A. O. Voorhees, now No. 296; evidently by an effort to get more business from the business center of the town.

John Potter, a capitalist of Princeton, offered to subscribe liberally if James Neilson, and a Board of Directors that he approved of could get control. Gibbons, who owned the steamboat "Bellona," run by Capt. Cornelius Vanderbilt, was also inclined to coöperate and bought a number of stockholders out at $1.00 for the lot of shares held by them. He was a wealthy steamboat man and had been in partnership with Ogden.

C. L. Hardenbergh, J. R. Hardenbergh's son and his successor, as President of the bank, made an offer of all the stock and $3,000 to wind up the bank. This did not meet with any response as in 1834, on Feb. 14, the bank suspended, and the receivers, Edward Wood, George Richmond and David W. Vail, took charge.

That Mr. Neilson made some efforts to save the bank and that his efforts were not appreciated is evident from a suit brought by the receivers for trespass, and damages of $40,000 were asked. As a bank, however, the suspension of Feb. 14, 1834, was the end. The mortgage it gave in 1825 was foreclosed in 1838 and the property passed to Thomas Fitch. On May 16, 1838, John DeGraw, Jr., announces that, 'having given up the Bell Hotel, he will open the Mansion House in the elegant building formerly occupied by the Bank of New Brunswick.' To those interested in this building I might add that Miss Hannah Hoyt bought it in 1847 for $5,750 for her Young Ladies' School, which she had been teaching in New Brunswick from 1837.

The Bank of New Brunswick's history furnishes a succession of surprises. The map and directory of the city for 1829 locate the bank on Burnet Street, south of Hiram, west side, and just south of an eight-foot alley. This property belonged to Abraham O. Voorhees, son of David and brother of Ira, who later appears as secretary for the receivers; and the deed from David to Ira (Book 21 of Deeds, p. 33) in 1827 for the next house and lot south of Abraham's recites in the deed that the brick house next north was "then occupied by the bank." This, at first seems unaccountable, but if we consider the fact that, when the bank bought and built on George Street, it was the only bank in New Brunswick, but that almost immediately another, the State Bank, opened on Albany Street, and that the bank building on George was practically out in the country, it is not hard to understand why it left its fine bank building and moved back into the business section, where it could compete on a better footing with the opposing bank.

On March 7, 1837, an Act was passed to enable the President and directors last elected to settle the affairs of the bank without compensation, and to replace the receivers; evidently to cut down expenses and save all that could be saved. The expiration of the charter required a supplement to this Act, on Feb. 26, 1840, which vested the powers of the receivers in the President and the directors notwithstanding. On May 22, 1839, the President—James C. Van Dyke—gave notice of a dividend to be paid at the office of the bank "on Albany St.," still another change in location.

The President, Van Dyke, was a son of Frederick and Lydia Van Dyke, and a brother of Dr. Frederick Van Dyke, of Philadelphia. He was a bachelor and met a sudden death in Princeton from heart trouble in October, 1843. The death of the President and the removal from the State of one of the directors seemed to require further authority, so, by supplement, Feb., 1850, the surviving directors were given power to wind up the bank but with no other powers. While this date in the Laws of 1850 is February 1, there is no doubt that the final dividend of 12¾ cents on the dollar, as advertised by Ira C. Voorhees, Secretary, in January, 1850, was paid at his office in Burnet Street, under the above authority.

After President Van Dyke's death there is one notice signed by Littleton Kirkpatrick as President, possibly an error on his part, as there is no authority in the Acts or supplements for the election of any additional officer, but the terms used are "The President and Directors last elected," and again "the surviving Directors."

While the Bank of New Brunswick suspended February 14, 1834, the Farmers' and Mechanics' Bank was incorporated February 6, 1834. It looked as if the Bank of New Brunswick held on as long as possible so as to give the new bank a chance to step into its shoes. From the unfortunate absence of the minute book, just what the inside connection between these banks was is at present conjecture, but, as a matter of fact, the new bank came into existence just in the nick of time and the bank of 1808 was followed without a break by the bank of 1834. This incorporation was to last until January, 1855, and no longer, which accounts for the formation then of a new bank, "The Bank of New Jersey," and for the movement in 1854.

The men who are named in the new charter in 1854 were: John Bray, James S. Nevius, Lewis Carmen, Peter N. Pool, Abraham Suydam, Charles Morgan, Littleton Kirkpatrick, David Mercereau, James C. Zabriskie, Andrew Agnew, Miles C. Smith and C. L. Hardenbergh. (C. L. Hardenbergh, it will be noted, was President of the Bank of New Brunswick which this new bank was to succeed). The above-named men were styled Commissioners to receive subscriptions, giving two weeks' notice of the opening of the subscription books; $5.00 was to be paid at the time of subscribing and the remainder as the President and directors should appoint, and the calls were $5 in August and $8 in September. There were 2,300 shares that paid the third installment of $8 per share, and 1,175 shares, or a majority, were held by three men, viz.: James F. Randolph, 372 shares; Lewis Carmen, 368 shares, and David Mercereau, 435 shares; and there were thirty-three other stockholders. The bank statement under date of September 25, 1834, is as follows:

Farmers' and Mechanics' First Statement, September 25, 1834.

Capital	$50,000	Discounts	$4,637
Discount	66	Real Estate	5,113
Bonds	3,000	Mechanics' Bank..	13,000
In Circulation	7,084	U. S. Bank, Phila.	10,000
Deposits	539	State Bank	16,733
		Foreign Funds ...	10,241
		Specie	525
	$60,749		$60,749

Quite naturally James F. Randolph became President and Lewis Carmen, Cashier. They purchased, in 1834, of Peter Dayton (Book 27 of Deeds, folio 477), the brick house on the westerly side of Peace Street, 35 feet 6 inches front, and lot 169 feet deep. This was the building that was for some time the Post Office. In its first statement as shown above, the Real Estate is put at $5,113. But the bank hardly got started before it got into trouble. On February 21, 1835, it notified its exchanges that, as the story would likely be much exaggerated, it wanted them to know the exact facts: That the bank had been entered and robbed of $13,229, $6,000 in its own notes and the balance in bills of other banks.

In 1836 the bank borrowed money of the Bank of the United States in Philadelphia, N. Biddle, President, as it supposed for a year, but on notes coming due in three and six months, and when the notes came due the Philadelphia bank did not care to renew them. Mr. Randolph writes, pleading for an extension, and saying: "The times, as you are aware, are sadly out of joint," but without success.

James F. Randolph, as President, signed the bank's notes or bills until some time in the year 1839, and then Abraham Suydam appears as signing the notes as President. And now there is a tragedy to record, for Abraham Suydam was murdered on December 3, 1840, by Peter Robinson, and so could not have been President over a year. A history of Middlesex names Charles Dunham as a President and he possibly succeeded Suydam, but there are no documentary evidences of it that I can find.

The bank managed to struggle along until 1842, when Peter Spader, John Van Dyke and David W. Vail, receivers, take charge. Vail, it will be remembered, was one of the receivers of the other bank in 1834, but he died soon after, in 1842, and the other two continued to act.

During this receivership continued efforts were being made to set the bank on its feet again, which was finally accomplished through an Act passed February 22, 1849, and two supplements in 1850 and 1854. As has been said: "After the receivership had lasted seven years this Act was to restore to the stockholders of the Farmers' and Mechanics' Bank of New Jersey its corporate rights and privileges," for it provided that, whereas it was represented that a final order had been made in the Court of Chancery of the State, and it appeared by the report of the receivers that they had moneys more than sufficient to pay principal and interest of all claims, and it further appearing that the said bank was really solvent at the time it was enjoined, and that the stockholders of the bank were desirous of being restored to their corporate rights and privileges, suspended by virtue of the writ of injunction issued from the said Court, and that it would be just and equitable to restore to them the same, therefore it was enacted: 1. That the corporate rights are restored. 2. The bank may commence business when $50,000 is paid in on the capital stock. 3. Receivers should fix value of assets. 4. Notice should be made by advertisement of the required payment of instalments. 5. A director must qualify by affidavit that he owns five shares at least of stock.

Under this Act the President pro tem, H. H. Schenck (the father of the late Hon. Abraham V. Schenck) called by advertisement in the "Fredonian" of March 21, 1849, pursuant to the above Act, for an assessment of $10 per share, to be made before April 25, or the stock would be forfeited. That the call was responded to was shown by an advertisement, May 14, 1850, for an election of eleven directors at Stelle's Hotel. Both notices were signed by H. H. Schenck, President pro tem.

The efficiency of the Receivers and the Acts for reinstatement can with safety be ascribed to John Van Dyck, an able lawyer, afterward Supreme Court Justice, who secured the necessary legislation at the time needed, and who stepped from the Receivership into the Presidency on the death of H. H. Schenck (who died March 22, 1851, at the age of sixty-three) with M. F. Webb as Cashier.

In the "Fredonian" of May, 1850, there are notices by M. F. Webb, Cashier, of a call for $10 a share on the stock to be paid June 17, dated May 8, 1850, to be made at the banking house, showing that it had one. Also a notice by Governor Daniel Haines, authorizing the directors to resume business, reciting that whereas Judge David Fitz Randolph and Abraham D. Titsworth certified, May 14, 1850, that $50,000 had been paid in on the capital stock, he, therefore, authorized the Directors to resume, May 15, 1850. On September 11, of the same year, there was a newspaper article which said: "An unjust effort to discredit the bills of the Farmers' and Mechanics' Bank has been made in New York; the capital of $50,000 has been paid in; the circulation has never been more than $25,000 and is at present less than $16,000. Bills of $5 and upwards will be redeemed at the Ocean Bank, New York, and small bills by S. Van Duzer of No. 170 Greenwich Street, New York;" and it went on to say that "The Farmers' and Mechanics' Bank is doing a small and we believe safe business, and is abundantly able to meet all its engagements, and is entitled to public confidence."

There are traditions that the bank resumed business in a building on Water Street, about opposite Janeway's factory. This building was at a later date, known as the Farmers' and Mechanics' Hotel. If this be true its stay there was brief, as it purchased the building at 11 Church Street, renumbered 15, from the executors of H. H. Schenck, on April 12, 1852, viz., 27 feet 6 inches on Church Street, and 51 feet deep, and the deed (B. 57-515) mentions the fact that it was then occupied as a banking house, so that it was already installed in the building as tenant before the purchase. Also, from the fact that its late President was the owner of the property, I am inclined to think that he provided them with quarters when the bank was authorized to resume.

That the bank soon became prosperous seems clear. The receivers sold the bank building on Peace Street and Commerce Square in 1843 to D. C. English; a building at one time the postoffice, under Fisher and Carson.

But the approaching expiration of the charter necessitated another move and was met by articles of association entered into, May, 1854, by B. D. Stelle, W. F. Randolph, James Dayton, Benjamin M. Clark, R. M. Honeyman and others, filed with the Secretary of State at Trenton, May 5, 1854, under the provisions of an Act "to authorize the business of banking," and the Farmers' and Mechanics' Bank, on June 30, 1854, deeded its banking house in Church St. to the Bank of New Jersey. This does not seem to have been entirely satisfactory, as almost immediately an Act to alter and amend the articles of association of the Bank of New Jersey, dated May 5, 1854, was passed at the request of Benjamin D. Stelle, David F. Randolph, James Dayton, Benjamin M. Clark, Robert M. Honeyman and others, shareholders in the Bank of New Jersey. The corporation under the articles of association, therefore, had but a brief existence, being only from the expiration of the charter of the Farmers' and Mechanics' Bank (Jan. 1, 1855) until the incorporation under the Act of April 6, 1855, a little more than three months, and while John Van Dyke, President, paid the last semi-annual dividend of 4% in August, 1854, for the Farmers' and Mechanics' Bank. He, as President of the Bank of New Jersey, March, 1855, two months after the change of name, paid a dividend of 4% before the incorporation of April 6, 1855 became operative. This is probably the shortest life of a banking institution on record, and its only act of record is the payment of a 4% dividend and the purchase, Jan. 22, 1855, from A. F. Randolph of the property, corner of Church and Neilson Streets, for $1,800.

The principal features of the Act of incorporation of April 6, 1855, and its twenty-two sections, are its name, "The Bank of New Jersey"; its capital stock, $300,000; shares at par to be $50; its first directors to be Peter Spader, Benjamin D. Stelle, John Van Dyke, Robert Miller, David F. Randolph, Isaac Fisher, Mahlon Runyon, Augustus T. Stout, James Dayton, William T. Runk, James Van Nuis, Jr., James T. Dunn, Robert M. Honeyman, John V. M. Wyckoff, Benjamin M. Clark and Robert S. Herbert, being the sixteen directors continued; the election of directors to be held the second Monday in May, the majority to be of New Brunswick and all from the State, and all to own at least twenty shares of stock; lastly, the officers to be elected by ballot.

An effort to start a competing bank had been begun in 1811, when an Act was introduced to incorporate "The Farmers Bank of New Brunswick." This was read a second time and also a third time, and then was finally disagreed to and failed to pass. This effort, though unsuccessful, was taken up again the next year in another form. An Act for the incorporation of State banks generally was passed on Jan. 28, 1812, and under this law the following six banks were incorporated: those of Camden, Trenton, New Brunswick, Elizabeth, Newark and Morristown. The charters were to run 20 years, the par of stock was to be $50 per share, and half the capital was to be reserved for the State. The books in New Brunswick were opened March 2, 1812, with Asa Runyon, 'Squire Martin and H. V. Low Commissioners to receive subscriptions. (See notice in "Fredonian" of Feb. 13, 1812). The first and second installments of $5 were payable March 2 and May 12; the third and fourth, also of $5 each, on Aug. 8 and Nov. 12, were called by J. J. Margerum, Cashier, and notice was given that the bank would open for business on July 2, 1812, from 9 to 3, in the building No. 21 Albany St. (new No. 39), which has been added to and now has an iron fire escape down the front. (This building was Geipel's in 1871). The bank removed to the corner of Albany and Peace in 1815. Its capital originally was $80,000. This building was remodeled and reopened for business Oct. 17, 1871.

On July 16, 1813, the stockholders of this bank met to consider an Act passed Feb. 15, 1813, altering the charters and transferring the State's rights to subscribers. Jan. 8, 1814, a further installment of $2.50 was called, and on Feb. 7, 1814, another installment of $2.50 was called, this time by D. W. Disborough, Cashier, while on Oct. 6, 1813, the first dividend of 4½% was declared by D. W. Disborough, Cashier, and notice of it appeared in the "Fredonian." In April, 1814, the dividend was 60 cents; in Nov., 1814, 70 cents; May, 1815, 70 cents; Oct., 1815, 4%. The dividends vary from 40 cents to 70 cents, from 3% to 4½%. Sometimes they were declared one way, and sometimes another. Disborough was Cashier till 1826, perhaps longer. In 1830 Peter Spader was Cashier and, until 1841, when John B. Hill became Cashier; in 1854 G. R. Conover; in 1855 M. Coddington.

March 15, 1855, the two banks joined in announcing that they would discontinue giving notice of the day of payment of notes; this was signed by M. Coddington, Cashier of the State Bank, and Moses F. Webb, Cashier of the Bank of New Jersey.

From the best obtainable data the First National Bank of New Brunswick was incorporated in 1865, for the purpose of securing a National bank charter for the State Bank (if it was thought desirable). The First National was located on the south side of Albany near Peace in the Sanderson building; Ira C. Voorhees was President and Israel H. Hutchings Cashier. This bank disappears from the City Directory list of banks of 1868, as it was merged into the State Bank.

The State Bank had a career of prosperity, continuously and almost uniformly, until 1873; this was the panic year, but it was not the panic that crushed the Bank. The President, J. R. Ford, was in Europe for his wife's health; H. Richmond was Vice-President and acting President. The bank statement of July 7, 1873, signed by G. W. Appleton, Cashier, appeared to be all right, but on Oct. 2 it closed its doors, and a loss of $552,984.44 was announced. G. W. Appleton and R. N. Woodworth were held responsible. This loss turned out to be even more than reported. Twenty-six men then subscribed $695,750 to save the bank of that amount. J. R. Ford and Christopher Meyer subscribed $225,000 each. Abraham Voorhees was now elected temporary President, and G. R. Conover Cashier; the latter had been cashier 20 years before. At an election of directors the following men were elected (many of the old directors refusing to serve again): Christopher Meyer, Garret Conover, James Bishop, Joseph B. Ford, Joseph Fisher, Peter C. Onderdonk, B. V. Ackerman, Abraham Voorhees, H. L. Janeway, T. B. Booraem, John Waldron, Miles Ross and Frederick Staats—thirteen. But even this great and generous effort did not save the bank. The loss was even greater than supposed. The Carpet Co.'s indebtedness proved a loss, as did the Masonic Hall Ass'n loan, and a claim of the Mercantile Bank of New York for $30,000 turned out to be $130,000. Confidence was lost, depositors withdrew gradually, the surplus of $250,000 and the capital of $250,000 were gone, and on Saturday, March 31, 1877, the Bank closed its doors, not to open again, and the Court appointed Col. J. W. Newell receiver.

For the next ten years New Brunswick had but one bank, when the troubles of the Bank of New Jersey in 1884 brought home the objection to this condition in a most convincing manner. For a brief period New Brunswick had no bank at all. The Charter of the People's Bank was obtained in 1887, and the bank started on the southeast corner of Neilson and

Church, T. E. Schenck Cashier. In 1890 the President was G. W. DeVoe, and in 1891 Benjamin F. Howell succeeded, and still is (1924) President, and the Bank is now at the southeast corner of George and Church Sts. While the Bank of New Jersey remained on the north side of the street, the People's adhered to the south side.

So briefly, the original line and the competing line of Banks were as follows:

1808. *Bank of New Brunswick* in brick building on Neilson St., now the Wieda Bakery. Then purchased site in 1809 and built the Banking House in 1810, afterwards the Mansion House and Miss Hoyt's School; now the United Cigar Co. occupy the altered building. Getting into trouble in 1827, it moved to Burnet St., four doors south of Hiram. (See map of 1829). Suspended Feb. 14, 1834.

Succeeded in 1834 by the *Farmers' and Mechanics'*, which purchased at once the house west side of Burnet, afterwards the Post Office on Commerce Square. Moved to No. 11, afterwards No. 15 Church St. in 1852 and was the Green Stamp Trading Co. in 1816.

Succeeded in 1854 by the *Bank of New Jersey*, which occupied the same building, moving later to northwest corner of Neilson and Church, and now on northwest corner George and Church Sts.

State Bank July 2, 1812, first at No. 21 (now No. 39) Albany St.; then corner Albany and Peace Sts., northwest corner, where it remained until its failure in 1877.

National Bank of N. B., incorporated in 1865, on south side of Albany.

1877 to 1887 ten years gap. No competing bank.

Then *People's Bank*, 1887, corner Church and Neilson, and corner C h u r c h and George Sts.

Bank of New Jersey (succeeding Farmers' and Mechanics'). (1854) Same President and Cashier. (Aug. 1, 1854) last dividend 4% paid by Farmers' and Mechanics'. March 20, 1855, first dividend 4% paid by Bank of New Jersey. (1854-1859) John Van Dyke, President; Moses F. Webb, C a s h i e r. (1859) Moses F. Webb, President; John T. Hill, Cashier; Israel H. Voorhees, Cashier. (1861) Garret G. Voorhees, President. (1864) John B. Hill, President. (1874) J a m e s Dayton, President. (1877) Mahlon Runyon, President. (1884) New Charter. (1886) Lewis T. Howell, President. (1903) V. M. W. Suydam, President. (1909) H. G. Parker, President.

NEW BRUNSWICK IN HISTORY 175

The officers of the various banks, in part, were as follows:

Bank of New Brunswick, Inc 1808—J. R. Hardenbergh, President; James Phelan, Cashier. (1816) Edward Wood Dunham, Cashier. (1821) I. N. Simpson, Cashier. (1830) C. L. Hardenbergh, President; Lewis Carmen, Cashier. (Jan. 1, 1833) C. L. Hardenbergh, President; F. Richmond, Cashier; Rutson Hardenbergh, Cashier. (Oct. 2, 1833) James C. Van Dyke, President; F. Richmond, Cashier. (1834-1836) Edward Wood, George Richmond and David W. Vail, Receivers. (1838-1839) James C. Van Dyke, President (died Oct. 15, 1843). (1848, or 1849, and 1850) Final payment on claims and certificates of 12½ cents; Ira C. Voorhees, Secretary; Littleton Kirkpatrick, President.

Farmers' and Mechanics' Bank, Inc. (Feb. 6, 1834 to 1854) James F. Randolph, President; Lewis Carmen, Cashier. (1839) Abraham Suydam, President (murdered Dec. 3, 1840); Lewis Carmen, Cashier. (1840) Charles Dunham. (1844-1848) Peter Spader, John Van Dyke and David W. Vail, Receivers. (1849) H. H. Schenck, President pro tem. (1851) John Van Dyke, President; Moses F. Webb, Cashier.

Bank of New Jersey (succeeding Farmers' and Mechanics'). (1854) Same President and Cashier as above. (Aug. 1, 1854) last dividend, 4%, paid by Farmers' and Mechanics'. (March 20, 1855) First dividend, 4%, paid by Bank of New Jersey. (1854-1859) John Van Dyke, President; Moses F. Webb, Cashier. (1859) Moses F. Webb, President; John T. Hill, Cashier; Israel H. Voorhees, Cashier. (1861) Garret G. Voorhees, President. (1864) John B. Hill, President. (1874) James Dayton, President. (1877) Mahlon Runyon, President. (1884) New Charter. (1886) Lewis T. Howell, President. (1903) V. M. W. Suydam, President. (1909) H. G. Parker, President.

The officers of the State Bank as far as they can now be verified were:

Presidents	*Cashiers*
John Bray.	J. J. Margerum.
Charles Smith.	D. W. Disborough.
Fitz Randolph Smith.	Peter Spader.
John B. Hill.	John B. Hill.
John R. Ford.	G. R. Conover.
H. Richmond (Vice and Acting).	Moses Coddington.
	J. R. Fountain.
Abraham Voorhees.	G. D. Appleton.
	G. R. Conover.

In the State Bank Mr. Hill was Clerk for 10 years, Cashier 11 years, and President 12 years—total of 33 years; and then went to the Presidency of the Bank of New Jersey in 1864. The troubles of the Bank of New Jersey briefly referred to as occurring when there was but one bank in New Brunswick, culminated Sept. 8, 1884, when the Bank closed its doors, owing to the sudden death of its cashier Sept. 4, 1884, and of its President, Sept. 8, 1884, after a run of about two days, when some $240,000 was drawn out. As it was the only bank in the city, and this collapse came so soon after the smash of the State Bank, it naturally excited the greatest apprehension, and the rumors afloat were of the most sensational character. But after a careful examination of the Bank it was found that, while the surplus was gone, the capital was intact. The Bank was reorganized Sept. 22 and opened Sept. 24, after being closed 16 days. The new President was Lewis T. Howell and the Cashier E. S. Campbell.

In the "Fredonian" of March, 1822, there is a long account of the launching of the New Jersey Bank for Savings. The 128 Articles of Association are given, and the Associators were J. R. Hardenbergh, John N. Simpson, S. Holcomb, M. Edgerton, Dr. A. R. Taylor, James Neilson, Jerome Rappelyea, Jr., Miles C. Smith, Rutsen Hardenbergh, Dr. John A. Pool; with Trustees Samuel Bayard of Princeton, Andrew Howell, of Somerville, William Edgar of Bridgeton. They opened in the counting room of John N. Simpson, Burnet St., Saturday, March 23, 1822, from 6 to 9 P. M. and every succeeding Saturday. J. R. Hardenbergh was President; Jerome Rappelyea, Jr., 1st Vice-President; Matthew Edgarton, 2nd Vice-President; Rutsen Hardenbergh, Treasurer, and Miles C. Smith, Secretary. It was announced that semi-annual interest of 2½% would be paid on all sums above $5.00 on deposit for three months.

The military spirit was not allowed to be smothered in business. The New Brunswick Artillery Co. was formed in 1807. The muster roll of June 24, 1809, has 56 names upon it. This organization seems to have continued till merged into the regular State militia.

I have referred to John Stevens' steamboat, mentioned in Council minutes May 6, 1809. His boat, the "Phœnix," ran for a time to New Brunswick and then was taken to Philadelphia by his son, Robert Stevens. The "Phœnix" and the "Clermont" were built the summer of 1807. Then J. R. Livingston and R. J. Livingston, under rights purchased of R. R. Livingston and Robert Fulton, built the "Raritan" in the winter of 1807-08 at a cost of $26,000, and ran it to New Brunswick for two years at a loss. Then, by an arrangement with Stevens, the "Raritan," the Stages and the "Phœnix" combined on a through line from New York to Philadelphia, and after that the boat was moderately profitable. While the date of the "Phœnix's" trip by sea to Philadelphia is given as 1808, as Stevens was running a boat to New Brunswick in May, 1809, it is probable his sea voyage was in 1809 instead of 1808 (numerous authorities give the earlier date), and as a boat was advertised for New Brunswick every other day, or three times a week, to begin July 4, 1809 (neither name of boat nor owner given), that is probably the date that the "Raritan" began her trips, taking nine to ten hours each way. This arrangement is said to have lasted six years. But from 1811 to 1815 there were no boats to New Brunswick.

Other ventures during this period were: Col. Ogden's "Seahorse," for the ferry between Elizabeth, Jersey City and New York in 1811; Thomas Gibbons' "Stroudinger" on the same ferry in opposition to Ogden. They were partners in the ferry rights, but, owing to a quarrel, became competitors for the steamboat business. In 1815 the "Raritan" is advertised to sail at 5.00 A. M., instead of 6.00 A. M., from June to September, with stages to the Delaware, and on to Philadelphia by a new boat on the Delaware, making a through daily line to Philadelphia, called the Union Line. As this "Raritan" was so much speedier than the one on the route in 1808, which took two days for the round trip, either she must have been remodelled and greatly changed, or a new boat keeping the same name put in her place. I have seen the statement that the first "Raritan" was broken up after two years; perhaps only rebuilt. While the above was the Summer schedule, there was a Winter schedule. All stages would leave 5 Courtland St., at 9.00 A. M. (evidently by ferry to Powles Hook, then to Newark and to Elizabeth); dine at New Brunswick; going on and making Trenton the same day, where the schedule says "Lodge at Trenton," and arrive at Philadelphia at 10.00 the next morning.

Robert R. Livingston died in 1813, and Robert Fulton died in 1815. J. R. Livingston and Stevens ran the "Olive Branch," evidently a change of heart from the day when the opposition named their boat the "Retaliation." In 1817 Thomas Gibbons' "Mouse & Mountain," and the "Bellona" (Capt. Vanderbilt) followed. The latter was advertised as drawing less water (a great advantage in the crooked and narrow Raritan) and would leave at 6.00 A. M. and return at 4.00 P. M. In 1824 Capt. Vanderbilt put on his own boat, the "Thistle;" Gibbons' boat the "Bellona" being still run, but by Capt. Jenkins, and the "Legislator," in charge of Capt. Fisher, was also on the route, put on by the New Brunswick Steamboat Ferry Co., incorporated Feb. 15, 1815, by Robert Arnould, John Phelan and Isaac Lawrence, with three boats. Competition became intense and the fare to New York was reduced to 12½ cents.

While individuals had so far conducted the steamboat business (Fulton and R. R. Livingston, John Stevens, J. R. Livingston and R. J. Livingston, Ogden, Gibbon, Vanderbilt), singly or as partners, there was a Company formed in New Brunswick in 1814, the first Steamboat Company of which I know. It was called the Team & Steam Boat Co., known locally as John Simpson & Co. They built a team-boat, or horse-power boat, called the "Retaliation," and a steamboat called the "John Fitch." But, owing to the repeal of the State law giving exclusive rights to the waters of New Jersey as an offset to the similar law passed by New York State, they thought best not to go on at that time, though the Company was incorporated Feb. 15, 1815, as the New Brunswick Steamboat Ferry Co., to take over the Company formed in 1814 without incorporating. This Company, represented by five Commissioners, Lewis Carman, F. Mollison, Simeon Ayres, John T. Duyckinck and James Bishop, called for an installment of $10 a share. We find also where a second installment of $10 a share was called, though they seem to have been some time availing themselves of this right, as on March 3, 1824, there was a call for a meeting to elect directors; and in Feb., 1825, James Bishop gives notice of a meeting to elect directors, and, later, announces that Lewis Carman, Joseph C. Griggs, James Bishop, Matthias Freeman and Robert M. Russell of New York, in place of John T. Duyckinck (declined), were elected.

I have given some space to this original Steamboat Co., for, while there was incorporated on Feb. 11, four days before, the Shrewsbury & N. J. Steamboat Ferry Co., capital $40,000, to run from Tinton on the Shrewsbury to New York; and also on the same day the Penn. & N. J. Steamboat Ferry Co., capital $50,000, to run from Southwark (Philadelphia?) to Kaign's Point on the Delaware; still the Steamboat Ferry Co. of New Brunswick, capital $100,000, was in reality the incorporation of the Team and Steamboat Co. of a year earlier. It gives us the honor of the first Steamboat Company in New Jersey, if not in America. As Fulton's and Livingston's exclusive rights were maintained till 1824 that prevented any organization in New York. After the decision of the unconstitutionality of these exclusive rights, the "Legislator," advertised by Lewis Carman, President of the Company in 1824, was their first venture. Evidently they had awaited the decision of the Courts. In 1826 the Company sold the "Legislator" and put on the "Long Branch," and Feb. 12, 1828, the Columbian Steamboat Co. was incorporated to operate on the waters of the Delaware, the Raritan and New York. This seems to have been in anticipation of the opening of the Canal, incorporated in 1825. The incorporators were, William Sheepshanks, Nathaniel Davidson, George Peterson, Michael Newbold, Daniel Woods, David C. Dow and Wm. McKnight, mostly Philadelphians. This Company was followed again, in 1831, by the New Brunswick Steamboat & Canal Transportation Co., usually called the Napoleon Co., from the name of their boat run by Capt. Fisher, who had run the "Legislator." All apparently the same Company, but under new charters and with added or greater powers and privileges. The Napoleon Co. paid dividends of $40 and

$50 a year on the stock, which, I believe, was not even fully paid, and was highly successful.

In 1840 another "Raritan" was put on under Capt. Fisher; in 1844 the "Mount Hope," Capt. Hoyt; in 1848 the "Antelope," Capt. Van Wickle, and the "New Philadelphia, "Capt. Fisher, were on the river, and in 1850 the "St. Nicholas," Capt. Frazee; in 1852 the "John Neilson," Capt. Frazee. In 1835 the railroads began to offer still better accommodations. In 1838 an advertisement in the "Fredonian" of the N. J. R. R. & Transportation Co., dated March 21st, announcing a summer arrangement, gives notice that trains will leave New Brunswick at 7.00 A. M., New York 9.00 A. M., and also leave New Brunswick at 2.00 P. M., New York 4.00 P. M. Fares to Newark 37½ cents; to Elizabeth 37½ cents; to Rahway 50 cents; to New Brunswick 75 cents. John Forman, Agent.

An obituary notice in the "Fredonian" of Capt. Moses Rogers who died Nov. 15, 1821, aged 42, and who was Captain of the "Savannah" (built in N. Y.; sailed from Savannah May 24, 1819; was 26 days crossing on her trip to England; went thence to Stockholm and St. Petersburg and back to the United States, the first vessel to cross the ocean under steam), would seem to indicate that we had some connection with this venture also. Thomas Gibbons, who came here from Savannah, built the "Stoudinger" and the "Bellona" and might have had a hand in the "Savannah."

While the men were so busy with the revolutions in travel, the result of the steam engine, the ladies were doing their part. The Revolutionary War had left old soldiers or their widows who deserved well of their country, and I have been told the Dorcas Society was formed primarily with the purpose to meet this need, in 1813. I am able to give the Society's report for the year ending Nov., 1815. This report gives a list of Officers, Managers, and the Treasurer's and Secretary's reports.

First Directress—Mrs. Kirkpatrick
Second Directress—Mrs. Dr. Smith
Treasurer—Miss Scott
Secretary—Miss Dean

Managers

Mrs. Anna Dunham	Miss Smith	Miss Neilson
Mrs. Hardenbergh	Miss Croes	Miss Kirkpatrick
Mrs. Holcomb	Miss Hardenbergh	Miss Johnson
Mrs. Lawrence	Miss Livingston	Miss Grant
Mrs. Jas. Neilson	Miss Richmond	Miss Abeel
Mrs. Dr. Taylor	Miss Holcomb	Miss Hassart
Mrs. Williamson	Miss Maria Parker	Miss C. A. Lawrence

Receipts

Receipts $505 38
Expenditures 501 54

Balance in Treas.... 3 84

Work

Yarn spun .... 305 lbs.
Cloth woven ...... 228 yds.
Cloth on hand..... 197 yds.
Yarn at weavers .. 82 lbs.
Yarn on hand .... 128 lbs.
Flax purchased .... 177 lbs.
Flax on hand .... 100 lbs.

MARY DEAN, Secretary.

Miss Hannah Scott started a Sunday School with three teachers and five scholars in 1816 in connection with the Presbyterian Church, and was Superintendent for 31 years.

In 1815 the yellow fever in New York induced a number of storekeepers to move to New Brunswick but I presume only temporarily. In 1821 a meeting of the New Brunswick Society for the encouragement of manufactures was held—John N. Simpson, Pres., and D. W. Disborough, Treas., an early edition of our Board of Trade. Hat making was quite an industry in our city. John Dennis was making hats as early as 1778, and we had a chocolate manufactory in 1780. Peter Low and Henry Guest were engaged in whaling.

The Public Library, the Charity Organization Society with its subdivisions, the Boys' Club and the Penny Savings Fund were all originated and brought into successful operation through the efforts of Mrs. James Neilson (Mary Putnam Woodbury Neilson).

The New Brunswick Free Circulating Library was opened March 29, 1883, on the corner of George and Church Streets, with a donation of a hundred books by the Ladies' Book Club, which were increased during the year to 2,083. The growth of the Library was steady and continuous. Two changes of location were required by its growth and, in 1892, the Free Public Library was formed, as it needed to be supplemented by public funds, and the free circulating property was leased to it; then there were over 8,000 books.

In 1903 a Carnegie Library Building was obtained and again the Library was moved—then consisting of 9,500 books. In 1902 Mrs. Neilson withdrew from the management. The Library now reports 30,000 books.

The Charity Organization Society began work in Oct., 1884, and has continued till the present time, though, since July 15, 1920, the work has been carried on by the Red Cross Society. For forty years it has ameliorated the condition of the poor, checking impostors and bringing pressure on the idle, encouraging industry and finding work for many. The Society became so efficient that small towns, wishing to establish similar societies, were referred to New Brunswick for advice and assistance. In the same year Mrs. Neilson organized a Boys' Club, later obtaining a building and providing the apparatus as well as giving her personal assistance night after night to make it a success, providing amusement and entertainment. The result was a marked improvement in the behavior of the boys of the town. In 1888 a Penny Savings fund was added. Stamps designating the deposit were pasted on cards till five dollars enabled the opening of a Savings Bank account. The Club and the Savings Fund were continued until 1902, when the Savings had reached $22,178 by twenty-two hundred and twenty-two savers during fourteen years.

Truant officers, Kindergartens, Manual Training, recommended and urged by Mrs. Neilson and this Society, are now regularly installed as part of the public school requirements of this State and shows how advanced this Society was in its views.

The following tribute to Mrs. Neilson's memory was written by Dr. Austin Scott, ex-President of Rutgers College and appeared in the "Home News" of Saturday, January 24, 1914:

"After a period of illness, Mrs. James Neilson died Friday at Woodlawn, her home here, in the 68th year of her age. Mrs. Neilson was the daughter of the late Isaac B. and Abigail Putnam Woodbury. The funeral will be held from her late residence, Woodlawn, on Tuesday afternoon next, at 3 o'clock. An intimate friend of the family has written this tribute for the Home News:

"'A deep sense of loss entered New Brunswick homes last evening when it became known that Mrs. James Neilson had left the life on earth. Even of those who did not know her, very many have known of the blessings her life has brought to the community, and those who passed her on the street felt instinctively and rightly that the rare charm of the features of her face was matched by the excellence of her character.

"'Born in a refined New England home, of New England lineage, Mary Putnam Woodbury imbibed and cherished always the desire to learn, evermore to learn. The training of her home land was supplemented by study and travel in Europe and it was in Berlin, Germany, that she became the wife of James Neilson.

"'It is difficult to say what field of human thought and life and achievement most engaged her interest and zeal. Of music, especially that of Wagner, she was a devoted friend and skilled critic. The elder and younger Damrosch were often her guests. She had wide, accurate and intimate acquaintance with much of the best in literature in its various forms, of the past and in the present. The choicest modern works in pure literature, history, sociology, in English, German, French, or Italian formed a goodly part of her reading. She had a marvelous skill in analysis of thought and feeling and a rare power of expression.

"'But the motives and purposes which found expression in her deeds will never be lost out of the history of this community. Those whose happy lot it has been to sit at the table of her exquisite hospitality, those who in large numbers at her invitation thronged the spacious house and wide-stretching lawns and gardens, will always cherish the memory of her kindly welcome and gracious bounty.

"'More comprehensive still was the motive which reached out for the general good and happiness of the community. She instituted the Free Circulating Library, which for so many years, first at the corner of George and Church streets, next on Albany street, then at the corner of George and Paterson streets, formed the object of her constant care and solicitude, and was a very fountain of blessing to the citizens for more than twenty years. It was she, too, who founded the Charity Organization Society. She established and for many years maintained the Boys' Club, and during that period gave at times entertainments to its members on the grounds of her home, which brought to the urchin off the street as keen delight as that felt by the most refined among her friends. If she had any chief joy it may well have sprung from her desire to make children happy, whether their lot were high or humble. Of her charities in private, many a grateful one could tell.

" 'She had fully deserved many of the best blessings which this life can bring; she was the mistress of a spacious and lovely home, filled with the treasures whose possession enriches mind and heart.

" 'She had a wide circle of admiring and devoted friends among her neighbors, friends in other cities of our land, close friends in England, friends in Italy; friends among the lowly and among those whose names nations delight to honor.

" 'New Brunswick has had a rare privilege; for more than forty years it has been the home of Mrs. James Neilson. There will be no lack of deepest sympathy for her devoted husband, our honored fellow-citizen.' "

Another writer, in speaking of Mrs. Neilson's work, says:

"With her vision and keen business judgment she chose the corner of Church and George streets for the first home of the Library and, when the site was taken for the New Brunswick Savings Institution, the old State Bank was bought, and soon after the building, corner George and Paterson streets, long before business discerned its value. Her plan was to secure the adjoining properties and erect a fire-proof building on this central spot, where the factory operatives and others could readily exchange their books, and consult books of reference.

"Many of the boys who attended the clubs and many who got their ideas of economy in the Savings Society have become today our most substantial and useful citizens, and cherish a warm spot in their hearts for Mrs. Neilson. An evidence was shown in the address of Mr. Harry Feller at the opening of the Hebrew Community Building recently, and in a tribute to her in the October number, 1922, of the 'Triad,' published by St. Peter's High School, New Brunswick."

From another source I quote:

"In 'My musical life,' by Mr. Walter Damrosch, he refers to Mrs. Neilson's cleverness in obtaining the orchestral score of Brahm's symphony, No. 1, in C minor, for his father, Dr. Leopold Damrosch, for its first production in America, which Gustave Schirmer was reserving for the Dr.'s arrival, Theodore Thomas."

Mrs. Neilson who inherited great musical ability from her father, referred to as "that musical genius—Isaac B. Woodbury," was a pupil and warm friend of Dr. Leopold Damrosch, and the whole Damrosch family. She was always a serious student of music.

CHAPTER IX

The Parker Family of Woodbridge, Perth Amboy and New Brunswick—James Parker, the Printer—The French Minister, de Neuville—The "Boom" in the Thirties—Early Finances of the City—Issuance of Paper Money—City Population in 1829—Town Meeting Minutes—The Increase of Taxes After the Legislature Began to Tax.

THE Parker family by tradition came from Kent, England, and used the seal of John Parker, of Sibertswold. Elisha and Robert Parker are found at Barnstable about 1657. Elisha married Elizabeth, sister of Gov. Thomas Hinckley; was born July 16, 1635 and married July 15, 1657. He joined the migration of part of the congregation of Rev. Thomas Parker of Newbury to Woodbridge, New Jersey. His children were:

1. Thomas, born May 15, 1658; left descendants.
2. Elisha, born Nov., 1660.
3. Sarah, born May, 1662; married Matthew Moore(?)
4. Samuel, born March 1, 1669; died Dec. 27, 1672.
5. Mary, born Dec. 3, 1672; married Nov. 27, 1691, Daniel Robins and left issue.
6. Samuel, born June 1, 1674; married Janet—, and had issue, including James Parker, the printer.

The will of Samuel Parker (cooper), of Woodbridge, made 1725, proved July 28, 1725, mentions wife Joanna, and four children, Samuel, John, James and Elisha. Witness to the will was Matthew "Mores," who was husband of his sister Sarah.

Elisha (2), born November, 1660, of Woodbridge, merchant, Captain, Sheriff, Assemblyman, and in 1711 appointed to the Council, moved to Perth Amboy between 1712 and 1715, and died June 30, 1717. The "Castle lot" was conveyed to him in 1715. He is described by Governor Hunter as an "old planter, a very large trader and owner of the best estate in the place." He was Captain of the Middlesex Troops 1707, Member of Assembly 1708-'10, and in the Council of East Jersey 1713-'17.

He married Hannah Rolph Feb. 5, 1672. She died Oct. 14, 1696. His children by Hannah Rolph were:

1. Elizabeth, who died young.
2. John, b. Nov. 11, 1693; m. Janet Johnstone, daughter of Dr. John Johnstone, and built the stone part of the Castle on land deeded to his father Elisha August 2, 1715.

Elisha by a second wife, Ursula Crage, or Craig, m. Sept. 27, 1697, and had issue:

3. Elizabeth, b. March 21, 1698-9; m. James Johnston of Monmouth.
4. Ursula, b. Dec. 21, 1700; died unmarried.
5. Mary, b. Dec. 22, 1702; died unmarried.
6. Elisha, b. 1704; died 1727.
7. Edward, of whom we do not know the subsequent history.

John (2), born Nov. 11, 1693, married Sept. 16, 1721, Janet, who was born Apr. 7, 1699, and was daughter of Dr. John Johnstone; she died Feb. 16, 1741. John was Colonel and merchant; lived in Amboy until his death in 1732, and was of the Council after 1719. He was Captain of the Middlesex Troops 1715; vestryman 1727 to 1732 and buried in the churchyard. He was in the East Jersey Council 1718-'32; Judge of Special Court to try pirates in 1718; Chairman of Committee of Ordinances, Court of Judicature, 1724; several times Chairman of Committee to regulate expenditure of public money; member of the New Jersey Bar. His children were:

1. John Parker, b. 1722, died April 30, 1725.
2. Elisha Parker, b. 1724; m. Catherine, daughter of James Alexander, 1749; was a lawyer licensed May 3, 1740, and died March 14, 1751. No children.
3. James Parker, mentioned hereafter.
4. Mary Parker, b. Oct. 27, 1727; died unmarried, Feb. 25, 1813, aged 86; buried in St. Peter's.
5. John Parker, b. Nov. 7, 1729. Midshipman and afterwards Captain and Colonel in the French War, 1755-'6, and in the West Indies. Died Feb. 15, 1762, unmarried.
6. Lewis Johnson Parker, b. Dec. 9, 1731; died Feb. 2, 1760, unmarried.

(The above genealogy was kindly furnished to me by Rev. W. Northey Jones, Rector of St. Peter's, Perth Amboy.)

Of the sons of John (b. 1693), James, born 1725, was a Captain in the Provincial service in 1746; Captain of a home Troop of Horse in 1760; in business in New York with Beverly Robinson; a member of Governor Franklin's Council, 1764-1775; Judge of the Court of Common Pleas, 1766; conducted the lottery for building straight roads through the Province, 1766; was President of the Proprietors; Mayor of Amboy in 1771; a large landholder and merchant; Delegate to the Provincial Congress in 1775. Adjudged a Tory, he was interned in Morris county Court House in August, 1777, released in October, but again returned to jail, released conditionally in December, and released finally in February, 1778. Then he removed to Bethlehem, Hunterdon county, to avoid taking any part in the Revolutionary movements, where he remained till after the War. In December, 1783, he removed to New Brunswick and bought, in 1787, a large part of Philip French's lands in the northern portion of the city, over 600 acres, at sheriff's sale, but failed to take up his purchase, so the lands were again put up and sold to James Cole (see Book G., 397, of Somerset County Deeds) and to Thomas Fitz Randolph (G.400), and Cole and Fitz Randolph deeded to Parker. The land bringing much less at the second sale, after a brief stay in New Brunswick he returned to Amboy, where he was vestryman and warden of St. Peter's Church, 1763-1797. He died October 4, 1797, aged seventy-two. His first wife was Gertrude Skinner of Amboy. His second wife, Catharine Ogden, survived him. His children were:

1. John, who married Ann Laurence.
2. Elizabeth, unmarried.
3. Janet, who married Edward Brinly.
4. Gertrude.
5. Sarah.
6. Maria, who married Andrew Smythe.
7. William, who died young.
8. James, born in Hunterdon Co., 1776; succeeded his father, and married Penelope Butler in 1803. Their children were: (1), James, who married Anna Forbes. (2),

William, who married Lucy C. Whitwell. (3), Margaret, who married W. A. Whitehead. (4), Gertrude, unmarried. (5), Sarah, unmarried. (6), Cortlandt, who married Elizabeth Stites, (a Newark family). (7), Penelope. (8), Catherine. (9), Lewis, who married Elizabeth Gouverneur. All by his first wife. James was long engaged in disposing of the New Brunswick lands with his stepmother as executrix. In 1808 we find a deed from him to Queen's Campus, six acres, and in 1813 one for the site of the Baptist Church, formerly Philip French's family burying-ground, and subsequently the railroad station, both historic sites.[1]

We have drifted some distance from John Parker, b. 1693, and his two sons in following the James line. John, the other son, b. 1729, d. 1762 unm., will require but a few lines. He was active in military service in the French frontier wars and served under Colonel Peter Schuyler.

To continue with Elisha, who married for the second time, when about 64, Ursula Crage, on September 27, 1697, and had 5 children: Elizabeth, b. 1698, who married James Johnson of Monmouth; Ursula, b. 1700; Mary, b. 1702, d. unm. and Elisha, the Weaver, b. 1704, d. 1727 unm. and left his property to his sisters, and Edward of whom there is no record.

James Parker, "the Printer," son of Samuel and Janet (6 under first numbering above) was a hard working, ambitious man, and was born about —— 1715. When eleven, (his father being dead) he indentured himself to William Bradford, the famous printer (January, 1726) for eight years, to be taught the art and mystery of a printer and bookbinder. In May, 1733, Bradford advertised him as having run away, his time not being quite up, lacking about nine months. It is thought likely that he found employment with Franklin in Philadelphia, who was then Postmaster and also had his own printing office. Nine years later he returned to New York and in January, 1742-'43, he, with Franklin as silent partner, who furnished the press and 400 pounds of letters, started an office in New York and revived the newspaper of his old master, William Bradford,

---

[1] For mention of other Parkers with hitherto published conflicting items respecting them, see Appendix.

which he called "The New York Gazette, Revived in the Weekly Post Boy." He is also, in 1752, credited with a paper called the "Independent Reflector," edited by William Livingston, containing essays but no news; but he declined to continue printing it on account of the character of the articles. A "Guide to Vestrymen" came from his press in 1747, and, as he was a vestryman himself, he probably saw the need of such a work. He associated Weyman (one of his fellow-apprentices while with Bradford), as partner and manager of his newspaper in 1754, and they printed the charter of the College of New York, later Kings, now Columbia, that year. Franklin appointed him Postmaster of New Haven in 1754, and in January, 1755, as James Parker & Co., the "Co." being John Holt, he brought out the "Commercial Gazette" and opened a printing office in New Haven. Holt was a brother-in-law of William Hunter, who shared the office of Deputy Postmaster-General with Franklin.

In 1751 Parker opened the first printing office in New Jersey, at Woodbridge, his native place, of which he was made Postmaster in 1754. Printing newspapers and post-offices seemed to go together, for a surprising number of the early newspapers were published by postmasters. In 1756 he was appointed Controller and Secretary of General Post-offices in the British Colonies, with territory from Quebec to Florida, to succeed William Franklin. In 1765 the territory was divided, and he had charge of the northern district; notices show that the mail service between New York and Philadelphia was controlled from Woodbridge. In 1743 he was Public Printer for the Province of New York, and Government Printer for New Jersey; in 1758 he printed Woodbridge money and legal documents; he was styled King's Printer in 1762 and until his death in 1770, printing all laws, ordinances, votes and proceedings.

His office in New Haven printed the laws of Yale College in Latin in 1755. Among the important papers that he published was the "Elizabeth Town Bill in Chancery," the most noted bill in the country, in 1747, which sold at three pounds, and the "Answer," printed later, was printed at his New York office. He printed the second volume of the Laws of the Province (1753 to 1761), compiled by Samuel Nevill. In 1756 his bill for printing the votes of the House was £61.9.6, and in 1768 it was £48.9.6. In 1758 he issued the new American magazine, "Sylvanus Americanus," (Samuel Nevill, Editor). The first number of 48 octavo pages contained: History of North America; the Traveler; Monthly Miscellany; Political Essays; Chronological Diary; Historical Chronicle and Naval Engagements. It has been stated that this was the first magazine in New Jersey and the second in America. As Bradford printed the "American Magazine" in 1757, and Rogers & Fowle published a magazine for a few months in 1743, the statement is not quite correct. In 1760 his nephew, Samuel Parker, had charge of printing the "Post Boy," and again in 1766. In 1764-65 James Parker was author, printer, and publisher of a bulky octavo volume, entitled "Conductor Generalis," setting forth the powers and duties of a Justice of the Peace, an office he held himself and, like his "Guide to a Vestryman," in 1747, the office doubtless suggested the need of the book. This work was in great vogue for twenty years or more and was reprinted in 1788 by Hugh Gaine at New York. In 1766 Parker also published a New York edition of the Stamp Act which is very rare. William Nelson lists seventy-nine issues of the Woodbridge press, 1754-'88; twenty-five orations, sermons, discourses and the like; the rest being acts and votes of the Legislature.

The usually-accepted story that Parker moved his press from Woodbridge to Burlington to print "Smith's History" is upset by the late William Nelson, who says that the facts were that Franklin had a press stored with Parker in New York, which Parker sent around to Burlington by water, as being less likely to receive injury from its transportation. This was the press used, and he was negotiating with Franklin for the purchase of the press, and contemplating continuing an office in Burlington permanently, in addition to his other offices. That he had definitely purchased this press appears from the statement that he left one press at Burlington, one at Woodbridge, one at New Haven, and two at New York.

He was fifty-six when he died and had been thirty years engaged in the printing business. His connection with Holt proved disastrous and his loss seems to have been very heavy. Parker had his share of the risks that beset the printer of that day. In 1756 both Parker and Weyman were taken into custody by the Sergeant-at-Arms, Weyman on the 18th, and Parker on the 23rd, on his arrival from Woodbridge, for an article on the conduct of people in Ulster and Orange. They were discharged on the 30th, after acknowledging their fault, begging pardon of the House, giving up the name of the writer of the article and paying fees. The writer, being the Rev. Hezekiah Watkins, Missionary of the Society for the Propagation of the Gospel in Foreign Parts, who lived in Newport, was taken into custody and was served about as Parker and Weyman had been.

The other trouble occurred the year of his death and was caused by a paper "To the betrayed inhabitants of New York," signed "A Son of Liberty" and printed privately by Parker. There being a hundred pounds reward for the author, one of his journeymen informed against him and he was taken into custody January 7, 1770. Parker finally admitted that General Alexander McDougall was the author. McDougall refused to plead and was committed to prison, where he remained several months. Parker in the meantime died and the evidence against McDougall was lost.

There was still another paper that would have brought Parker into serious trouble had it been proved that he printed it. It was called the "Constitutional Courant." Isaiah Thomas, in his book (1810), "Printing and Printers," says that it was printed by William Goddard at Parker's press in Woodbridge, Parker then being engaged in Burlington printing "Smith's History," and Goddard, who had been an apprentice of Parker's, had permission to use the press occasionally.

The papers for the "Sons of Liberty" were purported to have been printed by Andrew Marvell at "The Sign of the Bribe Refused on Constitution Hill, North America," and it had a device of a serpent cut into eight parts, with the letters NE, NY, NJ, MD, VA, NC, SC and GA, to represent the Colonies, with the motto: "Join or Die." That it was never certainly known whence the paper came is borne out by Mr. Nelson who, in trying to prove its authorship, says: "A careful comparison of the type found in the 'Courant' and in Parker's New York paper convinced me that they were both printed on the same type," but adds that Governor Colden said one or more of the bundles of this paper had been given the Post Riders at Woodbridge by Parker. However, there was no proof at the time that Parker printed it and he escaped. His press at Woodbridge was burned by Tories during the Revolution.

Samuel Eugene Parker said of him: "Looking at his work as a publisher in Connecticut, New Jersey and New York, and his direct connection with the country from Quebec to Florida and London, the conclusion seems right that he was a man of greater importance than a modern publisher or an assistant Postmaster-General of to-day." A most moderate and temperate conclusion. Barber & Howe say of Parker that "he was ever an opponent to the oppression of the higher power."

James Parker married Madame Mary Ballareau, a French lady. Their only daughter, Jane Ballareau Parker, married Judge Gunning Bedford, Jr., of Wilmington, Delaware. James' son, Samuel Franklin Parker, was a Major in New Jersey State Troops, who died December 6, 1779, aged 33, leaving a wife, Mary, a daughter, Mary, and a son, James Eugene Parker.

James Parker was Captain of the Local Troop of Horse, a lay reader in Trinity Church, Woodbridge, and was buried in the Presbyterian churchyard there (Trinity Church having no graveyard). In his will he mentioned his son, Samuel Franklin Parker, his daughter Jane, his brother's widow in Woodbridge (omitting the name), and her children, his granddaughter Mary, sister, and his nephew James Parker; also his dwelling in New York City in which was his printing office; a small house, lot and stable; a house and three lots in Woodbridge; a small house and lot in Woodbridge; property in New Haven; pine land and a saw mill in Monmouth county and land in Wyoming, Pa. His wife was the Executrix.

James Parker was probably the first and also the foremost printer in the State, where the earliest newspapers were:

1777. New Jersey or United States Magazine.
1777. New Jersey Gazette, at Trenton.
1779. New Jersey Journal, Chatham, Feb. 10, 1779, by S. Kollock, who d. July 28, 1839, aged 88; an officer in the Revolution.
1784. New Jersey Journal, Elizabeth.
1786-'92. Gazette & Weekly Monitor—Shelby Arnett, New Brunswick.
1786-'92. New Brunswick Gazette—Abraham Blauvelt.
1792. N. B. Advertiser & Guardian—Blauvelt and Arnett.
1793. Guardian & Advertiser—Blauvelt to 1807.
1795. Jersey Chronicle.
1811. Fredonian, of New Brunswick.
1815. New Brunswick Times.

Nor was New Brunswick thought to be an unsuitable residence for an Ambassador. The Baron Paul Hyde de Neuville, French Minister from 1816 to 1822, made his home in New Brunswick, or, to be exact, just north of New Brunswick on the Easton Ave. road. This probably arose from his having made this his home when an exile here in 1809. At a dinner given him at the termination of a three years' term as Minister in 1819 he says: "Ten years before I reached these happy shores as an exile." He negotiated a treaty between France and the United States signed by himself and John Quincy Adams as Secretary of State, Aug. 15, 1822. He was Baron, Member of the Society of St. Louis, and had received the decoration of the Legion of Honor, etc. His farm was lately the Mailler place, and now I believe is the McCurdy place. He bred merino sheep on his farm and sold blooded stock, as an advertisement in the "Fredonian," June 2, 1814, shows.

In the land speculations of Suydam and Graham, and the Daniel Ewen map and plan for opening streets, parks, etc. (see Legislative Act of Oct. 4, 1837, approving it) New Brunswick was treated to a boom in the '30s. Abraham Suydam, in the early '30s, picked up most of the vacant farm land within the city limits, as shown by deed after deed to him. He interested some New York parties in the venture and, in 1836, he deeded to James Lorimer Graham, of New York, probably 1,000 acres (some of the parcels included in the deed have no acreage given) for $250,000. Daniel Ewen, also from New York, came here and mapped and plotted the property on the same plan as New York was laid out, in blocks 200x500. While this was not an incorporated company, a number of gentlemen were interested in the venture. The land lay in five large sections, and lots from each section were selected and lumped to make a share, and all of these allotments were put into a hat and drawn out till all were allotted. The venture was not a success; the property was covered with mortgages; lots were not in demand; taxes and interest had to be met; mortgages were foreclosed, and lots were sold for nominal prices. The map, however, was accepted, although it was plotted to cover not only the Suydam-Graham lots, but other property as well. The development of the city in the main has been along the lines of this map, and has resulted in a uniform and generally satisfactory arrangement of streets and blocks, although, in some cases, due to a misconception as to the public and private rights in unopened streets, many persons supposed that all streets marked on the map were public property, and, where a street was not opened, that the party using it was a squatter.

The finances of the "early city" were, I presume, largely those as found in New Brunswick, taking the 20 years from 1730 to 1750 of which we have minutes. The first and second expenditures we find are £20 for support of the poor, a tax assessed and collected. Paving was done by each house or lot owner (not done for him), under penalty of 40s. The Court House was built without tax, (presumably by subscription). The stone arch bridges were paid for by the city without tax. Just where the money came from is not clear. 3s. 6d. for a padlock for the stock is duly entered in the minutes. The streets and roads were made and repaired by the inhabitants when summoned; anyone failing to do so was fined 3s. In 1742 the tax for the poor had grown to £50, and was still the only tax, and was assessed not over 10s., or less than 1s. 2d. upon the inhabitants, according to their estates. Later in this year a tax of £40 was levied to finish the Court House, begun ten or twelve years before; and the money for "freedoms" to be applied to repairing the city engine. Imagine a fire department that got along without an appropriation raised by tax!

Next, we find a lot given and money subscribed to build a market house. In 1745 the city finances were in the hands of the collectors, the managers of the two bridges and the Court House, and the overseer of the poor. The city treasurer was constantly paying small bills; just where his funds came from is still a question; certainly not raised by tax. When a night watch was established in 1746, an exact list of the inhabitants was made, showing about 91 freeholders, or, say five hundred inhabitants, and, excepting ministers and doctors, every man had to take his turn when called. In 1747 a tax of £25 was assessed, without specifying the object, but evidently for the poor, as that was an annual tax. In 1748 £30 was assessed for the poor. In 1749 £40 for the poor was raised, the tax being not over 14s., nor under 1s., according to their respective estates. Here our minutes close, but show that for the 20 years the city tax varied from £20 to £40, and only for the poor and to build the Court House.

The next fifty years will have to be judged by what has gone before and what comes after. On a resumption of the minutes in 1796 we find the amount of tax fixed by town meeting on the first Monday in May. Beginning with 1801 as per minute book (really with the 1784, or third charter, and possibly with the 1763, or second charter, as we have no record of this period), for six years the smallest amount voted was $250 and the largest $500; then come two years with none voted, though the next year, 1809, $1,000 was voted to make up the deficit, dropping to $400 for the next two years. In 1812 $2,300 was voted, dropping to $150 the next year; in 1813 it rose to $1,500, in 1814 it was $1,400, and in 1815 none; and for the next eight years the citizens refused to vote the money recommended by Common Council. And so it goes along. In 1843 the appropriation was rejected, and again in 1850, though the 1849, or sixth charter, allowed Council $1,000 independent of town meeting. From the records it would appear that $700 was about the average in the 50 years. Some years there would be voted one item and the balance rejected; for example, in 1829 there was voted $500 for the Lancastrian School; another year $600 for a new engine; in 1838 $500 for streets and pumps; in 1842 $150 for school; while in the epidemic of 1845 $300 for a hospital was voted down. In 1802 there were seven reductions allowed in the taxes of that year, so that dissatisfaction with the assessments of to-day is no new thing. But it is of interest to look at the reductions: Louis Reimer, 45 cents; Benjamin Meyer, 42 cents; John Van Nuis, a large land owner, $2.20; John Auten, 60 cents; Peter Wyckoff, $1.10; Jasper Smith, 60 cents; Robert Eastburn, $1.15; $6.52 in all. In 1813 the city treasury was directed to open an account with each fund, or sum raised at town meeting, and charge orders to the fund out of which they are ordered paid; practically the beginning of a Budget System of Accounts.

In April, 1817, the city decided to cease the issue of paper money. They had then $3,574.10 in circulation. The establishment of banks in the city undoubtedly had something to do with this decision. Estimated receipts and estimated expenses were made up each year and largely determined whether a tax was necessary. One of these, May, 1823, has been preserved and is as follows:

Estimated Expenses

New fire hose	$124 40
Keeping fire engines and apparatus in order	75 00
Repair of streets	200 00
Repair buildings	125 00
Debt to State Bank	210 00
Salary Clerk C. C.	25 00
Salary Marshall	25 00
Incidentals	150 00
	$934 40
Treas. Com. 2½% in lieu of salary	23 36
	$957 76

Sources of Income

Int. John Wick's note	$31 78
Int. Andrew Agnew's note	42 44
Judgment I. Johnson	20 00

Int. Robt. Watt's note	7 86
Int. J. R. McChesney's bond	28 00
Int. Henry Perrine's bond	42 00
Int. John & Peter Voorhees' bond	17 50
Div. on U. S. 6% stock	104 80
Div. due this time next yr.	61 44
Rent hay scales	176 00
Revenue market house	200 00
Tavern licenses	240 00
Bal. in treasury	151 40
Bal. clerk market	87 50
	$1,210 72

The expenses being $957.76 and income $1,210.72, therefore a tax was not necessary.

In 1829 the population was; 1st Ward, 1,070; 2nd Ward, 1,100; 3rd Ward, 750; 4th Ward, 800; 5th Ward, 280; 6th Ward, 600; total 4,600.

In 1829 it was suggested that King and Queen streets have but one name, and Columbia was suggested; residents on Prince street also desired the name changed and Bayard was given. Things moved slowly in those days, as some persons had been trying to get the name of Prince street changed for 20 years, and it had been unofficially called Maiden Lane in 1808. In 1803 the Common Council refused a petition to mend the street to the steamboat wharf on the ground that it would establish a precedent that they would be entirely unable to live up to.[2]

---

[2] As a comparison with 1823, here is the full list of expenditures for 1856 (A. V. Schenck, Mayor, thirty-three years, or a generation after):

Suppers for Common Council	$40 00
Paving, city share	263 43
Paving, persons failing to pay	454 22
Lamps	1,477 18
City surveyor	37 50
City Solicitor	106 67
Assessor's and Collector's fees	225 00
Repair hay scales	10 75
Expenses of market	49 27
Relief family of late policeman	100 00
Clocks	57 00
Fire Department	261 58
Discount	94 30
Care buildings	77 07

According to the minutes of Town Meetings, at the first meeting under the new charter on Monday, May 10, 1801, there were elected: Staats Van Deursen, Town Clerk; Common Councilmen, Moses Guest, William Dunham, John Dennis, Jr., John Baker, Robert Boggs, Abraham Blauvelt. The meeting was held at the Court House (Prince and Queen), James Schureman being Chairman; the Chairman and Mayor were the same. Appropriations voted: 1801—$660; 1802—$250; 1803—$445; 1804—$500; 1805—$300; 1806—$500; 1807—0; 1808—0; 1809—$1,000; 1810—$400; 1811—$400. An extra meeting was held in July to vote money desired by Common Council; negatived. 1812—$2,300, for Market and school. 1813—$1,500, vote being 256 for, 106 against. 1814—$1,400. July, 1814, special town meeting was held to fill vacancy in Common Council and Peter Dayton was elected unanmiously. 1815—0; 1816—$975; D. D. Williamson then Town Clerk. 1817—0; 1818—refusal to vote money recommended by Common Council. 1819—0; 1820—0; 1821—0; 1822—0; 1823—appropriation negatived. 1824—10 candidates up for 6 Councilmen; 291 votes were cast for candidate polling highest no.; 109 for lowest. 1825—9 candidates; 29 votes for highest, 3 for lowest, and 2 got none. 1826—13 candidates, 162 votes for highest, 2 received 1 each for the appropriation of $1,000; for lighting the vote was 8 against and 13 for. 1827—0; 1828—$500. At a special meeting in 1828 to raise $1,250, Common Council were requested to publish the receipts and expenditures in both news-

Pumps and reservoirs	151 63
Extension of Neilson St., balance	50 00
Celebration July 4th	44 79
Printing and stationery	18 49
Night Watch	178 50
Salaries	581 99
Police	165 24
Sewer	35 49
Removal of nuisances	54 25
Expenses of council chamber	25 42
Treasurer's commission, 2½%	114 42
Balance due city	94
	$4,692 43

Expenditures thus increased from 1823, from $957.76 to $4,692.43; not quite 500%.

papers the week preceding the annual Town Meeting; money not voted. 1829—voted $500 for Lancastrian School; 1830—election by plurality of voices; C. L. Hardenbergh, Mayor. 1831—election by plurality of voices, $1,000. 1832—nothing voted. 1833—election by plurality of voters, $1,500. 1834—election by majority of votes, $800. 1835—nothing voted. In 1836 the election was by majority of votes; C. L. Hardenbergh, Mayor. 1837—vote on appropriation 160 for, 162 against, $1,000. 1838—special for raising $1,300 (engine $800, yeas 57, nays 164; streets $300, yeas 37, nays 184; lamps $200, years 53, nays 168). 1838—under Act amending charter to raise $1,500; current expenses, $530, yeas 134, nays 238; to pay debts, $970, yeas 133, nays 239. 1839—election. 1840—Mayor, D. W. Vail. At special election refusal to vote $1,600 by yeas 148, nays 203. At second special election same year to vote $1,600, yeas 209, nays 203. 1841—for Mayor, D. W. Vail, 304; L. Kirkpatrick, 358. Two full tickets, parts of each were elected. 1841—special, $2,200 to pay a judgment and other pressing debts; vote 217 for, 210 against, and 2 rejected. 1842—special election for same, $2,200; 258 for, 170 against. 1842—Mayor Fitz Randolph Smith, 257; Kirkpatrick 1. Special election, $1,500, pumps $200, 83 yeas, 86 nays; pavements, $150, 75 yeas, 94 nays; Lancastrian School, $150, 95 yeas, 74 nays; Town Hall $500, 82 yeas, 87 nays. 1843—$600 to satisfy judgment; 92 yeas, 106 nays. 1843—Mayor, John Acken, 224; Kirkpatrick, 1. Special election, voted, 287 yeas, 216 nays. 1844—Mayor, John Acken, 300; John W. Stout 1. 1845—Mayor, Wm. H. Leupp, 187; A. S. Neilson, 1. Special election voted $2,250. Special election Dec. 1, 1845, to vote for night watch, $1,000, and $300 for Hospital expenses; 14 yeas, 284 nays for first; 35 yeas, 263 nays for second. 1846—Mayor, John Van Dyke. 1847—Mayor, Martin A. Howell; special vote, $2,800. 1848—Mayor, A. F. Taylor; $1,000, 308 yeas, 205 nays. 1849—Mayor D. F. Randolph, 377 votes for Hospital during prevailing epidemic; yeas 106, nays 58. 1850—Mayor D. F. Randolph; whole no. of names on poll list, 297; to raise $1,000, yeas 91, nays 204, rejected 22. 1851—Mayor, Peter N. Wyckoff; $100 voted at special. 1852—Mayor,

John Van Dyke; special voted $2,000. 1853—Mayor, J. B. Hill; special voted, $3,000. 1854—Mayor, J. B. Hill. 1855—Mayor A. V. Schenck; special voted, $5,600. 1856—Mayor Lyle Van Nuis; special, $6,000, refused; special, $4,000 refused. 1857—Mayor, J. B. Kirkpatrick; special voted $7,000. 1858—Mayor, J. B. Kirkpatrick; special voted, $2,500. Special, Nov. 29, for Mayor: J. B. K. resigned; T. V. D. Hoogland, Mayor. 1859—Mayor, P. C. Onderdonk. 1860—Mayor, E. M. Patterson. 1861—Mayor, Lyle Van Nuis. 1862—Mayor, Lyle Van Nuis.

The above is a brief glance of 62 years of government by town meeting. The appropriation asked for by Common Council was frequently refused, or reduced.

In 1858 (the last town meeting of record) votes cast were 181 for, and 104 against $2,500 over and above the sum allowed to be raised by law, which was $1,000 (see Charter of 1849). This meeting was held June 1, 1858, and the tax levied and collected for 1858 was $3,243.76, or $743.76 more than the amount voted at the town meeting. The Legislature began to pass tax laws in 1851 and the government at Trenton began to supersede the good old town meetings of our fathers, when they met and stood up and counted noses, and from now on one may see how rapidly the taxes and expenditures of the city increased.

The Civil War added greatly and at once to our cost of government. Bounties and the care of families of the volunteers, which increased the cost of the poor, together with new items of expense never before seen, such as the election expense in 1861, first time; care of lunatics, 1862; as well as largely increased school expenses, beginning in 1852, when the district school system was replaced by a city school plan, and school houses and greatly increased expenditure became necessary. This period may be properly carried along to 1878, and the only real permanent improvement to show during it was the city water system, introduced by private enterprise but taken over by the city. The county tax had now become equal to the city budget, so that city, school and county had about $45,000 interest for this period, and we now have a bonded debt of $613,900, in addition to an increase of expenditure for the 27 years of 30 times as great, compared with five times as great, in the preceding 33 years, or from $5,000 in round figures to $150,000. In 1877, through a Commission on Streets and Sewers, the city promptly added a million to its bonded debt; taxes were collected with difficulty, and the city credit was at a low ebb. Elizabeth was in much the same situation and became bankrupt. Then a number of public-spirited citizens made an effort to pull the city credit up. A Sinking Fund was established; a city treasurer of character and standing was appointed, and the debt was slowly refunded from 7% and 6% bonds, to 5%, 4% and even 3½% bonds. Expenditures were held down for about ten years, when a change of policy resulted in another large increase in the yearly expenditure, though the debt remained about the same. The amount cancelled by the Sinking Fund was replaced by a new debt from time to time.

Going now forward to 1911, when W. Edwin Florance was Treasurer, we find the most complete financial statement ever presented to the city was prepared. The balance sheet of that year totaled $639,773.23 above balance, but when debit and credit items are eliminated it brought the expenditure of the year to $382,298.74 as compared with 1878 (33 years earlier) of about $150,000, or an increase of $230,000, over 1½ times as much more. One and a-half times in 33 years against 30 times in 22 years seems modest, until one considers that the 30 times amounted to about $145,000, while the 1½ times amounted to about $232,000. A per capita cost is more clearly grasped. In 1823 the per capita cost of the city government was about 25 cents; in 1856 about 50 cents; in 1878, after the Civil War, about $10, with a debt of $613,900; in 1911 about $16 with a debt of $888,785. Under the Commission government the cost became about $17 per capita and a debt of $1,084,939, although the gross bonded debt is $1,993,373, from which must be deducted the amount of the Sinking Fund.

Deductions are always rather dangerous, for there are so many elements to be considered. But I think the foregoing review of the city finances very fairly raises the question between the city of our fathers and the city of to-day, and makes very doubtful the advantages of the "Greater New Brunswick" that is so continually dinned into the public ear.

CHAPTER X

School History in New Brunswick—Growth of the Buildings and Their Cost—The Public Library Facilities Beginning in 1796—Data Concerning Proposed Canals, and the One Finally Completed, Its Beginnings, Progress, Cost, Etc.—The Camden and Amboy Monopoly.

AS early as 1693 there is to be found (in the "Colonial Laws" by Leaming and Spicer, folio 328) a School Act showing the provincial fostering of schools. There is mention of a meadow in Woodbridge "set apart for the free school and minister's accommodation," and next to Hugh Dunn's; on Dec. 18, 1672, there is noted a Free School in Bergen. Jacob Schureman was a schoolmaster in 1719, choir leader and reader. John Cholwell, in Burnet St., New Brunswick, in 1724, received a legacy in 1741, as it was to "John Cholwell, Schoolmaster." Edward Cooper taught school in New Brunswick in 1760, and in 1768 Caleb Cooper, A. B., of Kings, conducted a school under the supervision of a board; this was the beginning of Queens College Preparatory School, while Queens College acquired a building for a college in 1771. Both Preparatory School and College continue to-day.

There were other private schools in the late seventeen hundreds. In 1784 the New Brunswick School Company had a school at Church and Dennis; it was a stock company of 40 shares, probably not associated for profit. Free Public School History begins with the Trustees of the Hall Fund for a School for Poor Children. In 1812 the Hall Fund proposed to operate the "Lancastrian School," both a free and pay school, and the first to receive city aid. This school was in the discarded College Hall, that was purchased and moved to Schureman street at the city expense: was opened April 6, 1814, with 143 pupils. In the "Times" of August 17, 1815, appeared the first report of Col. John Neilson, first President of the Trustees of the Hall Fund. Council made an appropriation irregularly to help out the Hall Fund and to keep the school going. In 1824 the city appropriated $125 to help the school, and the same amount in 1825-'6-'7-'8-'9, and $500 in 1830.

In 1829 there were the Grammar School, Union Academy, Black's School and the Hobart and Lancastrian of pay schools. A Township Free School was started in 1840 but drifted into a pay school and was taught by A. W. Mayo as late as 1872. Mr. Charles D. Deshler, in writing a sketch of the Free Public School, passes over the Township schools and dates New Brunswick Public schools from a town meeting held in April, 1851.

That we may better understand the public school situation, it may be noted that the Freeholders' report for May 12, 1847, gives the amount received for County School Fund as $2,049, together with interest on surplus revenue, $1,350.20—$3,399.20 in all; of which North Brunswick Township received $813.60 as its share. The Act of 1846 provided for a report on schools to the Legislature by the School Superintendent, who was Dr. H. B. Pool, while the Rev. Dr. How, of New Brunswick, and the Rev. J. F. Halsey, of Perth Amboy, were examiners of common school teachers. North Brunswick Township consisted of nine districts, and three parts of districts, and New Brunswick was School District Number 1, as we find from a Trustee meeting held in the Lancastrian School on April 21, 1848, the officials being A. P. Provost, Stephen Moore, and John Page; the School Superintendent was Dr. H. B. Pool. The Trustees report orders drawn for Dr. Pool, Town Superintendent, for $318.98, "the whole amount due the District." In 1850 the School Fund apportioned North Brunswick Township was $653.91. On June 17 there was a town meeting called, to be held July 2nd, to vote for an appropriation of $1,000—$600 to repair the Market, $200 for the Lancastrian School, and $200 for the Fire Department. The election was held, but the appropriation rejected by a vote of two to one. From the above notes it would seem that the only New Brunswick free public school up to the opening of the Bayard School in 1851 was the Lancastrian School held in the city school house on Schureman St., which for a short time was operated under the Township Act.

The North Brunswick Township Report for 1853 states the School Fund from State to be $752.84, and interest on surplus revenue, $200.75. Mr. C. D. Deshler reports as received $752.84. School Meeting of District No. 1 at City Hall, New Brunswick, reported $1,641.83. By report of April, 1854, in accordance with the Act of 1846, by Mr. Deshler as Township Superintendent of Schools, North Brunswick had nine districts and three parts of districts, 2,861 children; 1,938, or 62%, had attended school; 100 had attended school twelve months, 979 six months, 1273 three months; schools were open for 9½ months; there were 35 teachers, 12 males and 23 females, with an average salary of $271. Four of the nine districts he commended—No. 10, Old Bridge; No. 11, Washington; No. 12, Weston's Mills; No. 1, New Brunswick. In 1853-'54 the whole cost was $7,070 for 1,030 children; the law allowed a tax of $3.00 per child.

In 1851 I find a school census, showing a total of 1,754 children between five and eighteen, of which 757 had received instruction.

New Brunswick was not satisfied with the Township School Law and undertook to provide better school accommodations; so purchased the old jail lot on Bayard street for $1,800, and two adjoining lots for $550; total for site, $2,350. On this lot they contracted for a school building with P. M. Wyckoff, Jeptha Cheesman and I. B. Inslee. The architect, John Hall, received $100. A cupola was added at $350; furnaces at $468.56; furniture, $1,660; fence, $263.50; blinds and lightning-rod, $317; bringing the cost of the completed building and lot up to $12,619.06. This building had in the main part twelve rooms and in the front were four rooms more—sixteen in all. On Aug. 2, 1853, the new Bayard School would not accommodate the children and the session room of the Presbyterian church was rented at forty dollars per annum. Children aged from five to seven were moved into it and it was called the Junior School. In July, 1854, a lot was bought of Phœbe Harriot on Liberty Street as an outlet for the Bayard Street School. A lot was bought of Clark Letson on Old Trenton Road (French St.) at four dollars a front foot, a note being given for $500 in payment, and a one-room school for colored children decided upon, to accommodate one teacher and sixty children. The plan was made by E. B. Wright, for which he was paid three dollars; the building was built by John Inslee and fenced for $1,050; this was known as the French Street School. Forty desks were brought from the suspended Juvenile School in the Presbyterian Session House, and a new school was opened Monday, June 22, 1855. In this year the law provided for a School Board of twelve, two from each ward. There was also a night school opened in the Bayard School the same year.

In 1856 the census was 2,520 children. In 1858 nineteen teachers were employed and the basement of the Methodist Church rented for fifty dollars per annum. One janitor took care of all the schools for $350 per annum. In 1859 the census was 2,755 children; 1,033 at the public school, 509 at the private school, 618 at work and 595 who did not attend. The census of 1860 was 2,897 children. The Bayard and French Streets, and a building rented of John Lyle in the rear of the Bayard, were the buildings in use; Mr. Lyle's house was rented for $45 annually in place of the Methodist Church basement. In 1861 the school census was 3,010; attendance, 1877, viz., at Bayard, 1,100; French St., 60; and a lot was bought of James Bishop on Carmen St. for $750. In 1862 the census was 3,051 —1809 attending school. The Bayard colored school, Robert Lyle's and the Methodist Church not accommodating the children, all outside districts were barred. Still some children were obliged and willing to stand, so as to attend school. To relieve the situation the Carmen Street lot was built upon; a brick school of eight rooms, designed by Duncan J. McRae; the architect received 1% or $33; E. B. Wright, carpenter, $1,532; John Cheeseman, mason, $1,468; John Johnson, painter, $162; John Jenkins, slater, $236.73, at 6½ per square; the tinner, $94.10; blinds and extras, $250.24; fence $275; making $619.-34; furnace, $200, furniture $431.38; paving $371.24. The lot cost $750. The total was $5,803.69. It was opened April 6, 1863, with appropriate special ceremonies and the Bayard was relieved, so that instead of 1,100 it had 771 pupils; Carmen

Street School 349 in five rooms; French Street School 58, while a mission building had been secured for the colored children. St. Peter's asked for a share of the school money in 1862. The Bayard then had 18 rooms; Carmen Street, 5 rooms; French Street, 1 room; house rear of Bayard, 2 rooms; Methodist Church, 3 rooms—total 29 rooms. Five classes were accommodated at the Carmen Street School, and the teaching force was one principal, 4 vice-principals, 9 primary teachers and 3 teachers at Carmen Street.

A suit for a share in the school money was brought in the Supreme Court by St. Peter's Church. The colored children were moved to a mission building on Hamilton Street, rented at $25 per annum, and the French Street School building was enlarged to a two-room school for white children. The colored children were moved again later from the Mission on Hamilton Street to Mrs. Ryno's, 94 Church Street, rented at $50 a year.

The cost of school property fifty years ago, including three school buildings, was $20,975.75. The Bayard School and rented building in the rear, eighteen rooms, enrolled 1,400 children; house was leased at Bayard rear for five years at $50 a year, and 94 Church Street, Mrs. Ryno's, colored children, three years, at $100 a year. Mrs. Masterson, janitress of Carmen Street School, was paid ten dollars a month. The French Street building was enlarged to three rooms at a cost of $3,843.20. There was purchased a lot on Hale Street of John T. Jenkins for $1,000; it was 100 ft. square. A plan of building was accepted for colored children: a two-room building, $6,873.52; grading and fence, $249; drain $125; total $7,247.52. This building had 158 children in 1900, but was closed in 1901; it was located near French and must not be confounded with the Park School, also on Hale Street, and later called the Nathan Hale School. Livingston Avenue having been graded in 1861 a lot was bought in 1872 of Boundy and Letts, 100 x 210, for $15,000 and in 1873 a lot was bought of Campbell on Guilden Street for $2,433.05.

The schools had again outgrown their quarters and five rooms were rented in the Hoyt building at $400 per annum.

A written contract was entered into with a janitor to take charge of all the schools for $800, he to pay his assistants, and in 1873 this amount was increased to $1,200.

A five-room brick school was built on Guilden Street, one story, costing: Voorhees & Brown, masons, $6,990; Stephen DeHart, carpenter, $4,474; slater, $623.08; stone, $1,500; painting, $228; drainage, $697.11; heating, $600—total, including lot, $17,545.24.

About the same time a new High School had been begun on the Livingston avenue lot; it was completed and opened in 1876. It was a three-story, brick and stucco building, and, when finished, contained six rooms on the first floor, four rooms and an assembly room on the second floor, and an auditorium on the third floor. $30,000 was borrowed of the State. Stephen H. DeHart was architect, and a special Act of the Legislature authorized an issue of $50,000 in bonds to pay for it. The bills were: E. B. Goltra, carpenter, $21,350; Bassonet, mason, $22,612; McKeag, heating, $3,750; plumbing, $447; gas fitting, $447; architect, 2½%; stuccoing, $1,550; grading, $275; furniture, $825; painting and fence. These items total $52,281, and lot $15,000, altogether $67,281, but the payments show that the full amount of cost was $70,728.05. In 1890 the auditorium was altered to correspond with the floor below and the second floor assembly was altered to hall and two class-rooms; again in 1916 the assembly was changed to an auditorium and two class-rooms, and another class-room made in the front out of two small rooms; the cost of these changes is not given. This building, with the Guilden Street School, provided ample accommodations; in fact, for fifteen years the schools were gradually growing and filling up, and it was 1890 before lack of room began to be felt. In 1888 the Board purchased four lots on Hale Street, on the Park, for $900, with a view to a school there, and built a four-room structure costing $6,927.96. The school was opened in 1896.

In 1882 separate schools for colored children were terminated by law and the French Street wooden building was rented in 1884 to the Fourth Reformed Church at three dollars per week. In 1885 additional rooms at Carmen Street were put to use, not all of the building having been used, and there were two vacant rooms at Hale Street.

In 1893 the Bayard School had a new front added, making six class rooms and a Board room in place of the old front and four rooms; so the school, less the rented building in the rear, had then only eighteen rooms, costing $9,373.96. In 1895 the rear of Bayard School and the Carmen School were remodeled, making coat rooms, which they did not have before, at a cost of $10,800; divided 12/17 to Bayard, $7,623.60, and 5/17 to Carmen (on the basis of 12 and 5 rooms), $3,176.40. Thirty years ago the cost of school buildings was $121,339.76.

In 1898 a lot was bought on French Street for $4,700, and a building contracted for at $27,820. Paid over the contract $7,752.26, a total of $35,572.26.

In 1906 the four-room Park School, built in 1895, was enlarged to an eight-room building at a cost of $13,582; total cost, $21.409.96. The cost of school buildings to 1906 was $203,195.94.

The Lord Stirling replaced the Carmen Street School, having nine rooms and an auditorium, at a cost of $43,183.93; and the Lincoln replaced the Guilden on a new site, with nine rooms and auditorium, costing $53,820.86. These buildings enabled the doing away with part-time classes and left one vacant room over, but part-time began again the next year. $4,500 was spent for a new heating plant in the Washington School and $3,000 for improvements to the Bayard, including twelve new windows, floors, etc.[1]

A part of the educational history of New Brunswick relates to the public library facilities. The Union Library Company, formed Jan. 15, 1796, was the beginning of library conveniences, which have continued through varying vicissitudes to date. The Union Library Co. was organized by thirteen gentlemen at the "New Coffee House," when a constitution was drafted, shares fixed at $5, with dues of $1.50 per annum per share. The following gentlemen were stockholders: Dr. Charles Smith, John Baker, Thomas Hill, Timothy Brush,

---

[1] For a full tabulated form of the growth and cost of school buildings in New Brunswick, see Appendix.

Moses Guest, John J. Voorhees, David Abeel, J. W. Scott, Abraham Blauvelt, John Vredenburgh, Mr. Leupp, Mr. Cholwell, Mr. Van Norden, James Neilson, James Swift, Aaron Hassert, Andrew Ryder, Rev. John Croes. In 1811 the treasurer reported "$86 due and likely to remain so." In 1816 Mr. Hill, who had been Librarian for fifteen years, died, and Miss Hannah Scott undertook to be Librarian and had the books moved to her house, northwest corner Albany and Neilson streets. Finally, the New Brunswick Library Company, formed about 1820, proposed to unite the two libraries, and a committee, Dr. Croes, James Crommelin and C. L. Hardenbergh, effected the consolidation. The first annual meeting of the combined libraries was held Apr. 26, 1821, and a statement made that they had 600 volumes and that the shares would be $10. Abraham Blauvelt was Librarian, and books were to be at his house, open Wednesday and Saturday, 6 to 8 P. M. Rev. John Croes was President. At some later day the Rutgers College Library acted as custodian of the books, and in 1868 transferred them to the Y. M. C. A. as a nucleus of a library.

In 1882 the New Brunswick Free Circulating Library was formed, the outgrowth of a private "Book Club;" this Library continued for 23 years, when it was consolidated with the Free Public Library, which, as a combined Library, is now (1924) in its 42nd year, having a handsome, commodious building and being one of the city's permanent institutions.

The following matters in connection with this subject of the city's Libraries are interesting:

[From "The Guardian, or New Brunswick Advertiser," for Wednesday, November 14, 1792].
"TAKE NOTICE:
"The subscriptions to the New Brunswick LIBRARY will be called for on MONDAY next.
"November 13, 1792."

[From the same, Tuesday, February 16, 1796].
"Mr. Blauvelt:
"Being a member of the Union Library Society lately established in this city, I anxiously wish to promote its usefulness,

and will thank you to publish the following abstract from the constitution for the information of such gentlemen as live in the country, who may be inclined to patronize an institution founded on the most liberal principles. The object is to disseminate useful knowledge by enabling almost every one to subscribe, and consequently have an opportunity of perusing a variety of the most approved authors on very easy terms. Any person inclining to become a member may have an opportunity of examining the constitution and laws, of which the following is a summary extract, by applying to J. W. Scott, Secretary, in Albany Street.

"It may be proper to add that the subscribers are already so numerous, that a committee has been appointed to purchase books to a considerable amount, which in a few days will be ready for delivery.

"S. G. B.

"N. Brunswick, Feb. 12, 1796."

[Abstract from the Constitution of the Union Library, Instituted the First day of February, 1796].

"1st. The terms of subscription are five dollars for each share to be paid in monthly instalments of one dollar each, commencing the first instant.

"2nd. Any person may become a member previous to the first of February, 1797, by applying to the Secretary, subscribing the constitution, and paying the sum specified in the first article.

"3rd. Every share shall be liable to quarterly payments of thirty seven and an half cents.

"4th. Monthly meetings of the Society are to be held till the first of July next, and quarterly after that period.

"5th. Any person desirous of becoming a member of this Society after the first of February next is to be proposed at one meeting and balloted for the next.

"6th. The property of subscribers is transferable by will, inheritance or assignment.

"7th. Each member at any meeting is at liberty to propose such authors as he may think proper, which are to be voted for at the next meeting.

"8th. The Librarian shall take a receipt for every book he delivers.

"9th. Folios may be retained 21 days, Quartos 14, Octavos and all smaller books 7 days, provided, nevertheless, that members in the country be allowed double those periods."

We come now to the matter of the Delaware and Raritan Canal, which once played an important part in the history of the city.

On April 18, 1676, William Penn, Gawen Lowrie, Edward Byllynge, Nicholas Lucas and Edward Warner gave authority to James Wase, Richard Hartshorne and Richard Guy or any two of them to secure information of one Augustine Heermans, an able surveyor, to go up the river Delaware as far as Newcastle, or farther (as far as a vessel of 100 tons could go) as "we intend to have a way cut across the country to Sandy Hook." Here we have the first move looking towards a canal across New Jersey.

In the New Brunswick "Guardian" of Nov. 15, 1804, the adjournment of the Legislature on the 13th is referred to with a list of Acts passed. No. 16 was an Act to incorporate certain persons for the purpose of opening a communication by water from the tide-water of the Raritan River, at or near New Brunswick, to the tide-water of the Delaware River at or near Lamberton (now in Trenton). The same newspaper, of May 16, 1805, gives a detailed route for a canal under the above Act, under a charter to William Paterson and others, copying it from the "Aurora and General Advertiser," published in Philadelphia from 1797 to 1824, as follows:

"The elevation from a point at Lamberton at tide-water to tide-water at Raritan, was found to be 40 ft., 10', 4-8", to the Landing Bridge, 50 ft. 11' 8". The route as surveyed is from Lamberton 1 mile, 5 ch.; through low ground at Trenton; thence via Assanpink Creek to Burroughs Mills, 1 mile, 4 ch., 50 l., thence to Burnt Mills, 1¼ miles, 5 ch., 44 l., water 4½ ft. deep in shallowest place; thence to Miry Run, 32 ch., water very deep; thence to head of pond, 36 ft., and water 1 to 2½ ft. deep; thence a canal to be dug, 48 ch., through a soft meadow to Coleman's; the fall is 4' 7". From Coleman's Bridge to bend of the creek below Hutchinson's Mill, canal 62 ch., and fall 2 ft. 4". From Hutchinson's Mill to Cranberry Pond, 32 ch., 11 l., water 5 to 6 ft. deep and very wide; thence on the Assanpink to Duck Pond on Stony Brook, 2 miles, 57 ch. through Maidenhead, great meadow, deep black meadow, nearly on a level, through which a canal is to be cut, which is estimated can be done for $40 a rod. From Duck

Pond down the Long Reach on Stony Brook to the bend is 55 ch., water 3 ft. deep, at lowest tide. From Long Reach to the inlet, 43 ch., a canal to be cut through a line (?) meadow ground; thence down Schenck's Reach, 39 ch., water about 3 ft. deep. Thence a canal to be cut 114 ch., to the bend below the bridge on the road leading from Princeton to Rowley's Mill; from bridge to mouth Stony Brook on Millstone is 53 ch., water deep. Thence to Mayor Gulick's Mill, where road to New York crosses Millstone River, 150 ch., 87 l., water 4' to 8' deep. Thence a canal to be cut 38 ch. through Mayor Gulick's meadow full 6' 5½ in.; thence to Cruger's Mills is 74 ch., 50 l., water 6' to 10' deep; thence to Oppie's Cove is 150 ch., 60 l.; water 3½ ft. to 4 ft. deep; thence canal across Oppie's Cove 25 ch.; thence down river to Van Doren's Mill, 89 ch., 3 l., water 5' deep; thence a canal 32 ch. through meadow to bend of river below Griggstown bridge; thence to Sythoff Mill is 276 ch., 26 l., water 4 to 4½ ft. deep; thence to bridge at Millstone village is 167 ch., 77 l., water about 4½ ft. deep; thence to mouth of Millstone, 132 ch., 8 l., water about 200 yards is rapid and shoal; thence to mouth of river broad and deep, 4 to 4½ ft. deep; from thence to tide water of Brunswick Landing is 7 mi., 18 rods, which may be made navigable at small expense."

Upon reviewing the report of the Commissioners appointed to make the mensuration as above plotted, I find the distance from Delaware tide water to Raritan tide water at Brunswick is 40 miles; the whole distance of canal to be cut to make good inland navigation from Philadelphia to New York is 8 miles, 44 ch.; all the rest of the water is, at the lowest, 3 ft. deep. It would be necessary to place 13 locks, the expense of each lock about $1,000. A capital stock of 4000 shares at $25 each would be required, on the supposition that it would cost $100,000. It was believed that the whole expense would not be over $12.50 a share.

The newspaper article referred to was signed by A. Celgen of New Jersey. The route follows the Raritan, Millstone, Stony Brook canal to Skippetanken branch of Assinpink Creek and down to Lamberton and Delaware; there were 8 mills on the route. This is the same route along which the canal was finally dug, only the water courses were paralleled instead of being deepened, thus avoiding the mills, dams, etc.

The New Brunswick "Times" of Feb. 29, 1816, mentions an Act of the Legislature of Feb. 13, 1816, appointing a Committee to examine and suggest a canal route. The Committee were John Rutherford, John N. Simpson and Dr. George Holcomb. Simpson was a merchant of New Brunswick and had a book store in 1811; was a member of the Team and Steamboat Co. in 1814 (I believe the first Steamboat Co. in America), and Cashier of the Bank of New Brunswick in 1821. Three routes were suggested:
    a. By South River and Manalapan.
    b. By Lawrence's Brook and Heath Cole's Brook.
    c. By the Millstone.

In 1823 George Holcombe, L. Q. C. Elmer and Peter Kean were appointed a Committee by the State to report on the practicability and expediency of a canal. This Commission reported recommending the State to undertake the work. This report was referred to Messrs. Griffith, Woodhull, McDowell, Drake and Wurtz, and this Commission reported that, in view of its problematical success and immense expenditure, the charter be given a private company. At the last session of the Legislature in 1824 the Delaware & Raritan Canal Co. was incorporated. The charter was granted on December 30. This enacted that John N. Simpson, James Neilson and Floyd S. Bailey, and all and every person who shall hereafter subscribe according to the mode prescribed in the Act, shall be incorporated. The capital stock was to be $800,000, with power to increase it to $1,000,000. Subscriptions were to be opened on the first Monday in April at Trenton and New Brunswick, and to continue open for three days, $10 to be paid at date of subscribing. The Company was to be managed by 17 Managers. Benjamin Wright, Canvass White and Ephraim Beach, Jr. were appointed Commissioners to determine the route of the canal. The tolls were limited to 2 cents per mile per ton on coal and 4 cents per mile per ton for merchandize.

As the uses of the Delaware had been defined by a Convention between the two States of New Jersey and Pennsylvania in 1783, the Act provided for the consent of the State of Pennsylvania to be obtained, and, in case it was not obtained by June, 1826, the Act was to be void. The Legislature of Pennsylvania was at once petitioned for the desired permission to divert the water necessary to operate the canal, estimated at 1/40 of the water of the Delaware when at its lowest. Efforts were made at once to get the permission of that State. Mr. Bailey and Mr. Neilson went to Harrisburg to influence the Legislature. J. M. Bispham assisted in Trenton and presented a bill of $75.45 itemized for his services, including numerous hot punches, which were 25 cents a glass at that time.

The engineers, Wright, White and Beach reported that the canal should begin at the south-west corner of a dock on the Raritan known as "Martin's Dock," thence up the valley of the Raritan to the junction of the Millstone; thence up the valley of the Millstone, passing near Kingston, to the junction of Stony Brook; thence up the valley of Stony Brook south of Princeton, and thence through Lawrence meadows to Trenton, crossing Assanpink Creek and easterly up to the penitentiary, passing the village of Lamberton to the bank of the Delaware. While awaiting the action of the State of Pennsylvania the Committee to receive subscriptions, John N. Simpson, James Neilson, Charles Parker, Garret D. Wall and Floyd S. Bailey, and the Board of 17 Managers, who were:

John N. Simpson	Joseph Bullock	Joseph Rogers
Jas. F. Randolph	Samuel Clement	John Marshall
Lambert Rickey	Ephraim Bateman	Aaron O. Dayton
John T. McDowell	Richard L. Beaty	Floyd S. Bailey
James Neilson	Wm. Halstead, Jr.	Pierson Hunt
Nathl. S. Wyckoff		John Davisson

were left uncertain how they should proceed, owing to legal questions due to the action of Pennsylvania. In April, 1825, the opinion of Chancellor James Kent was obtained, and, acting under it, the Managers organized at the house of Joseph M. Bispham, Trenton, May 19, 1825, by the appointment of John N. Simpson as Chairman, Charles Parker, Treasurer and James Neilson, Secretary. A form of subscription was drawn by Garret D. Wall and copied into the subscription book. Still feeling uncertain on the whole subject, at a meeting to open the subscription books on May 23, Richard Stockton being at the place of meeting in the tavern, they obtained his opinion as to opening the subscription books. It being favorable, the books were opened, and, on May 26, the books were closed, when lawyer George Wood, William P. Dear (sheriff?) and James Wood were asked to witness the making up of the list. For the 6,000 shares offered for subscription (2,000 having been reserved for the State of New Jersey, which had reserved the right to subscribe for one-quarter of the stock in the Act granting the charter) there were found 77,480 shares subscribed, twelve men having subscribed for 6,000 each. There were 48 subscribers in all. So, in scaling down the subscriptions, the twelve men who subscribed for the entire capital stock got each 462 shares. It will be of interest to state who the twelve men were who intended to divide up the canal stock between themselves. They were:

Floyd S. Bailey,
Peter Remsen,
Francis Depaw,
Francis Staunton,
Levi Coit,
William Bayard,

Joshua Blake,
Levi Baker,
James Crane,
David Meeker,
Horatio H. Fish,
Thaddeus Nichols.

James Neilson, who had modestly subscribed for only 1500 shares, or one quarter of the stock, got scaled down to 120 shares.

The Commissioners again felt the need of advice, and on June 12, 1825, obtained the opinion of Gen. Garret D. Wall (who drew the Act of Incorporation) upon their past action in receiving subscriptions and upon the next step of paying the $100,000 bonus to the State required by the Act of incorporation. This opinion being favorable, Charles Parker, as treasurer of the Canal Company, paid to himself as Treasurer of the State of New Jersey the $100,000. This it was thought best he should retain for the present. This payment is dated May 26 on the Canal Co.'s accounts in one place, and June 24 in another. The receipt given by Charles Parker to the

Commissioners is put on record in Trenton in the secretary's office as of July 7, 1825. As a matter of fact, Charles Parker, Treasurer, had had the money after May 26, the day the subscriptions were paid in.

Floyd S. Bailey was then directed to invest $50,000 in U. S. 6% stock, and on June 9 he purchased, through an order of Levi Coit, $50,000 U. S. Scrip of 1813 at $101\frac{1}{4}$ and $101\frac{3}{8}$, and interest and commission, paying therefor $50,846.72. So, out of the $160,000 received from the first installment of $26\frac{2}{3}$ a share paid at the time subscriptions were made, but $9,153.28 remained. This was in the hands of Floyd S. Bailey, the entire $60,000 having been turned over to him to make the purchase of U. S. stock, although Charles Parker was the treasurer of the Board of Commissioners.

The Board of Managers now elected James Neilson as the treasurer of the Canal Co. and he gave a bond, July 20, 1825, for $40,000, with himself, his brother, John Neilson, and David Voorhees as sureties. There was some delay in turning the accounts over to the treasurer, as F. S. Bailey had been acting as disbursing officer and had paid Canvass White, the engineer engaged in locating the canal, $1,500 on account, together with some other bills.

The obtaining of the charter and the effort to secure corresponding action at Harrisburgh seem to have been left to Garret D. Wall and James Neilson, and while the Legislatures of the two States were in session, they spent much time at Trenton and Harrisburgh. They were at Harrisburgh by appointment of the Board of Managers on Dec. 13, 1825, and were there continuously 17 days from Dec. 22 to Jan. 6, 1826, their bill of expenses amounting to $81.68.

On Jan. 28, 1826 the stockholders elected a new board of managers, the meeting being held at George Follet's Tavern in New Brunswick, which was as follows:

John N. Simpson	Richard Stockton	Elisha Tibbits
James Neilson	Thos. Cadwalader	James Kent
John T. McDowell	Gen. G. D. Wall	Peter Remsen
William Halstead	Peter Kean	John Potter
Floyd S. Bailey	Rich'd Hartshorne	Francis Depaw
Levi Baker	George Griswold	

Wall and Neilson returned to Harrisburgh and remained there till March 24, fifty-three days. The expense bill, including printing and traveling expenses, was $477.23. As compared with present day methods, when important corporation legislation is being procured, this expense is impressive. The Act finally obtained from Pennsylvania dated March 28, 1826, was so unsatisfactory that it brought the Managers to a standstill.

The canal had now been located; a map of the route and elevations made; the engineers' bills were $4,931.95. Peter Forman and Staats Van Deursen were paid $65 for services for obtaining the right of way. Terhune & Letson received $36 for a set of books, $183.47 for expenses of various meetings of managers, and $85 for printing. The legal expenses were as follows:

Gen. Garret D. Wall, services and expenses........$3,283.50
Charles Parker, Treasurer to Commissioners........ 150.00
George Wood, Counsel 500.00
Horace Binney, Counsel 200.00

$4,133.50

There were legal opinions by James Kent, Richard Stockton, and Daniel Webster, which I presume are included in Gen. Garret D. Wall's expenses.

James Neilson as Commissioner, Agent and Treasurer, covering about three years' services from before the charter in December, 1824, until the Company was wound up in February, 1827, received $2,500.

In noting these expenditures we are a little ahead of certain events. After the unsatisfactory Act passed in March, 1826, the Treasurer, James Neilson, was authorized to loan the Company funds to the stockholders to the amount of $6 on each share, taking notes and the stock as security. Francis Staunton, Horatio Fish, Thaddeus Nichols and Joshua Blake availed themselves of this offer, borrowed $2,772, and put up 462 shares each as security. The Company sold some of its United States 6% stock to enable it to make these loans. The Managers now felt that they needed more legal advice, and this time, Sept. 11, 1826, they went to Horace Binney, and, Oct. 9,

1826, he advised them that the charter had failed owing to legislation by Pennsylvania; that the bonus paid the State should be returned and repaid to the subscribers. Daniel Webster, on Oct. 3, gave exactly the same opinion, rather intimating that he did not exactly consider it as an "opinion," as it was so evident a matter that there was no room for any other view.

The Managers, in view of the above opinions, on Feb. 24, 1827, paid the subscribers $20 a share, or $120,000 of the $160,000 which had been paid in. That ended the first effort for a canal across the State of New Jersey. Three years of hard work and $40,000 were sunk in the effort, and canal transportation was put back six years, as it was Feb. 4, 1830, when the second Act was passed under which the canal was finally built. The fatal error in the first Act was making the consent of Pennsylvania necessary. Under the second Act of 1830 Pennsylvania was not consulted and full power to construct the canal was conferred.

The Commissioners to receive subscriptions now (1830) were: James Parker and James Neilson, of Middlesex; John Potter, of Summit; William Halstead, of Hunterdon; Garret D. Wall, of Burlington. The general provisions of the Act were much like the one of 1824. The books were opened at Trenton on March 23, 1830, and 375 shares of the 500 necessary to incorporate were subscribed. The next day, at Princeton, 410 shares were subscribed, and the third day, at New Brunswick, 349 shares were subscribed—1134 in all. A contrast to the subscriptions to the same object in 1825! Matters dragged along till Apr. 6, when Richard Stockton stepped forward and subscribed for 4800 shares, "putting his entire fortune into the venture," and the Company was incorporated and a board of nine directors elected, viz:

James Parker	John Potter	James Neilson
William Halstead	Gen. G. D. Wall	Rich. F. Stockton
John R. Thomson	Joseph McIlvain	James Green

and they organized by electing Stockton, President; Neilson, Treasurer; Thomson, Secretary and Canvass White, Engineer.

The reluctance to subscribe was due to two reasons: first, the failure of the original effort and its contingent loss of $40,000; and, second, the fact that on Feb. 4, 1830, the very date of the Act to incorporate the Canal Company, another Act to incorporate the Camden and Amboy R. R. Company was also passed. The opinion of Alexander Brown & Sons of Baltimore then given, "that railroads would entirely supersede canals," was undoubtedly shared by others.

The report of the Commissioners is in the handwriting of James Parker; the list of subscribers, 29 in all, for 5,539 shares (the number voted at the first election for nine directors) are all interesting, and should be incorporated into any historical record of the Canal movement.

The rivalry between the Canal and the Railroad bade fair to be ruinous to both, but better counsel prevailed, and, a year later, Feb. 15, 1831, an Act allowing the two companies to consolidate, if seven-eighths of the stock voted to do so, was passed; and the men who controlled the Canal at once stepped to the front in the Railroad, dividing the honors and responsibilities with the Stevens' party.

While Stockton stepped into the gap and enabled the Canal Company to go on by subscribing for 4800 shares, John Potter, of Princeton, seems to have been really the financial support of the enterprise, for in a later list of stockholders, made shortly afterwards, John Potter appears as the holder of 3599 shares, while Stockton held 1680 shares, James Craig of Philadelphia 1000 shares, and William Gaston of Savannah had become interested to the amount of 200 shares. It is of interest that John Jacob Astor thought well enough of the venture to loan Richard F. Stockton $100,000 on 1000 shares of the joint stock and his personal bond as security. The stock was paid for in sixteen installments running from May, 1830, to Sept., 1832, and in October, 1832, an additional issue was made.[1]

---

[1]For the Articles of Agreement of the Canal Company and the owners and occupants of wharves and lands adjacent to the Raritan river in the city of New Brunswick, see the Appendix.

It is of interest to New Brunswickers to know that Canvass White, the engineer of the Canal, urged upon Stockton and Neilson as a private speculation the buying of lands on Sonman's Hill.

The Canal Company began paying dividends on July 1, 1833, when the first dividend of 3% was paid, amounting to $42,000, and it continued this dividend at regular intervals of six months, although the canal was not opened till about June, 1834, and the earnings for 1834 were only $11,604.19. In 1834, however, the earnings were $49,108.38, and, in 1836, $54,574.62.

Still needing money to complete the Canal after the stock was all sold, the Company issued, Aug. 27, 1833, at 6%, a 30-year loan of $800,000 at 108, of which John Potter alone took $405,000, Nicholas Biddle $245,000, R. L. Stevens $100,000, and the Trenton Banking Co. $50,000. This "with some chuckling," as the New York financiers had demurred over the issuance of such a loan and their ability to float it. The Canal was now an assured success and the further history appears in its annual reports.

One word in conclusion about the Canal's rival, the Camden and Amboy R. R. The Committee to receive subscriptions to the Railroad stock was Samuel G. Wright, James Cook of Middlesex, Abraham Brown, Jeremiah H. Sloan, Henry Freas. Alexander Brown & Co., of Baltimore, whose opinion on the two methods of transportation has been quoted, were importing rails for a road running 13 miles out of Baltimore, and they were consulted as to the best rail to use on the Camden and Amboy; they described the rail they were importing as follows: rails 20 ft. long, 2¼ in. wide and half an inch thick; 15 holes in each rail for nailing down and ends mitred to avoid jar in running off one end upon the next. 4560 rails weighed 139 tons, nearly 61 lbs. to the bar or rail, and cost £8 per ton, or about $56 in this country. Canvass White was engineer of both Canal and Railroad and, on Oct. 28, 1831, reported 28 sections of the Canal under contract, excavation having commenced in November, 1830.

In 1841 the Canal net earnings were $32,034.35, while those of the Railroad were $372,682.12—over ten times that of the Canal. The Directors stated, however, that the Canal had only just got into good operation, and they expressed great confidence that in a few years it would add largely to the profit. It had not, however, in 1846 realized over 1% on its cost. But this prediction was justified by later earnings, as in 1847 the Canal earned $161,707.06 net, while the Railroad earned $408,465.30 net. Instead of ten times, the Railroad earnings were now only more than 2½ times that of the Canal. In 1852 the net earnings of the Railroad were $478,413.94; that of the Canal, $244,556.68, so that for the five years then past the Canal had advanced to net earnings of one-half that of the Railroad. In 1857 the net earnings of the Railroad were $667,811.79; that of the Canal, $289,921.88. The Railroad now began to draw ahead of the Canal, as its earnings were considerably over twice that of the Canal, for in 1863 the Railroad net earnings were $1,172,724, the Canal's, $537,482.

New Jersey was long known as the "State of the Camden & Amboy." This arose from the fact that special and exclusive favors to the Camden & Amboy R. R. were granted, and the right to subscribe to one quarter of the stock was reserved by the State, which also received in addition to dividends 10 cents for each passenger carried across the State (that is, passengers between New York and Pennsylvania). The amount paid the State by the Company in 1844 was $51,502. Up to Jan. 1, 1846, they had paid a total of $531,213.04. For the year 1845 the State received $59,497 (one-fifth of the net income), while the stockholders the same year received $252,000.

When the rail route, Camden to Jersey City, via New Brunswick, was opened Sept. 25, 1848, a transit duty of 18 cents was paid the State on each through passenger. The transit duty, dividends and interest for 1848 to the State amounted to $78,576.81, and the total transit duties for the eight years, 1840-1847, was $273,721.12. This state of affairs led to much controversy. The amounts received by the State from the Railroad and the Canal went far to defraying the State's expenses, but, on the other hand, the feeling against the monopoly was very bitter.

CHAPTER XI

The Great Tornado of 1835—The Destruction It Caused in New Brunswick, Piscataway and a Few Nearby Places—Full Accounts from a Local Newspaper of the Time and from Professor Lewis C. Beck—Great Business Period of a New Sort—The Mayors from 1840 to the Civil War.

THE following account of the great tornado in June, 1835, is taken from the "New Brunswick Times' Extra," of Saturday morning, June 20:

"Our city experienced a most awful visitation about five o'clock yesterday afternoon, a TORNADO having swept through it from the western suburbs down to the river, and in its resistless course destroying a vast amount of property, to which, we regret to say, must be added a number of lives. It was first seen approaching from the west, and, from the clouds of dust, shingles, etc., that rose in the air, was supposed by the inhabitants of the lower and central parts of the city to proceed from a heavy fire, and the alarm bells were rung; but the flying of roofs, rafters and trees in every direction soon taught them that a hurricane was rushing with awful violence through the town, leaving a complete mass of ruins to mark its track. Where it first commenced we cannot correctly learn, but it is said in the vicinity or north of Trenton; and report says that many of the farm houses and barns northward of the turnpike are blown down or otherwise injured. Having struck several houses a little distance from the town, it reached the hill, where it remained apparently fixed for a minute or two, presenting the appearance of a pillar of fire, its base resting on the earth, and its top reaching a mass of black clouds. It then took an eastern course, threatening Albany and Church streets, but, suddenly changing its direction, swept across the town lot towards the dwellings of Mr. B. Myer, Drs. Deare, Prof. McClelland, Rev. John Croes, L. Kirkpatrick, Esq., Mrs. Kirkpatrick, and Rev. Dr. Janeway, tearing the roofs off of some, making literal wrecks of the barns and outhouses, and either uprooting or twisting off the largest trees, in some instances carrying the latter 20 or 30 paces. It then crossed to the buildings at the head of Paterson, Liberty, Bayard and Schureman streets, unroofing the house of Mrs. Harrison, leveling the store of Mr. Little and burying beneath the falling timbers Nicholas Booraem, Esq., and his eldest son Henry. Both were extricated a short time after; the son in a dying state, in which he lingered until 9 o'clock last night, when death relieved him from his sufferings; the father seriously, but, we believe, not dangerously hurt. A young lad about 8 years of age, son of Captain Baird, was also killed near this spot, a rafter from the blacksmith shop having struck him immediately above the eyes and almost severed his head. A female, a widow named Van Arsdale, was found dead under a building in Schureman street.

"The tornado now swept with increased force across George street, down Liberty, Schureman, New streets, crossing Neilson to Burnet street, a quarter of a mile in distance, down to the river, unroofing or tearing off the tops of the houses, and sweeping the lower doors and windows from their fastenings. Schureman and Liberty streets, from top to bottom, may be said to be a complete mass of ruins, as is likewise part of Burnet street. The Methodist church, a brick edifice, is damaged beyond repair, having been unroofed, and the eastern and southern walls blown down; and the rear wall of the Catholic church, also of brick, is drove into the body of the building. The pottery of Mr. Newell, in George street (part of it strongly built of brick), the carpenter shop of Francis F. Randolph, and the extensive coachmaking establishment of Mr. Richard Voorhees, on Schureman street, the stores of Brush & Probasco, and George H. Stout in Burnet St., together with some few dwellings, are entirely destroyed.

"The loss to our citizens in the destruction of buildings and other property must be immense. Various estimates place it at from one hundred to one hundred and fifty thousand dollars; and, as upwards of one hundred and twenty dwellings, besides stores, storehouses, etc., are either greatly damaged or entirely ruined, we scarcely think the latter sum will exceed the amount of loss.

"The accounts of the country lying in the track of the hurricane, particularly east of the Raritan, are fearful, and, we hope, much exaggerated. The village of Piscataway, two miles from this city, is said to have suffered much; and anxiety is felt for other parts of the country both east and west of us.

"As the mails are now closing, we are precluded from making further remarks, but will give a more particular account in our next number."

Later it continued:

"Since the above Extra was issued, we have ascertained that the tornado first commenced on the Millstone, within a few miles of Griggstown, a gentleman near the spot having his attention attracted to two dark masses of clouds, rapidly approaching each other, and which, furiously commingling, rushed to the earth. Suddenly bounding again into the air, a lofty black column was left resting on the earth, surmounting which appeared a mass of clouds in the wildest confusion. For a minute or two the pillar seemed fixed to the spot; the next it dashed to the south-east with inconceivable speed, though, as far as we can learn, doing but little damage until arrived in the vicinity of Middlebush, where, gathering power, it prostrated the stoutest forest trees. It first struck the buildings of Daniel Polhemus between Middlebush and Six-Mile Run, which were slightly injured; then passed to the barn of Joseph Suydam, doing but little injury; thence to the barn of John French, levelling it with the ground; thence passed to the farm of David Dunn, about two miles from this place, which it left a complete scene of desolation; thence to the outhouses of J. P. Wyckoff, which it levelled; thence to the house of Theophilus Holcomb, which it unroofed. Coming swiftly onward, it struck in succession the houses and barns of the Messrs. Sillcocks, James Fisher and Tunis Sillcocks; a few rods below the house of the latter the column remained for some minutes, observing a rapid rotary motion, and carrying up, in concentric circles, beams, boards and branches of trees, which it threw to a great height in the air, until they fell beyond the sphere of its influence, or, retained in air, were forced with terrible violence either against or into the houses in the city, or swept before it across the river.

"The following, as far as we are able to ascertain, are the principal sufferers, though there are doubtless others; the manner in which they have been scattered through the city—many families being houseless and obliged to seek for refuge in its most distant parts—rendering the closest inquiry, in some cases, abortive.

"Princeton Turnpike

"The farm house owned and occupied by Henry and James Sillcocks; right wing unroofed, walls cracked, chimneys down, barn and outhouses prostrate.

"New house, owned by James Fisher; considerably injured, two barns down, and peach orchard destroyed.

"A house owned by James Fisher, on the commons, and occupied by Tunis Sillcocks, entirely destroyed, as likewise is the furniture of the occupant.

"Albany Street—Upper Part

"A barn owned by Dr. Charles Smith destroyed.

"A house owned by Mr. Shepardy, Jac. Suydam occupant; unroofed, chimneys down.

A house near the town lot, owned and occupied by Mr. Benj. Myer; much injured.

"A cottage, owned by Mrs. Duyckinck, occupied by Levi Stout; unroofed and shattered.

"Bayard Street

"A large new house, (unfinished) belonging to Jos. C. Griggs; window sashes blown out and otherwise injured; considerable lumber blown away.

"Mrs. Deare's barn, occupied by S. G. Cook as a stable; destroyed, house uninjured.

"House of Prof. McClelland injured.

"The house occupied by Rev. J. H. Jones, and owned by the Presbyterian Church; slightly damaged.

"House of D. W. Vail, Esq.; slightly.

"—— SQUARE

"The house of L. Kirkpatrick, Esq.; partially unroofed, barn down.

"House of Rev. Dr. Janeway; left wing and body unroofed and shattered, barn down.

"The house owned and occupied by Widow Kirkpatrick, partially unroofed.

"The house owned and occupied by David Mercereau; chimneys down.

"The house owned and occupied by Asa Applegate; considerably injured.

"The house owned by Mrs. E. H. Harrison, occupied by her and Wm. Little; much shattered, upper part taken entirely off.

"GEORGE STREET

"J. C. Ackerman; house slightly injured, chimneys down.
"Rev. John Croes; house partly unroofed, chimneys down.
"Wm. Little's grocery store; entirely destroyed with most of his goods.
"Mrs. McKay's house; unroofed, chimneys down and otherwise injured.
"The extensive pottery, occupied by Jas. H. Newell and owned by Mrs. McKay; entirely destroyed.

"LIBERTY STREET

"Benjamin Cook; house much shattered.
"The house occupied by Rev. M. Bull, owned by James Bishop; unroofed.
"House occupied by Ralph Stout, owned by Mrs. Van Liew, unroofed.
"House occupied by Mrs. Harriott, owned by Mrs. Van Liew; unroofed.
"House owned and occupied by Mr. Nafey; slightly injured.
"The Brick Church occupied and owned by the Methodist denomination; entirely destroyed.

"NEILSON STREET

"Three-story brick house of Dr. Frederick Buckelew; gable end blown down, store house destroyed.

"A frame building owned by Dr. Buckelew, occupied by Mr. Graham, and Mr. Dunn, partially unroofed.

"Shop owned by Richard Manly, occupied by Mr. Addis; unroofed.

"The house owned and occupied by Henry Richmond; slightly injured.

"House occupied by James O'Brien, owned by H. Richmond; slightly injured.

"Do. occupied by widow Creamer, owned by Jacob Wyckoff; unroofed.

"Schoolhouse of Benjamin Mortimer; partly unroofed.

"House occupied by John Bray, owned by Elias Conover; top blown away.

"Do. owned and occupied by Jacob Doty; slightly injured.

"Do. owned and occupied by widow Tunison; destroyed.

"Do. owned and occupied by Dr. A. S. Launy; unroofed, chimneys down.

"Do. and store owned by Mrs. Furman, dwelling occupied by her, store by Van Syckle; greatly damaged.

"Do. owned and occupied by H. Sanderson; slightly injured.

"Do. owned and occupied by Mrs. Plum; destroyed.

"Carpenter's shop of F. F. Randolph; destroyed.

"House of Garret Nafey, occupied by Abram V. Schenck, slightly injured.

"Do. of P. P. Vanderhoof, occupied by Horatio H. Chittenden; partially unroofed and much shattered.

"Do. owned and occupied by Clarissa Rogers; roof and gable end off.

"NEW STREET

"House owned by Dr. Richmond, occupied by widow C. Van Nostrand and Farmer Perdun; unroofed.

"House of Dr. Richmond, occupied by Geo. Wilson and Sarah Johnson; slightly injured.

"Do. of John Blauvelt, occupied by Jos. Morton and James Stillwell; unroofed.

"Do. of Staats Van Deursen, occupied by Cornelius Whitlock; gable end torn out, barn down.

"Do. of Dr. Richmond, occupied by Mr. DeHart; unroofed.

"Do., occupied by a colored family; destroyed.

"Do. of Judge Hentz; slightly damaged.

"Do. of Capt. John Taylor; considerably injured.

"BURNET STREET

"Thomas J. Strong's Tavern, owned by John P. Quick; partly unroofed, stable down.

"House owned and occupied by Francis F. Randolph; slightly damaged.

"Do. of Richard Voorhees; much damaged.

"Do. of James Cox, occupied by Mr. Baldwin; unroofed.

"Do. of Staats Van Deursen, occupied by Charles Ennis and Mrs. Boice; unroofed.

"The three story brick house of Dr. Fitch, occupied by Miss Hubbell; unroofed.

"Barn of Andrew Agnew; destroyed.

"The house of Staats Van Deursen; store house and stable down, carriages destroyed, and cow killed.

"Do. of Staats Van Deursen, occupied by A. James; unroofed and much shattered.

"Store of N. C. Richmond; front blown in.

"House of C. H. Hutchings; chimneys down and roof drove in.

"Do. of John Hicks; partly unroofed, store house down.

"Do. of Dr. Fitch, occupied by Judge Outcalt; slightly damaged, store house down.

"Do. and office of Charles Dunham; much injured.

"Do. of Everett Egerton; much damaged.

"Do. of Dr. Van Deursen; much injured, stable and coach house down.

"Do. of Jeptha Cheeseman; chimneys down, much shattered.

"The dwelling and cabinet warehouse of Matthew Egerton; much damaged.

"House, store house and stable of George H. Stout; destroyed.

"House, two store houses and stable of Brush & Probasco; destroyed.

"Store, two store houses and stable of James Bishop; destroyed.

"House of James Bishop, occupied by Mr. Brant; destroyed.

"Do. of Daniel Dunmead; much injured.

"Do. of Henry Frazee; considerably shattered.

"Do. of Joseph C. Griggs; slightly injured.

"Do. of N. E. Baynon; slightly.

"Do. of L. Fisher, occupied by Lawrence Frazee; slightly.

"Do. of do., occupied by Otis D. Stewart; slightly; hatter's shop in the rear down.

"Do. of John Hatfield; unroofed.

"SCHUREMAN STREET

"Coachmaking establishment of Richard Voorhees, with carriages, etc.; destroyed.

"House of widow Vredenbergh; destroyed.

"Do. of Clarkson Stelle; much injured.

"Do. of Andrew Agnew, occupied by James McLaughlin and John Stewart; partly unroofed.

"Do. of A. Agnew, occupied by Samuel Carlisle and James Smith; considerably shattered.

"Do. of D. Oram, occupied by Captain Ashmore; shattered.

"Do. of S. Van Deursen, occupied by Mrs. Adams and Mrs. Lovett; considerably damaged.

"Do. of S. Van Deursen, occupied by William Long and Mrs. Rowett; much injured.

"Do. of Mrs. Corel; destroyed.

"Carpenter's shop of Richard Voorhees; destroyed.

"House of M. Egerton, occupied by Isaac Smith and Sarah Picket; much injured.

"Do. of M. Egerton, occupied by Capt. Stephen Moore and Amy Smith; considerably damaged.

"Do. of James Bishop; much injured.

"Do. of Miss Mary Dunham, occupied by Mr. Charloc and Mr. Provost; nearly destroyed.

"Do. of Charles Dunham, occupied by widow Dunham and Mrs. Deshler; slightly damaged.

"Do. of Mrs. Van Syckle; destroyed.

"Do. of Mrs. Furman, occupied by Charles Smith and Mrs. Davett; much injured.

"Do. of Isaiah Rolf, occupied by Mr. Rolf and widow Outcalt; much injured.

"Do. of L. Eldridge, occupied by Mrs. Eldridge and Mrs. Moore; slightly.

"Do. of estate of Mrs. Van Doorne, occupied by Vroom Hall; slightly, stable down.

"Do. of Mrs. Stoothoff; slightly.

"Unfinished building of Nich. Wyckoff; destroyed.

"House of John W. Stout, occupied by John Jackson; shattered.

"Do. of Mrs. Huyler; destroyed.

"Do. of Mrs. Boggs, occupied by James Fouratt; slightly.

"Do. of Widow Van Liew, occupied by T. Orchard; slightly.

"Do. of B. M. Voorhees, occupied by Mr. Williams; much injured.

"Do. of Walter Henry, occupied by Robert Lyle and Miss Van Doorn; slightly.

"Do. of Nicholas Wyckoff, occupied by Judge Ford; much injured.

"Do. of N. Wyckoff; much injured.

"Do. of N. Wyckoff, occupied by John Hager; much injured.

"Do. of Common Council, occupied as the Lancastrian School, the dwelling by Elihu Cook and Enos Fouratt; much injured.

"Do. of Cornelius L. Hardenbergh, occupied by Mr. McMechin and widow Lowe; destroyed.

"Do. of Miss Rachel Randolph, occupied by the Misses Voorhees; unroofed.

"Do. of Miss R. Randolph, occupied by Rulef Van Nostrand and widow Drake; unroofed.

"In addition to the above, the Catholic Church, in Bayard St., had the rear wall drove in; the tiles on the roof of the jail were torn off in several places, and the roofs of the houses occupied by Mr. Manly and Mr. Bellis, and others, were more or less injured by pieces of falling timber.

"Killed

"Henry Booraem, son of Judge B., formerly of the U. S. Navy.
"Widow Van Arsdale.
"DeWitt, son of Maj. Baird, aged about 10 years.

"Wounded

"Aaron Smith, badly, ribs broken, and head much cut.
"Nicholas Booraem, Esq., severely.
"A son of Jeptha Cheeseman, 9 years of age, dangerously.
"A. S. Van Deursen, Esq., severely.
"Capt. Richard Montgomery, do.
"Mrs. Booraem, of New York, seriously.
"Mr. Nicholas Wyckoff, severely.
"Wm. Atkinson, slightly.
"——— Atkinson, do.
"Richard Van Arsdale, slightly.
"Tunis Sillcocks, wife, wife's mother, and 2 children, severely; 2 other children slightly.
"Wm. Henry Frazee, slightly.
"Isaac Frazee, severely.
"A son of O. D. Stewart, 6 years old, severely; arm broken, head cut.
"A son of widow Harrison, 13 years, severely.
"John Nafey, much bruised and head cut.
"Stryker Conover, back hurt.
"Theodore Myer, head, hands and arms cut, and otherwise hurt.
"Isaac Sillcocks, dangerously.
"Mr. Provost, carpenter, badly.
"Jane Jackson, colored woman, arm broken.

"Probably this list does not comprise more than half the number hurt, but it is impossible at present to obtain a more perfect list. Having made such parts of the city through which the Tornado passed a complete wreck, it crossed the river and struck the woods, uprooting some of the largest trees, twisting off the body of others, and throwing several 40 and 50 yards from the places where they stood.

"In one place it appears to have played for some time, in a circle of about 100 feet, tearing up the grass, and leaving the earth completely bare of any signs of vegetation. It then passed over part of the farm of James T. Dunn, Esq., threatening the house, but, changing its direction, went a few paces to the rear, razing the barn and all the outbuildings, and dashing in a few of the window casements of the dwelling. A lad named Jerome Finch was here hurt, but not dangerously, by a falling tree.

"Now striking the woods, it passed on to the house of Joel Randolph, tearing off the gable end part of the roof, and considerably injuring the barn. It now changed its direction, taking again to the woods in a course about N. E. until near Piscataway town, where its course was east. Here, rushing with terrible violence, it swept over the devoted village, leaving scarcely a house untouched, and strewing the road and adjacent fields with the ruins. We have been enabled to gather the following particulars:

"At the widow Goodfellow's house; comparatively uninjured; barn and outhouses leveled, orchards destroyed, one horse killed.

"Joel Dunham; house unroofed, blacksmith shop and barn razed.

"Episcopal Church; thrown 20 feet from its foundation and lies a heap of ruins.

"School house; razed, the children fortunately dismissed an hour before in consequence of the anticipated rain.

"Elijah and James Dunham; barn and outhouses destroyed.

"Henry Sutton; house down.

"James Gillman; house uninjured, workshop and two barns down.

"James Arnold, Sr.; house and barn destroyed; James Arnold, Jr., severely hurt.

"Thomas W. Harper, formerly of New York; brick house destroyed; Mr. H. wounded, mortally. Since dead.

"Jeremiah Sofield, house razed; Mr. S. wounded severely.

"Mr. Perry; house razed, wife or daughter dangerously wounded, supposed mortally.

"Immediately after the Tornado had passed the village displayed a horrible scene; the isolated situation of the houses and barns presenting a fair mark to its terrible ravages. In some places we marked whole orchards prostrate, and the trees carried over the road into fields opposite.

"Having gone through the village, it demolished the barn and fulling mill of David Dunham, and passing on through Woodbridge township, threw down the barn of James Ross, thence took a direct course for Amboy, slightly touching a house on the southwestern edge of the town, and passed into the Bay, throwing an immense body of water into the air, and striking, it is said, the southerly point of Staten Island, when it was lost sight of.

"No pen, (at least it would require a more able one than ours) can do justice to the passage of the Tornado through our town. It would seem as if the Spirits of the Air had gathered in the pride of their might, and in their wrath would sweep the besom of destruction over our devoted people, leaving naught but death and desolation to mark their track. None but an eye witness can conceive the awful scene: houses toppling and crashing to the ground, or completely riven, flying through the streets, and scattered in every direction; heavy beams and rafters driven with fearful impetus into and through the houses; women and children, frantic, screaming for aid, and men, who had been strangers to fear, with blanched cheeks running in breathless haste to seek shelter from the impending danger; while with a deep roar, like that of a heavy, unremitted cannonade, or a vast building in one sheet of flame, the Tornado sped upon its way, sucking up everything within reach of its horrible vortex. The intense noise which accompanied it may be inferred from the fact that many who had sought refuge in the lower apartments of the buildings partly destroyed were unaware of their loss until the hurricane had passed; they heard nothing but its awful roar. Many of the escapes from death are wonderful; we have not time nor space to recount a tithe of them. Men who threw themselves upon the ground were lifted up and thrown violently down, while others who were clinging to posts or other supports, with the desperate strength which fear calls into action, were torn from them and dashed to the earth. One lad, 12 years old, a son of Wm. G. Dunham, was carried from his father's house at the head of New St. down to the wharf, a distance of half a mile, passing through a tree, the branches of which he attempted to grasp, with no other injury but a sprained wrist. Heavy oak beams, 18 feet long, and pieces of roof 10 feet square and upward were blown across the river, and fell into the woods, which were strewn with boards, window sashes, door panels, tile, shingles, bedding, wearing apparel and glass. Boards, shingles, etc., are said to have fallen on Staten Island. The trees are broken, shivered and uprooted on the opposite side for a thousand yards along its banks, and the vegetation is scathed as if a flame had been quickly passed over it.

"The alarm of fire just previous to the hurricane striking the city was most providential, as it was the means, no doubt, of saving many lives, it having called out the men from the workshops of Messrs. Voorhees & Randolph and the store of Mr. Little, which a few minutes after were a heap of ruins, and drawn many of the citizens from that vicinity to the head of Church and Albany Sts., where the fire was supposed to be raging.

"The loss is great, though not so heavy as at first supposed. $100,000, it is said, will cover the damages. Every storehouse from J. C. Griggs' down to A. Agnew's is prostrated. Our citizens have had a meeting, and measures have been taken to afford immediate assistance to those who are in need. We understand that our neighbors in Princeton, with their characteristic liberality, have already made proffers of aid, an example which will no doubt be followed by other cities in our State.

"N. B.—Carpenters and masons will find steady employment in our city for some time."

The following "Notes on the Tornado" were by Professor Lewis C. Beck:

"At about half past five o'clock, while on board the steamboat 'Napoleon,' which was then six or seven miles from New Brunswick, my attention was called to a singular appearance in a north-westerly direction. A very dense and low cloud stretched itself along for some distance like a dark curtain, which, near the center, was dipping towards the earth in the form of a funnel or inverted cone, whose basis rested exactly on the surface. At one extremity of this dark cloud was a smaller one, having a flecculent appearance, which soon also became conical in its shape, but which did not descend to the earth. These cones seemed to have been formed by gyratory or whirling movements, produced by currents of wind passing in opposite directions, viz., from the north-west and south. In a few minutes the well-defined character of these united cones was changed, and there arose a column, spreading at the top, and which had every appearance of the eruption of a volcano. A vast body of smoke, as it seemed, rose up and again descended, producing a sort of rolling upward and downward movement.

"The opinion now became general that it proceeded from the burning of some large building, which it was thought had been caused by lightning, a vivid flash or two of which had preceded the formation of the cones. This idea was, however, soon abandoned, for in a few minutes the dense column was dissipated, and we could distinctly observe the gyratory motion of wind, as was proved by the dust and fragments of timber which were carried upward in its course. Onward it swept, with incalculable velocity, until another black and well-defined cone was again formed, which remained stationary for a short time and then, as before, gave place to the eruptive appearance and gyratory movements before mentioned. These alternations continued, although much less distinctly characterized, until the whole vanished from our view.

"On approaching New Brunswick we witnessed the devastation which the tornado had occasioned; but it was in this city alone that its mighty power was fully exhibited.

"From the facts which I have collected, there can be no doubt that the cone above described was formed about three miles nearly west of New Brunswick, and that it remained stationary, that is, revolving on its axis, for some minutes. But when the second movement occurred, a dense cloud overshadowed the city. Slight but distinct explosions, as of the bluffing of sails, were heard from the column. The heat of the air became oppressive; volumes of smoke and even flames were thought to be issuing forth and rolling over in various directions. Under these circumstances the idea of an extensive and rapid conflagration would naturally be suggested. Immediately the alarm bells were rung, the firemen repaired to their engines; but, while all eyes were directed to the black and terrible column which was approaching apparently toward the head of Albany St., no one could fix upon the exact spot to which effort should be directed. This state of uncertainty, however, did not long continue, for soon a tremendous rush of wind passed through the city, and in a moment the dense column, which had been an object of so much wonder and dread, stood on the opposite bank of the river, as it were, rallying for another desolating march.

"The force of the wind, in its passage through the city, it would be idle to calculate. Men were thrown down, buildings of wood and brick were unroofed and even completely demolished, large trees were torn up by the roots and scattered promiscuously in all directions. The air was filled with dust and missiles of various kinds. The crash of the timbers was scarcely audible in consequence of the roaring of the tornado. Many of the inhabitants who had watched the appearance of the column were apprized of the coming danger and fled to the cellars of their dwellings for safety, and, in several cases, where the doors of the buildings were firmly closed, they suffered little or no injury, though in the midst of destruction.

"Thus far the course of the tornado had been a little north of east, a direction which it pursued to the village of Piscataway, about three miles distant, and which it almost totally destroyed; then, inclining somewhat to the south, it held an easterly course, passing over Amboy and thence to the ocean. It terminated, as I have seen it stated, by a fall of ice or hail, and by a great commotion of the water. The fall of ice is said also to have characterized its commencement, but on this subject I have not yet obtained authentic information.

"I will at present add only a few words concerning the cause of this, at least, in our latitude, very remarkable occurrence. The formulation of the inverted cone or funnel, so often mentioned, was undoubtedly produced by the currents of air from opposite directions. But whether these currents were caused by a vacuum arising from the electrical discharges from the cloud, or whether the supposed vacuum was the result of these currents, it is, perhaps, impossible to determine. But if this funnel may be compared to that of the tube which forms the water spout—and it certainly bore a close resemblance to that phenomenon—we may suppose that there was a current established from the earth to the cloud. This upward movement is indeed indicated by the occurrences which succeeded, and by many facts which have since been ascertained. Among these may be mentioned the unroofing of those houses into which the air rushed through the doors and windows, and the lodgement of these roofs nearly in front of the houses to which they belonged. This upward movement was distinctly visible at a distance, and it was this which gave the phenomenon the appearance of a volcanic eruption. At the same time, also, there was a gyratory motion to which the destruction produced by the tornado is to be chiefly ascribed. This motion appeared to us on board the 'Napoleon,' to succeed the upward movement just mentioned and characterized the progress of the tornado until it passed from our view. This gyratory motion is also evident from the appearances which are presented everywhere in New Brunswick and its vicinity. According to my measurement, the track of the tornado through the city did not exceed 300 yards, although the circle seems to have been much larger where the cone was first formed, and, also, on the opposite side of the river, where the column is supposed again to have rested. Near the circumference of the supposed circles was the line of the most destructive force of the wind. Several buildings in their centres remain altogether uninjured.

"I cannot subscribe to the opinion which has been advanced that the violence of the wind was produced by two currents making towards each other, and having at the same time an onward motion. If there was not a gyratory as well as upward motion, I must discredit my eyesight, and be blinded to the appearances which are everywhere presented, both in this city and its vicinity. Having had a fine opportunity of witnessing the phenomenon in its most interesting stages, and of studying its effects, it is perhaps more difficult for me to form a satisfactory theory on the subject than it is for those who were less favorably situated. I shall, therefore, still continue the humble and frequently too much neglected business of collecting facts, in the hope that they may hereafter lead to views more worthy of notice."

After the Tornado had passed a subscription was immediately circulated and the amount of $2,770 was subscribed. The original subscription with the original signatures has been preserved. It reads: "We, the subscribers, agree to pay the sums annexed to our respective names, for the relief of the sufferers by the present awful visitation of a just but merciful Providence." Among the subscribers were: J. J. Janeway, F. Richmond, Miles C. Smith, John W. Stout, C. L. Hardenbergh, James Neilson, Dr. Carroll, Charles Smith, F. R. Smith, John Clark, Ph. Milledoler, James J. Cannon, Theodore Strong, J. W. Scott, James W. Nevius, C. W. Terhune, Robert Butler, John B. Hill, J. C. Van Dyke, Josiah Stout, Sam'l Holcomb, Abraham Suydam, Terhune & Letson, John Van Nuis, John Acken, D. W. Vail, Peithessophian Society of Rutgers College.

The Committee who collected the fund were James Neilson (Chairman), J. D. Ogilby, James Zabriskie; and the Treasurer was Dr. F. Richmond.[1]

After C. L. Hardenbergh's second term as Mayor, in 1836, we enter on a long term (nearly 25 years) of one-year Mayors, with an occasional second term; quite a striking contrast to the long terms of the city's first Mayors—Farmer, 17 yrs.; Hude 15 yrs.; Ouke 16 yrs. respectively; in all 48 years.

This was a great business period of a new sort when most of New Brunswick's manufactories were established, making certain specialties for which New Brunswick became noted, as carriages, wall-paper, rubber goods, hosiery, wall-paper machinery, rubber machinery, knitting machinery, sash and blinds, shoes, etc. The carriage factory of Lyle Van Nuis is a little earlier (1811), while McCrellis' carriage factory dates from 1851; the first had a wide reputation.

Johnson Letson started a flourishing hardware business in 1835; Martin A. Howell a wall-paper business in 1837, although there are people who will state that the wall-paper business practically started with the Philadelphia Centennial Exhibition. J. P. Hardenbergh and H. L. Janeway started another wall-paper factory in 1843, while Waldron's Machine Shop was noted for its wall-paper machinery, being started in 1848.

---

[1] For the complete circular of a committee appointed at a Town Meeting in New Brunswick to solicit donations from outside persons and the subscriptions received, see "Proceedings of the N. J. Hist. Soc.," New Series, vol. VI, p. 236.

The New Jersey Rubber Shoe Co., was started in 1839; Onderdonk and Letson began the rubber business in 1842; the New Brunswick Rubber Co. in 1850. Then there was the Novelty Rubber Co., a hard rubber manufactory of buttons, etc., while the National Iron Works of Elijah Kelly made a specialty of rubber machinery in 1847. The Norfolk and New Brunswick Hosiery Co. started in Norfolk, Conn., in 1857, but in New Brunswick between 1863 and 1866, and Munn's machine shop specialized in knitting machinery after 1858. Then there was Wm. Wright's Sash and Blind factory, 1852, and Felters & Co. Shoe Manufactory. P. C. Onderdonk, before going into rubber in 1842, had a saw-mill at the Upper Lock.

The foregoing were the lines New Brunswick specialized in during the terms of the Mayors named below:

David M. Vail, 1840.

Littleton Kirkpatrick, 1841.

Fitz-Randolph Smith, 1842.

John Acken, two terms, 1843, 1844.

Wm. H. Leupp, 1845 (epidemic year).

John Van Dyke, 1846; second term, 1852.

Martin A. Howell, 1847 (born 1804; married, in 1828, Mary White).

A. F. Taylor, 1848 (born 1809; son of A. R. Taylor our 11th Mayor).

D. F. Randolph, 1849, 1850.

Peter Wyckoff, 1851.

John B. Hill, 1853, 1854 (married Henrietta B. Chapman; died Feb. 28, 1874).

A. V. Schenck, 1855 (born 1821; died 1902; counsellor-at-law; Senator).

Lyle Van Nuis, 1856, 1861 (son of John and grandson of the Van Nuis who built the Van Nuis homestead on Livingston Ave., later Sheriff Fick's house).

J. B. Kirkpatrick, 1857, 1858 (Y. M. C. A. established this year).

P. C. Onderdonk, 1859.

E. M. Patterson, 1860.

This brings us up to 1861 and the Civil War period.

CHAPTER XII

Some Prominent Visitors to and Citizens of New Brunswick in Early Days—Danker, the Earliest Traveler to New Brunswick—Dr. Henry Greenland—Cornelius Van Langvelt and His Son, Cornelius Longfield—Thomas Lawrence, the Baker—John Inian—The Two Tennant Ministers—Thomas Farmar, First Mayor—Capt. Christopher Billop—James Hude, Second Mayor—Governor Belcher—William Ouke, Third Mayor—The Bayard, Heermans and Kemble Families—Philip French—The Schuylers—Dr. John Cochrane, Etc.

ABOUT the first person of any note who passed through New Brunswick was Jasper Danker. He and Peter Sluyter, of Wilverd in Finland, were looking for a suitable place for a Colony, and were on their way to Augustine Heermans, whose Bohemian Manor of 20,000 acres was partly in Delaware and partly in Maryland. They were pleased at the location and bought 3,750 acres. The deed was made in the names of Peter Sluyter, Jasper Danker, Petrus Bayard and John Moll, in 1684, and a Labadist Colony was made there. It was in 1679 that Danker passed across the State of New Jersey, writing his journal at night as he went along. On Nov. 14 he writes:

"We rode two English miles from Pescatteway to Mr. Greenland, who keeps an Ordinary or Tavern, at the place of crossing the Millstone River, which they call the Falls. Close by was the dwelling of some Indians, who were of service to Mr. Greenland in many things. As the water was high we were set across in a canoe and the horses swam. It was about nine in the morning when we got across. From here to the Falls of the South river the road runs W.S.W., and then west, crossing a Rocky Hill, and a little further we crossed the Millstone again, where we dined. About three we crossed it again for the third time, it runs so crookedly, and arrived at the Falls of the South river at sundown. The Falls is simply a place two miles in length, where the river is full of stones and very shallow."

He went on to Maryland, having Ephraim, Heerman's oldest son, of whom we shall speak presently, as guide. On their return, Dec. 30, he continues in his diary:

"About three this afternoon we took a road on the right, leaving the road to Mr. Greenland's and arrived at dark at Cornelius Van Langvelt's, step-son of Thomas the Baker of New York. He lived alone with an Indian, and some neighbors were beginning a village on land of this Thomas directly opposite Pescatteway, upon the point where the Millstone river unites with the Raritan Kill and flows down to Acktor Kol, which they intend to call Nassau."

Here is the first known traveler to, and the first mention of a settlement on land that is now New Brunswick. He goes on to say:

"Millstone river is not, as supposed, the Raritan Kill, for that runs near the house on the right, due west; and this one before the house runs on the left, west-north-west."

I hardly think one will recognize these descriptions. Longfield's house was on the point made by the Raritan and Cromelin's creek or Lawrence's brook. As the head of Lawrence's brook is quite near the South Branch of the Raritan, he very easily got off of the Millstone and on to Lawrence's brook without knowing it, and so thought he was on the same stream he had crossed three times going to the Falls of the South river; hence his badly mixed description of the location of Longfield's house. The Raritan Kill, is, of course, the Raritan river, which he calls the Millstone when he crossed it at Greenland's. Longfield, the lonely Indian trader, and Longfield, the grandson of Admiral Cochradth of the Dutch Navy (his mother's father), Member of the House of Deputies, and of the Assembly, and one of Gov. Hunter's Council, hardly seem like the same person; the two views almost irreconcilable. But the quality that enabled him to persist in the first vocation equipped him to fill the others.

That Longfield's mother was something of a character herself I should judge from an item of Nov. 26, 1679, in the "N. Y. Historical Collections," which says:

"Upon the report of Mary, the wife of Thomas Lawrence, the Baker, about losing her ducks, which he said Thomas Clark had stolen or employed someone else to doe it—Ordered, that Thomas Lawrence on behalf of his wife give security in £10 to answer as an accessory to the theft of her husband's hoggs, hens and ducks. And Thomas Clark is left to the benefit of the law by order of the Governor.—MATTHIAS NICOLL, SEC."

Henry Greenland, where Danker stayed on his westward trip, was a man of equal ability though of less well-balanced and dependable character. He was what we call a scrapper. He represented a different element. He was one of the Churchmen on the Piscataqua; a skillful physician there from 1662 until banished by his Puritan neighbors in 1673, having been convicted of many high misdemeanors, which consisted mainly of being a Churchman, Royalist, quarrelsome, contentious, and a thorn in the flesh of his staid Puritan neighbors. From there he came to Piscataway and seems to have been in favor at once with all parties. He was appointed Captain of a military company, and, when Governor Andros in 1680 came to Elizabethtown to see Governor Carteret, whom he was trying to intimidate, Capt. Greenland, at the head of his Company, and "without colors," and several other Companies, were drawn up to receive him on Elizabethtown Point, so that Andros was obliged to be diplomatic instead of dictatorial. But, shortly afterwards, Governor Andros evened things up by abducting Carteret, taking him from his bed at night without any clothes.

"Greenland kept an 'Ordinary,'" as Danker said, and was appointed by Andros as one of the Overseers of Piscataway. In Nov., 1681, Capt. James Bollen, Capt. Henry Greenland and Samuel Edsal attempted to dissolve the House of Deputies; the same old tactics that he was charged with on the Piscataqua. Even the dispute over the partition line between East and West Jersey was carried on at his house, where an agreement was reached in 1688 and witnessed by Henry Greenland. His daughter, Mary, married Cornelius Longfield; Frances married Daniel Brinson, whose son, Barefoot Brinson (or Brunson) married Mary Lawrence, and was sheriff of Somerset County. Greenland's son, Henry, was also a doctor on the Millstone and lived near Princeton.

Quite the equal in importance with Longfield and Greenland was John Inian, the man who established the Ferry, and here again the Ferry-keeper will be always remembered, while the man of affairs who sat in Gov. Andrew Hamilton's Council and who had important mercantile ventures makes no impression. Inian's lands in New Brunswick, of 1280 acres, made a corner at Albany and the river and his house was there. As he represented Somerset county his house must have been north of French St., and in 1716 a two-rod road, now Little Burnet St., began over against his house, pretty near locating it. He was also sheriff of Somerset.

From Fernow's "Court Records of New Amsterdam" we find in numerous small causes tried that Cornelius Van Langvelt, the father of Cornelius Longfield, was a Dutch trader in 1653. He was a partner of Jan Geraerdy, son of Philip Geraerdy, who is mentioned in Valentine's "History of New York" as being one of the earliest Dutch settlers, having received in 1643 a grant of a house and lot on a road now called Stone street. The little disputes in the New Amsterdam Court over differences of understanding regarding trading show that Van Langvelt dealt in tobacco, cloth, boots, apples, beaver, etc., and took goods in pawn as well. He and his partner owned a vessel, over which they had quite a dispute; it was called a bark and also a yacht. In 1655, in a settlement between the partners, Van Langvelt claimed half of the vessel; but this dispute does not seem to have been satisfactorily settled, as next year Van Langvelt complains that his partner sailed away and left him. The vessel trips were long, for, in 1653, a suit having been brought in his absence, it was deferred a month to give the partner a chance to appear in his own behalf; they were *"at the north,"* and it was there his partner sailed away and left Van Langvelt to get home as best he could.

In 1655, in a record of a voluntary tax raised that year, Cornelius Van Langvelt is listed for 1 beaver and 8 florins.

These cases, which almost without exception were decided in favor of Van Langvelt, were of considerable amounts, as one for 38 florins for apples and 58 florins in beaver, one-half of 9 hhds. of tobacco. One case he lost and he was quite stubborn about it. He had traded a bed for a pair of gold pendants with pearls and was sued by Janeke Heermans, who claimed she gave them to Lookeman to sell for her. Van Langvelt refused to give up the earrings and was ordered to prison. He then appealed the case, but the final decision does not appear.

April 14, 1657, Cornelius Van Langvelt appears in the list of small Burghers, there being but 204 of them at that date in New Amsterdam. In 1661 there is mention of Van Langvelt's wife, Merritje (Mary), and also mention of Thomas Laurens (or Laurensen), the Baker's wife, called to Court by Peritje Pieter as witness in a case of defamation of character. This Thomas Laurens, the Baker, later married the widow of Cornelius Langvelt and became step-father of Cornelius Longfield, New Brunswick's first settler. "Thomas Laurensen" appears in Court to answer for failing to pay the minister's quota on Oct. 15, 1667; church support evidently not being optional at that date.

There is in all the Dutch Records of New Amsterdam but one other Langvelt mentioned, and that is in April 28, 1666, when Jan Langvelt is given as guardian of Aernout Rynders, son of Ryndert Arensen and Annetien Hermans, dec'd. (Flatlands, Liber D, fol. 61).

In the New York "Directory" of 1665, the names of Thomas Laurensen and his wife, Marritje Jans, appear on Pearl street. "Scot's Model," in 1680, mentions Thomas Lawrence (English spelling of the name), the Baker, and Cornelius Longfield, his step-son, as land owners on the Raritan. Jasper Danker, as we have seen, mentions in his journal in 1679 staying with Cornelius Longfield at the river. While at the Raritan he married Mary, the daughter of Dr. Henry and Mary Greenland, but evidently he took his wife to New York, as the Dutch Domine, Henricus Selyn, in his list of church members with their residence, mentions "Cornelius Van Langvelt and his wife Maria [Mary] Groenlant" [Greenland], so that he and his wife preferred to make their home for a while at New York rather than among Indian friends on the Raritan.

Evidently the first Cornelis Van Langvelt died before 1679. From the fact that his name is omitted from the Directory of 1665 it would seem that he died before 1665.

On November 10, 1681, the son, Capt. Cornelis Van Langvelt, made an affidavit regarding his purchase of land on the Raritan river, to which he had some difficulty in securing title. In 1689 his step-father deeded him his land on the Raritan (it would appear for the purpose of disposing of it for him). In 1690 he was a Deputy to the Assembly. In 1691 his father-in-law, Henry Greenland, deeded him more land on the east of the Raritan, 150 acres at the ford, where he had lived. In 1694 he acted as executor of his father-in-law's will. In 1695 Jedediah Higgins and himself were elected to represent Piscataway in the General Assembly, and it was not until then that he succeeded in perfecting the title to any of his lands; probably as a member of the Government he was better able to get his claims listened to. In 1698 he was again member of the House of Deputies. Between the first and second division to the Proprietors he acquired one-fifth of Robert Barclay's Propriety, and received his share of that dividend. In April, 1700-'01, he acted as executor of the will of his neighbor, Mary Inian, in which document he is called "good friend, a neighbor."

In 1708 Cornelius Longfield was nominated by Lord Cornbury for Council, and in 1710, as one of Gov. Hunter's Council, took the oath in Burlington. In 1711 he is again proposed for Council.

By his own early purchases in 1681, with that of his step-father in 1678 and the land from his father-in-law, and as Proprietor, his land holdings were very large. He held one tract from Livingston avenue in New Brunswick to the mouth of the South River, and he, or his son Henry, make deeds to all of this tract. His other lands were on the Passaic, the Matcheponix, Manalapan, up the South river, etc.

Of his children, Henry petitioned for the charter for New Brunswick in 1730 and remained here. His daughter, Catharine, married William Cox, whose son's (Col. John Cox's) daughter Rachel married John Stevens and was the mother of the distinguished engineers of that name—John, Robert, James and Edwin; while *her* sister, Catherine, married Samuel Stockton, the brother of the Signer, Richard Stockton.

In the genealogies of their families the Longfields are claimed to have sprung from two Dutch admirals—Admiral Langvelt and his wife's father, Admiral Cochradth, of the Dutch Navy, but no references are given.

In 1700 Rachel Longfield married Thomas Lawrence, Mayor of Philadelphia, and Octavo Coenraat, in his will, 1718, mentions his father-in-law, Cornelius Longfield, of Raritan Manor. Of this daughter we have no record. He left one daughter and Thomas Lawrence was his Executor. Coenraat was tutor (legal guardian) of Helena de Vries, and her husband Albertus Hodson.

From deeds by his widow it appears Cornelius Longfield died about 1733, and from deeds of the son Henry that his mother died about 1742. Henry died in 1770.[1]

John Inian, the second purchaser of lands on which New Brunswick stands, and who filled many positions of honor and trust, has but a brief and little known history.

In Shannon's "New York" he is noted as merchant and Alderman in 1677, and Deputy Mayor in 1678. In 1681 he purchased the two lots on the Raritan on which the north half of New Brunswick stands.

On May 14, 1683, the sheriff of New York was ordered to attach in the hands of John Inian, or any other person, 38 negro slaves carried away by Capt. Christopher Billop from the ship "Providence," the ship and negroes being the proper estate of John Bowdon and John and Thomas Temple, citizens of London. The sheriff attached the negroes in the hands of John Inian, also the proceeds, some of which had been converted into 40 bbls. and 24 half-bbls. of flour, and 8 hhds. of bread, put on the ship "Charles." Judgment was obtained against Capt. Billop for £1,140 sterling and appeal refused. He then appealed to the King and was granted an appeal if he put up £2,000 security bonds.

---

[1] For some additional notes respecting the Longfield, Greenland, Lawrence, etc., families, see Appendix.

Governor Dongan selected Inian on Nov. 24, 1683, as Alderman of Dock Ward (see James Grant Wilson's "New York," and Shannon's "New York"). In September he was on a jury to try a man accused of being a pirate; the jury acquitted the defendant.

In 1684 he received a patent for the first two and the fourth of the twelve lots (thereafter known as Inian lots), obtained for himself and his associates. In 1685 he deeded one lot to Andrew Bowne. In 1686 we find him "at the fording place on the Raritan," and this same year he built the road running from Inian's by the Crosswicks Bridge—the best road to Burlington—and the road to the Falls of the Delaware, six miles shorter, also the road to Piscataway, and he established the Ferry, though the exclusive rights were not granted to himself and wife for life until Feb. 5, 1697.

In 1686 he had an action against Mordecai Boudinot, at the September Middlesex County Court, and was himself a Justice of the Middlesex Court of Sessions.

In 1687 Thomas Budde, of West Jersey, was taken from Inian's house on the river by the sheriff, having barricaded himself there for three days.

In 1687 he mortgaged his Inian lots, of 1,280 acres, to Capt. Christopher Billop, thus keeping up his connection with Billop.

In 1688, when Somerset county was set off, Inian was made Treasurer, his home being in that county.

Sept. 24, 1692, he was in Governor Hamilton's Council, and in 1695, up to March, 1698, in Governor Basse's Council.

He died in 1699 and his wife in 1700, and he left his lands to Cornelius Longfield. So we have a record of Inian of ten years in New York City and thirteen at Raritan river, but no word as to his origin or social standing. He was honored by three Governors with an office. The only other mention of a name similar to Inian that I can find is of a Seymon Inons, with four in his family, listed as of St. Jones and Duck creek.

Another of this group of early settlers was Capt. Enoch Vreeland, son of Elias Mickaelson, and grandson of Mickael

Jansen, Captain of the first military company on the south or west side of the Raritan. He bought the farm on the south side of Inian's, and on this farm the first houses of New Brunswick were built along Little Burnet, Burnet and Peace streets. These early house lots were all sold by Enoch Vreeland, as far as New street. His own house was on Commerce Square. He had another farm, now the College Farm, with a mill at the College Farm Pond, about 1717.

About 1726 Rev. Gilbert Tennent came to New Brunswick to minister to the Presbyterians. Dr. Robert Davidson, in his "Historical Sketch of the Presbyterian Church in New Brunswick," says: "He was a noticeable man in his day, a member of a remarkable family and a companion of Whitefield," who came here first on Nov. 13, 1739, when he read the Church Liturgy and preached in the evening at Mr. Tennent's Meeting House, for there was no place of worship of the Church of England. On the 20th he returned and preached at noon for about two hours; in Mr. Tennent's Meeting House at three and at seven he preached again. Then, on Saturday, Apr. 26, 1740, he was again in New Brunswick and preached to about 2,000 in the evening. The next day, Sunday, he preached morning and evening to 7,000 or 8,000 people. Friday, Nov. 6, 1740, he was in New Brunswick for the last time and preached in the evening. Mr. Whitefield had a high regard for Gilbert Tennent and, after hearing him preach, wrote: "Never before heard I such a searching sermon. He went to the bottom indeed and did not daub with untempered mortar."

Gilbert Tennent's father, William Tennent, was an Irish clergyman of the Established Church, which he renounced and became a Presbyterian. All of his four sons became ministers. William, of Freehold, had a remarkable trance at Gilbert's house on Burnet street.

Thomas Farmar, the first Mayor of New Brunswick, in 1730 came to New Jersey from Philadelphia, his family having come there from England in 1685. It is said the family were friends and neighbors of William Penn. It consisted of Major Jasper Farmar and his wife, Mary Gamble; of Jasper Farmar, Jr. and wife Katharine, their children and twenty servants. They took up 5000 acres in White Marsh Township, Philadelphia county, south of the Skippock road. Both Jasper's father and son died on the voyage, and the widow Katherine married Capt. Christopher Billop, a widower with two children. Whether there was an acquaintance between the two families in England does not appear, but it looks likely, or how did the widower in Staten Island find the widow in Philadelphia? Or it is possible that Capt. Christopher Billop and his son Capt. Christopher Billop are more or less mixed up. Capt. Christopher, the father, was in the Royal Navy, and commanded the "Victory," 100 guns, "Greenwich," 54 guns, "Suffolk," 70 guns, and a number of others. He was a friend of the King and sailed his ship "Bently" around Staten Island in a day and got the manor of 3165 acres as a gift from the Duke of York. Cornelis Melyn originally held the whole of Staten Island under a patent as Patroon under date of June 19, 1642, but left the island and lost his rights, after which it was divided up in 1675 and one of the divisions was Bentley Manor.

Capt. Christopher Billop was in command of Delaware Bay and the river, under Governor Andros, in 1677. Katherine Billop Farmar had a son, Thomas Farmar, who was Sheriff of Philadelphia, but resigned his office in 1704 to go to England (and Charles Farmar Billop, who wrote the "Billop-Farmar Genealogy," says: "without doubt to marry Captain Billop's daughter, Ann"). His oldest daughter, Mary, had married a missionary named John Brooke, who returned to England leaving his wife in America. He was lost on the voyage, and his widow married William Skinner, another missionary. Having no children, her father left his estate to his second daughter, who married Thomas Farmar, with the provision that a son named for him (Christopher) should take his name of Billop and be his heir. Thomas came to Amboy, and was Collector of the Port of Amboy, and filled many of the offices of the Province. He was Member of the Assembly, Judge of Common Pleas, Commissioner in 1709 for provisioning the expedition into Canada, Chief Justice in place of Robert Lettice Hooper in 1727. Governor Hunter said of him that he was "a man of the first estate and ability in the Province."

In addition to these various offices he was Mayor of New Brunswick from 1730 to 1747. Capt. Billop had an early interest in the city, as he held a mortgage on John Inian's two lots of 640 acres each; and on these lots the city to the north of Livington Ave. is now built. Thomas Farmar and several of his children made their homes there. Jasper Farmar, the oldest son, was in the army and made his home in New York. Christopher died young; Thomas, the next son, changed his name to Billop and inherited the Staten Island property; Robert, William and John were in the British army; Brooke, named for the missionary, was an innkeeper; Samuel was a merchant in New York; Mary married Paul Miller; Annie married Philip French as his second wife; and Elizabeth married Dr. William Farquhar.

The installation of the second Mayor, James Hude, was the occasion of a visit from Governor Belcher, appointed Governor in room of Lewis Morris, deceased. He arrived from London, June 4, 1747. As the Charter provided that the Governor should assign, nominate, ordain and appoint a new Mayor, and as he had been sworn in Aug. 10, the Governor probably combined pleasure with business, and, while inducting the new Mayor into office, was also entertained and welcomed as the new Governor.

James Hude presided for the first time at a Council meeting Aug. 17, 1747, and a bill "for the entertainment of his Excellency, Jonathan Belcher, Esq., our Governor," at the house of Paul Miller was ordered paid out of the money in the hands of William Ouke, Treasurer of the City. We have no account of this visit, not even the amount of the bill is given, but one can imagine it was a great occasion in the young city. On that same day, August 17, he was being welcomed in Elizabeth.

James Hude is said to have lived in the one-story stone house afterwards enlarged into the Indian Queen Tavern; but I think this is a mistake, as his executors disposed of his three houses on Burnet and Little Burnet Sts., and he certainly did not own the Tavern site. But his widow, without doubt, lived there after his death, as records of 1769 and 1774 show. James Hude's obituary concisely and conveniently sums up his career by saying that "he passed through almost all the honorary offices and employments of the Government where he lived, as well those in the gift of the Crown, as those in the voice of the people," serving the city of New Brunswick as Recorder and Mayor for 32 years. His son, James Hude, Jr., became a Trustee of Queen's College.

Jonathan Belcher was born in Cambridge, Mass., 1682, making him in 1747 about 65 years of age. He was married in Burlington (where he had established his residence) the next year, on Sept. 9, to Mrs. Leal, a lady "of great merit and handsome fortune." A month later he "requested" the degree of Master of Arts at the first Commencement of the College of New Jersey (held at Newark Nov. 9, 1748) and his request was "heartily granted." He was not pleased with the religious atmosphere of Burlington, there being only an Episcopal and two Quaker congregations there, and the shops sold their goods on Sunday as on any other day. But, as it was only 20 miles by a good road to Philadelphia, he proposed "to go Saturdays and spend the Lord's Day with my good and trusty friend, Mr. Tennent." He removed later to Elizabeth, where he died Aug. 31, 1757, and Rev. Aaron Burr, President of the College of New Jersey, preached his funeral sermon.

The third mayor of New Brunswick, William Ouke, on taking office in 1763, made it again necessary for the Governor to come to the city, and this time it was William Franklin. He was entertained at the White Hall on March 1st and was escorted back to Amboy by the Middlesex Troop of Horse. Franklin was the last of the Provincial Governors. His last Council met in Burlington, Nov. 16, 1775, and the Journal ends Nov. 24, 1775, although they continued in session until Dec. 6th, when the Provincial Legislature of New Jersey terminated. Governor Franklin was then sent to Connecticut for safe keeping (June 20, 1776) and put under guard; there he remained until Nov., 1778, when he was exchanged.

In the meantime, July 10, 1776, the State of New Jersey was formed, and at Princeton, Aug. 31, 1776, William Livingston was chosen Governor. Richard Stockton was the opposing candidate, and the first ballot was a tie. He was reëlected in 1778 by 31 votes against Gen. Dickinson's 7 votes.

A Jacob Ouke was in New York in 1718 and in New Brunswick the same year. William came to New Brunswick in 1729, or before, and purchased land of Van Nuys, who had bought Enoch Vreeland's tract. Jacob and Abraham are noted as being in New Brunswick about the same date. A note in the "N. J. Archives" says that William Ouke was baptised in 1708 and was a son of Auke Janse, sometimes called Janse Ouckerse Van Nuys. Jacob Ouke and Auke Janse I take to be the same. Abraham was executor of John Van Nuys and died in 1751, and Jacob not very long after. Mary Ouke married in 1747 Abraham Heyer; probably William's sister. William was Alderman, Recorder, Mayor for 42 years. New Brunswick had a new charter at the beginning of Ouke's term of office, which was a progressive one. He dealt in bills of exchange, offering bills of 1000 to 5000 guilders and upwards. He died in 1778.

Contemporaneous with Mayor Ouke there were several other families of note in New Brunswick. The Bayard family was one. Samuel Bayard married Anna Stuyvesant, and Governor Peter Stuyvesant married a Bayard, making a double relationship. Samuel Bayard having died, the widow and her three sons, Nicholas, Belthasar, and Peter, came with her brother, Gov. Stuyvesant to New York in 1647. The widow Bayard married, second, Nicholas Varleth, one of Stuyvesant's Council, whose sister, Jane Varleth, married Augustine Heermans of New Jersey, and afterwards of Bohemia Manor, Maryland, where Lord Baltimore granted him 30,000 acres and Manor rights. This was also a second marriage on Heermans' part, and proved unfortunate, as she drove his children out of the house.[2] Heerman's oldest son, Ephraim, was, as has been

---

[2]Augustine Herman (according to the Bohemian orthography) was born in Prague, about the year 1605, the son of Augustine Efraim, an esteemed merchant and an alderman of Prague, and Beatrice, the daughter of another patrician family. The elder Herman became involved in the political disturbances that led to the Thirty Years' War, and in 1618 was exiled. In 1628 his wife and son are found in Amsterdam, Holland. The exact date of Augustine's appearance in the New World is uncertain, but in 1629 he is recorded as having introduced the cultivation of tobacco in Maryland. So far as known Augustine had seven children, three boys and four girls.—[Note furnished by Dr. Hadlitha, Smithsonian Institute].

stated, Danker's guide to Maryland. Augustine was looking for settlers and Ephraim met in New York the Labadists and guided them, hoping to get the proposed colony to settle on their lands. Once there, they were left to get back as best they could. Ephraim was appointed by Governor Andros as Clerk of the Court of Delaware until he relinquished authority over it.

This connection by marriage through the Varleths accounts for Peter Bayard's going to Maryland and the founding of the branch of the family there. Col. John Bayard belongs to this line. He first came to Philadelphia and formed the firm of Hodge & Bayard, and married Margaret Hodge in 1759. After the Revolution, his wife having died in 1780, he settled down in New Brunswick (in 1784), and married, second, Joanna White. He bought in 1793 on Albany St., and built the house now the Mansion House. He was Mayor of the city in 1793, and Judge in 1800; one of the seven stockholders who built the Albany St. bridge in 1791; and was President of the Trenton and New Brunswick Turnpike Co. in 1805, as well as a stockholder in the New Brunswick School Company. One daughter, Jane, married Judge Andrew Kirkpatrick; another, Margaret, married Samuel Harrison Smith and went to live in Washington. "The First 40 Years of Washington Society" are mainly from her letters and diaries. Judge Bayard died in 1807. But he was not the first Bayard to come to New Brunswick. Nicholas had a son Samuel who married Margaret Van Courtlandt and he came to New Brunswick before 1733, about 50 years before Colonel John came. He lived on Burnet St., and his daughter, Gertrude, married Peter Kemble, which brings us to another family of note.

In 1769 Peter Kemble wrote a short account of his family. Richard Kemble, his grandfather, was an Alderman of Bishopgate Ward, London. His father, also Richard, was a Turkish merchant of Smyrna, who married a Greek lady named Mavrocordato. He died in Smyrna. But Peter, born in Smyrna in 1704, came to America and to New Brunswick, where he married into the Bayard family as before referred to. An older brother, William, born 1696, was in the English Navy, and Samuel, who married Catherine French, daughter of Philip French, in 1758, lived next to him.

Peter Kemble was member of City Council in 1747; member of the Governor's State Council, 1745-1775; was Speaker and presided in the absence of the Governor; was in the vestry of Christ Church, and one of those named in the deed of the church lot in 1745. He removed to Morristown about 1765 and died there 1789, aged 85. It was said of him that he was one of the most prominent men in the Colony. Of his ten children, three were by a second marriage to Elizabeth Taite, an Irish lady. Three sons were in the British army. Margaret married Gen. Thomas Gage, who was in New Brunswick June 23rd, 1769, to review the 26th Regiment, John Scott, Colonel, and called Cameronians. This Regiment was in the barracks from 1767 to 1776, when the 29th Regiment took its place; New Brunswick being for some years a barrack town, or military post. Stephen was in the army from 1757 to 1805, was retired a Brigadier General, and returned to New Brunswick, where he died in 1822. His diary has been printed by the New York Historical Society in two volumes, and it says there that he died in the house in which he was born. This house stood on the middle lot of the five 50 feet lots between Neilson St. and the Alley, east of the Mansion House. His father must have moved up town from his house on Burnet street. Stephen, though a British officer, escaped confiscation, perhaps on account of the eminent services of his father.

Another Peter Kemble was a student in the first class at Queen's. This Peter was a son of Samuel Kemble and Catherine French, and a grandson of the trustee, Philip French, and in 1806 subscribed himself as of Halifax, while his two sisters were of "the parish of St. Marylebone, County of Middlesex, Kingdom of Great Britain." He and his sisters made a deed to the White Hall Hotel. The other and fourth heir was his brother, Sampson Gideon Kemble.

Philip French, whose daughter married Samuel Kemble, certainly deserves special notice. His father, Philip French, married Anatje, daughter of Frederick Philipse, the Dutch millionaire, who was very prominent in New York City affairs. During the Leisler troubles he was thrown into jail. Under Governor Belmont he was Speaker of the Assembly. In 1702 he was Mayor of New York and he died in 1707. He made several trips to England and had a most eventful life. He left a son, Philip, and three daughters. His wife, brother-in-law and Col. Lewis Morris were his executors.

The son, Philip French (second), married, first, Susannah, daughter of Lieut.-Gov. Anthony Brockholst and acquired very early the north half of the present city of New Brunswick, from Livingston Ave. north to Mile-Run. He was one of the first trustees of Queen's College. His daughter, Susannah, married, in 1747, Governor William Livingston; another, Mary, married the Hon. William Brown, of Beverly, New England; and Elizabeth married Cornelius Van Horn. Later, Philip French married (2nd), Ann Farmar and we know certainly of but two children—Catherine who married Samuel Kemble as before referred to, and Philip, who died in 1803, and noted then as one of the oldest inhabitants of New Brunswick, his father having died in 1782.

Philip French's business habits were peculiar in that instead of selling any of his lands he sold long leases on them, and on a number of these leased lands he placed mortgages; but neither the money from his leases nor the mortgages sufficed, and we find the Sheriff attaching his lands to satisfy judgments, amounting to £3,240; to James Parker, £800; to Madeline Beekman, £200; to William Beekman, £228; to Ann Chambers, £1,232; to Joseph Ryall, £380; to William Willocks, £400. Robert Stockton, Sheriff, sold a number of properties to satisfy the judgments. Then he was adjudged a Tory and the Commissioners of Forfeited Estates laid claim to what had escaped the Sheriff. Probably 60 properties were sold as Tory estates in Middlesex and as many more in Somerset.

Another family of note, which came down from Albany to New Jersey, was the Schuyler family. Arent came to New Jersey in 1710, though he had bought land here in 1695. He is the founder of the Newark branch of the family. Two of his sons, Col. John and Col. Peter, were not only prominent as business men, operating the copper mines at Second River, or Belleville, now Newark, and ranked as the richest men in New Jersey in 1731. Col. John was rated at £60,000 to £70,000. They were also great Indian and French fighters. Col. Peter asked in 1755 for 500 men and 1,000 offered. He and his command were captured at Oswego; Col. Peter was paroled to go home and the Colony was to return an officer of equal rank. This was not done in time, and Col. Peter returned to Montreal and gave himself up. He was finally released in 1759, and set out on a third campaign. The name "Jersey Blue" was first applied to Col. Peter's men in 1747, because they were such thoroughly trained soldiers.

To New Brunswick, before 1740, came the brothers, Dirck, or Derrick, and Abraham, sons of Abraham, and grandsons of David Pieterse Schuyler. Abraham's line is preserved in a Dutch Bible, of which I have the translation. From this we find that by intermarriage the Coejman, the Voorhees and many other Brunswick families trace back on the female line to the Schuylers. One Abraham Schuyler was Mayor of New Brunswick in 1796. That the family connection between the Newark and New Brunswick branches was kept up appears from some of the old records. Mrs. Joanna (Coejeman) Neilson's will is witnessed by her sister, Mrs. Gertrude Lott, by John Voorhees, the father of her son's wife (whose wife was a Schuyler), and by Dr. John Cochrane, husband of his cousin, Gertrude Schuyler. Mrs. Neilson's brother, Samuel Coejeman, had married Arentje Schuyler; so this family touched the Schuylers in three different ways.

Dr. John Cochrane, just mentioned, was one of the founders of the New Jersey Medical Society in 1766 and its President in 1769. He was an intimate friend of both Generals Washington and Lafayette, as he was a member of Washington's military family and had a cottage at Morristown, and was addressed by both Washington and Lafayette as "Dear Dr. Bones." He was appointed Surgeon-General of the Middle Department in 1777, and Director of the General Hospital of the United States in 1781. There is some discrepancy in the accounts as to whom he married. The New York Historical Society's volume of "Wills," in a note says he married a daughter of Col. John Schuyler and Cornelia Van Courtlandt, named Cornelia, while the "N. J. Archives" states he married Gertrude, daughter of Philip Schuyler. The fact is that Dr. John Cochrane married Gertrude Van Cortlandt, widow of Col. John Schuyler, and his step-daughter, Cornelia Schuyler, married Walter Livingston. In the will of Margaret, widow of Philip Schuyler, she leaves her estate to Gertrude, wife of Dr. John Cochrane. Before the Revolution Dr. Cochrane lived on the corner of Somerset and Water, west of Water and south of Somerset street. His house was burned by the British. Some years later Dr. Ira Condict lived on this same lot in a house, which, I presume, he built.

A word here as to Water St., which was at one time quite fashionable. The east side of the street was so restricted that no buildings could be built on it. In addition to Dr. Cochrane and Dr. Ira Condict, Col. John Taylor, Dr. William Mercer, Samuel Holcomb, Mary, the widow of James Hude, J. R. Hardenbergh and Benjamin Price lived on Water street. Mayor William Ouke had a shop on the lot where Col. Taylor lived later, next door to Hude and the corner.

CHAPTER XIII

Continuation as to Other Prominent Citizens of and Visitors to New Brunswick—Governor William Paterson—Col. Anthony Walton White—Mary Ellis—Gen. Charles Lee—Rev. Abraham Beach—Dr. Samuel Auchmuty—Bernardus Le Grange—Dr. William Farquhar —The Morris Family—General Washington's Visits—President John Adams—Baron de Neuville—Louis Andre Pichon—Gen. Lafayette's Visit—The Lyle Family—The Livingstons—Rev. John Croes—The Neilson Family.

THE next group of citizens to be noticed are those who have in one way or another some Revolutionary history. William Paterson, for instance. In addition to his house down on Burnet St. he had a farm about 14 miles up the river, bought of the Commissioner of Forfeited Estates, it having been Bernardus Legrange's.

While claimed by New Brunswick Judge Paterson was really a State and a National character. His father, Richard Paterson, came from Antrim, Ireland, in 1747, bringing his son, William (b. 1745) with him. He settled in Princeton and introduced the tin industry. William graduated from Princeton College in 1763 and received his degree of M. A., Sept. 24, 1766. There were four professors in Princeton then. He studied law with Richard Stockton, was member of the Provincial Congress, and May, 1775, Assistant Secretary. In October he was made Secretary, and again in February, 1776. He was Attorney-General of the State during the Revolutionary period and until 1783, when he resumed his practice in New Brunswick and was acting as surrogate in Bridgewater at the same time. He was a member of the Convention of 1787 to frame the Constitution; United States Senator in 1788-'90; appointed in 1790 to complete Governor Livingston's unexpired term and was reëlected. In 1793 he was appointed by Washington Associate Justice of the Supreme Court, which he held until he died in Albany, N. Y., Sept. 9, 1806.

He married his first wife, Cornelia Bell, in 1779, in Anthony White's house. She died in 1783. He married, second, Euphemia White, 1785. Anthony White married Joanna Staats.

His son, also Anthony, married before 1751, Elizabeth, daughter of Governor Morris, and came to New Brunswick to live. His house (now in Buccleuch Park) is cared for by the Daughters of the Revolution. His son, Anthony Walton White, served through the Revolution and married Margaret Vanderhorse Ellis of Charleston, S. C. She died May 23, 1850.

William Paterson made his home in New Brunswick for 23 years. He was a prominent citizen in every way, and when he died Council wore mourning on the arm for thirty days.

Anthony Walton White, born at Buccleuch July 7, 1750, was with the Army of Lafayette in the winter of 1782-'3 before Savannah and at Charleston, and it was without doubt at this time that he met Margaret Vanderhorse Ellis, whom he made his wife in the spring of 1783, while she was but a girl of fifteen. Colonel White came out of the War with a shattered fortune, partly from a lavish expenditure most patriotically made to hasten the equipment of two troups of cavalry, and which he expected the Government to repay; and partly from unfortunate speculation, entered into, presumably, in the hopes of recouping himself for previous losses. That he and his bride returned to New Brunswick about 1790 is indicated by the appearance here of his wife's sister, Mary Ellis, who seems to have devoted herself to her sister, Mrs. White. She bought the house on Livingston Avenue long known as the Janeway house, now the site of the Y. M. C. A. Here her sister and brother-in-law made their home with her, so completely in fact that the house is very frequently referred to as, and is supposed to have been Col. White's house. There he entertained his friends and brother army officers. This is the day of the new woman, and Mary Ellis, as a woman of affairs, of courage and independence, will, I think, measure up with any of our business women of to-day.

Colonel White inherited from his father a three-hundred acre farm in the southern end of the city, and, to try to save it from the wreck, he transferred it to his sister-in-law. In 1798 she made an effort to sell half of it, the half lying between the road and the river. The other half lay between the road and Lawrence's brook. Her advertisement of this farm is most interesting reading. She has been held to have been a most romantic person and tales of a lover, an officer of the Revolutionary Period, have been told of her, with how much truth I do not know, but the advertisement certainly shows a romantic bent of mind. Her next business venture was the purchase of Pine Tree Hill, now the site of the New Jersey Women's College. This she purchased, Col. White acting for her, in 1799, and it included rather more than the College site, taking in the quarry next to Burnet St., and down to the brook that has its source in the College Farm pond. But while she was waiting for her rents from Charleston to make the payment on the Hill, Judge Morris became, in some way not quite clear, the owner, instead of old Mrs. Voorhees, with whom Col. White had negotiated the purchase, probably through holding a mortgage on it, and it became necessary for Mary Ellis to complete the transaction through Judge Kirkpatrick, as Col. White and Judge Morris had reached a point where their negotiations were broken off. Mary Ellis' letter is of much interest, showing a clear business head, and a most punctilious sense of what was right and just, insisting on no favors to herself, but for a strict carrying out of Judge Morris' contentions.

On Livingston Avenue, in front of and just across the street from her house, was her garden, a lot of perhaps an acre; through this garden in 1805 the city insisted on opening Schureman St., which at that time ran only to Queen or Neilson. This she felt to be a great and unnecessary hardship, and she at once proceeded to a sale of her garden, cutting it up into lots, which she advertised as on "Oppression Street."

This destruction of her garden and the death of her brother-in-law, Feb. 10, 1803, resulted in the disposal of her town house in 1813 and the purchase of the place so long known by the name of her niece's husband as the Evans' place. Real estate was very slow of sale in New Brunswick, and perhaps this was the first opportunity that offered to sell; or it may be it was the waiting for a suitable place to buy that delayed the change. The place she bought immediately adjoined the farm she tried to sell in 1798, and all that she put in the advertisement of that place applied with equal and exact force to the place she had now bought. And it is a little singular that the

Pine Tree Hill, bought of the widow Voorhees and left to her niece and niece's daughter, long in the tenure of women, is now a Woman's College. The other place, by our first knowledge of it, was owned by Mary Neville, widow of Samuel Neville, left by her to her nieces, Lucia Vickers and Mary Lupp, and sold for their account to Benjamin Taylor.

The name "Lupp" by the way, becoming "Leupp" in later days, is thus explained (as to the change) by the late John H. Leupp, Esq., in a letter to the author as follows: "The family originally came from Nieuweid on the Rhine. When my uncle, Charles M., of New York, was visiting that place about 1840 he saw on the old gravestones the name spelled Lüpp, and thought the dots over the *u* indicated *e* and, that the spelling should not be lost entirely, incorporated the *e* in the name, and, the other members of the family agreeing, the spelling was changed to the prevailing mode."

To return now to Mary Ellis:

The following are the rather curious advertisements by Miss Ellis:

[From "The Guardian," July 24, 1798]

"A Country Seat for Sale.

"That valuable and beautiful part of Cool Spring Farm on the bank of the river Raritan, bounded by the river in the rear, and in front by the main road leading from the City of New Brunswick to Taylor's Mills, South River, Spottswood, Perth Amboy and Monmouth. The farm contains about 150 acres of land, in which is included a sufficient quantity of fire-wood, the best timbered land in the neighborhood of New Brunswick; a swamp in which may be procured a sufficient quantity of the very best manure to enrich the tillable fields with, and which the crops of Indian corn and oats of this year is the best evidence of their being already good, that can be given. The soil is also natural to clover, the field now in grain having without any manure produced the year before last enough clover to support a large flock of horses and horned cattle through the winter. There is also a piece of lowland meadow, and an orchard containing 260 grafted trees bearing the best kind of fruit. The meadow contains about eight or ten acres, and can be watered with very little expenses and trouble, there being a never-failing stream of water which runs through part of it. A good oak and chestnut fence encloses the tillable land, orchard and meadow. There are on the premises a comfortable farm house, a good barn, and a well of excellent water. The situation of this farm is in every respect delightful and advantageous. From the center can be brought to view at the same time the most variegated and pleasing objects, with boats gliding through the meanders of the river on their way to and from the City of New York. Perth Amboy can be seen with the naked eye, and New Brunswick is in full view from the same spot. In the rear of the place, on the banks of the river are many handsome pine and cedar trees interspersed with noble and majestic oaks and other forest trees, which, while they together secure the farm from the northwest winds in winter, afford the coolest retreat in summer. Through these, vistas may be cut so as to display the beautiful windings of the river, and the most romantic clumps and shady walks formed that imagination can depict. The advantages attending this situation will be as great to the purchaser as the objects surrounding it are agreeable to the eye. By a very good footway along the river it is but little more than half a mile to the first wharf in New Brunswick, and about three-quarters of a mile to the brewery and distillery where the city commences, and in the front of the farm is a good road leading from the city, to which produce can be conveyed in a less distance than two miles from the house. Mr. Taylor's grist mill and saw mill are but a few hundred yards from the premises; and here, boards, joists, and building stuff may be sawed for the use of the farm, and grain ground for the family, or exported to New York or Amboy by water, as the tide ebbs and flows from the River Raritan up a creek to a bridge at the mill, to which a large shallop or scow can go with care at high water. Shad in the season and small fish of different kinds are also frequently taken in the creek. The famous cool spring—the most agreeable ride and walk from New Brunswick, and which, in consequence, is frequently visited by those whose society is agreeable—is very near the dwelling house, and perhaps no farm in the state has the advantages of a better neighborhood. Though the beautiful situation and advantages of the farm are well known, yet it is supposed no one will purchase it who is unacquainted with them without first viewing the place; they are therefore referred to Mr. Peter Wyckoff, who lives near the premises and will attend any gentleman who may please to call on him for that purpose, and who is possessed in writing of the terms of sale. If not sold by the first of October it will then be exposed for sale on the premises.

"N. B.—Those who are unacquainted with the situation of the City of New Brunswick are informed that it is on the Post Road from New York to Philadelphia, 36 miles from the first place and 60 from the latter; the best of passage boats go once a week to New York. There is a College, three churches, a good market house and excellent schools. It is a very healthy place and provisions of every kind remarkable good and cheap."

The 150 acres (143.60) is that part of Cool Spring Farm of 300 acres that lay between Clifton Avenue and the river; the other half lay between Clifton Avenue and the brook, as the road up the hill continuing out Burnet St. was not opened until 1810.

[From "The Guardian," Oct. 28, 1805]

To Be Let

"A lot of land adjoining the College Lot and the street, lately opened, which I call *Oppression St.* leading into Schureman St. The said street was run through my garden lot, in a diagonal form, so as to leave the above lot in a triangle; for the injury done me no compensation has been made. Any person desirous to lease the said lot may know the terms by applying to the subscriber living opposite said *Oppression St.*
"Oct. 28, 1805. MARY ELLIS."

General Charles Lee was twice an unwilling visitor in New Brunswick. The first time was after the British had captured him at Mrs. White's Tavern at Basking Ridge and brought him here on his way to New York, January 20, 1778, as a prisoner. The second time was when his court-martial was begun here, July 4, 1778, just after the unfortunate events at the Battle of Monmouth. I have no doubt that he attracted no little attention on both occasions.

Abraham Beach, Rector of Christ Church, and later the assistant at Trinity, New York, born 1740 and appointed to New Brunswick in 1767, married his ward, Ann Van Wickle, about 1771, when she was, I believe, but fourteen. Through his daughter, Cornelia, wife of Isaac Lawrence, and their daughter Julia, wife of Thomas Lawrence Wells, the property bought by the Van Wickles in 1703, part of Raritan lot No. 8, is now the Wells place. During the Revolution the Rev. Doctor found much inconvenience from living outside the lines, for, having Washington's men using his house as a screen from which to take shots at the British who were holding New Brunswick, and going back and forth through the lines from his house to his church, it probably gave him many an exciting ride. A story has gone the rounds giving Dr. Beach the credit of being the only minister who kept his church open all through the Revolution. This story belongs to John Beach of Newton, Conn., who was first a Congregationalist and afterwards an Episcopalian. (See "Doc. Hist. N. Y.," Vol. 3, folio 639).

Another Episcopal clergyman of note was Dr. Samuel Auchmuty, Rector of Trinity, practically the business head of the Episcopal Church in America, judging by his correspondence with Sir William Johnson, Governor Colden, John Rand, etc. He left New York when it became the seat of war and came to New Brunswick, where his daughter, the wife of General William Burton, lived at Buccleuch. But as soon as the British took possession of the city he was anxious to return, especially on account of the great fire in New York, by which he lost, as he estimated, $12,000 and when Trinity lost £22,000, exclusive of the rents from buildings on 262 lots that belonged to Trinity. His three sons were all in the British army. Sir Samuel was presented by Parliament with a service of plate. Robert and Richard surrendered with the army at Yorktown. Dr. Auchmuty married Mary, daughter of Richard Nicholls. When the "Mischianza" was gotten up in Philadelphia as a parting compliment to General Howe on the eve of his return to England, Miss Auchmuty took part, and in the tilt and tournament her Knight was Lord Cathcart, Chief of six Knights, there being seven of the Blended Rose and seven of the Burning Mountain. Gen. Burton was a nephew of Bartholmew Burton, late Governor of the Bank of England. He took his family to England in 1766, and his marriage to Isabella Auchmuty in 1774 was evidently a second marriage.

Of other prominent Loyalists, one was Bernardus Legrange, nephew of Ari Molinaer and a very prominent lawyer; a member of Christ Church vestry. His two daughters married officers of the 26th and 29th while stationed in New Brunswick.[1]

Dr. William Farquhar, who married (1st) Elizabeth Farmar and lived on the corner of Albany and Water Sts., where Mrs. Hude lived afterwards, later moved to New York and married (2nd) Jane Colden.

Edward Antill, who built Ross Hall, had a son in both armies. Stephen Kemble mentions "finding my old schoolmate, Antill, among the prisoners on the prison ship." John and Lewis Antill married Margaret and Alice Colden respectively, and so were connected with Dr. Farquhar and Dr. Auchmuty. Mrs. Antill and Miss Colden had permission from the Continental Congress, Philadelphia, to proceed from New Brunswick to New York after taking an oath to carry no information to the enemy. After the war this group of citizens was lost to New Brunswick. Some returned to England, others moved to Canada. Their property losses must have been very heavy.

Another famous family that had New Brunswick representation was the Morris family. Capt. Richard Morris married Sarah Cole. He came to America via Barbadoes. His brother, Col. Lewis Morris, married Mary ———. Capt. Richard Morris and wife both died when his son Lewis, born 1751, was about six months old, and his uncle became his guardian in 1674 and died in 1676. Lewis inherited large landed estates, one at Morrisania, N. Y., and another at Tinton, (3540 acres), Monmouth Co., to which Morris gave the name of Tinton.

Colonel (and Governor, 1738) Lewis Morris was born 1671; married Isabella Graham 1691, and had 12 children:

---

[1] I should revise my assignment of Bernardus Legrange as a Loyalist and write him down just plain Tory. Johannes De La Grange, a Huguenot from La Rochelle, France, about 1656, settled in New Amsterdam and left four sons: Johannes, b. 1658, d. 1742, at Bergen; Isaac, Jacobus and Omie (usually written Omy), who came to Albany in 1665, bought a house in Albany in 1716 of Rip Van Dam, and purchased a patent at Harmans Kill; married Annetee De Vries in 1666 (?). His children were Johannes, Omie, Christiaan, Isaac, Christina and Jacobus. Johannes had two sons, Johannes and Christiaan. Isaac had three sons, Omi, Isaac, Coenraad. Jacobus had five sons. Bernardus was bapt. Mch. 11, 1721. Jacobus married Eugettie Vaeder, Oct. 24, 1717. Bernardus became a lawyer, came to New Brunswick and married Frances Brasier. His son, James Brasier Lagrange, married in 1776 —— Warrington, and died in 1822, leaving one son, James Warrington Lagrange, who married Harriet Demarest of Waterford, N. Y.

1. Robert Hunter Morris, named for Gov. Robt. Hunter; died 1764.
2. Lewis, born 1698; died 1762.
3. Mary, married Capt. Vincent Pearse, England.
4. Euphemia, married Capt. Mathew Morris.
5. Anne, married June 2, 1739, Edward Antill (died 1787) of New Brunswick.
6. Arabella, married James Graham.
7. Margaret, married Isaac Willets.
8. Elizabeth, married Col. Anthony White (died 1780-'7), of New Brunswick.
9. Sarah, married Michael Kearney, Treas. of East Jersey, 1724.
10. Isabella, married Richard Ashfield.
11. ———, married Capt. Morris, England.
12. John.

Lewis (2 above), b. 1698; d. 1762; m., 1st, Tryntie Staats, who died 1731; 2nd, Sarah Gouverneur, 1746; had 9 children, viz.:

1. Mary (Molly) married Thos. Lawrence, Jr., Philadelphia, 1742.
2. Lewis, born 1726; married Mary Walton (he was signer of the Declaration).
3. Staats Long Morris, Member of Parliament.
4. Richard, born 1731.
5. Isabella, married Rev. Isaac Wilkins.
6. Sarah, married V. P. Ashfield.
7. Gouveneur, born 1753.
8. Euphemia, married Samuel Ogden.
9. Catherine.

Robert Hunter Morris was Chief Justice and also Governor of Pennsylvania. He was born between 1691 and 1696; died 1764, unmarried, but left a natural son named Robert Morris, b. 1745, who also became Chief Justice; lived in New Brunswick and died 1815.

The Morrisania tract in New York and Tinton, N. J., were the two principal great tracts of the Morris family. Robert Hunter Morris and James Alexander bought of Ormiston (a brother-in-law of Peter Sonman), a Proprietary interest, one 1/24th and each obtained 6,000 acres. Judge Morris died in New Brunswick in 1815.

James Alexander was the father of William Alexander, commonly called Lord Stirling, one of Washington's Generals, who married Sarah Livingston, a sister of Gov. William Livingston. There is a note of his coming to New Brunswick in 1775 to inspect the Barracks, which were wanted for the new troops, and which he found full of refugees from New York City. John Schureman and Hendrick Fisher were appointed Barrack Masters, and Capt. Conway, who had raised a company in the city, was directed to march his men five hours a day by way of drill and discipline. His seat was about two miles from Basking Ridge. His mother, Mrs. Mary Alexander was the daughter of Dr. John Johnston of Amboy, and sister of Andrew Johnston, owner of Peapack lands in Bridgewater Township.

The Morris, Alexander and Livingston families together with the Antills and Whites were very intimately associated.

Washington visited New Brunswick only a few times, of which we have record, that is, during the War. His first visit was when on his way from Philadelphia to take command of the army at Boston. He left Philadelphia June 23, 1775, with a military escort under Generals Lee and Schuyler and W. S. Baker on horseback, and was in New Brunswick on the 24th and at Newark, Paulus Hook and New York on the 25th. It rained most of the trip, and the bill of expenses in New Brunswick was paid in bulk. It is probable that he stayed at the White Hall, as it was then the only hotel of note. His second visit was when his army retreated across the State in 1776. He arrived November 28, and left December 1, after the British had shown themselves on the Bluff opposite the city. Stephen Kemble in his diary says that Washington was reported in New Brunswick June 25th, just after the British had evacuated on June 22nd. He probably came to see in what condition the British had left the city. July 4, 1778, his army camped on the river just above the town, after the Battle of Monmouth. If Washington made any other visits during the Revolution I do not find any note of them.

On his first visit Washington was tired and wet from traveling on horseback in haste. On the second visit he had some trying and humiliating experiences, retreating before a superior force with his army melting away every day on account of the expiration of enlistments. He wrote some bitter letters from New Brunswick on this visit and used some very plain language. On his third visit Lee's inexcusable behavior and the pending court martial made it anything but pleasant. His fourth visit was to view a city held for six months by an army of the enemy and one that had done much damage during its stay.

After the Revolution, Mr. James Neilson, son of Col. John Neilson, said that General Washington always stopped to see his father when passing through New Brunswick.

John Adams, when President, made us a much more ceremonious visit than any of Washington's. The "New Brunswich Guardian" of Nov. 14, 1797, says:

"Wednesday, Nov. 8, President John Adams, Lady and Suite on his way from New York to Philadelphia, by invitation of a committee" [composed of Col. Neilson, Col. Bayard, Cornelius Ten Brook and Mr. Clarkson, who went to New York to tender the invitation], "stopped over at New Brunswick at Mr. Drake's Indian Queen Hotel, and was entertained at the White Hall at dinner, where fifty sat down."

Colonel Neilson made the address on behalf of the citizens of New Brunswick. The two hotels were on the east and west corners of the same block and the Presidential Party walked from one hotel to the other between lines of citizens anxious to get a glimpse of it. Adams left Thursday morning at 8 o'clock escorted by Major Dunham's Troop of Horse, commanded in his absence by Lieut. Voorhees for eight miles on his way.

Baron Paul Hyde de Neuville came to New Brunswick, as he says himself at a dinner given in his honor, as an exile, in 1809. He lived on the Easton Ave. Turnpike, lately Mr. McCurdy's, and made a specialty of breeding merino sheep. But the wheel turned, and from 1816 to 1822 he represented France as Minister Plenipotentiary. He negotiated the treaty with France, signed by himself and John Q. Adams, Secretary of State, on Aug. 15, 1822. He bore many titles and honors; was Baron, wore the Legion of Honor decoration, was member of the Society of St. Louis, etc., etc.

The French Charge de Affairs, Louis Andre Pichon, or Pochon, (both spellings), 1801-'5, also lived in New Brunswick, as I learn from a descendant, W. H. Perkins, Jr., of Baltimore, who corresponded briefly with me in regard to it. Both de Neuville and Pichon are mentioned in Mr. Hunt's "40 Years of Washington Society," and to-day one of the French Senators is a Stephen Pochon.

When Lafayette visited America in 1824, the City Council sent a committee to New York to invite him to New Brunswick. He accepted, and a reception and dinner were given to him. He left New York on September 23, crossed to Paulus Hook, thence to Newark, and arrived in New Brunswick September 24th. The Committee of Entertainment, consisting of A. R. Taylor, Mayor; C. L. Hardenbergh and William Van Deursen, met the General near Bonhamtown with the 1st Squadron of Horse Artillery commanded by Major Van Dyke. A military salute of 69 cannon was fired when he reached the bridge, where about 8,000 people had assembled to greet the distinguished visitor. Then the parade was formed as follows:

Escorts; then the General in a coach drawn by four white horses, supplied by Capt. Vanderbilt of the "Thistle;" the Governor of the State, Isaac Williamson; Committee of Arrangements; Common Council; Officers and Soldiers of the Revolution; Officers of the Navy; Militia; Military; Clergy; Judiciary; Bar; Strangers and Citizens.

After the parade there was a reception at the Court House, corner of Bayard and Neilson, followed by a dinner at Follet's City Hotel. (At President Adams' visit it was the Indian Queen and the White Hall that furnished the entertainment.) The Recorder made the speech; Col. John Neilson presided; the General sat on his right and the Governor on his left. After the dinner there was a reception to the ladies at 9.00 P. M. The 1st Squadron of Horse Artillery, the New Brunswick Artillery Co. and the City Guards participated. On Sunday Lafayette visited Joseph Bonaparte at his seat near Bordentown.

Robert Lyle went to Pennsylvania and John Lyle came to New Brunswick in 1732 from Scotland. He bought land of Peter Sleight on Burnet St., both sides, opposite to and adjoining Dr. Lewis Dunham. John Lyle was executor of William Ouke in 1779. When the pews of the Presbyterian Church were sold in 1784, John Lyle, Jr., Moses Lyle, John Lyle (2nd) and John Lyle (3rd) all took pews. In 1792 John Lyle, Sr., deeded his two houses to his two grandsons, John Lyle and Andrew Lyle. These two houses were the two he and his son John then lived in; and he deeded them also 17 2-10 acres on the top of Sonman's hill, extending to the river. This lot on top of the hill is now Mr. James Neilson's, while the part below the hill is known as the steamboat docks, and extends from the foot of the hill to Deep Gully. In 1801 John Lyle of New York, merchant, then in London, gave a power of attorney to Robert Lyle of New York, merchant, also then in London, to dispose of his lands in New Brunswick. This is the John to whom his grandfather deeded land in 1792. Next we have a numerous lot of deeds made by John Lyle (by his attorney Robert Lyle and joined in by Andrew Lyle) consideration nominal (20 shillings); partition deeds by which John and Andrew deeded to George Dunn and his wife, Martha Lyle, William Lawson and Mary Lyle, his wife, while the Dunns and Lawsons deeded to Andrew. Evidently John, Andrew, Robert, Mary Lawson, Martha Dunn and Samuel were brothers and sisters, children of John Lyle.

William Lawson and Andrew Lyle, merchants, were apparently in business together. One of these deeds recites that the deeds were made by John Lyle "now in France," by his attorney, Robert Lyle. One part of the property which went to George Dunn and Martha was a bark house and tanyard. Dr. Dunham was on Burnet St. south of the Lyle property. There was an alley between or adjoining the Lyle houses, called Pearl St., in 1801, but there is no such street or alley now.

Andrew Lyle was Sheriff and after him one John Lyle was Sheriff. The original John Lyle was in the city when the charter of 1730 was granted. John Lyle was Ruling Elder of the Presbyterian Church, March 22, 1790, and John Lyle Terhin was a member of the congregation; John Lyle (2nd) was one of the incorporators of the Presbyterian Church in 1784.

Jane Dunn, daughter of George and Martha Dunn, married David Dunham. Andrew, it would appear was father of Robert and of Samuel, a merchant of New Brunswick while Robert was a merchant of the island of Curacoa, where his father, John Lyle (2nd) was Consul.

John, executor of Andrew Lyle, and grandfather of Samuel, conveyed the 17 2-10 acres on Sonman's Hill to Samuel; and Elizabeth Lyle's son, John Samuel, lived in New York and was in the firm of Lord & Taylor. John N. Lyle, sole heir of Robert Lyle of New York, deeded to Mary C. Lyle and John Lyle was on Committee of Observation Jan. 16, 1775. (Some of this information comes from Louisa Ayres Patten, a descendant of the Lyles).

In New Brunswick City Council Minutes 1747, there is a Reuben Runyon who lived "on the hill" ("Pine Tree Hill"), lately Mrs. John Carpender's home, and the early houses were on Town Lane, the lower end of what is now Commercial avenue. Later in the Revolutionary period Reune Runyon was on the Committee of Correspondence in 1774, probably grandsons of the first Vincent (grandfather of Reune).[2]

There having been several Livingstons in New Brunswick, I have endeavored to place them in the well-known family of that name, with some success. A certain William Livingston, minister of Scotland, had a son John, born June 21, 1603, at Monyabroek, who married a daughter of Bartholomew Fleming, of Edinburgh, attended the College of Glasgow, was Master of Arts in 1621, called to Killenchie, Ireland, in 1630, sailed for New England in 1635, and got into so severe a storm off Newfoundland that the ship returned to Loch Fergus. In 1638 he was called to Stranraer in Galloway remaining until 1648; was called to Ancram, remaining until 1663, when he was banished and went to Rotterdam. He then had a wife and seven children and a stipend of £4 sterling a year. He had a tolerable insight into Hebrew, Chaldee and Syriac, and as much Italian, Dutch and Spanish as enabled him to make use of the books and Bibles in those languages. He spent his time in Holland in

---

[2]Some additional notes on the Runyon family may be found in the Appendix.

making a Latin translation of the Bible; but thought the Dutch the most accurate translation. From age, or constant sitting, he suffered with some bladder diffculties, and died August 6, 1672, in Rotterdam. The family descended from Lord Livingston, afterwards Earl of Linlithgow, who in 1547 had the care of Mary Queen of Scots. His daughter, Mary, accompanied the Queen to France.

Robert, a son of the Scotch minister, was more successful than his father and made the voyage in 1674, two years after his father's death, and settled in Albany; was Secretary of Albany from 1675 to 1721. He married Alida Schuyler, born in 1656. He was born in 1654, and was therefore 20 when he came over, and but 21 when he was made Secretary. Alida was the daughter of Philip and Margaret Schuyler and widow of Domine Nicholas Van Rensselaer. The license to marry is dated July 26, 1676; so he was then not 22. He purchased land of the Indians in 1680, as well as made other purchases, and in 1684 received a Patent from Governor Dongan. In 1682 he had a seat in the new Dutch Church, which he seems to have had a hand in erecting, and in 1686 helped to obtain a Charter for Albany, and was the first Town Clerk of that city. In 1675 or 1685 (both dates are given) he was made Indian Commissioner, though he is said not to have understood the Indian language at all. In 1691 he made a report on the Church pasture lot over which there was a dispute.

Now, in the meantime, his nephew Robert, son of his brother James, had also come over, just when we do not know, but in 1707 he says: "My nephew has been deputy clerk for 13 years;" and he added that he wished his son Philip, then just 21, appointed as Deputy. This nephew, Robert, Jr., as he was called (though Robert had a son Robert, and nephew Robert has a son Robert) seems to have been overshadowed completely by his uncle. The first positive date we have concerning him is his license, dated Aug. 26, 1697, to marry Margarite Schuyler, daughter of Peter Schuyler, brother to Philip, his uncle's father-in-law; so that his uncle's wife and his wife were cousins. Margarita was an only daughter.

There is a little evidence as to another marriage of Robert, Jr., as Annie (Van Schayck) Van Cortlandt in her will of 1707 mentions Mary, wife of Robert Livingston, Jr., and says she is the daughter of her sister, Engeltie Van Schayck. Col. Peter Schuyler married Engeltie Van Schayck also, and had at least two daughters, Anna ,born 1686, and Gertruy, born 1689; and Robert Jr.'s first child, baptised July 17, 1698, was named Engeltie (our Angelica in plain English) ; so there seems to be a mix-up somehow or somewhere in the names.

To go back to Robert, Sr. By his will in 1728 he mentions his sons as Philip, Robert and Gilbert; and his daughters as Margaret and Joannah. "Munsell's Collections" mentions another son, William, and a daughter Catrina, but leaves Margaret out. The will is, of course, the best evidence. I have already mentioned his son Philip taking his cousin Robert's place as Deputy Secretary, Robert being comforted by being made an Alderman of Albany. Gilbert, his third son, is noted as a surveyor in 1708, when but 18 years old.

These sons and Robert, Jr.'s, three sons, James (baptised Jacobus), Peter and Robert, give us six Livingston families, which, after the next generation, it is almost impossible to sort out.

Philip Livingston married Catharine Van Brugh and had nine children. He was the second Lord of the Manor, and his eldest son, Robert, was the third. The other children were Peter,[3] John, Philip,[4] Henry,[5] William, Sarah, Alida and Catharine. Of this line we are most interested in William, who was New Jersey's War Governor and who married Susannah, the daughter of that pioneer in New Brunswick, Philip French. His daughters—Sarah, Kitty and Susan—were great belles of Revolutionary days. But I shall refer to him later.

Robert Livingston, the third Lord's line, born in 1708, married Mary Thong, daughter of Walter and Catalyntje (Van

---
[3]Peter Van Brugh.
[4]Philip (b. 1717) was active in the movement to get a Presbyterian College, but the Episcopalians secured it 1744, though his brother William (b. 1723) made a powerful speech against the mistake of making it a sectarian college.
[5]Henry (b. 1719) settled in Jamaica and did not marry.

Dam) Thong in 1731 and had seven children; Walter, Robert C.,[6] John, Henry, Alida (who married Valentine Gardener), Catherine (who married John Patterson), and Mary (who married James Duane). Robert C. took the name Cambridge from the college from which he graduated in England to define which particular Robert he was. He came to New Brunswick for a wife and married Mary Hude, whose sister Susan married William Neilson; and his brother, Walter, married Cornelia Schuyler, a step-daughter of Dr. John Cochrane of New Brunswick, who had married Cornelia Van Cortlandt, widow of Col. John Schuyler. Walter was one of the managers of Christ Church Lottery in 1772, and is mentioned in 1766; was a member of the Provincial Congress in 1775.

Of the second group—the family of the second son Robert— Robert, who was born July 29, 1688, married Margaret Howarden and lived to be 88, leaving one son, Justice Robert, who married Margaret Beekman. He was born in 1719 and died the same year as his father, (1775), at the age of 58, at Clermont. In 1765 Governor Colden advised the removal of Justice Livingston on the ground that no case could come before him that the Livingston family were not interested in! He had ten children: Jane (1743), Chancellor Robert R., Henry B., John R., Gertrude, Joannah, Alida, Edward, Margaret and Catharine. The family connections are illustrious. Edward was Mayor of New York, and author of the "Livingston Legal Code." The daughters married Gen. Richard Montgomery, Gov. Morgan Lewis, Gen. John Armstrong; and the sons into Stevens and Shippen families, and back into the Livingston family.

It is the Chancellor, Robert R., who, with Fulton, ran their steamboat "Raritan" to New Brunswick, and later, under their unconstitutional exclusive water right, carried on the great steamboat war, who touches the city in this line, and it is probable that in this connection he bought the South Amboy Ferry, which he and his wife deeded in 1807 for $20,000, about 100

---

[6]Robert C. was a Vestryman in Trinity, New York, in 1790; this line seems to have become Episcopalians.

acres going with the ferry. John R. and Robert James succeeded Fulton and the Chancellor in the steamboat operations. As to the third group, or family of Gilbert. Gilbert was born March 5, 1690, and married Cornelia Beekman, daughter of Col. Henry Beekman, so noted as a land owner that once, when a boy asked if there was land in the moon, he was told to go ask Colonel Beekman, for, if there was, he certainly had a good slice of it. Gilbert got "Saraghtoge," just 12 miles wide by 22, along the Hudson River, as his share of his father's estate. He had ten or eleven children: Robert G., Henry, Gilbert, Philip, Samuel, Cornelia, Alida, Joanna, Catharine and Margaret. There is a will of Cornelius, 1757, which mentions his four sisters, Alida, Joanna, Catharine and Margaret, but not Cornelia, so perhaps Cornelia should read Cornelius. Robert G., the oldest son, married Catharine Mackphædrix, which I find handed down in history as Mac Feathers. This Robert got Rhinebeck as his portion. Henry, the second son, married M. S. Conklin, and his son the Rev. John H. Livingston, married Sarah, his third cousin, the daughter of Robert, son of Philip (1717), the son of Philip (1686). Born in 1746, Rev John H. was President of Queens in 1809, and removed to New Brunswick from New York City 1809. When he came he first bought 151 acres (the tract we call Livingston Manor) for $4,555, selling it again in 1818 for $8,000. In 1810 the farm on Livingston Avenue had a house on it. On June 25, 1810, he writes: "The new part of the house and the alterations to make it comfortable are in the hands of the carpenter." His church and college life are so well known that it is needless to follow it now.

Next we come to the families of the son of "Robert-the-Nephew," son of Robert's brother James. Jacobus (or James as it was in English usage) was baptised Oct. 21, 1701, married Maria, or Mary, Kierstede of the famous Aneke Jans family, the only child of Jacobus Kierstede. Their children were: Robert J., Elizabeth, Mary, Janet, Margaret. Janet married William Smith, the historian; Margaret married Philip R. Livingston of the Manor line; Robert married Susannah Smith, their children being Robert J., Jr., Col. Wm. Smith,

Peter R., Mary, Susannah, Maturin and James K. The line of Jacobus (James) was prolific and well-connected.

Janet married Col. Henry Beekman; as Janet was born in 1703, and as Col. Beekman's daughter, Cornelia, married Gilbert Livingston about 1712, this must have been a second marriage. Col. Henry Beekman did not die until 1784, a very old man.

Peter, the second son, married Zelia Holland in 1728, and their children were: Robert, Henry, Margarita, Thomas, Jane and a second Margarita (the first having died).

As to John, I cannot say whom he married, as there is a John in Philip's line, a John in Robert's line, and a John in Robert-the-Nephew's line. Philip's John seems to have married Catherine Depeyster; as to the other Johns, I can only note that a John married Mary Leroy; another John married Mary Winthrop; a John married Frances Saunders; a John married Margaret Sheafe; a John married a McEver; a John married Catherine ———, who was next of kin to Adolphe Philipse; and there was a John who was a nephew of John Chambers. A John, (Robert-the-Nephew's son?) married Catharine Ten Broeck. I place him there from the fact that the children were: Robert, Margarita and Dirck. Margarita is a family name. Robert-the-Nephew married Margarita; his son James had a Margarita; the son Peter had a Margarita; the son Robert, whom I have not yet mentioned, and whose wife I cannot name, had a daughter Margarita. In all of the other Robert's line I fail to find a Margarita, and I am a great believer in the persistence of things, not only in family names but in land lines as well.[7]

---

[7]It is disturbing to read in one family sketch a list of names, and then in another to find a different distribution. Second marriages bring in most confusing complications. For instance, of Dr. John Cochrane it is said he married Gertrude Schuyler, daughter of Philip Schuyler: another authority says Col. John Schuyler married Cornelia, daughter of Stephen Van Cortlandt, and that Cornelia Schuyler was Dr. Cochrane's wife, as if it were Col. Schuyler's daughter. Now, the fact is, that Peter Schuyler's daughter, Gertrude, married Stevanus Van Cortlandt, and their daughter, Cornelia, married Col. John Schuyler, and his widow, Cornelia Van Cortlandt Schuyler, married Dr. John Cochrane, while his stepdaughter married Walter Livingston; quite clear when one gets hold of all the facts.

This sums up very concisely the four Livingston family lines, on the male side. I have followed them out to include the first Governor, William; Robert R.; Walter; Robert C.; and Rev. John H., being those of local interest, as well as Peter Van Brugh, who, in 1821, owned the Ferry right and 60 acres in Highland Park, and Robert James who, in 1843, owned the manor adjoining.

There is more of interest, however, to be added concerning Robert's daughters. Margaret married Samuel Vetch, Governor of Nova Scotia; and her only child mentioned, Alida Vetch, married Stephen Bayard. The other daughter, Joanna, married Cornelius Gerrit Van Horne; and there are four sons mentioned—Gerrit, Augustus, Cornelius C. and David, who married Ann French.

Of the next generation I have referred to several—Sarah, who married William Alexander; Alida, who married Henry Hanson and (2nd) Martin Hoffman. Her cousin, Alida, married Gen. John Armstrong. Joanna married Peter R. of the "Nephew's" line; Gertrude married Gov. Morgan Lewis, and their only child, Margaret, married Maturin Livingston of the "Nephew's" line. Joanna, a cousin, married Pierre Van Cortlandt, Lieut-Governor of New York. Margaret married Henry Beekman, son of the old Colonel.

After the Revolution the entail comes to an end, though there had been previous liberal apportionments as in 1752. While Robert got the Manor at Clermont, Gilbert's line had the grant at "Saraghtoge," a no mean estate. After Robert, the third Lord's death, it was partitioned out to Walter, Robert Cambridge, John and Henry. Walter sold his portion of Clermont to Henry, who built a wonderful home there.

Of the later generations, one of the "Nephew" line, Robert James, came to New Brunswick and bought the tract now known as Livingston Manor in Highland Park; 97 acres, less six sold to the Railroad Company for right of way. He purchased in 1843 and held till 1891. This closes up the local connection with the Livingston family.

I have appended a family chart showing more clearly where the first members claimed come in. While the family goes back to a Dissenting Minister, persecuted and exiled, many of the family, a hundred years later, are members of the Episcopal Church, showing how time, a new country, broader and more liberal views, have softened feelings and views. Robert Livingston and James Hude's children were Episcopalians, though but one of the four parents was an Episcopalian, and I have noted many similar cases. The intermarriages of the Livingstons with the Beekmans, the Van Hornes, De Peysters, Ten Broecks, Alexanders, Stevens, Van Cortlandts and themselves, formed a little aristocracy that has been very persistent.

I think it is of special interest that three times members of the Livingston family should have purchased in Highland Park. First, the Rev. John H. Livingston went so far as to purchase there, though making another selection in the city and selling his first purchase. This was in 1809 and of 151 acres. Second, Peter Van Brugh Livingston acquired 60 acres of the old Ferry property. This is the piece south of and adjoining the piece bought in 1809 by the Rev. John H., and was bought in 1821. Third, Robert James Livingston and his wife, Louisa M., daughter of Garret Storm, bought the piece that was bought in 1809 by the Rev. John H. This was in 1843, and it was held till 1891, but is still called Livingston Manor.

One of the prominent figures in New Brunswick history and one with a state-wide reputation was the Rev. John Croes. As an instructor, with intimate relations to Queen's College; as a minister and rector of Christ Church, and as the first Bishop of New Jersey; born in poverty; unable to acquire a college education; he still forged his way to the first rank and to the head of it. Born at Elizabethtown June 1, 1762, he was the son of Jacob and Charlotte (Charlotte Christeana Reigert) Croes. His father, a native of Poland, received a limited education in Holland, where his real name "Kruitz" was spelled "Croes" and pronounced *Croose*. Charlotte, born in Germany, emigrated in the same vessel to America. Jacob is said to have been a saddler and Charlotte opened a bakery where John, when old enough, delivered the bread. Previous to the Revolutionary War the family removed to Newark and in 1778

John, though but 16, was called on for military duty. John was then unable to write and the drummer boy gave him lessons. That he was a good teacher and had an apt scholar, the Bishop's beautiful hand-writing in later years testifies. The teacher became Secretary of State and the pupil Bishop of New Jersey. He was soon advanced to Orderly Sergeant, and Quartermaster, then recruiting Sergeant, and Sergeant Major. His parents are thought to have been Lutherans, but in Newark became members of Trinity Episcopal Church under the Rev. Uzal Ogden, Rector.

The strong religious leading of his father is shown by a letter to John when his second son, Jacob, then in Virginia, was about to go to New Orleans (then under the King of Spain, for whom he had a strong dislike). He said: "I know not whence to fly for relief but to the Orphans' Court at the City of the New Jerusalem, where Emmanuel was Attorney-General, his old and tried Friend, his true Advocate, whose promise he had that He would never leave him nor forsake him."

At the close of the Revolutionary War John began teaching in Newark. He was a rigid disciplinarian, as might be expected after his military training. School hours were from 9 to 12 and 2 to 5. At this time he was corresponding with students at Princeton, to which place he hoped to go. Ashbel Green, May 21, 1782, wrote most interestingly of admission to the Whig College Society, of prayers morning and evening, of the Freshman and Sophomore speaking, recitations immediately after the ringing of the nine o'clock bell, with a daily lesson in Geography, Mathematics, and French, and an oration every fortnight. Zadoc Squier wrote that Congress was holding its sessions in the College Library June, 1783, and bantered John Croes on hearing that he is at the head of the Newark satirists.

While teaching he determined on the ministry as his life work. He married Martha, daughter of Elisha and Hannah (Mix) Crane of Newark. In 1789 he took a pedestrian trip, partly for his health and partly to find where a clergyman was required. He had letters from Rev. Dr. McWhorter, the Presbyterian minister of Newark, and from Judge Boudinot, to Joshua M. Wallace, of Burlington. He visited Dr. Colin and Bishop White in Philadelphia, and, by the advice of Dr. Colin, went to Swedesborough, where Bishop White proposed to confer Deacon's orders on him about March, 1790. He had read prayers and a sermon in the church in Newark by approval of Rev. Dr. Ogden, and now undertook to be lay reader at Swedesborough till ordained. Jan. 24, 1790, he received a conditional call to Swedesborough at £125 specie, with the parsonage house, woodland and meadow—all conditioned on his obtaining ordination. This took place as arranged in St. Peter's, Philadelphia, Feb. 28, 1790, Bishop White (who had been consecrated but four years before in England) officiating, again in the same church. March 4, 1792 he was advanced to the Priesthood, Bishop White officiating again. He attended the Convention held June 6, 1792, in Christ Church, New Brunswick and produced his letter of orders. The next year the Convention met at St. Mary's, Burlington, and Mr. Croes preached the opening sermon. In 1794 the Convention met in St. Peter's, Amboy, six clergymen present, and again Mr. Croes preached the opening sermon. In 1795, at Christ Church, Shrewsbury, Mr. Croes again preached the sermon. In 1796 Mr. Croes was appointed Treasurer of the Diocese and Dr. Ogden, of Newark, became his surety.

In 1796 Mr. Croes was chosen one of the delegates to the Geneva Convention. In 1797 Nassau Hall conferred on him the honorary degree of A.M., and in 1798 he received one vote for Bishop. His commemoration sermon on the death of Washington was published, and in 1800 the oration made before the Cincinnati Society at its meeting in Trenton was written by Mr. Croes and committed to memory and given by the orator of the day. In 1800 he also received a call to the rectorship of Christ Church, New Brunswick, which he declined. On May 16, 1801 the call was renewed, with an offer of $375 per annum for fifty-two sermons, and, under date of May 12, 1801, Queen's College Trustees extended an invitation to open a school in the College Hall building and offered $200 and the use of the college lot (about 2 acres); and then for seven years Mr. Croes carried this double burden of the church and school, when impaired health obliged him to relinquish the Academy (which had attained under him an enviable reputation, though the school was practically suspended when he took it).

Mr. Croes was described at this time as about six feet tall and of a portly frame; quite proficient in the Latin and Greek languages; and possessing the gift of government to a high degree, acquiring affection and esteem without extreme severity. The Hon. George Reed, of Delaware, who had a son at his school, wrote him on Sept. 9, 1805: "I am assured, Sir, that the correctness of your plan of education and the strict attention with which it is conducted must contribute in an eminent degree to promote the progress of your pupils and give the seminary over which you preside a character that is not surpassed by any on this continent." The success of this school encouraged Queen's Trustees to establish professorships and to recommence a collegiate course.

Mr. Croes, however, continued to do some teaching. In 1811 he taught in Miss Sophia Hay's Young Ladies' School, and in 1813 he taught a class of young ladies in Mrs. Isaac Lawrence's mansion, afterwards the Janeway mansion. Columbia conferred the degree of D.D. upon Mr. Croes in 1811, and on Aug. 15, 1815, he was elected the first Bishop of New Jersey, and was consecrated in St. Peter's, Philadelphia, where he had been made Deacon and Priest, and by the same man, Bishop White, assisted by Bishop Hobart, of New York, and Bishop Kemp of Maryland. The first Convention of his diocese met at Trinity, Swedesborough, Aug. 18, 1819.

Bishop Croes died July 30, 1832, aged seventy. His funeral was on the afternoon of the next day, precisely at three. The long procession moved with slow and solemn step to the church he had for thirty years served. The pall was borne by two of the clergy of his diocese, and by several ministers attached to Rutgers College, and the several religious bodies of the city.

Bishop Croes' prominent traits were industry, perseverance and a temper which never yielded to despondency; a strict uprightness; great dignity and urbanity of manners and kindness to the poor and afflicted. Early in life he formed the resolution never to turn a beggar from his door, because he thought it had a tendency to harden the heart. May 1, 1806, he bought the house No. 86 Carroll Place, where he lived the remainder of his life, and his family continued there till the death of Mrs. Croes in 1845. Dr. Alfred Stubbs, Rector of Christ Church from 1839, said: "He was in the truest sense of the word 'a self-made man.' Though not famed for popular eloquence he was the laborious parish priest, the sincere friend, the judicious counsellor, the watchful pastor, the instructive preacher, the thoughtful writer, the sound and well-read divine. He had the happy faculty of speaking the truth in love, and is generally spoken of as the 'good Bishop.'"

Of Scotch-Irish forebears on the side of his father, Dr. John Neilson, and of Holland ancestry on that of his mother, Joanna Coejeman, was John Neilson. Losing his father when but eight days old, he was adopted by his uncle James, his father's brother, and brought up in his family and to his business. On December 1, 1768, he married Catherine Voorhees, who was but fifteen years old, and he twenty-three. James Neilson's house was burned that year with his store houses, and his loss is put at eight thousand pounds; so the young couple rented a house of Levi Totten from May, 1769, for one year, at fourteen pounds. His uncle rebuilt his house and, as he was childless, the young couple without doubt made their home with him, though spending part of the time with his father-in-law, Captain John Voorhees, who had both a town house on Little Burnet Street and a farm house located at the College farm pond. There is little doubt that he was a member of the Sons of Liberty, but, as that was a secret organization, little is known of it. His uncle was a member of the Committee of Observation in January, 1775, and in August John was appointed Colonel of a battalion of Middlesex County Minutemen and left his little family for the War.

In 1776 New Brunswick was occupied by the British and Hessians. In August John was Col. of the Second Regiment, Middlesex Militia, and in 1777 Brigadier-General of Militia. He removed his family from New Brunswick when it was occupied by the British, and, while he might have placed them safely with his mother's family at what we now know as Raritan, his uncle, Abraham Lott, who married his mother's sister Gertrude, had removed his family to Beaverwyc (now called Troy Farms) not far from Morristown, and near Washington's Headquarters, and that was much the most convenient place for Col. Neilson.

Mrs. Washington was a guest at his home in Beaverwyc in 1777 and, in a letter from the General to Mrs. Washington, he said: "Mr. Lott's household have engaged you to spend the summer there. They are one of the finest families you ever saw. The old gentleman and his lady are as merry as boys of fourteen, and there are four or five young ladies of delicate sentiments and polite education." And it is a tradition in the Neilson family that Mrs. Col. Neilson had her seat at table between General and Mrs. Washington. In 1778 and up to May, 1779, he was in active service.

When in command of the post at Elizabeth, his friend, Major Van Emburgh, wrote: "I feel much for you, knowing your force to be weak, and the charge you have great and difficult."

The Declaration of Independence was sent to Col. Neilson by Congress and he read it standing on a table in Albany street, New Brunswick, to the assembled citizens. (His Militia Regiment was alternately in the field and at home to secure the crops).

That he was relied upon by Washington in times of stress is shown by letters of Washington. In December, 1776, he is directed to use his exertions to call together the State Militia, the British then holding New Brunswick, and the beleaguered state which they found themselves in was due principally to the activities of the State Militia. In June, 1779, Washington wrote to Colonel Neilson:

"HEAD QUARTERS, CRANBURY, 26th June, 1779.

"SIR: I have received your favor of this date and thank you for the intelligence contained in it. Various and uncertain information relative to the enemy's movements has made it difficult to determine the part to be taken by the Army. I shall rely upon you to advise me constantly of their situation. It is essential for me to know where they encamp each night and the extent of their encampment, at what hour they march, the length of their line, their halting places, in fine every minute particular that may assist me in forming my plans. Above all a frequency of distinct intelligence, whether the enemy change their position or remain stationary, will be of the greatest importance to me.

"With respect to your operations, if you find it impracticable to gain the enemy's front, as was intended, the next best thing is to fall on one of their flanks or rear, as opportunity may offer, and give all the annoyance in your power. The Monmouthshire militia may be of very great service by attaching themselves to one of the Continental detachments that are near the enemy. It will be best for them to coöperate with that which they can most readily join.

"I am, Sir, Yours most obed. etc.,
"Colonel Neilson   G. WASHINGTON."

There are other letters of like import. In September, 1780, Colonel Neilson was appointed Department Quartermaster-General and held that post at Trenton until January, 1783, renting a house and having his family with him. His uncle just lived to welcome peace, and Col. Neilson removed to New Brunswick to his uncle's house, which, by the death of his uncle at the close of the War, became his own. He entered at once into the shipping business, built up by his uncle and probably almost destroyed by the War. He bought the "Betsy," 70 tons, and the "Jersey," refitting the "Polly" and the "James," which brought cargoes to Robert Lenox's vessels at New York and traded actively with Lisbon, Madeira, London, Dublin and the West Indies.

The schooner "Favorite," Capt. John Voorhees, engaged in the West India trade. His son James, when eighteen, was assisting him in this business.

Colonel Neilson was a deeply religious man. His business did not interfere with serving his church, his city and his State. In 1784 he was one of the committee to build the Presbyterian church, the original church having been almost destroyed by the British; and he was a manager of the New Brunswick and Elizabeth church lottery. In 1791 he was one of the commissioners to build a toll bridge in New Brunswick.

In 1799 he made a horseback trip to Pittsburg in thirty-five days, in the interest of the estate of Abraham Nelson (not his own business). In 1800 and 1801 he was a member of the Assembly at Trenton, and kept interesting minutes of the sessions. He was a director of the New Jersey Turnpike Co., a member of the Grand Jury in 1804, and from 1795 to 1798 was Judge of the Court of Common Pleas. He was on the committee to raise money to build the new Court House in 1787 and was very active in its erection. It was opened Jan. 9, 1796, John Neilson then being Judge. He made a trip to Albany, going by horseback to New York and sloop to Albany, taking his horses with him. Andrew Coejeman, Capt. Farmar, Capt. and Mrs. Voorhees and General Floyd were of the party.

John Neilson was executor of Samuel, Andrew and Majeke Coejeman. He was Register and Recorder of the city of New Brunswick from April, 1798, to February, 1821, and resigned to avoid becoming Mayor. He was Secretary of his Church Board, or Session, from 1784 until his death, and the book of minutes is in his handwriting.

An incident of his Revolutionary career was the capture of Richard Stockton, known as the Land Pilot, Major of the Sixth Battalion N. J. Loyalist Volunteers, holding a fortification on the Island Farm, or Bennet's Island as it was then called. Col. Neilson and Capt. Farmar and his men captured the entire party of sixty-three, and Stockton was sent to Philadelphia in irons by order of General Putnam.

Col. Neilson's character was such that he was in constant demand as referee, executor, and other positions of trust. August 12, 1793, Col. Neilson wrote Governor Howell declining a commission as Brigadier-General, which, he said, he could not accept as a mattter of principle (though he does not explain that), but that his reasons were well known to his fellow citizens.

While the Neilsons were primarily business men, their connection with Queen's and Rutgers College was constant and their financial support most liberal. Col. John was a Trustee of the College in 1782. After his death in 1833 his son James (who, by the way, was also a Captain in the War of 1812, and a Colonel of militia) succeeded him as Trustee in 1834, and the hill where the Theological Seminary is located was a gift by him. His son, James, of the class of '66, and who is still living, followed as Trustee in 1886. His gifts to the College have been large and continuous. He gave most of the land known as Neilson Campus and the sites of the Agricultural Experiment Station Building, the Library, Gymnasium, Engineering, Chemical and Ceramic Buildings, Fraternity House, etc., as well as Neilson Field. In addition he has given the Agricultural Department land adjoining the College Farm, and to the Women's College a site for an athletic field, probably the most picturesque of any athletic field in the country, and, what is more than gifts, he has given freely of his time and interest to the three institutions.

In James the early settler, who helped build the city, enlarge its trade and commerce, and make firm its foundations; in Col. John who gave his best years to secure the freedom and establish the government of his country, now perhaps the greatest in the world; in James second of the name, son of Col. John, who carried on the first James' record for building up industries, and who stood in the first rank in fostering transportation, commerce and manufactures; in James third of the name, who has maintained the record established by his predecessors and has struggled to maintain civic virtue, promote education, and carry on the principles that have ever governed his ancestors, we have a record excelled by few, and, what is more rare in these days, the family has retained an exalted position in the same city for about two hundred years.

CHAPTER XIV

New Jersey As It Appeared to Early Observers and Travelers—Notices of and Extracts from Journals—Denton, Fox, Edmundson, Fenwick, Budd, Danker, Sluyter, Scot, Potter, Thomas, Brainerd, Hamilton, Kalm, Bernaby, Berkenhonts, Schoept.

THERE were two types of writers of the early history of New Jersey; one wrote for the hoped-for emigrant, and in a general description presented a sketch of the country in its most attractive light. Of such there is a very great sameness in what they said; the facts and arrangement would incline one to believe that they were reproduced by the successive writers or obtained from the same original source.

DANIEL DENTON wrote a brief account of New York under date of 1670, and describes New York as "all the land between New England and Maryland in Virginia." How far it extended back into the interior he does not attempt to say. He gives the rivers as the "Hudson," the "Raritan" and the "Delawarebay" Rivers, and of the Indians he says: "How strangely the Indians have been decreast by the hand of God, for since my time, where there were six towns they are reduced to two small villages," and adds: "The Indian name dies with him and must not be again mentioned, and any other Indian having a similar name doth change it and take a new one." Denton lived in Jamaica, Long Island, and was one of those who petitioned Governor Nicolls for the privilege of making a settlement in East Jersey; so it is quite probable that his little pamphlet was written and distributed to attract settlers to the venture made at Elizabethtown in 1664.

GEORGE FOX and WILLIAM EDMUNDSON were Quaker preachers, who came to Virginia in 1671 for the purpose of visiting the Quaker settlements and to encourage them, and to look into their spiritual condition. They both wrote journals and went over much the same ground; although not making the trip together, they met from time to time. George Fox, according to his "Journal," crossed the Delaware from New

Castle, "a Dutch town," and took a course through what are now the seaboard counties. These men came to see Quakers and saw little else. Fox says: "Not seeing man, woman or dwelling, except Indians, until they [we] arrived at Middletown, an English plantation in East Jersey." Middletown is said to have been the second town in East Jersey, Elizabethtown having been the first. He adds: "Were troubled to procure guides, which were hard to get and very chargeable." . . . "Then had we that wilderness country to pass through, since called West Jersey, not then inhabited by English. Sometimes we lay in the woods by a fire and sometimes in the Indian wigwam." From Middletown they went to "Middletown Harbour, where Richard Hartshorne carried us and our horses in his own boat over a great water, which held us the most part of the day in getting over, and set us upon Long Island. We got that evening to Graves End, the next to Flushing and the following to Oyster Bay, where the Quaker half-year meeting began next day." From there he went over to Rhode Island, and on his return, William Edmundson, whom he had left in Maryland, joined him at Shelter Island. "We came again to Richard Hartshorne at Middletown Harbour the 27th of the sixth month, 1672. We got at length to Shrewsbury and had a meeting there. Middletown is about five miles from Middletown Harbour. We set out on our return to Maryland and, on the 15th, we got safely to New Castle." At no place in New Jersey, except the three mentioned, does he note meeting a white man.

From the "Journal of the Life, Travels, Sufferings and Labor of Love in the work of the Ministry of William Edmundson," 1675 or 1676, on pages 105-109, we extract the following:

"The next morning we took our journey towards Long Island, and in three days came there, where friends received us gladly; but were much troubled in our meetings with several who had gone from Truth, and turned Ranters, i. e., men and women who would come into Friends' meetings singing and dancing in a rude manner, which was a great exercise to Friends. . . .

"When we were clear of that quarter, we took boat to East Jersey and came to Shrewsbury, where we staid some meetings, and were refreshed with Friends in the Lord; from thence went to Middletown and had a meeting there, at Richard Hartshorne's, which was full and large; to which there came several of those people that were tainted with the ranting spirit. One Edward Tarff came into the meeting with his face blacked, and said, 'It was his justification and sanctification;' also sung and danced, and came to me, where I was sitting waiting on the Lord, and called me 'old rotten Priest,' saying, I had 'lost the power of God;' but the Lord's power filled my heart and His Word was powerful and sharp in my heart and tongue, I told him he was mad, and that made him fret; he said I lied, for he was moved of the Lord to come in that manner to reprove me. I looked on him in the authority of the Lord's power, and told him, I challenged him, and his God that sent him, to look me in the face one hour or half an hour; but he was smitten, and could not look me in the face, so went out. The Lord's power and sense of it was over the meeting, in which I stood up, and appealed to the rest, whether this was not the same power of God in which I came among them at the first, unto which they were directed and turned when they were convinced of the truth, showing them how they (i. e. the Ranters) went from it, and were bewitched by a transformed Spirit into strong delusions. It was a blessed heavenly meeting. People were tender and loving and friends comforted and glad of that blessed opportunity.

"Next morning we took our journey through the wilderness towards Maryland, to cross the river at Delaware-Falls. Richard Hartshorn and Eliakim Wardell would go a day's journey with us; we hired an Indian to guide us, but he took us wrong, and left us in the woods; when it was late we alighted, put our horses to grass, and kindled a fire by a little brook, convenient for water to drink: so lay down until morning, but were at a great loss concerning the way, being all strangers in the wilderness. Richard Hartshorn advised to go to Rarington river, about ten miles back, as was supposed, to find out a small landing-place from New York, from whence there was a small path that led to Delaware-Falls. So we rode back, and in some time found the landing-place and little path; then the two Friends committed us to the Lord's guidance and went back.

"We travelled that day, and saw no tame creature; at night we kindled a fire in the wilderness, and lay by it, as we used to do in such journies; next day, about nine in the morning, by the good hand of God, we came well to the Falls, and by His Providence found there an Indian man, a woman and a boy with a canoe; we swam our horses, and, though the river was broad, yet got well over; and, by the directions we received from Friends, travelled towards Delaware Town along the west side of the river. When we had rode some miles we baited our horses, and refreshed ourselves with such provisions as we had, for as yet we were not come to any inhabitants. Here came up to us a Finland man, well horsed, who could speak English; he soon perceived what we were, and gave us an account of several Friends. His house was as far as we could ride that day; he took us there, and lodged us kindly.

"Next morning, being first day of the week, we went to Uplands, where were a few Friends met at Robert Wade's house, and we were glad one of another, and comforted in the Lord. After meeting we took boat and went to Salem about thirty miles; there lived John Fenwick, and several families of Friends from England. We ordered our horses to meet us at Delaware Town by land; so we got Friends together at Salem and had a meeting; after which we had the hearing of several differences, and endeavored to make peace among them.

"Next day we went by boat, accompanied by several Friends, to Delaware Town, and there met with our horses according to appointment, but for a long time could get no lodging for ourselves, or them; the inhabitants being most of them Dutch and Finns, and addicted to drunkenness. That place was then under the Government of New York, and is now called Pennsylvania. There was a Deputy-Governor in it; so, when we could not get a lodging, I went to the Governor, and told him we were travelers, and had money to pay for what we called for, but could not get lodging for our money. He was very courteous, and went with us to an Ordinary, and commanded the man to provide us lodging (which was both mean and dear), but the Governor sent his man to tell me, that what I wanted send to him for and I should have it.

"The next morning we took our journey towards Maryland."

JOHN FENWICK settled in Salem in 1673. While neither an observer nor a traveler, he was very much engaged and deeply interested in the settlement of the province of West Jersey, having (according to R. G. Johnson, Philadelphia, 1839), bought it of Lord Berkeley in 1673 for £1,000, and also of the Indians in 1675. Fenwick made captivating offers for immigrants: to each immigrant 70 acres of land with 70 acres additional for each man servant, and 50 acres for each female, feeble person or child. Fenwick himself brought his daughters and their families, children and servants; Elizabeth and her husband, John Adams, and three children; Priscilla, her husband, Edward Chamneys, and two children; Anna, who shortly married Samuel Hodge, Surveyor-General; and Fenwick's own ten servants. Fenwick kept 1/10 or 150,000 acres in Salem and Cumberland counties, and sold the other 9/10's of West Jersey for £900 to William Penn, Gawen Laurie and Nicholas Lucas. Fenwick was a Major of Calvary under Cromwell, and attended with his squadron at the decapitation of King Charles I. Three of those concerned in the execution fled to this country. Fenwick's wife (a second wife) remained in London for some reason, but corresponded with him. He died in the winter of 1683-1684.

THOMAS BUDD, whose prospectus is much like Daniel Denton's and is styled a true account of the country in Pennsylvania and New Jersey, made some interesting comments. Of the Indians he said they go up the Delaware from the Falls about eighty miles to an Indian town called Minesincks (or "the water gone"). This settlement was on alluvial flats on both sides of the river and extending for some forty miles, called Parquarry Flats, and is now indicated by Pahaquarry in the northeast corner of Warren county, New Jersey. In 1729 Penn's government learned for the first time that there was a settlement of Hollanders there, and Nicholas Scull, a surveyor, was sent there in 1732 to investigate. He found the settlement (after forcing his way up through the Water Gap) which was believed to be many years older than Penn's Charter of 1681. Scull began a survey, when an old Indian put a hand on his shoulder and said: "Put up iron string—go home." So Scull returned and made his report.

The outlet to this settlement was by a mine road to Esopus, some 100 miles. The Hollanders claimed to have no knowledge to where the river ran. The first settlers bought the improvement of the Indians, who largely moved to the Susquehanna. The date of the Esopus settlement is 1615, and Samuel Preston visited and talked with the old men in 1787, who were generally grandsons of the first settlers. General James Clinton and Christopher Tappan knew of the mine-holes and the mine road, and were of the opinion that it was the first good road of any extent ever made in any part of the United States. While there is some uncertainty as to the kind of ore that was mined, it has been stated that it was copper. The settlement, the oldest European settlement of equal extent ever made in the territory, was afterwards named Pennsylvania, and they maintained peace and friendship with the Indians for 100 years.

JASPER DANKER and PETER SLUYTER, Labadists of Wilverd, Finland, made a journey in search of a suitable spot for a colony and were travelers taking careful note of the country. Danker's "Journal" (1679) is a year later than Budd's. They went to Maryland and crossed New Jersey going and coming. They accompanied Ephraim Heerman, who was going to his father, Augustine Heermans, at Bohemia Manor, Maryland. The party consisted of Ephraim Heerman and wife (a daughter of Madam Van Burgh), on one horse; his younger brother and servant on another horse; while Danker, Sluyter and another servant each had a horse—seven people on five horses. Danker's "Journal" says:

"We came to Woodbridge by boat. Smoker's hook runs from the Kill up to Woodbridge. Here we took horses. In an hour we came to Piscatteway, the last English village in New Jersey. About two miles further we came to Mr. Greenland's, who kept an Ordinary [Inn] there; we had to pass the night because it is the place of crossing the Millstone [Raritan] River which they call the falls. Close by was the dwelling of some Indians. As the water was high we were set across in a canoe and the horses swam across. The road to the Falls of the South [Delaware] River is nothing but a foot-path for men and horses between the trees, although we came to places where there were large tracts grown over with long grass. We crossed the Millstone twice more during the day and arrived at the Falls of the South [Delaware] River about sundown. The Falls are nothing but a place where the river is full of stones for two miles or less, and very shallow, and the water breaks against them, causing some noise. After breakfast we continued down the river in a boat, but as Ephraim was suffering from the Quartan Ague, and it was now come on, we had to lie by the bank and make a fire, as he could not endure the cold in the boat. We had to row against the current to Burlington, a Quaker village. November 18th, during the night, it snowed and froze. Left Burlington about noon, and at dark came to Takanij, a village of Swedes and Finns, on the west side of the river. Next day, about 3:00 P. M., we arrived at the island Tinicum, the fifth we had passed. On it were three or four houses built by Swedes, and a little Lutheran Church and the remains of a block house, called New Gottenburgh. We came after dark to Upland" [now Chester].

Philadelphia it will be noted was not yet in existence. Ephraim Heerman was Clerk of the Court in New Castle and Upland, appointed by Gov. Andros, 1676. On the return trip across New Jersey they—

"left the Falls of Delaware about 2.00 P. M., spent the night in the open, in the rain, about a fire, waded across the Millstone, again crossed it in an Indian's canoe, as it was too high to ford. At 3:00 we took a road easterly to Raritan Kill, leaving the road to Mr. Greenland's and Piscatteway, and arrived at dusk at Cornelis Van Langvelt's, step-son of Thomas the Baker of New York. He lived in that house alone with an Indian, but he had some neighbors who are beginning a new village on the land of this Thomas the Baker, directly opposite Piscatteway, upon a point where the Millstone [Lawrence's Brook] unites itself with Raritan Kill; from here we returned by boat down the Raritan and through the Kill.

This journey is by quite a different route from that taken by George Fox eight years earlier. But the general type of country is about the same.

GEORGE SCOT, of Pitlochie, Scotland, sailed Aug. 1, 1685, with about 200 passengers on the "Henry and Francis." Some of the passengers from prisons brought the prison fever with them and the mortality on the voyage was very heavy. Both Scot and his wife died on the passage; a daughter, Upham, survived and married a fellow-passenger, John Johnston, and received the 500 acres promised her father. His "Model of Government," prepared for the Proprietors, mentions the seven towns: Shrewsbury, Middletown, Berghen, New Ark, Elizabeth, Woodbridge and Piscataway, and says Middletown was the second town settled. He also mentions Thomas Lawrence's and his wife's son's (Cornelius Longfield's) plantations, about 3,000 acres; that the Raritan is fordable at the Falls; that there were several tracts on both sides of the river located by Captain John Palmer, Thomas Coddrington, "Mr. White & Co.," John Robison, Samuel Edsal & Co., and Capt. Corson; that Elizabeth was the first place settled, 1664; that the type of house built in Amboy was 30 ft. x 16 ft., with double chimney, and cost £50, or in goods, £25; that an acre was 20 roods long by 8 roods broad, 16 feet to a rood (a little less than they are now). There were a few Indian natives. Land on the South Branch of the Raritan was, in his opinion, the best. The "Model" is reproduced in Whitehead's "East New Jersey under the Proprietors."

COL. CUTHBERT POTTER was sent by the Council of Virginia "to ascertain the truth of matters in New England and New York." He was a lawyer and large landholder, and he started July 6, 1690. On July 18 he reached the Falls of the Delaware, stopped at Mr. Penn's and lodged at Mr. Wheeler's. Next day he took a horse and guide (it was still necessary to have a guide across New Jersey) for Elizabeth, but got no further than "Onions" (John Inian's). On the 20th went from "Onions" to Elizabeth and stayed with Col. Richard Townley. He was traveling with a pass from Governor Nicholson of Virginia. He was in New York during the Leisler uprising and smuggled his papers in after dark for fear of being searched and losing them. It was just after the overthrow of the Andros government in Massachusetts when he arrived there, and Governor Bradstreet and Council sent an officer to seize and search Col. Potter. They found his portmanteau at the coffee house, and, when he refused to open it, broke it open and opened all his letters. After keeping what they wished they dismissed him with the remainder. He barely escaped arrest in New York on his return, but made the rest of his trip without event. Here was an envoy from the Governor of one Colony carrying a Governor's pass on a friendly trip of investigation barely escaping arrest in another colony, and arrested and despoiled of his private papers in a third; it shows on what terms one colony was with another.

GABRIEL THOMAS in 1698 got out a little pamphlet much like Daniel Denton's.

DAVID BRAINERD comes next, but we must now go ahead fifty years. In 1742 Brainerd, a missionary to the Indians in New Jersey, wrote a voluminous memoir, giving a sketch of his five years' work. He undertook three distinct missions; one above the Falls of the Delaware; a second on the Susquehanna at an Indian town called Shammoking; and a third at Croswicksung, not certainly located but probably Crosswicks, New Jersey. This mission was later transferred to land just out of Cranberry [now Cranbury], to which place his Indians removed and settled. He gives the distance from the forks of the Delaware to his Indian village on the Susquehanna as 120 miles and more, and from the forks to Cranberry as 70 miles and more. Having little success with the Pennsylvania Indians, either at the Delaware or the Susquehanna, he gradually concentrated his efforts on the Jersey Indians and, from not over ten at Croswicksung, when he first went there with two or three families in other places scattered six, ten, fifteen and thirty miles around, he gradually attracted them until, in 1746, he had about a hundred and thirty gathered at Cranberry. Three missions; Presbytery to attend; and then visits to clergymen, took him about continually, but his diary is solely devoted to his work with the Indians, and with no comment on other places except the bare fact that at such a date he was here or there, and occasionally with whom he stayed; as, for instance, that he went "to Mr. Dickinson's at Elizabethtown, came to a place named Cranberry and, meeting with a serious minister, Mr. MacKnight, I lodged there with him and went to Freehold to see Mr. Tennent. About thirty Indians having collected at Crosswicksung, walking a little from the place of meeting, the Indians killed three deer, which were a reasonable supply for their wants." He visited the Rev. Mr. Wales at Kingston and Mr. Stockston (Stockton) at Princeton; and on one of his trips from Fishkill-on-the-Hudson to the Forks of the Delaware he says he went "about 100 miles through a *desolate and hideous country,* where there were very few settlements." This, I think, is his only comment on the country through which he passed.

ALEXANDER HAMILTON, M.D., in 1744, made a trip across New Jersey from Annapolis. Travelling for his health, he set out on horseback, with his negro slave, Dromo, on Wednesday, May 30, 1744; went to New York via Baltimore, Havre de Grace, Philadelphia, Trenton, Perth Amboy, Staten Island, Brooklyn; thence to Albany and return; thence by Long Island to Southold, by ferry to New London, to Boston, Portsmouth; returning via Boston, Providence, Newport, New Haven, New York, Elizabethport and Trenton. I quote:

"Thursday, June 14, a little after five in the morning, I departed from Trenton. At half after eight I put up at one Leonard's, at the sign of the Black Lion, in Kingston. I breakfasted there upon a dish of tea. We arrived at six o'clock at Brunswick, a neat, small city in East Jersey Government, built chiefly of brick and lying upon the Raritan river, about sixty miles northeast of Philadelphia. I put up this night at one Miller's, at the sign of the Admiral Vernon, and supped with some Dutchmen and a mixed company of others. I had a visit from one Doctor Farquhar in town, who did not stay long with me, being bound that night for New York by water. Our conversation at supper was such a confused medley that I could make nothing of it. I retired to bed at eleven o'clock, after eating some very fine pickled oysters for supper. A little before six in the morning I forded the Raritan river, the tide being low and the scow aground, so that I could not ferry over. I went by way of Perth Amboy.

"Sept. 11th, after dinner, I took boat along with Mr. Rhea from New York to Elizabethtown Point and had a pleasant passage, making 15 miles by water in three hours. We passed through Elizabethtown at seven o'clock that night and arrived at Woodbridge at half an hour after eight. We put up at Heard's. We set off at seven and, before nine, passed through a place called Piscataway, about three miles from Brunswick. I have observed that several places upon the American main go by that name. We crossed the Raritan river and arrived in Brunswick at nine o'clock. We baited our horses and drank some chocolate at Miller's. We mounted at ten; put up at Leonard's at Kingston a little before one, when we dined."

PETER KALM, of the University of Abo, Finland, sailed for America Aug. 5, 1748. Before seeing land the vessel ran aground off the coast of Maryland, Sept. 13. It then sailed into the Delaware and up to Philadelphia, where Kalm lodged with a Quaker, having three meals a day at 20 shillings, Pennsylvania currency, per week, wood, washing and wine being extra. The site of Philadelphia had been obtained by Penn from three brothers called "Sven's Saeven Sons of Sven," who had settled there. Kalm speaks of Arch street 56 feet in width, and Market street over 100 feet, and of seven streets the other way, besides one on the river front called Water street; of the Presbyterian church built in 1704 on the south side of Market; of the two great Fairs every year, May 16 and Nov. 16. He mentions a traveler from Mount Lebanon in 1737, Scheick Sidi, also Count Sinzendorf, head of the Moravian Brethren in 1741; also that 12,000 Germans came to Philadelphia in 1749. In October he crossed the ferry to Jersey (four pence for ferriage), visited Trenton "of about 100 houses," and says the chief gain was from travelers between Philadelphia and New York by Trenton yachts going from Trenton to and from Philadelphia, and to Brunswick by "waggons." The yacht fare was 1s.6d, with baggage extra; the waggon 2s.6d, and baggage likewise extra. The greater part of the country was without woods; "a reddish brown earth is particularly plentiful near New Brunswick, under which was a sort of red limestone." He mentions Princeton and Rocky Hill. Of New Brunswick he says:

"The Germans have two churches, one wood and one stone; the English one of wood, and the Presbyterian one of stone" [not quite accurate, as the Dutch and English were stone and the Presbyterian wood, with an old Dutch of wood]. "Houses were of brick and wood, the wall next the street only of brick, a peculiar kind of ostentation. At each door was an elevation ascended by some steps, a sort of balcony with benches on both sides, where the family sate evenings and took the air and watched the neighbors pass by. The town has only one street lengthways and at its northern extremity there is a street across. One of the streets is almost entirely inhabited by Dutchmen who came from Albany, and so they called it Albany street. They get considerable profit from travelers, who every hour pass on the high road. An inhabitant built a house of the red stone, but it soon began to change so much that its owner was obliged to put boards all over the walls to prevent it from falling to pieces." [In tearing down old houses more than one has been found of that description, weather boards over the stone]. "We were ferried over the Raritan with our horses. In a dry summer at ebb tide it is by no means dangerous to ride through the river.

"Woodbridge is a small village; the houses mostly of boards and shingled on the side walls. Elizabethtown is a small town about 20 miles from New Brunswick; it has some stone buildings. It might truly be said of Elizabethtown that it was situated in a garden. We lodged in Elizabethtown Point about two miles from the town. In the morning we crossed the river (the Kil) to Staten Island, and at eight went aboard a yacht to go eight English miles by sea to New York, where we landed about 11 A. M. Besides the Christians of different sects there are many Jews in New York and they have a synagogue. Saw yachts from New Brunswick loaded with wheat, flour and linseed. William Burnet, son of the learned Dr. Thomas Burnet, is recorded the best Governor New York ever had."

Kalm was Professor of Economy in the University of Abo, in Swedish Finland. They continued his salary during his trip to America. The University of Upsala voted £150 and an Association for Promoting Manufacture contributed £45, and Kalm used £130 of his own money, Abo making up the rest.

ANDREW BERNABY, B.A. 1754, M.A. 1757, Queen's College, Cambridge, afterwards a minister of the English Church, travelled from Virginia to Massachusetts, much the same trip as that taken by Col. Potter seventy years earlier. He says:

"June 15 arrived in Philadelphia, a city of about 3,000 houses and 18,000 or 20,000 inhabitants. A house lets for £100 currency per annum. July 6th proceeded to Bristol, and 10 miles further up the river to Trenton, of about 100 houses, a church, Quaker and Presbyterian Meeting Houses, and barracks for 300 men. Thence to Sir John Sinclair's at the Falls of the Delaware, about a mile above Trenton, and spent an agreeable evening. Proceeded 12 miles further to Princeton— a handsome school and College for the education of dissenters, erected on the plan of those in Scotland; about 20 boys in grammar school, and 60 in the College Building, called Nassau Hall; but only two Professors besides the Provost. Two students occupy each apartment, consisting of a large bed-room, with fire-place and two studies. Student's expenses were £25 currency per year. The Provost's salary was £200 and the Professors' £50 each. In the afternoon proceeded 18 miles to Brunswick. There is a very nice barrack for 300 men; a church and a Presbyterian Meeting House. In this place and in Philadelphia were the handsomest women I saw in America. The next day I rode up the river to the Raritan Hills to see a small cascade which falls about fifteen or twenty feet very romantically between two rocks." [Buttermilk Falls, Chimney Rock, presumably]. "On the 7th I proceeded to Amboy, which contains about 100 houses and has a barrack for 300 men. In the afternoon travelled 16 miles further to Elizabeth, leaving Woodbridge, where there is a printing office, on my right hand. Elizabeth is on a small river; contains 200 or 300 houses; has a Court House and a Meeting House and barracks like those above mentioned. Thence to Newark, built in an irregular, scattered manner near two miles in length. It has a church erected in the Gothic taste with a spire, the first I had seen in America. Thence along Second, or Passaic, river 17 or 18 miles to the Falls, which are very extraordinary, different from any I had hitherto met in America. The river, about 40 yards broad, falls above 70 feet perpendicular in one entire sheet. Returning, crossed over to Col. John Schuyler's copper mine where there is a very rich vein of ore. Two miles further down is the park and gardens of his brother, Col. Peter Schuyler. In the gardens is a very large collection of citrons, oranges, limes, lemons, balsam of Peru, aloes, pomegranates and other tropical plants, and in the park several American and English deer, three or four elks, or moose deer. I arrived at Elizabeth not a little entertained with my expedition, but exceedingly fatigued with the violent heat and many mosquitoes that had infested me. The total inhabitants are supposed to be 70,000, of which the white males are obliged to serve in the militia between 16 and 60. The paper currency is about 70% discount, but in very good repute and preferred by Pennsylvania and New York to that of their own province. In Rhode Island the paper money is as bad as possible, the difference in exchange being at least 2500%, while that of New Hampshire is no better than Rhode Island."

To illustrate the curiosity of the New England innkeeper, he tells this anecdote of Franklin, who, because he could not get served till his curiosity was fully satisfied, assembled the master and mistress, sons and daughters, manservants and maidservants, and began thus: "Worthy people, I am Benjamin Franklin of Philadelphia, a printer by trade and a bachelor. I have some relatives in Boston to whom I am going to make a visit; my stay will be short, and I shall then return and follow my business, as a prudent man ought to. This is all I know of myself and all I can possibly inform you of. I beg, therefore, you will have pity on me and my horse and give us both some refreshment."

He refers to a strange and visionary idea that some people held—that empire was travelling west and was looking forward to when America would give law to the rest of the world. "But if ever an idea was illusory and fallacious, I am fully persuaded this will be so."

Dr. John Berkenhonts was another traveler, who gives an account of an expedition from New York to Philadelphia in 1778 with a pass from Sir Henry Clinton and under a flag of truce. He says:

"Landed the same evening at Elizabethtown. The rebel troops are extremely ragged. General Maxwell, after some hesitation, gave me a pass. After dinner set out for Brunswick, where I arrived late in the evening. A dismal town but pleasantly situated. I traveled with three intelligent Americans, had dinner at Princeton, remarkable for its fine College, now a hospital."

His trip, while under a flag of truce, seems to have been to pick up all possible information in regard to Washington's position and forces, and of the Continental Congress. His comments are so biased as to make his opinions worthless.

Johann David Schoepf, M.D., Surgeon to Ansbach Troops, arrived in New York July 4, 1777, but got no opportunity to see the country until July 22, 1783, when he left New York for Elizabethtown Point by water, making the trip between 5 P. M. and 2 A. M., remaining on the boat deck till morning amid millions of mosquitoes. Quoting from him:

"Here I made the acquaintance of an American Captain who volunteered to take me to Governor Livingston, whose country seat was in the neighborhood of Elizabeth. We had not the pleasure of finding the Governor at home, which I the more regretted as my companion had taken the trouble on the way to give me a high opinion of the man with the Roman nose. Instead, I was taken before certain other officers and furnished with a letter to a member of Congress near Princeton. When the greatest heat of the day was over we set out on the road to Brunswick. From Elizabeth we came to Bridgeton [Rahway] on the Raritan, mainly Quakers; from Bridgeton to Brunswick is 16 miles; here we underwent a general questioning on the part of the landlord of the Queen. There are no people in the world more curious than the innkeepers."

He gives here the anecdote given by Bernaby of Dr. Franklin and adds:

"At the Inn at Brunswick nothing was to be had till it was known where we came from and whither we were bound. I asked for a room and the woman of the house bade me in a most indifferent manner 'to be patient.' . . . Brunswick is pleasantly and advantageously situated. The Raritan here reaches no great depth, probably 10 or 15 feet, but with the help of the tide, which ascends two miles above the town, tolerable large vessels come up, and at one time it exported direct to the West Indies, and carried on more business than Perth Amboy, lying 10 miles further down at the mouth of the River. In Brunswick the Royal Barracks still stand, for which there are no soldiers, and an Episcopal Church remains for which there is no congregation. The Quaker meeting house and the Market House as well as many other buildings are in ruins. This section of Jersey, especially Princeton, Woodbridge, Newark, Bergen and Elizabethtown, etc., suffered the most during the War from the troops of both parties. From Brunswick we proceeded down [up] the Raritan through an incomparable landscape, neat country houses scattered here and there, the buildings forsaken and half ruined. Col. Steward's [Stewart's] house on a rising ground by the road, like so many in America, is thinly built of wood but after a tasteful plan. Two miles from Brunswick we again crossed the Raritan over a wooden bridge, and, after a few miles down [up] that stream reached Boundbrook and Middlebrook. At Boundbrook we visited Dr. Griffith, a practising physician, whose skill and upright character made him free of the general persecution other Loyalists were exposed to. In company with Dr. Griffith we made an excursion towards the mountain country where Captain Mosengail and Mr. Rubsaamen had establishments for smelting copper—the first in America (?). In this narrow valley we were unspeakably oppressed with the heat, and in Dr. Griffith's home the thermometer stood at 94° in the shade, and in the valley I am convinced that it was not less than 120°. The first chain is called First Mountain and extends from Newark to Pluckamin, about 28 miles. Van Horn's mine [copper] has been more than once profitably worked. It was found possible to prepare 2½ tons of sheet copper a week in 1775."

Of the Brunswick mine he says:

"About twenty-six years ago a mine was opened in a hill of red shell. A vein nearly 4 in. wide was a sufficient guarantee, but it was found to fall away almost perpendicularly. Solid copper was taken out in quantity, lying in a brown mould; however, it was a low hill and the Raritan was too near and the shaft filled with water and could not be kept clear. The owner became discouraged after taking out probably 2 tons mostly solid copper at an outlay of more than £12,000 current. . . .

"From Boundbrook we came to the mountain where Washington's army camped in 1779, and farther through an extremely well-cultivated region along the Millstone river. In the Raritan a law compels millers to leave a 40-yard passage way over the dams during the running of the shad, which formerly came up the Raritan in numberless schools. In the tavern at Black Horse we found quarters for the night. The landlord told us without any boasting that he was a weaver, a shoemaker, a farmer, a farrier, a gardener, and, when it can't be helped, a soldier. 'I bake my bread, brew my beer, kill my pigs, grind my axe and knives. I built those stalls and that shed, and I am barber, leach and doctor.' The man was everything and at no expense for a license. The following morning we came by a stone bridge to Rocky Hill which once had the hope of being one of the richest and most productive hills in America on account of copper being found there. A company was formed, with eight shares, which sold for as high as £1,500 current each, but it was unprofitable. One of the largest and most famous copper mines was that of the Schuyler family on Second River. For 40 years and more these works were carried on to great advantage. From Rocky Hill we went to Princeton, a little country town of one street, but its elevated site makes it especially agreeable, the view from it being splendid. In 1746 an Academy was established and given the privilege of bestowing the same degrees as Oxford and Cambridge. The College is in bad condition; the British used it for stalls and barracks, and left a Presbyterian Church near by in a state equally bad. At the present time there are only fifty to sixty students, and only Humaniora and Philosophy are taught. Princeton had the honor of being for a while the place of assembly of the American Congress, after a handful of indelicate soldiers, demanding such a trifle as five or six years' back pay, had frightened Congress from Philadelphia.

"A diligence, known as the Flying Machine, makes daily trips between Philadelphia and New York, a distance of ninety miles in one day—only changing horses three times on the journey. The diligences are large wooden carts with light tops, neither convenient nor neat, carrying ten or twelve passengers with luggage, and are drawn by four horses only. The charge is five to six Spanish dollars the passenger. I had the pleasure of meeting two members of Congress and General Lincoln, ex-Secretary of War, returning to his considerable landed property in New England. Six miles from Princeton we came to Maidenhead, of five or six houses; after sunset we arrived at Trenton. Here the landlord permitted us to go to bed unquestioned, being not yet done with several other guests arrived shortly before. The taverns on the way were in other respects very good, clean, well-supplied and well served. A mile from Trenton brought us to the Delaware, over which the passenger is set very cheaply in a flat, roomy ferry-boat. A little above the ferry is the lower Falls of the Delaware, the limit of shipping. At Lancaster I got to know a worthy man of great good sense in Mr. Henry, Judge of the Common Pleas, who showed me some inventions; one for moving a boat against the current."

From these extracts we get some fairly clear pictures of New Jersey in its beginning, and from time to time as the country became settled. But one almost invariably feels like wishing they had told us just a little more!

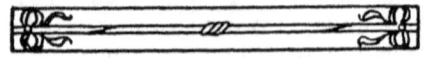

APPENDIX

I. Bibliography of Works, Etc., Consulted
II. The City Charters
III. Lotteries from 1723 to 1729
IV. First Revolutionary Movements
V. Prisoners' Bounds in New Brunswick, 1803
VI. Articles of Agreement with the Delaware and Raritan Canal Co., in 1832
VII. Some Expenses for Soldiers in the Civil War
VIII. Growth of School Buildings in New Brunswick and their cost
IX. Notes on Various Family Lines:
Bayard - Bennet - Billop - Ditmars - Drake - Farmar - French - Hardenbergh - Livingston - Low - Hude - Lawrence, Longfield, Inian, Greenland, Brinson and Cox - Livingston - Parker - Runyon - Schureman - Schuyler - Scott - Taylor - Van Wickle, Beach, Wells - Voorhees, Williamson.
X. Map of Hessian Fortifications.
XI. Index to Map of New Brunswick Lands, 1681-1800.

I. BIBLIOGRAPHY OF WORKS., ETC., CONSULTED

A Brief Description of New York, Formerly Called New Netherlands. By Daniel Denton, 1670 (Cleveland, 1902).
Journal of George Fox, (Phila., 1671).
Journal of William Edmundson, 1671 (Dublin, 1715).
Dictionary of National Biography, Volume 16.
Records of New Amsterdam from 1653 to 1674. By Berthold Fernow (N. Y., 1897).
An Historical Account of the First Settlement of Salem, in West Jersey. By John Fenwick, Esq., 1675. With additions. By R. G. Johnson (Phila., 1839).
The Bibliographer's Manual of American History, etc. By Thomas L. Bradford, M. D. Edited and Revised by Stan. V. Henkel. Vol. 3. (Phila., 1908).
Account of New Jersey. By Richard Hartshorn, 1676. (Reprint by Cox, London, 1878).
Good Order Established in Pennsylvania and New Jersey, in America, etc., By Thomas Budd, 1678. New edition, with Introduction and Notes. By Edward Armstrong. (N. Y., 1865).
A Journal of Jasper Danker and Peter Sluyter, of Wilverd, Finland, 1679, (Brooklyn, 1867).
George Scot's Model of Government. Edinburgh, 1765. (Reprint in N. J. Hist. Collections, Vol. 1, 1846).
Mass. Historical Society Proceedings, Dec., 1911, as to Dr. Henry Greenland.
A Journal and Narrative of a Journey Made by Me, Cuthbert Potter, from Middlesex County In Virginia to Boston in New England. 1690. (From Travels in the American Colonies, edited by Newton D. Mereness, N. Y., 1916).
Historical and Geographical Account of the Province and Country of Pennsylvania and of West New Jersey in America. By Gabriel Thomas, 1698 (N. Y., 1848).
The History of the Colony of Nova-Caesaria, or New Jersey, etc., by Samuel Smith. (Burlington, 1765).

W. A. Whitehead's Analytical Index, Vol. V, as to Ship "Catherine," Jaspar Farmar, Commander. (Dec., 1733-March, 1734).
Provincial America, 1690-1740. By Evarts B. Greene, Ph.D., in The American Nation: A History, Vol. 6, edited by A. B. Hart. (N. Y., 1905).
The Charter of the City of New Brunswick of December 30, 1730 and Early Ordinances of the City. By Austin Scott. (New Brunswick, N. J., Feb., 1913).
Hamilton's Itinerarium. By Alexander Hamilton, M. D. "Annapolis to Boston," May 30, 1744. (Reprint by W. K. Bixby, St. Louis, 1907).
A Bill in the Chancery of New Jersey, at the Suit of John, Earl of Stair, and others, Proprietors of the Eastern Division of New Jersey, etc. (N. Y., 1747).
Robert Eastburn's Captivity among the Indians. Preface by Gilbert Tennent, 1758. (Printed by William Dunlap).
Andrew Bernaby's Travels, 1759. Virginia to Mass. (London, 1775).
Leaming & Spicer's Grants, Concessions and Original Constitutions of the Province of New Jersey, etc. (Phila., n. d. Reprint, Somerville, N. J., 1881).
The Acts of the General Assembly of the Province of New Jersey, 1702-1761. By Samuel Nevill, 2 vols. (Woodbridge, N. J., 1761).
Glimpses of Colonial Society and the Life at Princeton College, 1763-1773, by One of the Class of 1763. W. J. Mills, editor. (Phila., 1903).
Manual of the Corporation of the City of N. Y. By Joseph Shannon. (N. Y., 1868-9).
Travels into North America: Containing its Natural History and a Circumstantial Account of its Plantations, etc. By Peter Kalm. (London, 1772).
History of the Late War in North America. By Thomas Mante. (London, 1772).
Paper by Mrs. S. B. Condit, Troy Hills, N. J., Von Beverhout in 1772, named "Beverwyck" (N. J. Hist. Soc. Proc., New Series, Vol. 4, p. 128).

W. A. Whitehead's East Jersey under the Proprietary Governments. (N. J. Hist. Soc. Collections, Vol. 1, 1846).
Valentine's Manual of the Corporation of the City of New York (1868-1869).
The History of the United States of America. By Richard Hildreth, Vol. 2. (N. Y., 1875).
History of the Church in Burlington, N. J. By George M. Hills. (Trenton, N. J., 1876).
The Magazine of American History with Notes and Queries. Vol. 1, on "New Jersey Blues" (1877).
Dr. John Berkenhonts' Excursion from New York to Philadelphia, 1778. From "Travels in the American Colonies," edited by Newton D. Mereness. (N. Y., 1916).
Rev. Talbot W. Chambers' Historical Sermon, 1879: "The Review of a Generation." (N. Y., 1880).
Works. By John Witherspoon. 4 vols., 1781. (As to Continental Money).
The John Bogart Letters, 1776-1782. (Rutgers College Publications, 2nd. series, 1914).
Travels in the Confederation (1783-1784). From the German of Johann David Schoepf. Translated and Edited by Alfred J. Morrison. 2 vols. (Phila., 1911).
New Jersey as a Colony and as a State. By Francis Bazley Lee. 4 vols. N. Y., 1902).
American Philosopical Soc. of Philadelphia, Proceedings and Transactions, Vol. 1. (1809).
Poems on Several Occasions, etc. During a Journey from New Brunswick, in New Jersey, to Montreal and Quebec. By Moses Guest. (Cincinnati, 1824).
Historical Collections of the State of New Jersey, etc. By Barber & Howe. (New York, 1844).
Colonial Women of New Jersey. By Mrs. S. N. Ogden. (N. J. Historical Society, Newark, N. J.).
The Women of the American Revolution. By Mrs. Elizabeth F. Ellet. 2 vols. (N. Y., 1848).
Documentary History of the State of New York. Arranged by Christopher Morgan. By Edmund Bailey O'Callaghan. Vols. 2 and 3. (Albany, 1849-1851).

The Weekly Register. H. Niles, Editor. Vol. 1, 1811, to Vol. 74.

American Archives, Fourth Series, By M. St. Clair Clarke and Peter Force. Vol. 1, 1837-Vol. 6, 1846; Fifth Series, Vol. 1, 1848, Vol. 3, 1850.

A Civil and Political History of New Jersey, etc. By Isaac S. Mulford, M. D. (Phila., 1851).

History of the City of New York. By David T. Valentine. (N. Y., 1853).

Contributions to the Early History of Perth Amboy, etc. By William A. Whitehead. (N. Y., 1856).

Life of Bishop Croes. By John H. Norton. (N.Y., 1859).

The Sons of Liberty in New York. By Henry B. Dawson. (Poughkeepsie, 1859).

Annals of the American Pulpit. By Wm. B. Sprague. 9 Vols. (N. Y., 1857-69).

History of Trenton, N. J. By John O. Raum. (Trenton, 1871).

History of the Land Titles in Hudson County, N. J. 1609-1871. By Charles H. Winfield (N. Y., 1872).

Official Register of the Officers and Men of New Jersey in the Revolutionary War. By Wm. S. Stryker. (Trenton, 1872).

Our Home. (Somerville, N. J., 1873).

Woodbridge and Vicinity. The Story of a New Jersey Township. By Joseph W. Dally. (New Brunswick, N. J., 1873).

Land Titles of Hudson County, N. J. By Charles H. Winfield.

The Pennsylvania Railroad, its Origin, Construction and Connections, etc. By William B. Sipes. (Phila., 1875).

The First Presbyterian Church of New Brunswick, N. J. By Robert Davidson, D. D. in 1852, and an Historical Discourse by Rev. Thomas Nichols. (New Brunswick, N. J., 1876).

NEW BRUNSWICK IN HISTORY

History of the City of New York: Its Origin, Rise and Progress. By Martha J. Lamb. 2 Vols. (N. Y., 1877).
Annals of Staten Island, from its Discovery to the Present Time. By J. J. Clute (N. Y., 1877).
History of Princeton and its Institutions. By John Frelinghuysen Hageman. 2 Vols. (Phila., 1879).
New Jersey Continental Line in the Virginia Campaign of 1781. By Wm. S. Stryker. (Trenton, 1882).
History of Union and Middlesex Counties, New Jersey, etc. Edited by S. Woodford Clayton. (Phila., 1882).
Stephen Kemble's Diary, 1773-1780 in N. Y. Hist. Soc. Publications, Vol. 1, 1883.
Old New York and Trinity Church in N. Y. Hist. Sec. Publications. Abstract of Wills. Vol. 1 to Vol. 15, 1665-1800.
History of Burlington and Mercer Counties, New Jersey, etc. By Woodward and Hageman. (Phila., 1883).
The Story of An Old Farm; or Life in New Jersey in the Eighteenth Century. By Andrew D. Mellick. (Somerville, N. J., 1889).
History of the First Baptist Church of Piscataway, N. J. By J. F. Brown, Pastor. (N. Y.; 1889).
History of Piscataway, By Oliver B. Leonard. (N. Y., 1890).
The Rise of the Republic of the United States. By Richard Frothingham. (Boston, 1890).
A Monograph on the Founding of Jersey City. By Charles H. Winfield. (New York, 1891).
The Memorial History of the City of New York from its First Settlement to the Year 1892. By James Grant Wilson. 4 Vols. (N. Y., 1892).
An Historical Sketch of the Rutgers Preparatory School. By Edward J. Meeker. In "The Argo," Vol. 3, No. 9, June, 1892.
John Whitehead's Judicial and Civil History, (1897).
Historical Handbook of New Jersey, etc. (Columbus, Ohio, 1898).
Voorhees Family. By Henry Pennington Toler. (N. Y., 1903).

The First Forty Years of Washington Society. By Gaillard Hunt. (N. Y., 1906).
A History of Thomas and Anne Billop Farmar, and Some of Their Descendants in America. With typewritten notes on the Farmar Genealogy. By Charles Farmar Billopp and Miss Kate Deshler. (N. Y., 1907).
Isaiah Thomas' Printers. American Antiquarian Society of Mass. Transactions, 1810. Proceedings, 1911.
Notes toward a history of the American Newspaper. By William Nelson, (1918).
The Cox Family in America, etc. Including the Cock-Cocks-Cox Genealogy. By Henry Miller Cox and George William Cox, Assisted by John Cox, Jr. (N. Y., 1912).
A History of the City of Newark, New Jersey, 1666-1913. By Frank John Urquhart. (N. Y., 1913).
The History of Tammany Hall. By Gustavus Myers. (N. Y., 1917).
New Jersey Archives, First Series, Vols. 1-30 (1880-1918). Second Series, Vols. 1-5 inclusive (1901-1917).
Proceedings of the New Jersey State Historical Society. Vols. 1845 to 1919 inclusive.
Index to Christ Church Minutes of Wardens and Vestrymen and the Congregation, with Historical Notes, 1790 to 1892. By Fred B. Kilmer. (New Brunswick, 1917-18).
The Eve of the Revolution. A Chronicle of the Breach with England. By Carl Becker. (New Haven, 1918).
Somerset County Historical Quarterly. Vols. 1-8, 1912-1919, (Somerville, N. J.).
Lawrence Echard's Gazetteer. Bounds of New Albion. (London, 1732).
David Brainerd's Journal. Edinburgh, 1765. (Reprint, New Haven, 1822).
Documents Relative to the Colonial History of the State of New York: Church of England and Episcopal Church. (O'Callahan, 1816).
History of Philadelphia, Pa. By James Rees. (1866).
Original List of Persons of Quality. By J. C. Holten. (London, 1874).

Churches of Piscataway and Woodbridge. By Rev. Mr. Halliday.
First Houses of Bound Brook. Address by Rev. T. E. Davis (Bound Brook, N. J., 1893).
The Battle of Bound Brook. Address by Rev. T. E. Davis (Bound Brook, N. J., 1895).
Life of Abraham Beach.
History of American Steam Navigation, by John Harrison Morrison.
Steam Navigation. By Zack Poulson, Vol. 2.
Social New York under the Georges. By Esther Singleton.
Newspaper Files, including New Brunswick "Guardian," "Times," "Fredonian," etc.

II. THE CITY CHARTERS

1730. First Royal Charter by George II, from Gov. John Montgomerie, Dec. 30.
1763. Second Royal charter by George III, from Gov. Josiah Hardy, Feb. 12. It established North and South Wards.
1784. Third Legislative charter of 1784. Bounds became 2 miles square. City divided into four Wards—North, Market, Middle and South Ward.
1801. Fourth Legislative charter of 1801, drawn by Mr. Boggs, of New Brunswick. Bounds extended from Mile-Run to Easton Ave. bridge, back to Garnet's gully and down to river. City divided into North and South Wards. Amended in 1818; again in 1829, making six Wards; again in 1837, 1838 and 1844, when city comprised about 800 (?) acres.
1845. Fifth Legislative charter. Bounds same as in 1801. Town meeting to vote money. Amended in 1846.
1849. Sixth Legislative charter. Down Mile-Run to river. Amended in 1856 and 1861.
1863. Seventh Legislative charter. Gives present bounds and six Wards as heretofore. Amended in 1864, 1868, 1869. Previous acts repealed.

This is our present charter and has been published by order of Common Council.

In the 25 years, 1870-1895, there were 168 Acts to amend, supplement, or affect the charter.

The City limits extend across the river to high water mark.

Is the made ground on Conover's dump and adjoining dump in the city of New Brunswick? It would so appear.

III. LOTTERIES FROM 1723 TO 1779

A list of advertised lotteries from 1723 to 1779 follows. It includes 22 churches and parsonages; 6 colleges and schools; 3 for charity; 3 for land; 2 for merchandise; 2 U. S. lotteries; 5 New Jersey Provincial—43 in all. Most of the lotteries were between the years 1745 and '65.

1723. John Stevens of Perth Amboy, offered £501 of silver and gold work (table service).

1741 to 1765. Lotteries beginning with the College of New Jersey; Peter Cochrane in New Brunswick and John Noe, in Woodbridge (both charity lotteries); Amwell Presby. Meeting House; Church in Bordentown; Burlington church steeple; parsonage in Hanover; Elizabeth parsonage; parsonage in "Turkey," or Provincetown; New Brunswick Episcopal church and parsonage; and Raritan Landing lots and bldgs.

1751. Trenton Church.

1753. School house in Trenton.

1754. Peter Gordon, 497 acres.

1758. Lutheran Church, Bedminster; New Brunswick Episcopal church.

1759. Lutheran Church, Hackensack; Parsippany parsonage; St. John's Church, Elizabeth; Newark Trinity Church; English Church, Second River; Bound Brook Presby. Church and parsonage; Province of New Jersey to raise £600 to pay Indian land claims.

1760. Hunterdon Charity, Michael Hundershut; Church at Shrewsbury.

1761. Acquackanonk Dutch Church; Wm. Dunlap, $10,000 importation of books, jewelry, bric-a-brac, etc.; Alexander

Alexanders, Petty's Island, opp. Philadelphia for gentleman's seat.
1762. Amboy Church; Bridge at Bound Brook; St. John's Church, Elizabeth; St. Mary's Church, Burlington.
1762, and '63. Colony of New York £3,000; Sandy Hook light house.
1763. New Jersey Provincial at Burlington; Third N. J. Prov. at New Brunswick.
1765. Road New York to Philadelphia £500. (via. S. Amboy to Burlington).
1777. U. S. Lotteries.
1779. Third class by Henry Van Dike, Mr. Caldwell and Aaron Ogden.

IV. FIRST REVOLUTIONARY MOVEMENTS

As to the first Revolutionary movements in New Brunswick and generally I am largely indebted to Force's "American Archives" (1851) for the following facts:

On July 15, 1774, a Middlesex Committee of Correspondence was formed, among whom were John Dennis and Reune Runyon and two general meetings of County Committees were held in New Brunswick on July 21, 1774, there being present 721 when it was resolved to send relief to Boston; James Neilson and others were to receive subscriptions. There were appointed five members to the Continental Congress, viz.: James Kinsey, William Livingston, John DeHart, Stephen Crane, Richard Smith, to meet in Philadelphia Sept. 1, 1774. Woodbridge, on Jan. 7, 1775, appointed a Committee of Observation; William Cutler and John Conway were two of it. The Middlesex Committee met Jan. 16, 1775 when Committees of Observation and Inspection were appointed, viz.: Azariah Dunham, John Schureman, John Dennis, John Lyle, Abram Schuyler, George Hance, Jacobus Van Huys (Nuys), John Sleight, John Voorhees; also a new Committee of Correspondence, consisting of James Neilson, William Ouke, Azariah Dunham and John Dennis, who was the clerk. On Jan. 24 Perth Amboy appointed James Kinsey, Stephen Crane, William Livingston,

John DeHart, Richard Smith, or any three of them, to attend the Continental Congress at Philadelphia in May. A memorial to Congress by merchants of New York City to know if they can ship flaxseed to Ireland was signed by seven, among others by William Neilson. Middlesex was required to raise two Regiments of militia and Somerset two Regiments.

On February 6 the following salaries were allowed: £1,200 to the Governor; £150 to the Second Justice Supreme Court and same to the third Justice; £140 to the Attorney-General; £40 to each of the two Treasurers; £30 to the Clerk of the Council; £100 to the Agent of Council; £20 to Clerks of Courts; £10 to Doorkeepers; £60 house rent of the Governor if in Amboy or Burlington. James Murdock, of Perth Amboy, Surgeon, challenged Lord Stirling sitting in Council Feb. 10, but apologized publicly. Middlesex was represented by John Wetherill and Hendrick Fisher was Chairman of the Committee on "Grievances."

On Feb. 14, Burlington appointed a Committee of Observation. On March 11 a cargo of the ship "Beulah" shut out of New York, was attempted to be unloaded at Elizabeth, but the goods were finally relinquished to Committee of Observation, and £200 allotted toward rebuilding the Hospital was offered as amends, John Murray of New York, merchant, being the owner. Hackensack on March 14, declared it would support the King and disavowed all riotous mobs; 37 signers. Freehold protested against the action of Shrewsbury in not forming a Committee of Observation and would break off all dealings with them.

The New Jersey Provincial Committee of Correspondence met at New Brunswick, May 2, summoned by Hendrick Fisher, Chairman, and called a Provincial Congress to meet at Trenton on May 23rd. Newark, May 4th, elected deputies to Trenton. Somerset sent 7 delegates to Trenton, Hendrick Fisher, William Paterson, etc. Middlesex sent 9 deputies, Azariah Dunham, John Wetherill, etc. Hendrick Fisher was President of the Trenton Congress, William Paterson, Assistant Secretary. Grievances stated were: A standing army maintained, expensive, and oppressive officers multiplied. Judges to receive salaries from effects condemned by themselves. Officer of Customs empowered to break and enter houses, without civil or legal authority, and others were also named. Cumberland County published Silas Newcomb, a member of the Committee of Observation, for drinking tea and refusing to discontinue use of same; whereupon he recanted. In May Morris Co. voted to raise 300 volunteers in five companies of 60 men each. Monmouth County, May 4, advised every man able to bear arms to enter into Companies to train, and subscribed £160 for powder and ball.

Governor Franklin called the Assembly for May 15 at Burlington, to be the first sitting of the 4th Session of the 22nd Assembly. Amboy voted whether to send delegates; decision in the affirmative. Middlesex sent delegates, John Wetherill, Azariah Dunham. Somerset sent delegates, Hendrick Fisher and John Ray. Newark, May 18, agreed to stop all exports to fishing coasts and islands. On July 27 John Dennis was Chairman of the New Brunswick Committee of Safety. On July 28, the Freeholders of Somerset met at the Court House in Hillsborough to appoint a new Committee of Correspondence, the old one having expired by limitation, and they instructed each township to appoint a new Committee of Inspection to consist of nine from each township. On August 30 William Paterson was Secretary of the New Jersey Committee of Safety at Princeton. Nov. 24, Lord Stirling was at New Brunswick to get the Barracks there put in order. They were then occupied by those who thought it not safe to stay in New York, New Jersey Continentals, first Regiment of foot consisting of two Companies from New Brunswick, John Conway's and John Polhemus "9," one Company from Raritan Landing, Daniel Piatt's; two Companies from Morristown, two Companies from Elizabeth and one Company from Monmouth. Dec. 11, 1775, John Conway and his Company were in Barracks at Amboy. Capt. Conway was instructed by Stirling to march his men five hours a day by way of drill and discipline. On Dec. 14, Capt. Polhemus was at Elizabethtown. On Dec. 15 the Barracks at New Brunswick were to be ready for Capt. Polhemus' Co. by "the end of next week." Dec. 16, John

Conway and Capt. Polhemus went into Barracks at New Brunswick. On Dec. 28 about 40 Tories in Sussex County were dealt with by the Committee of Observation, most of whom recanted.

On Jan. 10, 1776, the Chairman of the Committee of the North Ward of New Brunswick gave certificates to John Taylor as Captain, John Mersural as 1st Lieut., James Schureman as 2nd Lieut., and John Voorhees, Jr. as Ensign of a Company of Minute men. Colonel Heard and 600 or 700 militia from New Jersey and three Companies of Lord Stirling's Regiment had gone to L. I. Col. Heard sent Stirling's Companies back, as his militia were sufficient for the purpose of awing the Tories. Jan. 18-19 they crossed into Long Island and on the 25th disarmed the Tories, who delivered up about 500 arms and 4 colors of the Long Island militia (Tory) at Jamaica, Hempstead and Oyster Bay. Lord Stirling captured the ship "Blue Mountain Valley" in New York Bay, took her to Amboy and then through the Kill to Elizabethport, where she was unloaded. On the last of Jan., 1776, or first of February, the navy had its birth in a fleet of 5 vessels; the "Columbus" of 36 guns, the "Cabot" of 32 guns and three smaller vessels.

The Provincial Congress was sitting in February, 1776, in Myndert Voorhees' "large room," in New Brunswick and £15 was voted for the use of the room with wood and candles. Feb. 5, Lord Stirling took his regiment of eight Companies to New York and took command as General Lee left on Feb. 23. From the vast number of houses in New York shut up, one would suppose the city almost evacuated; women and children were scarcely to be seen on the streets. The troops broke open and quartered themselves in the houses found shut up. On Feb. 3 the Provincial Congress ordered the records in the Secretary's office in Perth Amboy removed to New Brunswick, and further ordered that John Demarest of Bergen attend the papers, books and records and deliver the same to Charles Pettit at Burlington, and take his receipt. On Feb. 12 a memorial from Colonel John Neilson, Middlesex Battalion of Minute Men, prayed they be placed on a respectable footing. On Feb. 14 it was ordered that Moses Scott be Surgeon to

2nd Regiment Foot, Middlesex Co. militia, under Col. Wetherill. On Feb. 23, John Voorhees, of New Brunswick, coming to New York in his sloop "Brunswick" loaded with bread, flour and butter, was stopped by the British ship "Asia," the cargo taken and put part in the "Asia" and part in the "Dutchess," and an order on Abram Lott of New York given him for the payment thereof, Lott being the Treasurer of the Colony in New York.

Washington on a trip to Philadelphia (at the request of Congress) went from New York by Woodbridge and Amboy, rest of the route not designated. On the fourth Monday in May an election of deputies to Provincial Congress was held at the New Brunswick Court House. Major Duyckinck and 450 Middlesex militia were at Amboy July 5th. On July 20 all New Jersey militia were relieved to secure their harvests. The Declaration of Independence on July 4 was not signed by New York whose delegates were not authorized to sign. July 16, it was duly agreed to by New York and was ordered read in New York City on Thursday, July 18th. It was read in the State House, Philadelphia, on July 8, in the Court House, Easton, Pa., July 8, in Trenton, July 8, in Nassau Hall, Princeton, July 9, in the Court House, Bridgeton, Cumberland Co., Aug. 7. No date recorded for New Brunswick.

On Aug. 1, it was ordered that John Neilson be Colonel of the 2nd Battalion Foot militia of Middlesex, and John Taylor 1st Major. A New Jersey State Convention on Aug. 12 ordered half of the militia, relieved July 20th, be immediately called out to serve one month and then to be relieved by the other half.

The British landed on Long Island on August 22. Gen. William Livingston, at Elizabethtown Point, writing Aug. 29th of Penna. Troops, says a "disciplin-hating, good living-loving, to eternal fame damned, coxcombical crew we lately had here from Philadelphia." On Sept. 15 New York was evacuated; Sept. 21 it was on fire; Sept. 23 Paulus Hook was evacuated. All the brass knockers were ordered taken from the doors of New York and sent to Newark. Continental Prisoners were held at the Somerset goal at Millstone.

At Brunswick, William Hunt went up one street and down another, and saw every house full of redcoats. Washington's troops partly broke down the bridge at the Landing when they retreated. The arrival of the British fleet in New York harbor and the Declaration of Independence occurring almost simultaneously made lively times. Washington's retreat across New Jersey was made Nov. 14, reported as south of Hudson, crossing Neck between North River and Hackensack and crossing another Neck between Hackensack and Passaic occupying nine days. Nov. 23 and 27 the army was at Newark. The British arrived at Newark and Washington left on the 28th at 7.00 A. M. and Washington was in Woodbridge at sunset. Next day he reached Brunswick; Friday 29th, 30th and Dec. 1, Sunday, he went 8 miles towards Princeton. Dec. 2nd Princeton and same day Trenton. On the 8th crossed to Pennsylvania. The British were detained at Brunswick by Washington breaking the bridge. On Oct. 19, 1782, 300 British troops are noted as being in New Brunswick.

V. PRISONERS' BOUNDS IN NEW BRUNSWICK, 1803

There is a map on file in the Middlesex County Clerk's office showing the lines of the prisoners' three-acre liberty bounds in 1803. Certain prisoners were allowed the privilege of freedom within certain designated bounds, which were fixed by the Court and limited to three acres. This map was made by William Plum, surveyor, and showed the lines both of the then present and proposed bounds. They included George Street (marked "Barrack" on the map) from the North side of Bayard (marked "Maiden Lane" on the map) to the south end of the street in front of Queen's College; thence on a line N. 45 E., the same course as Livingston Avenue to Bayard, going along the rear of the jail lot, which was where the Bayard School now stands; thence down Bayard to Queen (now Neilson); south on Queen to and including Van Arsdalen's well on the west side, and the tavern at the foot of Bayard on the east side; north on Queen to a line with the north side of the Court House; thence to the corner of the Court House; then northwesterly to the corner of the old Dutch church, which stood about the middle of the Church lot; thence around three sides of the church and back to Bayard; west on Bayard to a vacant lot on the northeast corner of George, taking in that lot; thence across George to the northwest corner of Bayard and George and to the beginning.

These bounds, beside two large vacant lots on George and Bayard, took in the jail and yard, the well on Queen and the Tavern kept by Colonel Peter Keenon, the Court House and yard, the Dutch church and part of the graveyard. Colonel Keenon was also keeper of the jail. These lines showed great consideration for the prisoners, who were mainly in jail for debt.

VI. ARTICLES OF AGREEMENT WITH THE DELAWARE & RARITAN CANAL CO., IN 1832

ARTICLES OF AGREEMENT made and entered into this ——— day of ——— in the year of our Lord One thousand eight hundred and thirty-two, between the Delaware and Raritan Canal Company of the first part and the individuals executing this Instrument, being owners and occupants of wharves and lands adjacent to the river Raritan in the City of New Brunswick, New Jersey, of the second part.

Whereas the river Raritan, at or opposite to the inhabited part of New Brunswick, is a tidewater navigation and allows at high water six or seven feet depth, or thereabouts, to the wharves, but at low water the bed or bottom of the river is in many places bare and vessels can come to or depart from the wharves only at high water, or for the period of three-quarters of an hour before, and after that time of tide, but below the Town, at or near the lower steamboat wharf, the depth of the river is greater and allows at low water a draft of five feet or thereabouts, and at one-third flood of seven feet; and whereas the Delaware and Raritan Canal Company proposes to locate the route of their canal so that the same shall enter the river

Raritan within the precincts of New Brunswick, but at the upper end of the settled part of the City, and to construct a Pier or Tow-path in the river at a convenient distance from the existing wharves of said City and down the said river as far as the lower Steamboat Dock, or thereabouts, where there is a sufficient depth of water, and to construct a lock at the termination thereof, so as to admit vessels not over seven feet draft of water to come to and depart from the said wharves at all times of tide, and to load and unload without grounding; and whereas it is expected and believed that the construction of such works are not only necessary and expedient to effect such a termination of the said canal at the City of New Brunswick as shall answer the fair and legitimate purposes of the canal as contemplated in the charter, but that it will also improve the navigation of said river at the City of New Brunswick and be beneficial to the persons owning, occupying and using the wharves of said City; and the Delaware and Raritan Canal Company will be at considerable expense not only in the construction of said Pier and Lock and the works and improvements incidentally necessary thereto and in keeping the same in repair, but also in employing persons to attend the said lock for the admission of boats and vessels passing and repassing the same to and from the said city:

Now it is agreed between the parties, each individual owner of said wharves and lands respectively for himself, his heirs, executors, administrators and assigns, severally, and not for another, as follows to wit:

First: The Delaware and Raritan Canal Company shall provide and keep at their own expense a suitable person or persons, as the case may require, stationed at the said lock, so as to allow vessels going to and from the wharves of the City of New Brunswick to pass through the said lock with as little delay and inconvenience as may be necessary in the use of such works at all suitable times and seasons when such vessels shall present themselves at the said lock for passage or repassage through the same.

Second: The said owners of wharves as aforesaid, the parties of the second part, their heirs and assigns respectively, shall pay to the Delaware and Raritan Canal Company, or to a person by them to be designated for the purpose, at their office to be located for that purpose at or near the said lock for the passage of vessels through the said lock to and from the City of New Brunswick, in order to load, unload or lay at their respective wharves or landing places in said city constructed, or to be constructed as aforesaid, opposite to the said Pier, or to depart therefrom, a compensation equal to the tolls payable for one mile of the said canal according to the quantity and quality of the cargo on board and the tonnage of the vessel, but that all vessels bound merely to and from the City of New Brunswick and not intending to pass up the canal, or not having arrived at New Brunswick through the canal, shall and may pass through the said lock at high tide and within the space or period of three-quarters of an hour immediately before and after high tide, without making any compensation.

Third: That the right of the Delaware and Raritan Canal Company to receive the compensation and at the rates aforesaid under the above covenants shall be a lien and easement upon the respective wharves and landing places aforesaid of the several parties of the second part, and the same are hereby charged therewith in the hands of themselves, their heirs and assigns respectively.

Provided always, nevertheless, that if the Delaware and Raritan Canal Company shall fail within the space of ——— years from this time to construct and complete said pier and lock so as to answer the purposes hereby intended, then these presents and every part thereof shall be void and of no effect.

In witness whereof the Delaware and Raritan Canal Company have hereunto caused their corporate seal to be affixed, and the parties of the second part have hereunto respectively set their hands and seals, the day and year first above written. Signed, sealed and delivered in the presence of:

A. S. Neilson	Henry Hutchings
John Manning	John Hardy
Peter S. Broberseo	Peter R. Stettle
A. S. Neilson	James Dunham
Samuel Thompson	A. S. Neilson
Johnson Letson	Frederick Richmond

Wm. P. Forman	James B. Cox
C. F. Randolph	Theo. M. Holcombe
James C. Van Dyke	Abigail Ayres
A. S. Neilson	George H. Stout
John Clark	James C. Van Dyke
A. S. Neilson	Frederick Richmond
A. S. Neilson	Josiah Stout
A. S. Neilson	Robt. Minturn
Ch. Dunham	John Henry
A. S. Neilson	James Clark
A. S. Neilson	Ellen Clark
A. S. Neilson	Ann F. Cole
A. S. Neilson	Littleton Kirkpatrick
A. S. Neilson	Trustee for Mrs. Cole
A. S. Neilson	Saml. Mundy
A. S. Neilson	Ch. Dunham
A. S. Neilson	N. Dunham
A. S. Ten Eick	H. Dunham
Samuel Thompson	Moses Smith
A. S. Neilson	Andrew Agnew
A. S. Neilson[1]	Miles C. Smith
Staatz Van Deursen	Walter M. Richmond
Jos. C. Griggs	Henry Outcalt
John Brusts	Gershom Dunn
James Wilcom (Holcomb?)	Samuel H. Day
John Neilson	John W. Hampton
James Neilson	Altie Satick
A. S. Neilson	Andrew Ten Eick
Vail & Acken	J. C. Ackerman
J. & H. Hutchings	Wm. B. Paterson

VII. SOME EXPENSES FOR SOLDIERS IN THE CIVIL WAR

In a Supplement to the "New Brunswick Times," Thursday, June 8, 1865, appeared a detailed statement of Middlesex Co. finances by the Board of Chosen Freeholders; the only state-

---

[1] The reason for this name occurring so often is because he signed as attorney for various dock owners.

ment known to exist of payments for men in Middlesex in the Civil War.

The disbursements totaled $154,529.10. In addition there were some interesting "Bounty matters," viz.:

Received, to pay for substitutes, from private individuals	$70,064.00
Paid 29 men as substitutes and commutation, $300 each	8,700.00
Paid 26 men, Co. H., $400 each	10,400.00
Paid 26 men, Co. D., $400 each	10,400.00
Paid 15 men for New Brunswick, $400 each	6,000.00
Paid 10 men for New Brunswick, $388.55 each	3,855.50
Paid 22 men for New Brunswick, $400 each	8,800.00
Paid 15 men for East Brunswick, $400 each	6,000.00
171 men guard money paid up to Aug. 25, 1864, $25 each	4,275.00
In substitutes, volunteers, German	5.00
Cash for list of men at Trenton	15.00
	$65,514.50

All of the above a war expense.

Bounty Committee .... { Elias Ross, New Brunswick. B. D. Stelle, "   " James T. Crowell, Perth Amboy.

VIII. GROWTH OF SCHOOL BUILDINGS IN NEW BRUNSWICK AND THEIR COST

1851. Bought old jail lot, 1,800 and two additional lots, $550	$2,350.00
Contracts, P. M. Wyckoff, Jeptha Cheeseman, J. B. Inslee	7,110.00
Cupola $350; architect, John Hall, $100; furnaces $468.56	918.56
Furniture, $1,660; fence, $263.50; blinds and lightning-rod, $317	2,240.50

1854. Lot of Phoebe Harriot for outlet to Liberty Street	1,000.00
	$13,619.00

1853. Rented Presbyterian Session House for $40.00 per annum, for children of five to seven, and called the Juvenile School; suspended 1855.	
Bought lot on "Old Trenton Road" of Clark Letson, at four dollars per foot..........	$500.00
Built one-room French Street School for colored children, equipped with forty desks from the Juvenile School, which had been held in rented building; Wright, architect, fee $3.00; John Inslee, builder, $1,050.....	1,053.00
	$1,553.00

Opened Monday, Jan. 22, 1855, and Night School opened at Bayard Street.

1856. Census, 2,520 children, 5 to 18.

1858. Nineteen teachers. Rented room in basement of Methodist Church in Liberty Street for one year for $50. One Janitor all bldgs., $350.

1859. Census, 2,755. Public school children 1,022; private, 509; at work, 618; out, 595.

1860. Rented building in rear of Bayard St., of John Lyle, at $45 annually, instead of Methodist Church. Census, 2,897.

1861. Bought lot of James Bishop on Carmen Street	$750.00
1862. Built eight-room school, McRae architect, fee 1%	33.00
E. B. Wright, carpenter, $1,532; John Cheeseman, mason, $1,468	3,000.00

John Johnson, painter, $162; John T. Jenkins, slater, $236.75	398.73
Tinner, $94.10; blinds, extras, $250.24; fence, $275	619.34
Furnace, $200; furniture $431.38; paving, $371.24.	1,002.62
	$5,803.69

      Twenty-five teachers. 1,892 attending school; all outside district and around. Census 3,051. Using now Bayard and Colored Schools, Robert Lyle's and Methodist Church. Some children obliged and willing to stand.

1863. Carmen School, opened April 1, 1863, with appropriate ceremonies and opened for school April 6. Bayard, 18 rooms; Carmen, 8 rooms; French, 1; wooden rear, Bayard, 2; M. E. Church, 3; total 32 rooms. The last 5 classes to be accommodated in the Carmen. One Principal, 4 Vice-Principals, 8 senior teachers, 9 primary teachers, 3 at Carmen; total 25.
Suit for share of school money brought in July in Supreme Court by St. Peter's Church.
French Street School changed in Sept. to two rooms for white children; colored children moved to Million building on Hamilton Street. Rented at $25.00 a year.

1866. Moved again to Miss Ryno's, 94 Church Street. Rent $50.00 per annum.

1867. Cost of school property for past 50 years.. $20,975.75

1868. Janitress of Carmen St. paid $10 per month—Mrs. Masterson. Two room house at rear of Bayard again leased for five years @ $50.00 per annum; also 94 Church St.

APPENDIX

of Mrs. Ryno, 3 years, @ $100.00 per annum.

1871. French St. School enlarged to three rooms 3,843.20
Modern building on Hale, near French, two rooms for colored children, lot 100 feet square, bought of J. T. Jenkins in 1871.... 1,000.00
Building, $6,873.52; grading and fence, $249; drain $125 .... 7,247.52
This building had 158 children in 1900, but was closed in 1901.

1872. Written contract with janitor at $800; he to pay his own assistants. 4,373 children in the city and 1,280 seats in the schools.
Lot 200x210 bought on Livingston Ave. at $15,000, of Messrs. Boundy and Felter.

1873. Bought lot on Guilden Street of Campbell 2,433.05
Rented 5 rooms in Sept. in Hoyt Building, @ $400 per annum.
Janitor, $1,200 for all schools.
Borrowed $30,000 of State for new High School. Architect, Stephen H. DeHart.
Act of Legislature authorizing $50,000.00 bonds for school.
Carpenter, E. B. Goltro 21,350.00
Mason, Bassonet 22,612.00
Heating, McKeag 3,750.00
Plumbing 447.00
Gas fitting 100.00
Stucco 1,550.00
Furniture 825.00
Painting and grading 275.00
Architect 2½%.

1874. Built five-room brick building, at Guilden Street; Voorhees & Brower, masons, $6,990; Stephen DeHart, carpenter, $4,474; slater, $623.08; stone, $1,500; painting, $228; drainage, $697.11; heating, $600 .... 15,112.19

1882. Separated school for colored children; terminated by law.

1884. Rented the French St. School to Fourth Reformed Church @ $3.00 a week.
1885. Added room at Carmen; same put to use. Two vacant at Hale, but Bayard needing enlargement. Opened in 1885.
1875. Built High School. Brick stucco; three stories; thirteen rooms as first built, six on first floor, four and Assembly on second, Auditorium on third and two rooms. Auditorium on third not used for fifteen years; then, in 1890, altered, the Assembly changed to Hall and two class rooms, and the auditorium changed to Assembly and recreation and coat rooms. The payments made in 1875-'6 and 1876-'7 were 55,728.05

Cost of school property forty years ago....$121,339.76

1888. In 1888 four lots were bought on the Park for $900.00
Four room brick building was built costing 6,927.96

$7,827.96

This school seems to have been opened in 1896.

1895. Bayard and Carmen remodeled, adding coat rooms.
Bayard, on basis of twelve rooms $6,480.00
Carmen, on basis of eight rooms 4,320.00

$10,800.00

1893. Bayard new front of six rooms and board room, removing old four-room front 9,373.96
1898. Bought lot on French 4,700.00
Contract for building 27,820.00
Paid over and above contract.. 7,752.26

$40,272.26

1906. Park School on Hale Street enlarged to eight rooms at a cost of	13,582.00	$81,856.18

1907. Cost of School property 17 years ago......		$203,195.94
1910. Carmen School replaced by Lord Stirling, same site	$43,183.93	
1911. Guilden Street School replaced by Lincoln on new site	53,820.86	
1912. Three manual training rooms in basement of High	1,500.00	
1916. High School, Livingston Ave. and Comstock Street	206,808.14	305,312.93
Cost of buildings to 1916................		$508,508.87

1914. In 1914 with eight part-time classes, the Board moved for a new High School. As the city owned half of the block, Livingston and Lee Avenues, Delevan and Comstock Streets, the Board bought the other half of the block for $25,000.00 so acquiring the whole block, 200 by 500 feet. The Board of Estimate allowed $175,000 for a new High School which the Board divided, $150,000 for building and $25,000 for furniture, equipment, grading, walks, etc. Alexander Merchant won the position of architect in a competitive trial of unusual requirements, namely, that, unless a bidder was secured at the price of $150,000 the Board was at liberty to select another architect.

Building, $121,974.21; plumbing and heating, $27,334.83	$149,309.04
Architect, $7,485.95; Inspector, $139.00; furnishing, $19,720.34; land, grading, walks, $29,480.64; advertising, $673.17....	57,499.10
	$206,808.14

Bonds, interest and appropriation $206,107.25
Amt. spent in excess charged to Budget 700.89   206,808.14

The part-time classes had increased to thirty-six, or eighteen rooms on part-time. This, the new building, did away with.

1916. Above High School opened February, 1916, and in December, 1917, there are so many part-time classes that more school room was essential.

1918. Addition to Nathan Hale; four class-rooms, two manual training and drill hall.
Addition to Washington; four class and drill hall.
Addition to Lincoln; four class, two manual training and drill hall. These three additions cost $138,000.00
A further addition to Nathan Hale; five classes, two manual training and two offices.

1919. To Washington, six class-rooms. The two cost 103,666.20

1921. To Lord Stirling, fifteen rooms and drill-hall, costing 221,608.95
Plans for rebuilding the old Livingston (made in 1917, but not carried out till much later), three stories and basement and about seventeen rooms to a floor, giving twenty-six class-rooms, with some thirty-two rooms to be used for manual training, domestic science, arts, etc., an arrangement in view of the part-time persistence, and the county vocational school in the city, at a cost of.... 505,478.12

1922. Total cost of buildings to date.......... $1,477,262.14

While these costs may not be absolutely exact, in the five years 1918 to 1922 inclu-

sive, there was alloted for buildings, equipment, land purchase, repairs, etc.........$1,058,621.98
From which deduct the buildings.......... 968,753.27

Leaves for the other items.............. $89,868.71
The eighty-five class-rooms in buildings costing 505,508.87
Including rooms used for other purposes, average nearly six thousand per class-room, while the forty-six class-rooms, including those for other purposes, costing $968,-753.37, average over twenty thousand per room, shows the greatly increased cost.

IX. NOTES ON VARIOUS FAMILY LINES

[The following notes are from various sources and, while far from complete in the family lines named, are given in the hope that they may prove useful. Necessarily many dates given should be verified by family, church or civil records, where such exist].

BAYARD FAMILY

Samuel Bayard left a widow, Anna Stuyvesant, who was sister to Peter Stuyvesant, and who came to New Amsterdam 1647 with three sons, and died in 1702. The sons were:

1. Peter b. 1635; died 1699; m. Blandina Kierstede, and went to Maryland. Children: (a) Peter, who m. (1) Rachel Van Bael and (2) Elizabeth Sluyter. Child by first wife, Susannah Bouchelle, b. 1677. (b) Sarah: m. Abraham Gaasbeek. (c) Samuel, b. 1675; died 1721; and had children: Samuel, James, Mary Ann, Col. Peter of Bohemia Manor and James, who m. Mary Asheton. This James was the father of Col. John Bayard of Hodge & Bayard, merchants, of Philadelphia, who lived at New Brunswick after the Revolution until his death. He was Major in 1774, Colonel in 1775, served at Princeton, Brandywine and Germantown; was Mayor of New Brunswick 1792, and Judge of the Courts in 1800. He m. (1) Margaret Hodge, 1759, who died 1780 by whom were 13 children; (2) Johanna White, 1781, who died 1785, and

by whom were 2 children, one being Jane, who m. Chief Justice Andrew Kirkpatrick, of New Brunswick.

(2) Balthazar, who m., 1664, Maria Lockermans, and was father of Col. William Bayard of Weehawken.

(3) Nicholas, b. 1644; died 1711 in New York City; m., 1666, Julia Varleth and had son Samuel, b. 1669; died 1745; m. Margaret Van Courtland. Samuel lived in New Brunswick in 1735, and his daughter, Gertrude, m. Peter Kemble of New Brunswick. He was a lawyer who prepared and had printed an "Abstract of the Laws of the United States" in 1804.

The Ann Stuyvesant, above named, widow of Samuel Bayard, m. (2nd) in 1656, Nicholas Varleth, whose sister, Jane Varleth, m. Augustine Heerman, of New Jersey, afterwards of Bohemia Manor, Maryland, where, in 1661, Lord Baltimore granted him 30,000 acres and manor rights. This accounts for Samuel Bayard's son, Peter, going to Maryland. Heerman bought immense tracts in New Jersey before going to Maryland.

BENNET FAMILY

According to Bergen's "Early Settlers," the Bennets came from Kings Co., N. Y., to New Jersey in 1708. But Jan Bennet purchased land on the Raritan in 1683. He m. Eyke Van Marter. From this early pair, there seems to have grown a large and ever spreading family of Bennets.

Adrian Bennet m. Maria Van Pelt about 1705.

Abraham Bennet m. Jane Suydam about 1725, and was elder in the Six-Mile Run church. He bought 400 acres in the rear of the Raritan lots in 1731. An Abraham built the Three-Mile Run church before 1717, and petitioned for the city charter of New Brunswick in 1730. Abraham and Jane's children were: Charles, Peter, Phœbe, Buckalew and Abraham Jr., the latter's wife being Ann.

A prominent Bennet was John, whose estate was settled in 1798 and divided into eighths, indicating 8 children. He lived on the Franklin Park road. So far as is known he had children: Isaac, of Three-Mile Run; Eleanor, who m. Richard Garretson; John; Leah, wife of Abraham Sperlin; Ann, who m. Abraham Hogelandt; and James, b. 1749, who m. Elizabeth Voorhees. The children of James, so far as mentioned, were: Eleanor, wife of James Bishop; Ann, wife of Isaac Brown; Phœbe, who got the tavern on Queen St; also Elizabeth, John, Jane and James.

BILLOPS IN STATEN ISLAND

Jacobus Billop m. Ann Stilwell, b. 1675.

Judge Joseph Billop, brother of Christopher, Escheator-General 1711; died 1712.

Lieut. Christopher Billop, New York Troops, 1674.

Mary and Ann Billop, spinsters, of London "1752" (date erroneous, or otherwise they were aunts of Christopher Billop's daughters, Mary and Ann).

Captain Christopher Billop, of Royal Navy, in command in Delaware, 1677; owner of Bentley Manor, 1679; took a mortgage on Inian's two lots in New Brunswick (640 acres each) at the ford of the Raritan, 1687.

Captain Christopher Billop, b. ———; m. ———. Children by 1st wife: 1. Mary, who m. (1) John Brook of the Missionary Soc. for the Prop. of the Gospel in Foreign Parts, and (2) William Skinner, Missionary of the same Society. 2. Ann, who m. Thomas Farmar, 1705. 3. Lieut. Christopher Billop, 1674, was a (supposed) son.

Capt. Christopher Billop m. (2nd) Katherine, mother of Thomas Farmar. Thomas Farmar, a grandson of Christopher Billop, took the name of Billop as his heir. (See Farmar Line).

DITMARS FAMILY

Jan Jansen Van Ditmarsen emigrated from Ditmarsen in the Dutchy of Holstein. He obtained a patent March 24, 1647, for 24 morgens of land on Manhattan Island; lived at Dutch Kills, Queens Co., L. I. He m. Altje Douwe and d. prior to 1650.

Douwe Jansen Van Ditmarsen, son of above, was b. May, 1642, and m., Sept. 22, 1687, Catherine Lott, dau. of Peter Lott, common ancestor of the Lott family, who emigrated in

1652. Children: John, Peter, Douwe, the latter born 1691 or 1700.

Douwe Ditmars, son of Douwe Jansen, m. Leitie Suydam, who was b. 1706. She was the dau. of Jacob Hendricks Suydam and Leitie Jacobs, the latter being born 1666 and died 1738. Hendrick Reycke Suydam, son of Jacob H. and Leitie, emigrated from Zutphen in the Netherlands and m. Ida Jacobs; died 1701. Alche, dau. of Douwe Ditmars and Leitie Suydam, b. Oct. 6, 1754, m. Nicholas Williamson.

DRAKE FAMILY

Francis Drake died 1687. Francis and Mary Drake moved to New Jersey in 1667-'8 from the Piscataqua River, New Hampshire. His sons, Francis, George and John, came with him, also his daughter Elizabeth.

George Drake m. Mary Oliver in 1677; sons George and Andrew. By his will of 1742, he left 11 children—George, Jeremiah, Edward, David, Johanna (m. Manning), Susannah (m. Smalley), Mary (m. Lee), Lydia, Sarah, Catherine, Randle. The elder George bought a large tract of land along the Raritan opposite New Brunswick before 1678.

John Drake m. Rebecca Trotten in 1677 and was a lay preacher in the Baptist Church. Children—John, Francis, Samuel, Joseph, Benjamin, Abraham, Sarah, Isaac, Rebecca, Jacob, Ebenezer, Ephraim.

Elizabeth m. Hugh Dunn, who was also a lay preacher.

There are many Drakes mentioned besides the sons and grandsons named above, as—

Jonathan Drake's mill, 1771.

David Drake on Burnet St., 1724.

Andrew Drake, died 1743, on Ambrose Brook.

James Drake, Indian Queen Tavern and Ferry, 1778.

James Drake purchased a pew in Presbyterian Church, 1787.

Joseph Drake died 1751; probably a brother of Andrew.

Andrew Drake's brother-in-law, John Clarkson.

Dr. Henry Drake, 1817; son James.

James Drake, 1804, innkeeper, Amboy.

Jacob Drake, 1816, innkeeper, New Brunswick.

Jane Drake, 1821, innkeeper Washington House, New Brunswick.

"N. J. Collections" mentions three lay preachers at Piscataway—Hugh Dunn, John Drake, Edmund Dunham.

FARMAR FAMILY

Jasper Farmar, Jr., having been in this country, returned to England for his father and for their families. The vessel arrived in Philadelphia, October, 1685. Jasper, father and son, died on the voyage. The line runs:

1. Jasper Farmar, Sr., who m. Mary Gamble. Children: Jasper, Edward (wife Rachel), Sarah, John, Charles.

2. Jasper, Jr., m. Katherine ———. Children: Thomas, b. 1675; Elizabeth, Katherine.

3. Thomas, first Mayor of New Brunswick, b. 1675; m., 1705, Ann Billop (dau. of Capt. Christopher Billop). Twelve children, viz.:

(1). Captain Jasper, b. 1707; m. (1), 1731, Anne ———; m. (2), 1742, Mary Gouverneur. Ch. (a). Major Jasper, b. 1734; m., 1758, Mary Grant; had son, Jasper, b. 1759. (In deed to twelve acres in Amboy made in 1792 he styles himself of the island of Jamaica). He d. Oct., 1793, at Barbadoes. (b). Peter, b. 1736; m., 1760, Mary Leacraft and had ten ch: Jasper, who m. Elizabeth Van Harlingen; George, who m. (1) Gertrude Coejeman, and (2), Jane Van Doren; Maria, who m. Mathias Vanderveer; Anne, who m. Jacob Berdine; Sarah, who m. (1), ——— Voorhees, and (2), Isaac Vedder; Peter, who m. Elizabeth Wall; Thomas, who m. Rachel Stelle; Elizabeth, who m. James Buckelew; Samuel, who m. Rhoda Smith; Cornelia, who m. Jacob Suydam.

(2). Christopher, who d. in childhood (heir of Bentley Manor, but in case of death it was to go to Thomas).

(3). Thomas, b. 1711; d. 1750; m. (1) Eugenia Stelle, and (2), Sarah, dau. of Captain Samuel Leonard. As heir of his grandfather he assumed the name of Billop. Had nine children, viz.: Christopher, b. 1737, who m. (1), 1762, Frances (dau. of Thomas Willet), and (2), 1773, Jennie Seaman, and removed to N. Y. between 1778 and '83, and, being a Tory, later removed to St. Johns, N. F.; Ann Billop, dau, of first wife; Mary, who m. Col. Davis; Elizabeth, who m. Peter Goelet in Christ Church, New Brunswick; Sally, who m. Alexander Ross, M. D.; Katherine, who m. Effingham Lawrence; Thomas, who m. (1), a cousin, Elizabeth (dau. of Samuel), and (2), Jasper's widow, but had no ch.; Jasper, who m., 1771, Susannah Skinner; Rachel, second wife of Peter Goelet. The children (all but Christopher) resumed the name of Farmar.

(4). Brooke, who m. ———. His widow m. John Hodge, of Princeton, and d. and was buried there. Brooke's house was burned while the British were in New Brunswick. It was next to the Bell Hotel on Albany Street.

(5). Edward, unmarried.

(6). Robert, Capt. in the British Army; went to West Indies in 1740.

(7). Samuel, merchant of New York City; m. Christina Peck; had ch.: Thomas, who m. Abigail Moore, who was b. 1770; Elizabeth, who m. her cousin, Thomas, son of Thomas; Annie, who m. Abraham Jarvis; Hannah, spinster; Christina, who m. John Marschalk, of New Brunswick.

(8). William Penn, in Captain Grant's Company in British Army, 1764.

(9). John, who went with Robert to the West Indies in the British Army, 1740.

(10). Mary Brooke, who m. Paul Miller, Jr., of New Brunswick.

(11). Anne Billop, who m. Philip French. Had three ch.: Anne Billop French, Philip French, 3rd, and Major Christopher French.

(12). Elizabeth, who m. William Farquhar, M. D.

FRENCH FAMILY

Philip French m. Susannah, dau. of Lieut.-Gov. Anthony Brockholst. He had three sisters: Elizabeth (who m. Cornelius Van Horn), Ann and Margaret. Philip m. (2nd), Ann Billop Farmar, dau. of Thomas, first Mayor of New Brunswick. By his first marriage he had four daughters: Susannah, who m. Gov. William Livingston; Mary, who m.

Hon. William Brown of Beverly, New England; Ann, who m. David Van Horn; and Elizabeth, who m. David Clarkson. By his second marriage the children were: Catherine, who m. Samuel Kemble; and Philip (3rd of the name), who died in 1803, being then one of the oldest inhabitants of New Brunswick, and was buried in his family burying-ground, later the site of the Baptist church. The first Philip died in 1782.

Gov. William Livingston and Susannah French had three daughters: Sarah, who m. John Jay; Susan, who m. John Cleve Symmes; Kitty, who m. (1) Matthew Ridley, and (2) Col. John Livingston.

HARDENBERGH AND LOW FAMILIES

Rev. Jacob Rutsen Hardenbergh, D. D. (son of Col. Johannes Hardenbergh), was b. 1738; died 1790; m. Dinah Van Berg, widow of Rev. John Frelinghuysen; she died in 1807. He was President of Queen's College 1785-1790.

Jacob R. Hardenbergh, lawyer of New Brunswick and merchant; d. 1841. He lived on Water Street; his wife, Mary Margaret, daughter of Cornelius and Catherine (Hude) Low, died Feb. 24, 1841, ten days after him. He was President of the first Bank in New Brunswick in 1808. His children were:

1. Cornelius Low, b. 1790; m. (1) Catherine Richmond; (2) Helen Mary Crook; (3) Mary Hude Warren, and (4) Marcella V. Graves. He was a graduate of Rutgers in 1810 and President of the Bank of New Brunswick, familiarly known as "Hardenbergh's Bank," and had sons—James R., of California; J. Rutsen, of New Brunswick; and Warren, who had sons A. Augustus and Cornelius L.

2. Jacob Rutsen, who d. 1829; m. Mary, dau. of John Pool.

3. Catherine Low, unm.; d. 1873.

4. John, who d. in infancy.

5. Dinah Maria, who d. 1822, aged 25.

6. James Hude, who m. Eliza McKnight and d. in early manhood.

7. Louis Dunham, lawyer, who d. 1857; m. Ellen V. D. Voorhees.

NEW BRUNSWICK IN HISTORY 339

8. Frederick Frelinghuysen, who d. 1846; m. Emeline Morgan.
9. Joanna, who d. 1878; m. Rev. Ransford Welles, D. D.
10. Theodore Frelinghuysen, physician, who d. 1877; unm.

A John Low, who had a will of 1728, had son Cornelius, who had a will of 1749; the latter had children—Peter, of New York City, afterwards chocolate manufacturer of New Brunswick in 1780; Col. John Low, of Second River in 1767; and Cornelius Low, Jr., of New Brunswick Landing in 1737. The first Cornelius Low m. (1) Johanna Gouverneur, 1729; (2) Catherine Hude. The house still standing at the Landing was built in 1741 (so noted in Family Bible) and was built by Cornelius Low.

HUDE FAMILY

Adam and Marion Hude came to New Jersey in the "Henry and Francis," Sept. 3, 1685; bought land in Woodbridge, 1701. Adam was Judge in 1718, and 1733. Marion, his wife, died Nov. 20, 1732, aged 71, and Adam died Jan. 27, 1746, aged 85. They had six children:

1. John; b. July 23, 1687.
2. Agnes; b. Oct. 29, 1689.
3. Robert; b. Sept. 25, 1691; d. Jan. 30, 1748-'9; m. Mary Moores, Aug. 6, 1746.
4. Andrew; b. July 13, 1693; died 1716.
5. James; b. Aug. 14, 1695; died 1762. Executor of Robert in 1749.
6. Mary; b. July 27, 1696.

James was one of the Commissioners for "Victualling and Transporting Troops" to the West Indies in 1740. His obituary says "he passed through almost all the honorary offices and employments in the government where he lived, as well those in the gift of the Crown as those in the voice of the people." He bought land in New Brunswick in 1732-1737. He m. Mary, sister of Simon Johnson, of New York who died in 1772, and their children were: (a) John, who died young; (b) Robert, married, 1765, Abiah Callender; was surrogate of Middlesex; (c) Ann, who m., Dec. 31, 1766, R. Kearney;

(d) Susan, who m. (about 1773) William Neilson, merchant in New York; (e), Mary, who m. Robert G. Livingston; (f) Catherine, who m. Cornelius Low; and (g) James W., counselor at law; d. 1820.

LAWRENCE, LONGFIELD, INIAN, GREENLAND, BRINSON AND COX NOTES

A Thomas Lawrence had a will in 1698. Thomas and Samuel Lawrence were merchants of Philadelphia and New York respectively. This Thomas, Jr., m., 1742, Mary (or Molly) Morris, dau. of Lewis and granddaughter of Gov. Lewis Morris, and lived in Philadelphia also, and in 1778 divided the island farm into three farms.

Henry Greenland's will, of Dec. 11, 1694, mentions his son Henry Greenland, and sons-in-law, Cornelius Longfield and Daniel Brinson. The latter immigrated in 1677 and m. Frances Greenland about 1680; was living at Millstone in 1693 and d. in 1694, while his wife died in 1748.

Barefoot (corruption of Barford) Brinson, often written Brunson, was sheriff of Middlesex in 1711, and of Somerset in 1750. Barefoot m. Mary Lawrence and had ch., John and Ruth. His widow m. John Horner, who d. in 1754.

John Brinson m. Miss Arrowsmith and had ch., Daniel b. 1768; d. 1840; m. Sarah Whitlock; and Mary, who m. John N. Simpson, merchant of New Brunswick.

John W. Brinson was b. 1800; d. 1866; m. Sarah Van Tine, who was b. 1798. Their dau. Sarah Ann Bronson, m. Abram Voorhees, b. 1826, and their dau., Sarah Voorhees, m. John S. Clark, of Middlebush.

Rachel, probably a sister of Cornelius Longfield, was the wife of Thomas Lawrence of Philadelphia.

Cornelius Longfield and his wife, Mary Greenland, had ch. (order uncertain): (1) Catherine, who m. William Cox and had ch.: Sarah, who m. ——— Beekman; William; Thomas; Longfield and Mary; (2) Henry, who m. Ann ———, and had ch.: Mary, who m. Alexander Connolly; and Thomas, a Lieutenant in 1759.

Col. John Cox m. into the Hoboken Stevens' family.

In N. Y. Hist. Soc. Wills, Vol. for 1899, folio 58, I find the will of Octavo Coenraats, merchant, who m. another dau. of Cornelius Longfield, name not given, but he leaves his estate to his only daughter, Morice, and mentions "my share of the land on the South Branch of the Raritan, purchased together with Col. Gerard Beekman, Barent Rynders, Thomas Laurence, John Spratt and Isaac Governeur, and mentions also father-in-law, Cornelius Longfield, of Raritan Manor.

LIVINGSTON FAMILY

The earlier generations of the Livingston family are believed to be as follows. The list given is mainly to show the two distinct Robert Livingston (uncle and nephew) lines, as gathered by me from Rev. Timothy Alden, Munsell's Collections, N. Y. Hist. Soc. Wills, Etc.

Rev. Dr. John Livingston, of Ancram, Scotland, b. June 21, 1603, at Monyabroek. (As to him, see ante, p. 272).

I. Robert, b. Dec. 13, 1654. He came to America in 1674 and settled at Albany, N. Y.; m. (license dated July 26, 1676) Alida (dau. of Philip and Margaret Schuyler and widow of Rev. Nicholas Van Rensselaer), who was b. 1656. He had three sons and two daughters, viz.:

1. Philip (the Manor Line), b. July 25, 1686; m., Sept. 19, 1707, Catherine Van Brug; d. Feb. 4, 1749. Succeeded as Lord of the manor; was Secretary of Albany. His six sons and three daughters were:

(a). Robert, b. 1708; m., 1731, Mary (dau. of Walter and Catalyntie Van Dam Thong). Had six children: Walter, who m. Cornelia Schuyler (and had son Schuyler), Robert Cambridge, John, Henry, Alida and Catherine.

(b.) Peter, b. 1710; m. Mary Alexander (sister of Lord Stirling), and had ch.: Catharine, who m. Nicholas Bayard; Peter Van Brug, Jr., who m. Susan Blundell; Susan, who m. (1) John Kean, and (2) Count Nemcawicx, and had son Philip.

(c). John, b. 1714; m. Catharina De Puyster.

(d). Philip, b. 1717; m. Christina Ten Broeck, and had ch.: Philip, b. 1741, Island of Jamaica, who m. Sarah ———, and had ch.: Sarah; Dirck, b. 1743; Catherine, b. 1745; Robert, whose dau., Sarah, m., 1775, Rev. John H. Livingston (of the Gilbert line).

(e). Henry, of Island of Jamaica, ship owner, b. 1719; unm.

(f). William, b. 1723; m. Susannah French, of New Brunswick, and had ch.: Sarah, who m., 1774, John Jay; Kitty, who m. (1) Matthew Ridley, and (2) Col. John Livingston; Susan, who m. Hon. John Cleve Symmes.

(g). Sarah, b. 1725; m. William Alexander, "Lord Stirling."

(h). Alida, b. 1728; m. (1) Henry Hanson, and (2) Martin Hoffman.

(i). Catherine, b. 1733.

2. Robert, b. July 29, 1688; d. June 27, 1775; m. Margaret Howarden. Had one son, viz.:

Justice Robert R., b. 1719; d. Dec. 9, 1775, at Clermont, N. J.; m. Margaret Beekman; had four sons and six daughters, viz.:

(a). Jane, b. 1743; d. 1828; m. (1772?) Gen. Richard Montgomery. No ch.

(b). Chancellor Robert R., b. 1746; m. Mary Stevens.

(c). Margaret, b. 1748.

(d). Henry B., b. 1750; m. (1) Ann Shippen and (2) Catherine Keteltas.

(e). Catherine, b. 1752.

(f). John R., b. 1755; m. and had a family.

(g). Gertrude, b. 1757; m., 1779, Governor Morgan Lewis, of New York. One ch., Margaret, m., 1798, Maturin Livingston.

(h). Joannah, b. 1759; m. Philip R. Livingston (line of James).

(i). Alida, b. 1761; m., 1789, Gen. John Armstrong.

(j). Edward, b. 1764. He was Mayor of New York City, 1801, and author of "Livingston's Code."

3. Gilbert Livingston, b. Mar. 5, 1690; m. Cornelia Beekman (dau. of Henry Beekman and Janet Livingston; the latter of the "Nephew" Robert line). Received "Saraghtoge," a plantation running 22 miles along the Hudson river and extending 6 miles back on each side. By his will of 1746 he has seven sons and four daughters, viz.:

(a). Robert G.; m. Catherine Mack Phaedrix. Left will of 1789. He received Rhinebeck as his portion of his father's estate, and had five ch.: Henry, Catherine, Reade, Helena and Gilbert.
(b). Henry, b. 1714; d. 1799; m. S. Conklin. Their son, Rev. John H. Livingston, b. May 30, 1746, m. his third cousin, Sarah, and had one ch., Col. Henry, b. 1775.
(c). Gilbert, of Bermuda; m., and had one son, John.
(d). Philip.
(e). James G. (See remarks under next family, James (2), bapt. 1701).
(f). Samuel.
(g). Cornelius.
(h). Alida, who m. Jacob Rutsen.
(i). Joanna, who m. Pierre Van Cortandt, Lieut.-Governor of New York.
(j). Catherine, who m. Thomas Thorne.
(k). Margaret, who m. Henry Beekman (son of Col. Henry Beekman).
3. Margaret Livingston who m. Governor Samuel Vetch, of Nova Scotia; the latter d. 1732.
5. Joanna, b. July 27, 1698, who m. Cornelius Gerrit Van Horn (son of Gerrit Van Horn and Anne Reade), and had seven ch.
II. James; did not come to America, but had a son Robert (herein called "the Nephew"), who did, and he also married a Schuyler. These facts have caused the two lines to be much confused. This Robert "the Nephew," was Deputy Secretary of New York from 1696-1707; m. (license dated Aug. 26, 1697) Margarita, only dau. of Pieter, (brother of Philip Schuyler). The children of this Robert were:
1. Engeltie, bapt. July 17, 1698; m. Johannes Van Rensellaer.
2. James, bapt. Oct. 21, 1701; m. Mary (or Maria) Kierstede (only child of Jacobus Kierstede); but her marriage and this line are also credited by some authorities to James Gilbert Livingston of the Gilbert Livingston line, and I am uncertain which is correct, but believe Mary belongs here.
3. Janet, bapt. Nov. 24, 1703; m. Col. Henry Beekman, and

had ch.: Henry, who m. Margaret Livingston; Cornelia, who m. Gilbert Livingston; and Margaret, who m. ———.

4. Pieter, bapt. Jan. 6, 1706; m., 1728, Letitia Holland, and had ch.: Robert, bapt. July 27, 1729; Henry, bapt. Sept. 25, 1730; Margareta, bapt. July 2, 1732; Thomas, bapt. Oct. 5, 1733; Jane, bapt. June 18, 1735; Margareta (2nd), bapt. June 23, 1736.

5. John, bapt. Mar. 6, 1709; m., 1739, Catherine Ten Broeck.

6. Robert, bapt. Aug. 31, 1718; m. and had ch.: Robert, b. 1740; Margareta, b. 1742; Dirck, b. 1744.

PARKER FAMILY

Benjamin Parker was b. 1670; d. 1731. John Parker was b. 1665; d. 1702. The first Elisha Parker m. in 1657; wife was Elizabeth Hinckley and they had children: Thomas, b. 1658 (m. Mary ———); Elisha, b. 1660 and d. 1717; Sarah, b. 1662; Mary, b. 1672; Samuel, b. 1674.

Elisha (first) m. (2nd) Hannah Rolph, and had children: Elizabeth, b. 1691; John, b. 1693. This John m. Janet Johnson and had children: James, b. 1725; John, b. 1729; Lewis, b. 1731 (the Amboy Line).

Elisha (first) m. (3rd) Ursula Crage (Craig) and had children: Elizabeth, b. 1698; Ursula, b. 1700; Mary, b. 1702; Elisha, b. 1704, who m., 1747, Catherine Alexander; died 1751; no children.

Thomas (above, who married Mary ———) had children: David, b. 1676; Elisha, b. 1684; Daniel, b. 1686; Joseph, b. 1692; Benjamin (twin), b. 1692; George, b. 1695, and Elizabeth (twin with George).

Samuel, (above) had children: James, (the printer) b. 1714; m. Mary Ballereau and had children: Samuel Franklin and Janet, who m. Governor Bedford.

Elisha (known as Captain), b. ———; also spoken of as, "the weaver," was unm. and removed to Amboy 1715; died 1727.

A John Parker of Somerset co. and New Brunswick had wife Elizabeth and will of 1750; names children: James, John, Janet and Ellender.

Other notes more or less conflicting are:
Elisha deeds to son Elisha seven acres in Woodbridge, 1680.
Benjamin, a joiner, owned 105 acres in Woodbridge, and land in Elizabeth, 1670.
John (named in second paragraph above), is in the list of Associates of Elizabeth, 1665.
Whitehead calls Elisha, "the weaver," a son of Elisha and Elizabeth.
Dally says Elisha, "the weaver," m. Elizabeth, and married three times; the second m. being to Hannah Rolph, and the third to Ursula Crage.
Colie says Elisha, Sr., m. Elizabeth Hinckley and that "Elisha, "the weaver," m. Hannah Rolph and Ursula Crage; while Whitehead says Elisha, "the weaver," died unm. and left property to sisters Elizabeth, Ursula and Mary, having removed to Amboy about 1715.
Besides the two Elishas who came to Woodbridge, there are Elisha, son of Thomas, and Elisha, son of Ursula Crage, who, Whitehead says, is son of John, b. 1690. Thus four Elishas were contemporary: Elisha of Barnstaple, Mass., his son Elisha, his grandson Elisha, b. 1684, and Ursula's son, Elisha (as per Dally), b. 1704.
Then there are James, the printer, d. 1770; James, Mayor of Amboy, d. 1797; the second James of Amboy, b. 1776 and d. 1868, at 92 years; and a third James of Amboy, d———. What is the relation between James of Amboy and James of Woodbridge?
Other Parkers are: Martha, b. 1683; Elizabeth, b. 1686, who m. Thomas Pike; Sarah, b. 1696, who m. Matthew Mores and Mary, b. 1691, who m. Daniel Robinds.

RUNYON FAMILY

Vincent Runyan, of Piscataway, N. J., m., 1668, Ann Boutcher. Children: Vincent, b. 1670; Darrich, b. 1672; Joseph, b. 1674, an innkeeper of Franklin Township; Reune, b. 1675; Ephraim, b. 1676; Mary, b. 1677; Peter, b. 1680; Jane, b. 1683; Sarah, b. 1685, m. Richard Sutton; and John, who m. Elizabeth Dunn.

Vincent, (b. 1670) m., 1691, Mary Hull. Children: Vincent, b. 1692; Sarah, b. 1693, and m. Robert Webster, who was b. 1695; Martha, b. 1697, who m. John Moulton; Susannah, b. 1698; Mary, b. 1700; Annie, b. 1702, and m. John Wetherbee; Rizpah, b. 1704, and m. George Martelle; Reuben, b. 1706, and m. Sarah ———, lived on Town Lane (and had ch.: Walter and Reuben); Vincent, b. 1709; Reune, b. 1711 (Town Clerk of Piscataway); Keziah, b. 1713.

Reune (b. 1711) m., 1732, Rachel Drake and had ch.: Mary, b. 1733, and m. Joshua Martin; Ephraim, b. 1735; Rachel, b. 1738; Rev. Reune, b. 1741 and m. Anna Bray; John, b. 1743; Rizpah, b. 1746 and m. James Compton and Zeziah, b. 1749. Chancellor Runyon was of this line. Reune and John applied to Committee of Correspondence for leave to go into enemy's line to get will of their father, who went over to and died among the enemy. Leave to write was given them.

Ephraim (b. 1735) m. Ruth Mollison, and had ch.: Mary, b. 1759; Ann, b. 1761; Lewis, b. 1765 and m. Jane (daughter of Benjamin, b. 1729, the son of Peter, b. 1704); Rachel, b. 1762; Lewis, b. 1765; John, b. 1767; Jeptha, b. 1769, and m. Osy Fitz Randolph.

John (b. 1767) m. Christina Stelle and had ch.: Abel Stelle, b. 1795; Ephraim, who m. Ann Pratt; Clarkson, who m. Matilda Mundy.

Abel Stelle (b. 1795) m. (1st), Catherine Manning, and (2nd), Mercy Runyon and had ch.: John, who m. Caroline FitzRandolph; Mahlon, who m. Susan (daughter of Peter P. Runyon (and had ch.: Mary, who m. Fitz Randolph Stout; Deborah, who m. Samuel Long, M. D., and had ch.: Pauline A., M. D., Lily and Dorothy Lillian; Charles, who m. Mary S. Cooke).

Peter (b. 1680) m., 1704, Prudence Blackford and had ch.: John D., b. 1705; Grace, b. 1706 and m. Daniel Cooper; Joseph, b. 1710; Rosannah, b. 1712; Peter J. R., Jr., b. 1715; Richard, b. 1719; Providence, b. 1723; Sarah, b. 1725; Benjamin, b. 1729 and m. Annie Van Court.

Richard (b. 1719) m., 1745, Jane Van Court and had ch.: Sarah, b. 1746 and m. Elias Corriell; Elias, b. 1749; Elizabeth, b. 1750 and m. Moses Carpenter; Jean, b. 1752; Rosannah, b. 1754; John, b. 1756 and m. Mary Conklin; Anna, who m. Daniel Sayre.

Elias (b. 1749) m., 1771, Deborah Clark and had ch.: Richard, b. 1771 and m. Phoebe Lewis; Annie, b. 1773 and m. Ludlow Squire; Daniel, b. 1776 and m. Hope Lewis; John, b. 1776 and m. Margaret Runyon; Jean, b. 1781; Isaac, b. 1782 and m. Polly D. ———; Elias, b. 1784 and m. Agnes Day; Peter P., b. 1789; Jane, b. 1790 and m. Savage Wright.

Peter P. Runyon (b. 1789) m. Phebe Ten Eyck (dau. of Tunis Ten Eyck and Susannah, dau. of Peter Trembly). Ch.: John, Deborah, Peter Trembly, Mary, who m. Peter Onderdonk, Elias and Susan.

Elias (son of Peter P.) m. (1) Emily Fitz Randolph, and (2) Cornelius Rue, and had ch.: Peter, who m. Josephine Leveridge; David Fitz Randolph, who m. Alice Wood and had child, Elsie B. Elias's ch. by 2nd wife were: Ernest, Elias, Emily, Clara and Grace, who m. E. L. Stevenson.

SCHUREMAN FAMILY

Jacobus Schuurman was b. in Holland after 1693; came to America in 1719 with Rev. Theodore J. Frelinghuysen as his accompanying schoolmaster, choir leader and reader. He settled with him at Three-Mile Run. Both m. sisters, Jacobus' wife being Antje, and Frelinghuysen's wife being Eve Terheun (Terhune), the two being daughters of Albert Terheun, of Flatbush, L. I. Jacobus had seven children:

1. Anne, b. 1721; d. 1800; unm.
2. Jacoba, b. 1724; d. before 1760; m. Archibald Thomson.
3. Margaret, b. 1726; d. 1745; m. 1743, Petrus Vredenburgh.
4. John. (See below).
5. Ferdinand; m. Eleanor Voorhees.
6. Jacob (sup.); m. Maria Van Voorhees.
7. Albertines, b. 1735.

John Schureman (4) was b. 1729; d. 1795; m., Feb., 1751, Antje (De Riemer) Stryker. He had a storehouse on the Raritan river at New Brunswick, at the foot of Dutch (now

Schureman) St. He was most active in the Revolutionary War, being on the Middlesex Committee of Correspondence, a member of the Provincial Congress and of the Committee of Safety. He was also a Trustee of Queens College and its Treasurer from 1780 to 1790. He had five children.

James Schureman, son of John, was b. 1756; d. 1824; m., 1778, Eleanor Williamson. He graduated from Queen's College in 1775 and served as Lieutenant and possibly as Captain in Col. John Neilson's Battalion of Minute Men. In 1777 he was captured by the British and confined near New Brunswick, and later in the "Sugar House Prison" in New York City, from which he escaped. On the Simcoe raid in 1779 it was Schureman in Neilson's 2nd Middlesex Regiment who took Simcoe prisoner. He was member of the N. J. Assembly for four terms and of the N. J. Senate three terms; was twice elected to Congress; then became, in 1799, U. S. Senator, and again served one term as Representative in Congress, 1813-'15. He was Mayor of New Brunswick in 1810 and again in 1821. He followed his father in the merchant business, foot of Schureman St., which was named for him. He also became Trustee and Treasurer of Queens College. He had 14 children. His son, William Williamson, who was b. 1799 and d. 1850, m. Anne Bennet, and lived on the Three-Mile Run farm owned by his father, grandfather and great-grandfather. His son, James, b. 1823 and d. 1901, m. Hannah Kocks (Cox) and lived on the same homestead. The latter had a son, Howard Bishop, b. in 1849.

SCHUYLER FAMILY

The Schuyler family came from Albany and descended from David Peterse Schuyler and Catalyntjie Ver Planck, whose third son, Abraham, b. 1663, m. Gertruy Ten Broeck, and the latter's fourth son, Abraham, b. 1704, m., 1732, Catriena Staats. This Abraham and his brother, Derrick, came to New Brunswick about 1729. This Abraham (second) also had a son Abram, b. 1741, who m., 1761, Altie Voorhees, of New Brunswick. His sisters were: Christina, who m. John Voorhees; Getani, who m. Peter Voorhees (brother of John); and

Arietta, who m. Samuel Coejeman, of Somerset Co., while their dau., Joanna Coejeman, m. Dr. John Neilson.

Abram (b. 1741) had children: Abraham, b. May 19, 1764, (fourth of the name); Catriena, b. 1764; Altje, b. 1767; Christina, b. 1771; Johanna, b. 1773; and Neiltie, was b. 1776.

Another Jersey Schuyler family descended from Philip Peterse Schuyler, David's brother, and settled on Second River, just above Newark, now called Belleville.

Arent, who settled here in or before 1709, had three sons, who operated a coppermine there. He died about 1734.

Col. John is the most prominent, and in 1731 was rated as worth £60,000 to £70,000. He lived in Belleville, (while Col. Peter is said to have lived next the mine; he died March 7, 1762 at his seat at Newark).

Adonijah was the third son, and there were two daughters, Eva (Mrs. P. Beyyers, or Mrs. P. Bayard; both names are given), and Cornelia, (Mrs. P. De Peyster).

A list of officers in Col. Peter Schuyler's regiment is given in 1759.

Nicholas Gouverneur left by will, 1786, to Mary, his wife, all of Peter Schuyler's personal property in his possession. Was she his daughter?

A Col. Peter Schuyler left a widow Margaret, who, in her will of 1782, leaves her estate to Dr. John Cochrane, who married her daughter, Gertrude Schuyler, and lived in New Brunswick, 1766-69. His house was burned by the British.

SCOTT FAMILY

Moses Scott, b. 1738; d. Dec. 28, 1821, aged 83; m. Anna Johnson, who was b. 1745 and d. Aug. 7, 1833, aged 88. Their children were:

1. Joseph Warren, who d. in infancy.
2. Hannah, b. 1765; d. 1847 aged 82; unm.
3. Jane M., b. 1768; d. 1826, aged 58; m., 1794, Abraham Blauvelt, the printer and publisher of New Brunswick, whose children were: Dr. Cornelius, Rev. William Warren, D. D., John Scott, Dr. Charles Cotesworth, Isaac Alstyne, and one

or two others who d. in infancy. (See, for further particulars, "N. J. Hist. Soc. Proceedings," for Jan., 1921).

4. Mary Dickerson, b. 1770; d. March, 1848; m. Dr. Charles Smith, who lived in the Leupp house on Albany St., with his sister, Mary Smith. He was born in 1770.

5. Phœbe, b. 1772; d. 1839, aged 67.

6. Margaret, b. 1774 (?); died 1785, aged 11 years.

7. Joseph Warren (2nd), b. 1778; d. 1871; m. May 31, 1804, Jane Griffiths of New York City.

8. Anna Johnson, b. 1780; d. 1785.

9. Margaret (2nd), b. 1785; d. 1811, in 26th year.

10. Anna Johnson (2nd), b. Apr. 12, 1789, d. June 5, 1851; m. Nov. 14, 1815, Dr. Fitz Randolph Smith. Their dau., Anna, m., Jan. 17, 1839, Rev. John D. Ogilby (his second wife).

11. Eliza, who m., June 4, 1822, Rev. Peter P. Rouse.

Joseph Warren Scott (7 above) had children:

1. Lavinia Agnes, b. Nov. 30, 1805; d. March 31, 1886; m. Sept. 11, 1822, Rev. Richard Varick Dey, and had 7 children; (a) Joseph Warren Scott, who died in infancy. (b). Richard Varick, who died in infancy. (c). Mary Laidlie, b. May 8, 1824; d. 1915. (d) Lavinia Agnes, b. 1826; d. 1852. (e). Anthony, b. 1829; d. 1912; m. Mary B. Humphries, who d. 1884; no ch. (f). Joseph Warren Scott (2nd), b. 1832; d. 1905; unm. (g). Richard Varick, b. 1835; living.

2. Anna Cornelia, b. Jan. 19, 1808; d. May, 1808.

3. Joseph Griffiths, b. Apr. 12, 1809; d. Oct. 10, 1884; m., May 23, 1839, Eliza Duryee; no ch.

4. Moses Warren, b. May 1, 1812; d. Aug. 25, 1857; m. Juletta Ann Cornell, who d. July, 1880. Children: (a) Joseph W., who d. Oct. 13, 1888, aged 37, leaving a widow, and a daughter, who m. Walter Pierson, the latter leaving two sons, Joseph Warren Scott Pierson, and Walter Scott Pierson, Jr., (b) William Earl Dodge Scott, who m. Marion ———; no ch.

5. Cornelia De Diemar, b. Mar. 13, 1815; d. Apr. 30, 1837; m., 1834 (as his first wife), Rev. John D. Ogilby.

6. Charles Smith, b. June 6, 1819; d. Dec. 24, 1893, **at** Buccleuch; **unm.**

TAYLOR FAMILY

Richard Taylor, of England, was Member of Parliament in 1620. Another Richard Taylor was Member in 1661. John Taylor, of Hawes, Bedfordshire, Eng., b. 1688, came to America in 1739 and settled on the Raritan. His son, Jacob, of Amboy, was b. Nov. 23, 1729; d. 1776; m. Rachel, dau. of John Potter of Springfield, N. J. Their son, Col. John, was b. Aug. 1, 1751; d. Nov. 5, 1801. He graduated from Princeton College in 1770; was Tutor at Queen's College; Major in 2nd Regiment of Middlesex; Captain in Col. Neilson's Battalion of Minute Men in 1775; Major in State Troops 1776, serving then both military and College. He m. Janet Fitzrandolph of Woodbridge, who was b. 1752 and d. 1840. They had three children. He was Clerk of the Board of Queen's College in 1780. He reorganized the Grammar School in New Brunswick with Andrew Kirkpatrick, which was suspended during the War and resumed in 1785. After 1783 he was Professor of Mathematics and Natural Philosophy in Queen's until 1790; then he went to Elizabethtown Academy, and in 1793 to Union Academy, Schenectady, N. Y., where he died. Col. John's son, Augustus R. Taylor, was b. Aug., 1782 and d. 1840. He graduated from Union College 1800 and studied medicine with Dr. Moses Scott. He m. Catherine S. Neilson in 1804 and was member of the N. J. Assembly in 1839. He lived in the John Van Harlingen house, southwest corner of Church and George Sts.

Dr. Augustus F. R. Taylor, son of Dr. Augustus R., was b. 1809; d. 1887, having been blind after 1866. He graduated from Rutgers in 1829 and assisted in the cholera epidemic of 1832. He m., 1833, Cornelia A. Holcomb.

VAN WICKLE-BEACH-WELLS FAMILIES

Evart Van Wyckelyn came to Long Island in 1664; m. Elizabeth Van Liew. He was in Flatbush, about 1687; bought 800 acres of William Dockwra about 1700. Thomas Cardale, of Jamaica, L. I., in 1703, sold Gerardus Beeckman, M. D., Leffert Peterse and Evart Van Wyckelyn, of King's Co., land on the south side of the Raritan, beginning at Richard Jones'

Raritan lot No. 7, north-west corner, about 3½ miles from Albany St., New Brunswick; south-west 140 ch.; north-west, distance omitted; east to Raritan and down river to beginning, in all 450 acres, for £200. (Book I, Sec'y State's Office, Trenton.

An Evart Van Wickle m. Elizabeth Van Liew; had son bapt. Mar. 5, 1699.

An Evart Van Wickle m. Cornelia Lupardus, and died 1757. His dau., Ann Van Wickle, m. Rev. Abraham Beach about 1771, when she was 14.

Rev. Abraham Beach was b. in Cheshire, Conn., Sept. 9, 1740. He went abroad to be ordained and returned under the auspices of the "Society for the Propagation of the Gospel in Foreign Parts" in Sept., 1767. On July 7, 1784, he became assistant in Trinity Church, N. Y., returning later to New Brunswick, where he died in 1828. Their children were (order uncertain):

1. Ann Chandler Beach, wife of Rev. T. Lyell.
2. Maria, wife of Rev. A. Carter.
3. Hannah, b. 1769; d. 1848; m. ―――― Ratoone.
4. Cornelia, wife of Isaac Lawrence.
5. Abraham, Jr., m., but has no present descendants.
6. Evart, d. unm.

Isaac Lawrence and Cornelia Beach's daughter, Julia, m. Thomas Lawrence Wells, and this branch of the family now occupy the old Van Wickle homestead near New Brunswick, which has been in the family occupancy since 1703, 221 years in 1924.

VOORHEES FAMILY AS RELATED TO THE WILLIAMSONS

1. Steven Coerte Van Voorhees, of Holland and Flatlands, L. I., and his wife, Willempie Roelofse, had ten children and eighty-six grandchildren. His eldest son was—

2. Coerte Stevense, b. 1637; d. 1702; m. Maretje Van Couwenhoven (daughter of Garret Wolfertse Van Couwenhoven). One of his sons was—

3. Steven Coerte, b. 1667; d. 1723; m. Agatha Janse. He purchased a tract of land on the west side of the Millstone

river and left it to his five daughters. The second dau., Lucresy, m., 1715, Nicholas Williamson, who was b. 1680.

2. Minne Lucasse, another son of Steven Coerte, m. Antie Wyckoff and had eight children. Lucas, his son, b. 1718 (the Joiner), m. Catrina Vandervoort and owned 16 acres through which Oliver, Hassert, Carmen, Abeel and Neilson Streets now run. Ch.: four sons and two daughters, among them Ann, (wife of Jacob Hassert), whose daughter, Jane, married David Abeel; Mary (wife of John Pool), whose dau., Mary Pool, m. Rutsen Hardenbergh; Captain Peter Voorhees, who was killed by Simcoe's men, Oct. 26, 1779.

David Abeel (sea Captain), had a dau., Mary Ann Abeel, who m. D. D. Williamson, father of Nicholas and D. D. Williamson, Jr.

3. Jan Lucasse Van Voorhees, another son of Coerte, had a son Johannes, b. 1700, whose son, John, b. 1729, m. Catherine Schuyler, and had ch.: Cap't John, b. 1750, who m. Sarah ——— and was in the Revolutionary War and died before his father without children; Catherine, b. 1753, who m. Colonel John Neilson and whose son, John, M. D., m., 1798, Abigail Bleecker. Julia, dau. of the last named John, m. Charles A. Bulkley, and their dau., Catherine, m. D. D. Williamson.

WILLIAMSON FAMILY

William Williamson was b. 1637; m. Mayke Pieterse Wyckoff, of Amsterdam, Holland. She was the dau, of Pieter Classz Wyckoff, who emigrated in 1653, and who m. Grietje, dau. of Hendrick Van Ness. William Williamson came to this country in the ship "Concord" in 1657, and settled at Gravesend, L. I.

Nicholas Williamson, son of above, was b. at Gravesend in 1680; m., 1715, Lucresy Voorhees, dau. of Steven Coerte and Agatha Janse of Flatlands and Gravesend.

Garret Williamson, son of Nicholas, was b. March, 1728; d. 1790; m. Charity Bennet, who was b. Apr. 30, 1731, and died Oct. 27, 1783.

Nicholas Williamson, son of Garret, was b. Oct. 8, 1762; d. Aug. 18, 1856; m. Alche Ditmars.

X. MAP OF HESSIAN FORTIFICATIONS, 1776-'77

The map of Hessian Fortifications at New Brunswick, 1776-'77, is a free-hand copy made from a photograph in possession of the Rutgers College Library, the original, by A. Sutherland, being in the Hill Collection in the Congressional Library at Washington. The notes to it, by the author of this volume, are made to assist in locating the earthworks.

XI. INDEX TO MAP OF NEW BRUNSWICK LANDS, 1681-1800

The following Index to the Map of New Brunswick, 1681-1800, inserted as a frontispiece to this work, and which has been carefully plotted by the author, will be readily understood by any searcher of titles, and will, it is to be hoped, prove of real value to those interested in early city lands. Under "No" appears the plot designated; "Acres" are given when known, also "Year," which is followed by names of owners. The figures or letters in parentheses after sentences or names indicate the deed books to which reference may be made, which are all in either the Middlesex or Somerset Clerk's office, unless "T" is affixed, when the reference is to deeds in the Secretary of State's office, Trenton.

PLOT A. CORNELIUS & MARY (GREENLAND) LONGFIELD

No.	Acres	Year	
A	870	1681	First Deed from Indians and Elizabeth Carteret, Executrix.
A	700	1678	Acquired part of Thos. Lawrence (his stepfather's) tract.
A	1280	1681	Inherited John Inian's two Raritan lots, by will of Mary Inian.
A	150	1694	Inherited of Henry Greenland half of his 300 acres at the Ford.
A	300	1706	Purchased of Osterland & Keyser part of Peter Sonman's Grant.
A	3300		West of Longfield were the farms of Edw. Van Harlingen, Jaques Van Liew, Dirck Schuyler and George Appleby. (K:32).
A	280	1699	To John Paterson Mellet. (K:114).
	200	1720	To Enoch Freeland. (K:32; K:254).
	100	1727	To John Van Nuys. Bounded by Livingston Ave., if projected to river on north; by Remsen Ave. on south, and from River southwesterly to and including Lot A 15. Rear to Roe-

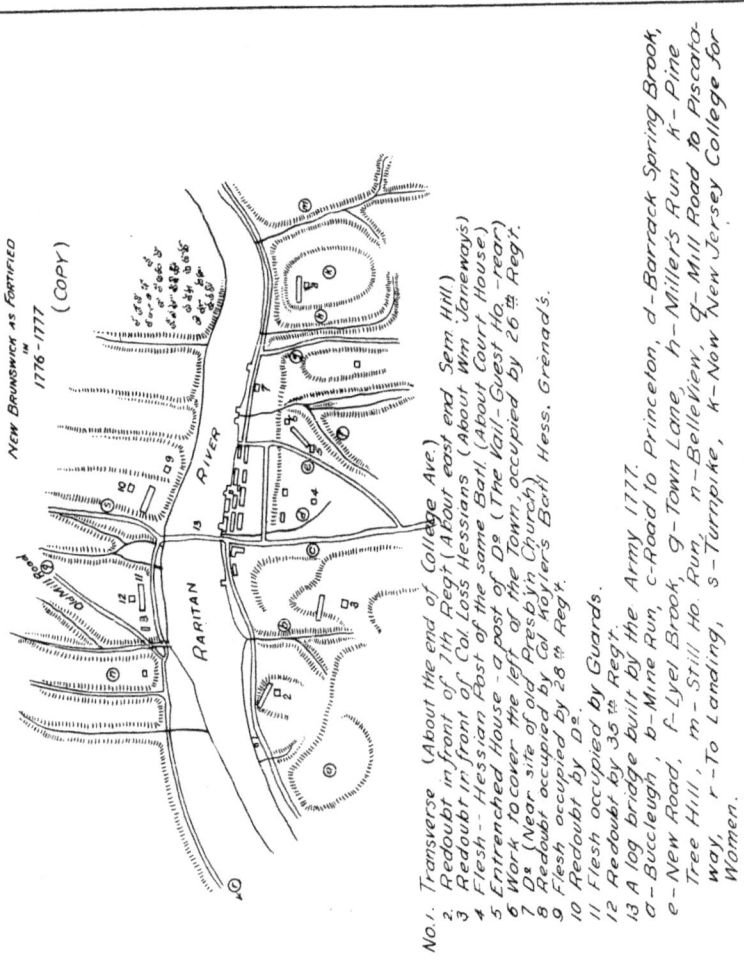

No. 1. Transverse (About the end of College Ave.)
2. Redoubt in front of 7th Reg't (About east end Sem. Hill)
3. Redoubt in front of Col. Loss Hessians (About Court House)
4. Flesh — Hessian Post of the same Bat'l. (About Wm. Janeways)
5. Entrenched House — a post of D? (The Vail-Guest Ho.-rear)
6. Work to cover the left of the Town, occupied by 26 th Reg't.
7. D? (Near site of old Pres'byn Church)
8. Redoubt occupied by Col. Koyler's Bath Hess. Gren'ad's.
9. Flesh occupied by 28 th Reg't.
10. Redoubt by D?.
11. Flesh occupied by Guards.
12. Redoubt by 35 th Reg't.
13. A log bridge built by the Army 1777.
a — Buccleugh, b — Mine Run, c — Road to Princeton, d — Barrack Spring Brook,
e — New Road, f — Lyel Brook, g — Town Lane, h — Miller's Run k — Pine
Tree Hill, m — Still Ho Run, n — Belleview, q — Mill Road to Piscato-
way, r — To Landing, s — Turnpike, k — New New Jersey College for
Women.

(Notes in parenthesis added by Wm. H. Benedict.)
(Locations indicated by letters (a,b, etc.) also added by Mr.
Benedict.)

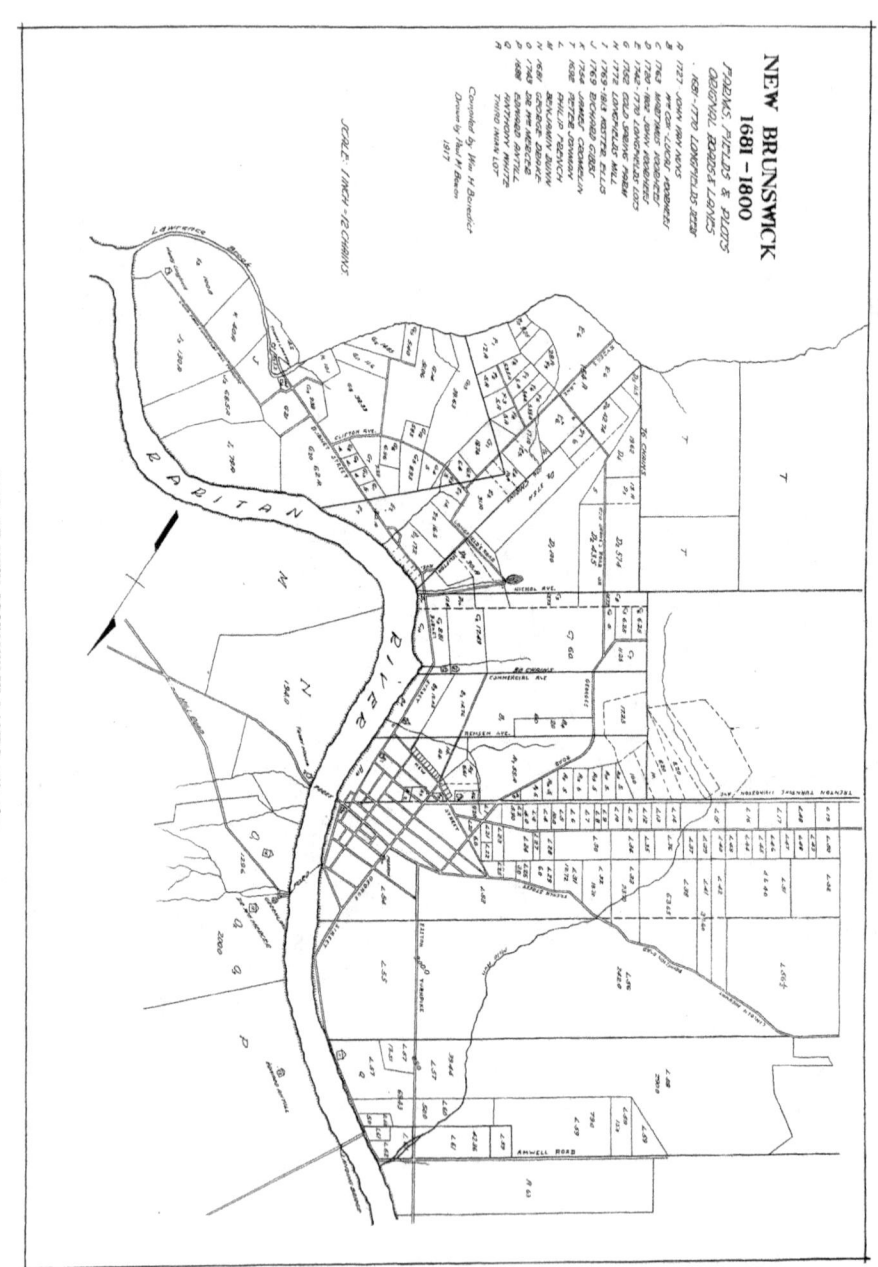

MAP OF NEW BRUNSWICK LANDS, 1681-1800
(See Index to this Map, XI of Appendix.)

		Ioff Voorhees and children, John P. Voorhees and Lena (Voorhees) Vanderbilt. Have not attempted to plot the lots, except those of an acre or more.
A1 ...	2............	Dutch Church burial plot. Confirmation deed by Dennis and Ida Van Liew.
A2 ...	?............	Queen's College Lots, on which stood the College Hall.
A3 ...	?............	Mary Ellis's garden; part of Van Liew tract. Point made by New & Livingston Ave.; also Van Liew's. As Van Liew owned both sides of the College lots, they were probably also originally Van Liew.
A4 ...	14.....1790....	Enoch Freeland, 14 acres. Also John Dumont and Koert Voorhees, successive owners. (1. 566, 632; 5:279; 7:432).
A5 ...	6.61...........	J. H. Livingston. (8:875; 17:771; 18:195).
A7 ...	55 ...1810....	J. H. Livingston. (30:193, 619; 34:138).
A8 ...	....	Ditto. A small piece to straighten road.
A6 ...	........1760....	Henry & Moses Guest. (9:546).
A8 ...	........1802....	James Schureman. (4:361).
A9 ...	5.....1802....	John Dennis. (4:361).
A10 ..	5.....1802....	A. Hassert. (4:424).
A11 ..	5............	Alpheus Freeman. (4:397; 12:884).
	2½...1818....	The Potters' Field was, later on, the East half of this lot—West end. (12:884).
	61/100..........	The old Van Liew burial-place next to it. 1830. (22:511; 84:193).
A12 ..	6.....1802....	Dr. Chas. Smith. (4:235).
A13 ..	5.....1816....	John Van Nuys, Jr. (26:504).
A14 ..	5.....1816....	Peter Wayckoff. (12:871).
A15 ..	5............	Nehemiah Vernon. (5:734). Livingston to Vernon, both inclusive, make 97.61 of the Van Nuys 100 acres.
A16 ..	10............	Samuel Brush. Lucas Voorhees bought 280 acres at rear of Longfield and sold same to Jan Voorhees. (69:423).
A17 ..	10	John P. Voorhees. (62:620).
A18 ..	8.2	John P. Voorhees. (61:353).
	8.2	John P. Voorhees. (82:366).
	17.25..........	John P. Voorhees. (60:394).
	61.11..........	Rutgers College. (40:245).
	74.66.........	Wilbur Farm.
	9.90..........	Atkinson Place.
		Abraham Suydam to Levinus Graham includes A5 and B1, 115 acres. (See Book 23, folio 476).

PLOT B. CORNELIUS LONGFIELD, 15 chains x 80 chains; between Remsen Ave. and Commercial Ave., and from the river 80 chains southwest.

	120.....1734....	To Wm. Cox, his son-in-law, husband of his
	1767....	daughter Catharine. Later, as 16 ch., 18 l., in 1767 mortgaged 116 (E:231) acres to Thos.
	1763....	Lawrence and, excepting some lots, sold same

			to Benjamin Designy. Same, Lucas Voorhees, son of Minnie (Will, 1783). Cut up as follows: (1:313, 566, 632:6:679; D3:266).
B1	60	1830	Robert Morris; Luke Voorhees. (6:679; 30:398, 614).
B2	14.76	1725	Koert Van Voorhees; Lucas Voorhees; The Hassert Abeel Lots. (5:249).
		1737	Wm. Ouke. (5:349). The old Abeel House. (1:313). Later, Dr. Helm's house, on west side of George, was on this plot. (1:566). Now a double brick apt. house. (1:632).
B3	12.48	1778	Bernardus LeGrange; Jas. Richmond. (1:604). Abm. Heyer (cooper), of N. B., and Jacob Heyer (hatter), of Princeton, successive owners. (3:334).
B4	20	1798	Jacob Heyer; Samuel Coates; Robert Morris. (24:261; 1:90; 627; 24:249).
B5	Lots	1749	Burnet St. lots, sold by Wm. Cox; reserved out in deed: Richard Stillwell, 74 feet front. Christopher Beekman, 40 feet. Presbyterian Meeting House, 54 feet. Wm. McKeath, 35 feet. Timothy Goodfellow, 30 feet. Thos. Marshall, 25 feet. John Smith, 40 feet. Capt. Richard Gibb, David Abeel, John Bergen, Court Van Voorhees and John Wiley; other lots; being about 2,000 feet front on both sides of Burnet St.

PLOT C. CORNELIUS LONGFIELD, 20x80 chains, between Commercial Ave. (Town Lane), (George's Road), and a line 5 chains East of Nicholl Ave.

		1725	160 Acres to Johannes Voorhees, who kept the 5 chains East of Nicholl Ave., and sold 15
		1763	x80 chains to his brother, Lucas Voorhees, son of Jan Lucasse; by inheritance to his son, Martymus, or John Martin Voorhees and children.
		1777	He died Sept., 1777; no will. The 120 acres cut up as below; the 40 acres cut up with Plot D.
C1	120	1790	Robert Morris, subject to prior sales, as follows:
		1789	110' front, 100' deep, cor. Commercial Ave.
		1788	30' front, 100' deep, to Abm. Van Tine, at turn in Burnet St. (5:72). 80' front, 100' deep, to Roeloff M. Voorhees (Executor of Martymus). 40' front, 100' deep, to John Voorhees, Jr.
C3	Includes		1 3/10 acres on George's Road west; Reuben Runyon to Col. Sam Hay. (17:49).
	3/20		On George's Road to John De Graff.

	14/10.....1783	....S. W. cor. tract on George's Road to John M. Voorhees.
		10 Acres, N. W. corner on George's Road, Martin M. Voorhees.
	3/20	............Strip 44' wide for road into Cornelius Vanderbilt's from George's Road.
C2 ...	17.49...1799 (?)	Reuben Runyon (Town Lane). (10:648).
	8.81 Quarry...	Pine Tree Hill, Woman's College.

14/10.....1783....S. W. cor. tract on George's Road to John M. Voorhees.
    10 Acres, N. W. corner on George's Road, Martin M. Voorhees.
3/20............Strip 44' wide for road into Cornelius Vanderbilt's from George's Road.

C2 ... 17.49...1799 (?) Reuben Runyon (Town Lane). (10:648).
  8.81 Quarry...Pine Tree Hill, Woman's College.
  Altogether about 44 acres, leaving about 76 for Morris.
C3 ... 17.49...1796....Mary Ellis, Pine Tree Hill; 8:81 acres, Quarry Lot to Eliza Evans, excepting out 1 3/10 to Col. Saml Hay and ½ int. in Quarry. (10:685).
C4 ... 5 ....C. H. Van Nortwick; Jas. Richmond; J. W. Stout.
C5 ... 6.25...........Dutch Church; Staats Van Deursen. (7:303).
C6 ... 6.25...........Dutch Church; Denice Vanderbelt. (7:303).
C7 ... 10 ....John M. Voorhees; West George's Road; N. W. cor.
  Afterwards Reuben Runyon and John Dennis.
C8 ....Divided in Plot D. (38:333).
C9 ....Divided in Plot D. (38:333).
C10 ....Burnet St. lots (110' + 30' + 80' + 40' + and balance.
  1747....The old house of Reuben Runyon on the Hill; see City Minutes, Common Council, folio 84.
  1790....The old house on Pine Tree Hill, Van Sickle, now Moses Ross. (Mary Ellis Papers).
  1792....Moses Wilcox. (6:106).
  1795....Ferdinand Van Sickle; G. Van Sickle; on corner of Burnet St. (5:349).
  1813....Francis Hathaway. (10:225). Town Lane, called George's Road in this deed.

PLOT D. CORNELIUS LONGFIELD. Also located by Peter Sonman as part of his first dividend, coming to a point on the River, and making a triangle of 106 chains on the East leg, 76 chains in rear, and 74 chains on North leg, containing 281 acres, which, with 40 acres in C, was cut up by John Voorhees as follows:

  1707....Longfield to Leonard Smock, 281 acres. (Not recorded).
  1717....Leonard Smock to Enoch Freeland, 281 acres. (Not recorded).
  1720....Enoch Freeland to Johannes Voorhees, 281 acres.
D1 ... 162.74...1793....To Peter Voorhees. (1:682).
     100 ...1794....To D. C. Otis & Fdk. Schuchardt; Rutgers College. (1:804).
      6¼...........To N. B. Water Co. (100:162).
D7 ... 6 ....To James Neilson. (92:130).
D6 ... 36¾...........To C. L. Hardenbergh. (17:17).
C9 ... 13.75..........To Warren Hardenbergh.
D2 ... 100.90...1801....Cornelius Vanderbilt to heirs. (3:562).

APPENDIX

D2 ... 57.40 .... Samuel Bush, part of Vanderbilts. (14:306).
D3 ... 13 .... Samuel Bush - Hardenbergh - Neilson - Rutgers College. (15:4).
D4 ... 19.62 .... James Richmond, Wm. Dunham, Jas. Neilson, College.
D2 ... 5 .... James Rappleyea. (16:437).
C8 ... 14.72 ... 1817 .... Peter Staats, E. Conover.
D5 ... 11.05 ... 1742 .... John Ryder, included in E6; part of Thos. Lawrence. (1:344).
D8 ... 37.50 ... 1802 .... John Neilson, by will; John Voorhees.
D9 ... 30 ..... 1795 .... Moses Wilcox. (6:110).
D10 .. 13.40 ... 1792 .... Peter Ten Eyke. Survey by Jas. Dunham. (2:179).
                            John Keyworth. (2:421).
                1796 .... John Jacob Astor. (5:136).
                            Road up Still House run. (5:342).
D11 .. 2 .... Between Burnet St. and River.
                            Old Road and to abolish Road. (5:376, 445).
                            John Keyworth of Andrew Lyle, across the road. (11:181; 275:228).
                            There is possibly some error in the acreage in subdivisions, which foot up more than the original.

                            PLOT E. THOMAS LAWRENCE TO STEPSON, CORNELIUS LONGFIELD, known as Longfield's lots, on road to Longfield's Mills, and on Lane opened by Longfield to sell lots and called Ryder's Lane after John Ryder, who made the first purchase on it. Subdivided to:
E1 ... 17.20 ... 1770 .... John Lyle. (1:425).
E2 ... 16.50 ... 1770 .... James Neilson. (1:425, 641; 5:245).
E3 ... 31.10 ... 1770 .... Richard Gibb; Longfield's Lots No. 3 and 4. (17:81).
E4 ... 10.40 .... Samuel Kemble; Longfield's Lots No. 2. (4:28).
E5 ... 17.10 ... 1761 .... Peter Sleight; Longfield's Lots No. 1. (5:247; 20:343).
                            Joseph Vickers' part of Samuel Kemble, Lot 2.
                            Jacob Klady, in Kemble; really overlap of Cold Spring Farm.
                            Mathew Sleight, part of Samuel Kemble, Lot 2.
                            Philemon Elmer to Wm. Hiller; part Peter Sleight's, Lot 1. (4:30, 386; 20:343, 346; 36:2).
E6 ... 154 ..... 1742 .... John Ryder. (1:344; 20:346).
E7 ... 30 .... Reuben Runyon; Hugh White; Jacob Carpender. (25:479; 47:178).
E7 ... 14 ..... 1770 .... Reuben Runyon; John Brown; Joseph Vickers; Webbs. (38:332; 64:256).

F1 to 10 inclusive ...... PLOT F. RICHARD GIBB.
         30 ..... 1770 .... Cut up into 3 lots. Lane opened between lots. (1:645; 3:278).
         36 .... Cut up into 7 lots. (9:697).

356.30 — 1742....Two rod road opened for purpose of sale of lots. (3:222; 12:457; 97:150; 31:19; 33:351).

PLOT G. COLD SPRING FARM. 300 Acres and Stone House, mortgaged, first, to Edw. Antill. Offered for sale by Henry Longfield Oct. 10, 1760.

1760....Bought by Anthony White about that date. Deed not found.

300.....1780....He by will, 1780, leaves it to his children: To son, A. W. White, 2/5; to 3 daughters, 1/5 each. (Isabella, unmarried; Euphemia, who m. Gov. Wm. Paterson; Joanna, who m. Judge John Bayard). Subdivided to (19:435; 10:897).

G 300	....	A. W. White to sister-in-law, Mary Ellis— not legal, and taken by sheriff and sold to satisfy judgments against White. (12:512).
G1 ...	18.74.........	John Dennis. (18:443).
G3 ...	5	Rev. Jos. Clark. (3:188).
G4 ...	5	James Richmond. (3:11).
G5 ...	8.93.........	Nehemiah Vernon. (2:489).
G6 ...	5.96.........	Sarah Wallace. (5:357).
	115.........	A. J. Rutherford; Peter P. Wyckoff. (19:435; 24:383).
G7 ...	7.29.........	Andrew Agnew. (11:193; 57:398).
G20 ..	60	Thomas O'Neil. (57:216).
G21	....	Thomas O'Neil.
G18 ..	38.33.........	Benj. Naylor. (66:502).
G19 ..	9.38.........	D. McLaury. (64:181).
G8 ...	2	Benj. Taylor; Lot 7 of the sale.
G9 ...	4	Andrew Agnew; Lots 5 and 6 of sale.
G10 ..	4	Eliza and Mary Evans; Lots 3 and 4 of sale.
G11 ..	4	Samuel Brush, Lots 1 and 2 of sale.
G12 ..	5.83.........	Robert Boggs; Kilbourne's. (2:407).
G13 ..	96.08.........	Wm. Paterson. (G2, G13, G14, as divided later). (2:412; 2:418).
G13 ..	38.62.........	James Neilson. (24:540).
G14 ..	51.06.........	Phineas Mundy; John N. Simpson; Dr. Phelps.
G2 ...	6.4.........	James Neilson.
G15 ..	5.40.........	James Dunham. (3:425).
G16 ..	14.85.........	George Farmer. (3:604; 2:416).
G17 ..	11.06.........	John N. Cummings. (4:127).

H ....10 1/10...1772....PLOT H. LONGFIELD'S MILLS TO JAMES NEILSON.

1783....Mill to John Neilson; to Benjamin Taylor.
1791....To John Outcalt; 1804 to Wm. Huffman.
1809....To Timothy Ericson and Mathew Perrine. (8:130, 315).
1816....To John D. Sutphen. (11:850, 830).
1833....To Hercules Weston and W. H. Merritt. (72:667).

APPENDIX

		To N. B. Water Company. (26:626; 106:340, 357).
	1873	To City of New Brunswick. (140:218).

PLOT I. 1769, LONGFIELD TO BENJAMIN KOSTER, 79 acres.

I	....	1770	Mary Neville.
		1792	By will to Jos. and Lucy Vickers and Mary (Vickers) Lupp.
		1796	Joseph Vickers and Henry Lupp, Executors to Benjamin Taylor. (10:28, 29).
		1813	Mary Ellis, sister of Mrs. A. W. White, whose daughter married an Evans, who inherited the place.
		1767	Benj. Koster owned 37 acres of the above; Thos. Say, Ex. ("Penna. Journal," April 16).

PLOT J. LONGFIELD TO RICHARD GIBBS, 1769, 198 acres, for £890.

			1769	Abraham Potts, same. (1:641; 8:884; 9:603).
J1 & 2	68.5	....		C. W. Tunison. (19:800).
J3	 130	 1811		Moses Wilcox. (25:432).

PLOT K. MARY, WIDOW C. LONGFIELD, 1739, 120 acres, to THOS. LAWRENCE.

		170	 1754	H. Longfield to Thos. Lawrence of Phila.
K	....	140	 1784	Stacy Hepbourn, of Phila., 140 of the 170 acres. (1:1).
		1173	....	To James Cromelin for £4,400, with Island farm.
K1, 2..	140	....		James Cromelin and Hugh Smith to Wilcox
K1	...	40	....	& Pennington. (41:126; 43:356, 396).

PLOT T. PETER SONMAN, ONE OF THE PROPRIETORS, 1692. First dividend 38.600 acres, of which 15.600 acres were located in the Valley of Lawrence's Brook, coming to the River, not at the mouth of Lawrence's brook, which had been purchased in 1678 by Thomas Lawrence, but by a triangle, which he claimed as unlocated between Longfield and Lawrence, but which was legally confirmed to Longfield and relinquished by Sonman. This triangle is Plot D on the Map.

T1	... 281	 1678	Same as Plot D.
		1692	Same as Plot D.
T2	...3500	 1703	Osterland & Keyser purchased 3,500 acres on east end next to Longfield, but outside city limits.
T3	... 203	 1784	Mathew Collins; Henry Guest; part of the 3.500 acres. (7:620).
T3	....		Vincent Wetherill; Reuben Runyon. (24:258).
T3	....	1796	Robert Morris.
T3	 203	...1784	Matthew Collins to John Wetherill; willed, 1784, to son, Vincent Wetherill. (24:258).

NEW BRUNSWICK IN HISTORY

		1794	To granddaughter, Ann Wetherill, wife of Ralph P. Lott; to Robt. Morris.
		1799	To Nicholas Bordine. (7:620).
T2			To Reuben Runyon.
T4			To John Van Harlingen; to N. Bordine.

PHILIP FRENCH LOTS Between Livingston Ave. and Drift St., mostly in 5-chain and 5-acre lots; so many of same size, difficult to positively locate.

L1	9.20	1785	French, by Abm. Schuyler, Sheriff, to John Schureman.
L2	5.9	1785	French, by Abm. Schuyler, Sheriff, to James Schureman.
L3	4.92	1785	French, by Abm. Schuyler, Sheriff, to James Richmond. Old Lot 3 in plot by French. (4:488; 4:497; 1:600).
L4 L5 L6	15	1796	A French Lot; Lewis Dunham to Nehemiah Vernon. (2:128).
L7	5	1805	French, by Abm. Schuyler, Sheriff, to John Dennis, Jr., 2½ ac.
L8	2½		East by John Dennis, Jr. (6:302).
L9	2½	1799	West by Jacob Klady; N. Vernon. (5:735). Old lot 15.
L10	5	1799	J. Schureman to N. Vernon; old lot 16. (5:732).
L11	5	1799	J. Schureman to N. Vernon, (French to Schureman, old lot 17). (5:732).
L12	5	1792	French, A. S. Sheriff, to F. Van Dike, 18x19 (old lot 18). (9:300).
L13	5	1794	Moses Scott to Charles Smith (old lot 19).
L14	5		J. R. Hardenbergh. (4:234).
L15	19.4	1810	S. Vernon; John and Mary Vernon Keyworth. (8:604).
L16 L17 L18 L19	10 10 10 10	1764	Philip French mortgage to Levinus Clarkson, Somerville; about 130 acres in the above lots. (A:238).

PHILIP FRENCH LOTS between Drift road and rear lot line on French.

L20	6	1784	French, by Abm. Schuyler, Sheriff, to John Bray. (8:26).
L21	2	1784 (?)	Ditto to Mathew Egerton; to H. Guest. (4:26).
L21	2.48	1793	Ditto to J. Hill. (3:554).
L22	2.52	1802 (?)	Mathew Egerton to R. Lupardus. (4:618).
L23	5	1786	J. Schureman to P. Vredenbergh.
L24	10	1786	French, by Abm. Schuyler, Sheriff, to Hannah Bull. (4:36).
L27	2½?	1795	Ditto to F. Van Dike. (7:25).
L27	2½?	1784	Ditto to Ephraim Loree. (4:16).
L28	5	1784	Ditto to Isaac Clawson. (6:668).
L30	20	1784	Ditto to Wm. Paterson. (1:74).

L34	... 10	1785	....Ditto to Wm. Wallace. (2:112). (Old lots 33 and 34).
L35	... 5	1785	....Ditto to P. Vredenbergh. (2:115). Same to Wm. Paterson.
L37	... 5		............Saml Munday (?).
L39	... 5		............James Bennet.
L40	... 5	1784	....French, by Abm. Schuyler, Sheriff, to Hermanus Ward. (6:145). Old lot 41, same Kinsey 10.8 A.
L43	... 40	1764	....Mtg. 160 acres to Levinus Clarkson, Somerville. (A:238). About 128 acres in the above lots.

PHILIP FRENCH LOTS between rear lot line and French or Princeton Road.

L25	... 2.01		...........Mathew Egerton.
L25	... 2.82	...1803	....Mathew Egerton to A. Kirkpatrick. (4:611).
L26	... 3	...1800	....Mathew Egerton to A. Kirkpatrick. (3:35).
L29	... 6.40	...1801	....Abraham Schuyler to John Clark. (4:239).
L31	... 12.72	...1792	....James Striker to James Cole (Peter Dumont, Lot 48). (8:274).
L32	... 18.70	...1785	....French, by Abm. Schuyler, Sheriff, to F. Van Dike. Lot 49 S. by 30, 31. (7:23).
L33	... 23.70	...1784	....Ditto to Moses Scott; west by Richard Stevens' Lot, 50. (1:405).
L38	... 63.65	...1789	....Ditto to Thos. Mackness. (1:440).
L41	... 18.30	...1789	....Ditto to Jas. Schureman. (4:532).
L42	... 18.90	...1785	....Ditto to John Schureman, ½ of 37.80 acres, Lot 53. (4:490).
L51	... 46.40	...1792	....Ditto to John Schureman. (4:492).
L52	... 35	1795	....Ditto to F. Van Dike; west by Cornell; N. by G. Verplank. (7:25).
L52½	.. 123	1784	....Ditto to G. Verplank. (1:24).
	175½	...1796	....Jane Cornell; formerly Adrian Cornell, adjoining Philip French from John Waldron's southerly corner to French's southwest corner, S. 49¼, E. 57 ch., 87 links. Tract of 175½ acres; roughly about 50 chains on each side. This bounds Philip French on the southwest. (2:19).
	137	1785	....Joanna Voorhees. White oak tree known as Indian tree, lately Philip French's corner tree. (5:736).

PHILIP FRENCH DEEDS between Princeton Road and North line of Inian's Lot No. 2; north from Livingston Ave., in Somerset Co.

L53	... 40	1786	....Robert Stockton, Sheriff, to James Cole.
L54		1786	....Robert Stockton, Sheriff, to James Cole.
L55	... 300	1787	....Robert Stockton, Sheriff, to Thos. FitzRandolph.
L56	... 242	1787	....Robert Stockton, Sheriff, to James Cole.
	About 600		Noted in above deeds that same had been sold to James Parker previously and sale fell through. (Somerville, G:397, 390, 400, 394).

L53 ... 40 ..... 1787 .... James Cole to James Parker. (G:399).
L54 .... 1787 .... James Cole to James Parker. (G:392).
L55 ... 300 .... Thos. Fitz-Randolph to James Parker. (G:406).
L56 ... 242 ..... 1787 .... James Cole to James Parker. (G:399).
About 600   Cut up and distributed by James Parker. All in Somerset Records.

                    PHILIP FRENCH DEEDS between second and fourth lots, i. e. (Inian's Lot, No. 3).
L59 ... 15 ..... 1783 .... John Bergen to J. M. Nevius and Chas. Stewart. (A:51).
                    Same Chas. Stewart to John Garnett. (C:597).
L57 ... 85 ..... 1783 .... Com. of Forfeited Estates to John Bergen (account Wm. Burton) (formerly land of Anthony White); same John Bergen to J. M. Nevius and Chas. Stewart. (A:51).
              1798 .... Same, Charles Stewart to John Garnett. (C:597).
L60 ... 50 ..... 1783 .... John Bergen to J. M. Nevius and Chas. Stewart. (A:51).
                    Chas. Stewart; same to John Garnett. (C:597).
L59 ... 79.90 ... 1796 .... John Probasco to J. R. Hardenbergh, 75½ acres. (A:356).
              1800 .... J. R. Hardenbergh to John Garnett, same. (C:589).
L59 ... 8.24 .... James Cromelin to J. R. Hardenbergh. (A:347).
                    J. R. Hardenbergh to John Garnett, same. (C:589).
L61 ... 42.36 ... 1799 .... John Booraem to John Garnett. (C:592).
L62 .... 1808 .... Less 17.75 previously sold Jacob Field. (E:299).
L62 ... 11 ..... 1799 .... John Booraem to John Garnett. (C:592).
L62 .... 1823 .... J. B. Field and part to Wm. Philips. (K:702).
L58 ... 290 ..... 1813 .... Hendrick Bergen to J. R. Hardenbergh and others. (H:184).
L63 ... 125 ..... 1792 .... Executors of Cornelius Low to Philip French; to John Voorhees; to H. Underdonk; John
L61 .... Voorhees to Patrick Riley.
Totals 573.50   Same, Anthony White to Martha Lafavor, Mch. 18, 1767; then H. Suydam and Conrad Overfield.
            75½ ... 1780 .... Elijah Philips, June 26, moved into his new house opposite Landing.

L57 ... 39.44 ... 1821 .... Mary Garnett to Abm. Degrau.
L57 ... 13.51 ... 1821 .... Mary Garnett to Chas. Wilkes.
        69.43 ... 1821 .... Mary Garnett to J. W. Scott, part of L57, L59, L60. (K:202).
L60 ... 6 ... 1821 .... Mary Garnett to Wm. Connors.
       137.75 ... 1821 .... Mary Garnett to J. H. Bostwick, part of L59, L60, L61.
       266.13   Est. of John Garnett; J. H. Bostwick to Miles Smith.
       137.75 ... 1821 .... David Freeman to Miles Smith; Mill and Lot on River.

APPENDIX

	1838....	Miles Smith to Hatfield Franklin and Digby Smith. 3 Lots. (K:243; N:76).
L62	....	"Osceola"; Eleanor, Oseola and Hatfield to Tom DeRussy. (144:332; 150:437).

OPPOSITE NEW BRUNSWICK, ACROSS THE RIVER.

O1 .... 129.6....1743....George Drake, 1681; boundaries uncertain, but what was later the Ferry farm (194 acres), and also Dr. Wm. Mercer's from Johnson's pond to the Donaldson farm line. (2:328).

1773....John Probasco; Dr. Mercer's, north of Ferry Farm.

141.....1750....John Wetherill. (16:182).

N ....Philip French to Ann (French) Van Horn, wife of David Van Horn.

N .... 194.....1784....By Sheriff Philip French mortgage to David Van Horn, July 9, 1788; 28 heirs. (1:10). David Van Horn, by Commissioners, the Ferry Farm; 28 heirs united on P. VanB. Livingston, at least the Clarksons, Livingstons, Floyds, Ludlows, Read, Howard, Morgan.

N .... 101.30...1846....Lot 1, 25.46 acres. (43:561).

1868....Lot 2, 41.73 acres. Lots 2, 3, 4, 5 and 10 to F. R. Smith, M. D., 101.30 acres. (97:114; 111:472).

Lot 3, 14.08 acres. Same to Luke C. Cowe (Coe Park).

Lot 4, 16.20 acres. Same to Wesley Benner (Benner Park).

Lot 5, 15.58 acres. Now Highland Park.

Lot 6, 10.07 acres.

Lot 7, 11.66 acres. Lots 1, 6, 7, 8, 9, 11; six lots and 89 acres.

Lot 8, 12.46 acres. Deeds 43; (F:554; 600-608).

Lot 9, 15.73 acres. Lot 12, John Hicks.

Lot 10, 13.71 acres. Philip French sold 10 a. of this to Richard Merrill.

Lot 11, 13.44 acres.

Lot 12, 10.98 acres. John Hicks' South Lot, next to Benjamin Dunn.

Total 201.28 acres.

M .... 83 ...1784....Lewis Dunham to David Dunham; to J. T. Dunn.

117.19...1762....Benj. and Jos. Fitz-Randolph to Benj. Dunn for £707.8s at 8s an ounce. (2:50). Dennis Condon. (167:308). John Hicks, by E. F. Roberts, Sheriff. (67:69). Christopher Meyer. James Bishop.

1884....James Donaldson. (103:109, 585).

O2 ... 200.....1768....DR. WM. MERCER (O1 and Part O2); Valentine

40.....1771.... Gardner; later the Belle View farm of Geo. Farmer, now Robert Johnson. (9:1002; 28:602).

1793....Meklemus Lupardus, 200 acres.

O2-O3 ....1717....Originally 300 acres, Henry Greenland's; same C. Longfield; Benj. Pridmore; Samuel Leonard; Dr. Wm. Mercer; Valentine Gardner; Meklemus Lupardus; John Probasco and Geo. Farmer.

P ....1688....Edward Antill.
               1763....Alexander Ross.
               1788....Chas. A. Howard.
                    Miles Smith. (1:309, 400).
361.............Ross Hall, built by Edw. Antill, 1739-'40. (34:438).

ADDITIONAL DEEDS ON ABOVE.
45.....1821....To Peter Van Brugh Livingston. (31:521).
       1758....Executor of Samuel Leonard; Ferry Rights.
6¾...1821....Part John Wetherill, south of above, 1753.
9.....1750....River front, 2 ch. x 45 ch.
       1843....To Louisa M., wife of Robert James Livingston.
       1845....To Louisa M., wife of Robert James Livingston. (38:179; 42:120).
151.....1809....To Rev. John H. Livingston. (8:133).
45.............Dr. Wm. Mercer (1743-1768) no deed to.
       1749....Samuel Leonard (1758); same as Mercer Ferry Rights in 1749.
                Benj. Pridmore (1717), same.

Index to Names and Places

Abeel, David, 210, 352, 356
  Mary Anne, 352
  Miss, 181
Abo, Finland, 297
Acken, John, 60, 200, 239, 240
Ackerman, B. V., 173
  J. C., 227, 324
Acquackanick, 15
  Bridge, 117
  Dutch Church, 314
Adams, John, 292
  John (President), 62
  John Q., 194, 269
  Mrs., 230
Addis, Mr. 228
Adrain, Dr., 53
  Garnet, 53
Agnew, Andrew, 167, 197, 235, 229, 324, 359
Agricultural Society, 135
Ahandewamock, 12
Aires, Obadiah, 74
Albany, 34, 47, 226, 286
  Street Bridge, 55, 254
Alden, Rev. Timothy, 341
Alexander, Alexander, 315
  Catherine, 187, 344
  Elizabeth, 93
  James, 26, 187, 268
  Mary, 268
  William (Lord Stirling), 268, 278, 342
Allen, Horatio, 160
Allison, James, 35
Alstyne, Isaac, 349
Alvey, John, 49, 50
  Mrs., 50
Amboy (1680), 15, 17, 19, 20, 22, 26, 34, 45
  Charter (1718), 26
  Church, 315
  Perth, 15, 19
  South, 15
Ambrose Brook, 335
Amwell Presbyterian Church, 314
Andros, Governor, 243, 250, 254, 293, 294
  Major, 32
Antelope (steamer), 180
Antill, Edward, 31, 34, 45, 46, 47, 50, 91, 115, 130, 266, 267, 359, 365
  John, 115, 266
  Lewis, 115, 266
  Mrs., 51, 115, 266
Appleby, George, 354
Applegate, Asa, 227
  William, 44
Appleton, G. W., 173
  Greenleaf D., 173
Arenson, Rynders, 245
Armstrong, Gen. John, 275, 278, 342
Arnett, Shelley, 44
Arnold, James, Jr., 234
  James, Sr., 234

Arnould, Robert, 178
Arrowsmith, Miss, 340
Arthur, Rev. Thomas, 44
Asheton, Mary, 332
Ashfield, Richard, 267
  V. P., 267
Ashley, Thomas, 35
Ashmore, Capt., 230
Asia (Man-of-War), 112, 319
Assunpink Creek, 212, 213, 214
Astor, John Jacob, 220, 358
  Place, 355
Atkinson, William, 232
Atlees, William, 66
Auchmuty, Dr. Samuel and family, 31, 114, 265
  Isabella, 114, 265
  John, 31, 114, 265, 266
  Judge, 115
  Miss, 115
  Richard, 115, 265
  Robert, 115, 265
  Sir Samuel, 115, 265
Auke, Jacob, 428 (see Ouke)
Aukerse, Jan, 38
Aurora & General Advertiser, 212
Auten (Aten), Anna, 53
  Jan (John), 42, 49, 52, 53, 197
  Nicholas, 53
  Thomas, 35
Authors, Thomas, 35, 36
Ayres, Abigail, 324
  Simeon, 178
  (see Aires)

Bach, Theopolis, 127
Bache, Richard, 90
Bailey, Floyd S., 214, 215, 216, 217
Baird, Captain, 224
  DeWitt, 232
  Major, 232
Baker, John, 44, 199, 209
  Levi, 217, 216
  W. S., 268
Balding (Bauldings, Baldwin), Ann, 34, 61
  John, 27, 34, 61
Baldwin, Mr., 229
  Widow, 29
Ballareau, Jane B., 193
  Mary, 193, 344
Baltimore, Lord, 253, 333
Bank, Farmers' & Mechanics', 162, 166, 168
  First National, 172
  History, 160
  Jersey, 163
  Ocean, N. Y., 170
  of New Brunswick, 62, 160, 162, 214
  of New Jersey, 162, 167
  of Savings, New Jersey, 176
  People's, 164, 173
  United States, Phila., 168

INDEX TO NAMES AND PLACES

Baptist, 53, 54
  Church, 52, 163, 189
Barbadoes, 17
Barber & Howe, 193
Barcalow, Conradt, 17
Barclay, David, 13
  John, 16
  Robert, 12, 13, 246
Barker, Thomas, 12
Barnard, Gov. Francis, 37
Barnhill, John, 77, 78, 79, 80
Barrack Springbrook, 41, 158
Barracks on Paterson St. (1758), 25, 111, 116
Barre, Isaac, 97
Barrens, 12
Basking Ridge, 268
Basse, Governor, 248
Bassonet, 208, 328
Bateman, Ephraim, 215
Battle of Monmouth, 264
Bayard, Belthazar, 253, 333
  Colonel, 269
  Family, 253, 332
  Gertrude, 254, 333
  Hodge &, 254, 332
  Jane, 254, 333
  James, 332
  Joanna, 130
  John, 56, 61, 144, 146, 254
  Judge, 130
  Leroy &, 56
  Mary Ann, 332
  Major and Col., 269
  Margaret, 254, 332
  Nicholas, 253, 254, 333, 341
  Peter, 253, 254, 332, 333
  Petrus, 241
  Samuel, 34, 176, 253, 254, 332, 333
  Sarah, 332
  Stephen (Alderman), 98, 278
  Street School, 204, 205, 206
  Widow, 253
  William, 100, 216, 333
Baynon, N. E., 230
Beach, Canal Engineer, 215
  Cornelia, 264, 352
  Ephraim, Jr., 214
  Family, 351
  John, 265
  Rev. Abraham, 114, 121, 139, 264, 352
Bealls, General, 117
Beattie, Dr. Reading, 136
Beatty, Richard L., 215
Beaverwyck, 284
Beck, John, 64, 75, 78
  Lewis C., 236
Bedford, Judge Gunning, Jr., 193, 344
Bedminster Church, 314
Beekman, Christopher, 356
  Cornelia, 276, 277, 342
  Gerardus (M. D.), 341, 352
  Henry, 276, 277, 342
  Henry, Jr., 278, 343
  Madeline, 256
  Sarah Cox, 340
  William, 256
Belcher, Jonathan, 33, 48, 251, 252
Belknap, Samuel, 35
Bell, Cornelia, 259
  Hotel (see Taverns)
Belleville (Second River), 117, 257

Bellevue Farm, 21
Bellis, Mr., 232
Bellona (steamboat), 85, 178, 180
Belomont, Governor, 256
Benbrigge, Joseph, 12
Benner, Wesley, 364
Bennet, Abraham, 27, 35, 41, 333
  Adrian, 333
  Ann, 333, 334, 348
  Arie, 37
  Buckalew, 333
  Charity, 352
  Charles, 333
  Eleanor, 333, 334
  Elizabeth, 334
  Family, 333
  Isaac, 333
  James, 333, 334, 362
  Jan, 333
  Jane, 334
  John, 125, 333, 334
  Leah, 333
  Peter, 333
  Phœbe, 333, 334
Bennet's Island, 121, 122, 286
Bentley Manor, 32, 33, 334
Berdine, Jacob, 336
Bergen (1682), 15, 20, 294
  Ferry, 74, 75, 78
  Hendrick, 363
  Jacob, 132
  John, 50, 133, 356, 363
  Maria, 50
  Teunis, 110
  Township, 15
Berkeley, 10
  Lord, 291
Berkenhonts, Dr. John, 301
Bernaby, Andrew, 299
Berrien, John, 45, 46
Bessonet, Charles, 81
Bethaven, Earl of, 136
Beveridge, John, 35
Beyers (Bayard), Mrs. P., 348
Biddle, Clement, 116
  Nicholas, 221
Biles, Island, 34, 76
  Jonathan, 76, 77
Billing, Edward, 12, 13
Billop, Ann, 32, 250, 334, 336
  Charles Farmer, 250
  Christopher and family, 334
  Christopher (Capt.), 32, 55, 247, 248, 250, 251, 334, 336
  Jacobus, 33, 334
  John, 33
  Joseph, 32, 33, 334
  Lieut., 32, 250, 334
  Manor, 32
  Mary, 32, 250, 334
  of Bentley Manor and London, 30
  Thomas Farmar, 251
Bilson, William, 35
Binge, Jacob, 35
Binney, Horace, 218
Bishop, James, 60, 150, 159, 173, 178, 206, 227, 230, 326, 334, 364
  John, 10
Bispham, J. M., 215
Black Horse, 303
  Padlock, 52
Blackford, Prudence, 346
Black's School, 204
Blackstone's Commentaries, 108

INDEX TO NAMES AND PLACES 369

Blake, Joshua, 216, 218
Blane, William, 35
Blauvelt, Abraham, 136, 199, 210, 349
 Dr. Charles Colesworth, 349
 Dr. Cornelius, 349
 John, 229
 John Scott, 349
 Rev. William Warren, 349
Blazing Star Ferry, 74, 78
Bleecker, Abigail, 352
Bliss, Mr., 79
Blue Mountain Valley, 112
Blundell, Susan, 341
Boat Travel, 177
Bodine, Peter, 33
Bogert, Jacob, 35
Boggs, Lawyer, 313
 Mrs., 231
 Polly Morris, 52
 Robert, 49, 52, 199, 359
Bohemia Manor, 293
Boice, Mrs., 229
Bollen, Cap't James, 243
Bonaparte, Joseph, 158, 270
Bong, Ruth, 50
Bonhamtown, 121
Booraem, Henry, 224
 John, 363
 Mrs. (of N. Y.), 232
 Nicholas, 224, 232
 T. B., 173
Borck, Christian, 142
Borden, Joseph, 67, 100
 Joseph, Jr., 69, 70, 72, 76, 81, 82
Bordentown, 67
 Church, 314
Bordine, Nicholas, 361
Bostwick, J. H., 363
Bouchelle, Susannah, 332
Boudinot, Elisha, 61
 Judge, 281
 Mordecai, 248
Boughton, John, 46
Bound Brook, 10, 12, 15, 43, 44, 123, 302
 Bridge, 315
 Church and Parsonage, 314
Boundy & Felter, 328
 & Letts, 207
Bounties, 324
 Civil War, 325
Bounty Committee, 325
Boutcher, Ann, 345
Bowdon, John, 247
Bowers, John, 51
 John, Jr., 49, 50
 Susannah, 51
Bowles, Metcalf, 100
Bowne, Andrew, 12, 247
 Gresham, 12
Boys' Club, 181
Braddock, General, 92
Bradford, William, 87, 90, 98, 189
Bradstreet, Governor, 295
Brain, James, 12
Brasher, Philip,
Brasier, Frances, 47, 266
Brainerd, David, 296
Brant, Mr., 230
Brass Knockers, 319
Bray, Anna, 346
 John, 44, 53, 143, 167, 175, 228, 361
Breaser, Francis, 34, 46, 47

Brewery, 41
Bridge at Landing, 39, 55, 320
 at Railroad, 59
 of 1791-3, 24, 56, 58
 on Burnet Street, 29
Bridgeton, 113, 302
Bridgewater (1749), 16
Brien, Daniel, 46
Bries, Hendrick, 42
Brinley, Simon, 19
Brinly, Edward, 188
Brinson (Brunson), Barefoot (Barford), 243, 340
 Daniel, 243, 340
 John, 340
 John W., 340
 Mary, 340
 Ruth, 340
 Sarah Ann, 340
Broadhead, Jacob, 142
Brockholst, Lieut. Gov. Anthony, 32, 256, 337
 Susannah, 32, 256, 337
Brook, Rev. John, 31, 32, 45, 48, 250, 334
Brooks, Mr., 68
Brown, Abraham, 221
 Alexander & Sons, 220, 21
 Captain, 128
 Doctor, 64
 Isaac, 334
 John, 358
 William (Hon.), 256, 338
Brunswick (see New Brunswick)
Brush & Probasco, 224, 230
 Elizabeth, 52
 Samuel, 85, 359
 Timothy, 209
Bryan, George, 100
Bryant, Joseph, 84
Buccleuch, 49, 53, 129, 136, 260
Buckelew, Dr. F., 227
 James, 336
Buckingham, John, 76
Budd, Thomas, 248, 293
Budget (1813, First), 197
Bulkley, Catherine, 352
 Charles A., 352
Bull, Hannah, 361
 Rev. M., 227
Bullock, Joseph, 215
Bunn, Sarah Langstaff, 53
Burlington, 21, 24, 40, 51, 52, 62, 119, 294
 Charter (1773), 26
 Church, 314
 Road, 18, 27
Burnaby, Andrew, 161
Burnet, Dr. Thomas, 299
 Governor, 299
 Street Bridge, 29, 195
 Street Church, 43
 Street Paving (1739), 29
 William, 290
Burnt Mills, 212
Burr, Aaron, 252
Burroughs Mill, 212
Burton, Bartholomew, 131, 265
 Governor of Bank of England, 131
 William, 113, 363
 General William, 114, 131, 265
Burying Ground (Philip French's), 189
Bush, Samuel, 358

Butler, John, 73, 75, 76, 77
  Major, 122
  Penelope, 188
  Robert, 239
Byllynge, Edward, 210

Cadwalader, Thomas, 217
Caldwell, Elias, 315
Callehan, John, 35
Callender, Abiah, 339
Camden & Amboy R. R., 159, 220
  State of, 222
Cameronians (or 26th), 39, 255
Campbell, Mr., 207
  E. S., 176
Cannon, James J., 239
  James Spencer, 142
  John, 35
Cannon's Point, 24, 30
Cardale, Thomas, 352
Carle, J. H., 142
Carleton, Gen. Guy, 93
Carlisle, Samuel, 230
Carman, Lewis, 167, 178
  Phineas, 163
  Street School, 206, 207
Carpender, C. J., 131
  Jacob, 358
  Mrs. John N., 272
Carpenter, Moses, 347
Carr, Jean, 46
Carroll, Dr., 239
Carteret, Gov. Philip, 10, 11, 19, 243,
  Lady Elizabeth, 11, 12, 22, 354
  Sir George, 10, 11, 12, 22
Carter, Rev. A., 352
Cathcart, Lord, 115, 265
Catholic Church, 54, 224
Cedar Brook, 16
Celgen, A., 213
Census (1746-1829), 158, 198
Chambers, Ann, 256
  David, 35
  John, 277
Chandler, Dr. Thomas Bradbury, 108
Channeys, Edward, 292
  Priscilla, 292
Channing, Rev. Dr. Charles, 108
Chapman, Henrietta B., 240
Charity Organization Soc., 181
Charles, First, King, 292
  Ship, 247
Charloc, Mr., 231
Charters (see City Charter)
Cheasman, Jeptha, 206, 229, 232, 325, 326
  William, 27, 35
Cheeseman, 154
Chesequakes, 45
Chimney Rock, 121, 125, 300
Chittenden, Horatio H., 228
Chocolate Manufactury, 181
Cholwell, Elizabeth, 41
  John, 203
  John (schoolmaster), 34, 41
  Mr., 210
Christ Church, 40, 52, 255, 283
  Church Lotteries, 33, 46
Churches, Baptist, 53
  Catholic, 54
  Dutch, 25, 30
  Episcopal, 30, 45
  Methodist, 53

Presbyterian, 25, 30, 43
  List of, 54
  of England, 25
  of Lawrence's Brook, 42
  (see Lotteries)
Circulating Medium, 160
City, Charters (1730, '63, '84, 1801, '45, '49), 19, 26, 37, 40, 143, 146, 196
  Debt authorized, 157
  Minutes (1730, '50, '96, 1832), 34
  Officers, 199
  Receipts and Expenditures, 197, 199
  Water, 357, 360, 201
Civil War, 240
Clark, Benjamin M., 170, 171
  Ellen, 324
  Deborah, 347
  James, 324
  John, 239, 362
  John S., 340
  Joseph, 359
  Mrs. John S., 340
  Thomas, 242
Clarke, Joseph, 144
Clarkson, David, 49, 50, 338
  Freeman, 50
  John, 335
  Levinus, 49, 50, 148, 361, 362
  Matthew, 49, 50
  Mr., 269
Classwicks Bridge, 21
Clawson, Isaac, 361
Clement, Samuel, 215
Clermont (steamboat), 177
Clinton, Gen. James, 293
  Sir Henry, 301
Clucks, John, 70, 71
Coates, Samuel, 356
Cochradth, Admiral, 242, 247
Cochrane, Dr. John, 38, 48, 139, 257, 258, 275, 349
  Peter, 35, 314
Coddington, Moses, 172
Codrington, Thomas, 295
Coe, Luke C., 364
Coejeman, Andrew, 286
  Gertrude, 52, 336
  Joanna, 256, 283
  Majeke, 286
  Samuel, 257, 286, 348
Coenraat, Morice, 341
  Octavo, 247, 341
Coit, Levi, 216, 217
Cold Spring Farm, 23, 262
Colden, Alice, 266
  Governor, 99, 103, 193, 265, 275
  Jane, 31, 114, 265
  Margaret, 266
  Miss, 115, 266
Cole, Ann F., 324
  James, 44, 188, 362
  Sarah, 266
  Trustee for Mrs., 324
Colemans, 212
Colin, Dr., 281
College, 53
  Brook, 18
  Building, 156
  Farm, 41, 287
  Grammar School, 41, 138, 141, 203
  Hall, 139, 203
  of New Jersey, 252

INDEX TO NAMES AND PLACES 371

of New Jersey Lottery, 314
Princeton, 42, 301, 304
Queens, 281, 282, 286, 320
Rutgers, 210, 286
Collins, Matthew, 360
Colonial Barracks, 25, 111, 116
Colony of New York, 315
Columbian Steamboat Co., 179
Combs, Jonathan, 44
Commerce Square, 30
Commercial Avenue, 23
Commissioners of Streets and Sewers, 202
Commissioners of Forfeited Estates, 32, 113, 256, 363
Committee of Correspondence, 110, 315
  of Observation, 110, 283, 315
Communipaw Ferry, 83
Compton, James, 346
Condict, Dr. Ira, 141, 258
Condon, Dennis, 364
Conklin, M. S., 276
  Mary, 347
  S., 343
Connelly, Alexander, 340
Conners, Wm., 363
Conover, E., 358
  Elias, 228
  G. R., 172, 173
  Garret, 173
  Stryker, 232
Constitutional Courant, 192
Continental Congress, 259, 110
Money and Proclamation, 161
Conway, Captain John, 111, 268
  John, 317
Cook, Benjamin, 227
  Elihu, 231
  James, 221
  Matthew, 35
  S. G., 226
Cooke, Mary S., 346
Coombs, John, 16
Cooper, Caleb, 41
  Daniel, 76
  Edward, 41, 203
  Ferry, 76
  Thomas, 12
Copper Mine, 303
  at Newark, 257, 303
  at Rocky Hill, 303
Corel, Mrs., 230
Cornbury (Lord), Governor, 14, 63, 246
Cornelisse, Michael, 77
Cornell, Adrain, 362
  Elias, 346
  Jane, 362
  Julietta Ann, 138, 350
Cornell's Brook, 146
Cornwallis, Lord, 118, 119, 123
Coroner, 29
Corson, Captain Joseph (Ferry, 1753), 295
Cortelyou, Hermanus, 146
  Jaques, 127
  Simon, 127
Coryell's Ferry, 64, 80
Costigan, Francis, 45, 46
  Francis, Jr., 46
Cotton, John, 101
Counties, 15
Court House, Barrack Lot, 25, 147
  House, Bell rung for Churches, 29, 30, 43, 147
  House, Burnet St., 29, 37, 147, 195
  House, Prince and Queen St., 38, 148, 158, 286
  House, Somerville, 21
  Houses, New Brunswick, 147, 155, 286
  Records, 17
  Street (Richmond), 19, 21, 25
Courts, 20
Cowen, Patrick, 72
Coyle, Cornelius, 35
Cox, Catherine Longfield, 246, 247
  Col. John, 246, 340
  Family, 340
  James, 229
  James B., 324
  Longfield, 340
  Mary, 340
  Sarah, 340
  Thomas, 340
  William, 18, 23, 25, 27, 34, 35, 40, 43, 246, 340, 355
  (see Kocks)
Coxe, Governor, 10
  John, 91
  William, 102-105
Craig (Crage), Ursula, 187, 189, 344
  James, 220
Cranbury, 296
  Brooks, 17
  Pike, 62
  Pond, 212
Crane, Elisha, 280
  James, 83, 216
  Joseph, 80
  Martha, 280
  Stephen, 111, 315
Creamer, Widow, 228
Crecy, Ellit, 44
Crochran, "Mih.," 33
Croes, Jacob, 279
  Rev. Bishop John, 50, 52, 54, 134, 210, 223, 227, 279, 283
  Miss, 181
  Mrs. Martha, 135, 280
Cromelin, Creek, 21, 23
  James, 144, 148, 149, 210, 360, 363
Crook, Helen Mary, 338
Crooked Billet Tavern, 63
  Billet Wharf, 63, 69
Cross Keys Tavern, 81
Crosswicks, 62, 296
  Bridge, 68
Crosswicksung, 296
Crowell, James T., 325
Cruger, John 100
Cruger's Mill, 213
Cruser, Abraham, 153
Cummings, John N., 359
Curtis, Edward, 159
Cutter, William, 315

Dally, John, 28, 35, 90
Dam on Raritan (1825), 158; (1779), 41
Damrosch, Leopold, 184
  Walter, 184
Danker, Jasper, 23, 24, 241, 245, 254, 293
Daughters of the Revolution, 260
  Jersey Blue Chapter, 129, 130

INDEX TO NAMES AND PLACES

Davenport, Josiah F., 80
Davett, Mrs., 231
Davidson, Dr. Robert, 42, 249
  Josiah, 35
  Nathaniel, 179
Davis, Colonel, 337
  Commander (Ship Edward), 102
Davison, John, 215
  Josiah, 27
Dawson, Henry B., 109
Day, Agnes, 347
  Samuel H., 324
Dayton, Aaron Ogden, 215
  House, 167
  James, 170, 171
  Peter, 167, 199
Dean, Aaron, 46
  Jonathan, 44
  Miss, 180
Deare, Jonathan, 49, 50
  Mrs. Frances, 50, 223, 226
  William P., 149, 216
DeCamp, John, 125
Declaration of Independence, 284, 319
DeGraff, John, 356
DeGraw (DeGrau), Abraham, 135, 363
  Garret, 18, 29, 35
  John, 35, 44, 147
  John, Jr., 165
DeGrove, John, 82
DeHart, John, 111, 316
  Mr., 229
  Stephen, 208, 328
DeKay, Agnes, 132
Delamontayne, Tunis, 35
Delaware, 24
  and Raritan Canal Co., 159, 212, 214, 321
  Bay, 288
  River, 23, 34, 212
  Town, 291
Dellaman, 63
Demaine, William, 82
Demarest, John, 318
DeMorest, Cornelius, 142
DeNeuville, Baron Paul H., 194, 269, 270
Dennis, John, 44, 49, 151, 315, 355, 357, 361
  John, Jr., 48, 56, 164, 199, 359
  John, Sr., 47, 48, 52, 56, 57, 110, 111, 181, 317
  Judge Daniel, 20
  Mary, 151
  Robert, 10, 11
Depaw, Francis, 216, 217
Depeyster, Catherine, 277, 341
  Elizabeth, 50
  Gerardus, 34, 35, 41
  Mrs. P., 348
Deputies (Piscataway), 20
DeRussy, Tom, 364
Descent of the British, 116
Deshler, Charles D., 204, 205, 231
DeVoe, G. W., 174
DeVries, Annetee, 266
  Helena, 247
Dey, Anthony, 84, 133, 138
  Colonel Theunis, 139
  Joseph W., 128
  Livinia Agnes, 138
  Mary Laidlie, 138
  Richard Varick, 136, 138, 350

Dickinson, General, 40, 121, 252
  John, 100, 101
  Mr., 296
Dilke, Joseph, 157
Disborough, D. W., 172, 181
Disbro, Hassert & Freeman, 41
Ditmars, Alche, 335, 353
  Douwe, 335
  Family, 334
Dividend to Proprietors, 13
Dockwra, William, 14, 352
Doles, Isaac, 74
Donaldson, James, 364
Dongan, Governor, 248, 273
Donop, Colonel, 123
Dorcas Society, 180
Doty & Ford, 60
  Jacob, 228
Doughtie, Samuel, 17
Douglass, James, 143
Douwe, Altje, 334
Dow, David C., 179
Downey, John, 78
Drake & Grummond, 83
  Abraham, 335
  Andrew, 335
  Benjamin, 335
  Catherine, 335
  David, 19, 335
  Ebenezer, 335
  Ephraim, 335
  Edward, 335
  Elizabeth, 335
  Francis, 17, 20, 335
  George, 20, 21, 335, 364
  George (2nd), 335
  Henry, 335
  Isaac, 335
  Jacob, 335
  James, 44, 55, 56, 83, 335
  Jane, 336
  Jeremiah, 335
  Johanna (Manning), 335
  John (Lay Preacher), 20, 54, 335
  Jonathan, 335
  Joseph, 335
  Lidia, 335
  Mary, 335
  Mary (Lee), 335
  Mill, 41
  Mr., 214
  Mr. (of Indian Queen), 269
  Rachel, 346
  Randle, 335
  Rebecca, 335
  Samuel, 335
  Sarah, 335
  Susannah (Smalley), 335
  Widow, 232
Drummond, Evan, 27, 35
  John, 12
Duane, James, 275
Duck Pond, 212
Duckets, Mrs., 74
Duffy, Michael, 90
Duke of York, 10
Dumont, Peter, 44
  John, 113, 355
  Peter, 143, 362
Dunham, Azariah (5th Mayor, 1784), 37, 40, 44, 111, 143, 315
  Charles, 168, 229, 231, 324
  David, 234, 272, 364
  Edmund, 336
  Edward Wood, 164

INDEX TO NAMES AND PLACES 373

Elijah, 233
H., 324
James, 57, 233, 323, 358, 359
Joel, 233
Lewis (M. D.), 44, 61, 141, 143, 164, 271, 361, 364
Major, 269
Mayor (8th, 1793), 146
Miss Mary, 231
N., 324
Widow, 231
William, 199, 358
William G.'s son, 235
Dunlap, William, 314
Dunmead, Daniel, 230
Dunn, Benjamin, 364
  David, 225
  Elizabeth, 345
  George, 271
  Gershom, 324
  Hopewell, 11
  Hugh, 11, 54, 336
  Hugh (Lay Preacher), 335
  James, Jr., 364
  James T., 171, 233
  Jane, 272
  John, 315
  Macajah, 16
  Mr., 228
  Thomas H., 157
Duryee, Eliza, 138, 350
Dutch Church (before 1717), 41, 42
  Burying Ground, 43
  in Colony, 54
  Official and Legal Title, 43
  on Burnet Street (1735), 42
  on Neilson Street, 321
  Street, 19, 42
  Settlers, 298
Dutchess (Man-of-War), 113, 319
Duyckinck, James, 49
  John, 39, 51
  John T., 149, 178, 179
  Mary Taylor, 51
  Mrs., 226
Dyer, Eliphalet, 100

Early Cities (N. B. Typical), 26
Early Railroads, 220, 160
East and West Jersey Line, 16, 22
Eastburn, Robert, 197
Easton Pike, 269, 114
Eaton, Margaret, 46
  Thomas, 46
Eatontown, 46
Edgar, William, 176
Edgerton, Everett, 229
  Matthew, 49, 50, 176, 361, 229, 230
Edmonds, Jacob, 152
Edmundson, William, 76, 288, 290
Edsal, Samuel, 243, 295
Education, 20, 41, 144, 203, 205, 207, 209
Efraim, Augustin, 259
Egbert, Thomas, 44
Eldridge, L. and Mrs., 231
Election Expenses (The 1st), 201
Elizabeth (1664), 11, 19, 20, 34, 45, 62, 118. 294
  Charter (1739-40), 26
  Ferry, 74, 75
  Parsonage, 314
  Port, 24
  Town Point, 10

Town Point Associates, 10
Township. 15
Elizabethtown, 11, 12, 15, 19, 26, 121, 295
  Bill in Chancery, 11, 190
  Grant, 12
Ellis, Margaret Vanderhorse, 130, 260
  Mary, 130, 131, 133, 260, 262, 264, 355, 357, 359, 360
Elmer, L. Q. C., 214
English, D. C., 170
Ennis, Charles, 229
  Killen Dragoons, 133
Episcopal Church, 54
  New Brunswick, 45, 126, 314
  Piscataway, 45, 126, 233
Erickson, Eliza, 357
  Mary, 359
  Timothy, 359
Esopus, 292
Evan, Mary, 139
Evans, Misses, 131
  Place, 23, 131, 261
  Thomas, 130
Everson, N., 16
Ewen, Daniel, 194
Ewing, James, 159
  Rev. Dr. John, 136
Express Riders, 125

Fairbanks, Richard D., 86
Falls (or Ford) of Raritan, 23, 24
  of Delaware, 24
Farmar, Anne, 336, 337, 30-1, 251, 256
  Anne Billop, 337
  Brook, 31, 35, 48, 90, 251, 337
  Capt George, 49, 52, 286, 336, 359, 364
  Charles, 336
  Christina, 337
  Christopher, 31, 33, 251, 336
  Cornelia, 336
  Edward, 31, 336, 337
  Elizabeth, 31, 114, 251, 265, 336, 337
  Genealogy, 336
  Hannah, 337
  Jasper, 30, 52, 251, 336, 337
  Jasper and Family, 336
  Jasper (Cap't), 336
  Jasper, Jr., 249, 336
  Jasper (Major), 249, 336
  John, 31, 251, 336, 337
  Katherine, 31, 249, 334, 336, 337
  Maria, 336
  Mary, 31, 48, 251, 337
  Mayor, 30, 32, 48, 52, 114, 337
  Peter, 52, 336
  Rachel, 337
  Robert, 31, 251, 337
  Sally, 337
  Samuel, 31, 251, 336, 337
  Sarah, 50, 336
  Thomas, 21, 22, 27, 30, 35, 50, 55, 239,249, 250, 251, 334, 336, 337
  Thomas (Judge), 31, 250
  Thomas Billop, 31, 33, 55, 336
  Thomas Family, 336
  William, 31, 251, 337
Farmers' & Mechanics' Bank, 162, 166, 168
Farquhar, Dr. William, 31, 34, 35, 114, 251, 266, 297, 337

INDEX TO NAMES AND PLACES

Feller, Harry, 184
Felter & Co., 240
Fenwick, Anna, 292
  Elizabeth, 292
  John, 292
  Priscilla, 292
Fernow's Court Records, 244
Ferry, Bergen Point, 74, 76, 78
  Abraham Vantile, 75
  John Beck (1764), 64, 75, 78
  John Mersereau, 75
  Joseph Corson (1753), 75
  Otto Van Tuyl, 75
  Bordentown, Dunk's, 64, 77
  Delaware, Coryell's, 64, 80
  Elizabethtown Point, 74, 75
    Jesse Johnson, 75
    John Watson, 75
    Mrs. Ducket, 74
    Simonson, 75
    Wm. Douglas, 75
  Five (New York to Phila.), 78
  Hackensack (1768), 64
  Hudson Communipaw, 83
  Pavonia, 64
  Phila. to Burlington, 64
  Phila. to Camden, 64, 76
  Powles Hook, 64
    Abraham Mesier, 75, 77
  Raritan, Inian's (1686), 18, 20, 24, 55, 64
  Redford's (South Amboy), 65
    Abraham Webb, 71
    Daniel O'Bryant, 64
    John Clucks, 70
  Staten Island, Billop's, 64, 74
    David Mersereau, 75
    Hilliker's, 75
    Isaac Decker, 75
    Isaac Dole, 74
    Jacob Fitz Randolph, 75
    John Ryer, 75
    Joshua Mersereau, 75
    New Blazing Star, 64, 74
    Old Blazing Star, 74, 78
  Trenton, Ramsey's, 64
    To Phila., 64
Fever (1793), 140
Fick, Sheriff, 240
Field, J. B., 363
  Jacob, 363
  Jeremiah, 16
Finances (1730-'45), 195; (1801-50), 196; (1823-56), 197, 198
Finch, Jerome, 233
Fire Engine, 158, 204
First Railroad, 220, 221
  Thanksgiving Day (1676), 19
Fish, Horatio H., 216, 218
Fisher, Capt. Isaac, 171, 178, 179, 180
  Hendrick, 43, 100, 111, 139, 268, 316
  James, 226
  Joseph, 173, 225
  L., 230
Fitch, Daniel, 28, 35
  Doctor, 229
  Gov. Thomas (of Conn.), 100
  John (steamboat), 178
  Thomas, 165
Fitz, Nathaniel, 49, 52
Fitz Randolph, A., 171
  Benjamin, 364
  Caroline, 346
  David, 170, 171
  David (Judge), 169
  Emily, 347
  Isaac, 75
  Jacob, 75
  James, 167
  Janet, 351
  Joseph, 364
  Mr., 57
  Osy, 346
  Reuben, 75
  Samuel, 152
  Stelle, 57
  Thomas, 188, 362
  W., 170
Flatlands, 34
Fleming, Bartholomew, 272
Florance, W. E., 202
Floyd, General, 286
Follett's City Hotel (1824), 58, 85, 157, 217
Folwell, Joseph, 81
Fondee's Tavern (Savannah, Ga.), 109
Forbes, Anna, 188
Ford, Ebenezer, 118
  John R., 173
  Joseph B., 173
  Judge, 231
Foreman, George, 12
Forenekes, Mrs., 35
Forfeited Estates, Commissioner of, 32, 113, 139
Forman, Captain, 122
  John, 180
  Peter, 218
Fort Constitution, 116, 118
  Lee, 116, 118
  Washington, 116
Fountain Co. Inc. (1801), John Bray, 158
Fountain, J. R., 175
Four Lanes End, 82
Fouratt, Enos, 231
  James, 231
Fox, George, 127, 288, 294
Franklin, Benjamin, 63, 89, 90, 189, 300
  Court House (1716), 22
  Gov. William (1763), 38, 40, 93, 115, 188, 189, 252, 317
  Park, 22, 34, 41
Frazee, Captain H., 180
  Isaac, 232
  Lawrence, 230
  William Henry, 232
Freas, Henry, 221
Fredonian, 194
Free Public Schools, 156
Freedom of City, 37
Freehold Township, 15, 45, 296
Freeholders, Chosen, War Bounties, 60
  List (1750), 35
Freeland, Enoch, 18, 25, 354, 355, 357
Freeland's House, 18
Freeman, Alpheus, 355
  Anna Margaretta, 50
  David, 363
  Hassert & Disbro, 41
  Matthias, 179
Frelinghuysen, Col. Frederick, 125, 132, 134, 143
  Gen. Frederick, 137

INDEX TO NAMES AND PLACES 375

Rev. John, 338
Rev. Theodorus Jacobus, 43, 98, 347
French, Ann, 337
 Burying Ground, 52, 53, 189
 Catherine, 47, 255, 256, 338
 Christopher (Major), 337
 Elizabeth, 50, 55, 256, 337, 338
 Family, 337
 John, 225
 Margaret, 337
 Mary, 256, 337
 Philip, Sr., 32, 255, 337
  Jr., 25, 31, 34, 35, 36, 37, 43, 45, 48, 53, 55, 114, 188, 251, 255, 256, 337
  3rd, 49, 52, 256, 337, 363
 Pucklehammer & Horn, 41
 Susannah, 250, 337, 338, 342
 William, 44
Froeligh, Rev. Solomon, 142
Fulton & Livingston, 177, 178
 Robert, 84, 177, 178
Fulton's "Raritan," 85, 275
Furman, Moore, 61
 Mrs., 228, 231
Fushee, Margaret, 35

Gaasbeck, Abraham, 332
Gadsen, Christopher, 100, 101
Gage, Gen. Thomas, 39, 93, 99, 255
Gaine, Hugh, 191
Gamble, Mary, 249, 336
Gano, David, 37
Gardener, Valentine, 275, 364
Garnett, Anna Maria, 134
 Fannie, 134
 Harriet, 134
 Henry, 134
 John, 49, 53, 134, 363
 Julia, 134
 Mary, 134, 363
Garrigues, 154
Garretson, Richard, 333
Gaston, William, 220
Geipel, 172
George, Nicholas, 70
 II, 12
 III, 107
Geraerdy, Jan, 244
 Philip, 244
Gibb, Andrew, 12, 44
 Capt. Richard, 17, 35, 356, 358, 360
 Master, 17
Gibbons & Ogden, 177
 "Bellona," 85
 Edward, 12
 "Mouse and Mountain," 85
 Thomas, 164, 177, 178, 180
 William, 85
Gibson, William, 12
Giddiman, John, 35
Gillman, J., 20
 James, 233
 John, 11
Gilman, Charles, 11
Glentworth, George, 14
Goddard, William, 192
Godfrie, John, 35
Goelet, Peter, 337
Golden Ball Tavern, 77
Golding, Louis, 150
Goltra, E. B., 328
Goodfellow (Widow), 238

Timothy, 356
Gorden, Peter, 314
 Robert, 12
Gosman, Mr., 57
Gould, Major William, 94
Gouverneur, Elizabeth, 189
 Isaac, 341
 Johanna, 339
 Maria, 336
 Nicholas, 349
 Sarah, 267
Governor, Andros, 243, 295, 250
 Basse, 248
 Bedford, Gunning, 244
 Belcher, Jonathan, 33, 48, 251
 Belomont, 32, 256
 Bernard, F., 37
 Boone, Jonathan, 29
 Bradstreet, 295
 Brockholst, Anthony, 32, 256, 337
 Burnet, William, 299
 Cartaret, Philip, 10, 11, 19, 243
 Colden, 99, 103, 193, 265, 275
 Cornbury, Lord, 14, 63, 246
 Coxe, William, 10
 Dongan, 248, 273
 Fitch, Thomas (Conn.), 100
 Fletcher, 87
 Franklin, William, 38, 40, 93, 115, 188, 252
 Haines, Daniel, 169
 Hamilton, Andrew, 20, 63, 87, 244, 248
 Hamilton, John, 91
 Hardy, Josiah, 37
 Harrison, William, 40, 45, 46
 Howell, 94, 95, 286
 Hunter, Robert, 21, 26, 186, 242, 246, 250
 Lewis, Morgan, 275, 278, 342
 Livingston, William, 40, 252
 Lovelace, Francis, 87
 Lovelace, John, 88
 Montgomeree, John, 28
 Morris, Lewis, 46, 251
 Nanfan, 32
 Nicholson (Va.), 295
 Nicoll, 9, 10, 11, 12, 288
 Paterson, William, 44, 56, 61, 144, 259
 Stuyvesant, Peter, 87, 253, 332
 Sumner, Increase, 115
 Ward, Samuel, (R. I.), 100
 Williamson, Isaac, 270
Graham & Suydam, 194
 Isabella, 266
 James, 267
 James Lorimer, 194, 355
 Mr., 228
Grammar School, 204, 351
Grant, Captain, 337
 General, 123
 Mary, 336
 Miss, 181
 Thomas, 44
Graves, Marcella, 338
Gray, Richard, 212
Green, Ashbel, 280
 Brook, 16
 James, 219
 Gen. Nathaniel, 119
Greenland, Captain, 243
 Frances, 243, 340
 Henry, M. D., 17, 20-22, 24, 41, 243, 246, 340, 354

INDEX TO NAMES AND PLACES

Henry, Jr., M. D., 243, 340
Mary, 22, 243, 245, 340
Mr., 241, 293, 294
Griffith, 214
Griffiths, Dr., 302
Jane, 137, 350
Griggs, Joseph C., 179, 235, 226, 230
Griggstown, 225
Bridge, 213
Griswold, George, 217
Groenlant, Maria, 245
Groom, Samuel, 11
Groosbeck, Nicholas, 35
Grummond & Drake, 83
& Johnson, 83
& Young, 83
Guardian, 210
Guest, Henry, 37, 44, 49, 50, 127, 143, 181, 355, 360, 361
Moses (Capt.), 125, 144, 199, 210, 355
Gulick's Mill, 213

Hackensack, 15, 118
Church, 314
Ferry, 64
Hager, John, 231
Haight, Joseph, 80
Haines, Gov. Daniel, 169
Hale School, Nathan, 207
Half Moon Battery, 70
Hall Fund, 203
John, 205, 206, 325
Vroom, 231
Halsey, Rev. J. F., 204
Halstead, William, Jr., 215, 217, 219
Hamilton, Alexander, 84
Alexander, M. D., 297
Andrew, 98
Col. John, 88
Gov. Andrew, 63, 87, 244
Samuel R., 159
Street, 24
Hamilton's Council, 248
Hampton, John W., 324
Hance, George, 44, 111, 315
Hancock, Frances, 13
Joseph, 73
Hand, Colonel, 116
Hankins, John, 127
Hanover Parsonage, 314
Hanson, Henry, 278, 342
Hardenbergh Bank, 160, 163, 165
C. L., 146, 150, 157, 167, 200, 239, 270, 210, 231, 357
Charles, 142
Family, 338
Rev. J. R., 139, 338
J. R., Jr., 56, 61, 138, 141, 163, 164, 176, 258, 338, 361, 363
Miss, 181
Mrs., 181
Rutsen, 352, 176, 175
T. P., 239
Warren, 357
Harding, Thomas, 35
Hardy, Gov. Josiah, 37
John, 323
Harper, Thomas W., 234
Harra & Wesner, 60
Harriott, Mrs. Phœbe, 205, 227, 326
Harris, Dr. Robert, 44
Harrisburgh, 215
Harrison, Mrs., 223

Mrs. E. H., 227
Widow, 232
William, 35, 45, 46
William (Mayor), 40, 47
Hart, Joseph, 81
Thomas, 11, 13
Hartshorn, Hugh, 11, 13
Richard, 212, 217, 290
Hartwick, John, 44
Hassenclever, Peter, 99, 139
Hassert, Aaron, 210, 355
Freeman & Disbro, 41
Jacob, 352
Jane, 352
Mary, 352
Miss, 181
Hatfield, John, 230
Hathaway, Francis, 357
Haviland, Nathan, 158
Hay, Col. Sam, 356, 357
Hays, Sophia, 282
Haywood, John, 11
Heard, Colonel, 318
General, 117
Heard's Tavern, 297
Heathcoat's Brook, 17, 213
Heermans, Annetien, 245
Augustine, 212, 241, 245, 253, 254, 293, 333
Augustus, 9
Beatrice, 253
Ephraim, 23, 241, 253, 254, 293, 294
Janeke, 245
Hegeman, Dollius, 17, 27, 35
Helm, Dr., 356
Hempstead, 318
Hendricks, John, 138
Hendrickson, John, 44
Henry and Francis (ship), 249
Alexander, 35, 45, 139
John, 44, 53, 324
Mr., 304
Patrick, 96
Walter, 231
Hentz, Judge, 229
Hepburn, Stacy, 360
Herbert, Robert S., 171
Hessians, 117, 119, 121, 123
Heyer, (Hyer), Abraham, 18, 35, 253, 356
Jacob, 356
Hickels, Mrs., 35
Hicks, John, 229, 364
Higgins, Jedediah (or Judiah), 16, 20, 34, 35, 245
High School, 12
Highland Park, 24, 52
Highlands of Navesink, 23
Hill, J., 361
John B., 172, 239, 240, 201
Mr., 210
Thomas, 159, 209
Hiller, William, 358
Hilliker's Ferry, 75
Hillsboro (Millstone), 22, 125
Court House, 125
Hillyer, Capt., 51
Simon, 49
William, 358
Hinckley, Elizabeth, 344
Gov. Thomas, 186
Hoagland, Hendrick, 35
Sarah, 132
Hobart, Bishop, 282

INDEX TO NAMES AND PLACES 377

Hobart's School, 204
Hodge & Bayard, 254
  John, 48, 337
  Margaret, 254, 332
  Samuel, 292
Hodson, Albertus, 247
Hoffman, Josiah Ogden, 84
  Martin, 278, 342
  Samuel V., 59, 258
Holcomb, Cornelia A., 351
  Dr. George, 214
  Miss, 181
  Mrs., 181
  Samuel, 164, 176, 239
  Theophilus, 225, 324
Holland, Letitia, 344
Hollingshead, Francis, 46
Holman, Francis, 73, 75
Holt, John. 98, 190, 191
Honeyman, Robert M., 170, 171
Hood, Zacharias, 99, 102
Hoogland, Abraham, 334
  T. V. D., 201
Hooper, Robert Lettice, 250
Hooton, Thomas, 66
Horn, Pucklehammar & French, 41
Hornblower, Chief Justice, 154
Horner, John, 340
Hortwick (Hartwick), James, 44
  John, 44
Hospital, 197, 200, 301, 316
How, Rev. Dr., 204
Howard, Dr. C. A., 49, 50, 365
Howarden, Margaret, 275, 342
Howe, General, 115-6, 118-9, 124, 265
  Sir William, 117, 119
Howell, Andrew, 164, 176
  B. F., 174
  Governor and Mayor, 95, 286
  Lewis T., 174
  Martin A., 200, 239, 240
Hoyt Building, 207, 328
  Captain, 180
  Hannah, 62, 165
Hubbell, Miss, 229
Hude, Adam, 22, 37
  Catherine, 339
  Family, 339
  James, 27, 33-6, 44, 47, 48, 91, 239, 251, 258, 339
  James, Jr., 37, 252
  Marion, 37, 339
  Mary, 48, 258, 275
  Mrs., 266
  Robert, 339
  Susan, 48, 275
Hudibras Tavern, 79, 82
Huffman, William, 359
Hull, Benjamin, 11
  Mary, 346
Humphries, Mary B., 350
  William, 105
Hundershut, Michael, 314
Hunt, Major David, 84
  Mr., 270
  Pierson, 215
  William, 320
Hunter, Gov. Robert, 26, 186, 242, 246, 250, 267
  William, 90, 190
Hunterdon Charity Lottery, 314
  County, 16
Hunt's Forty Yrs. of Wash. Soc., 270

Hutchings, C. H., 229
  Israel H., 173
Hutchinson, Duncan, 27, 35
  Henry, 323
  Mill, 212
Hutton, Thomas, 68
Huyler, Adam, 127
  Mrs., 128, 231
Hyer, Jacob, 356
  Mary, 38, 253

Indian Deeds, 22
  Paths, 24
  Queen Tavern, 55, 56, 62, 83
  Trails, 17
  Wampum, 160
Indians, 9, 10, 12, 13, 24, 43
Ingersoll, Jared, 97, 102
Inian, John, 12, 16, 17, 18, 20-22, 24, 25, 244, 247, 248, 249, 250, 295, 354
  Line, 25
  Lots, 13, 22
  Mary, 21, 22, 246, 354
  Seymon, 248
Inian's Ferry, 16, 17, 21, 24, 27
Inons, Seymon, 248
Inslee, J. B., 205, 325
  John, 206
Island Farm (Bennet's Island), 121, 122, 360, 286

Jackson, John P., 59, 60, 231
  Jane (Colored), 232
Jacobs, Ida, 335
  Leitie, 335
Jacques, Henry, 10
Jail at New brunswick, 148, 205, 320, 325
  Liberty Bounds, 320
Jamaica, L. I., 110
James, A., 229
  Major, 102
Janeway, Agnes DeKay, 132
  Capt. George, 132
  H. L., 132, 173, 239
  House, 260
  Jacob, 132
  Jacob J., 239
  Rev. Jacob, 132, 223, 227
  William, 132
Janse, Auke, 38, 253, 276
  Agatha, 352
Jansen, Charles W., 83
  Michael, 248
Jarvis, Abraham, 337
Jay, Sir James, 128
  John, 338, 342
Jenkins, Capt., 178
  John T., 207, 327, 328
  John, 206
Jersey Blues (1747), 91, 93, 96, 124, 257
  Charter, 84
  Chronicle, 194
  Company, 84
  Flying Camp, 118
Johnson, Anna, 137, 349
  Aletta, 52
  Colonel, 92
  George, 83
  Gerard, 35
  Gershom, 82
  & Grummond, 83
  I., 197

378 INDEX TO NAMES AND PLACES

Isaac, 35
Janet, 344
John, 206, 294
Dr. John, 327
Mary, 339
Mary Hude, 37
Mary Stewart, 133
Miss, 181
Nicholas, 37
R. G., 291
Samuel (Judge), 133
Sarah, 228
Simon, 339
Stephen W., 159
& Twinning, 83
Sir William, 265
William S., 100
Johnson's Place, 21, 24, 41
Robert, 364
Johnstone, Andrew, 268
James, 187
Janet, 187
Dr. John, 187, 268
Jones (Lot 7), 352
Rev. W. N., 188, 226
Richard, 12, 352

Kaign's Point, 179
Kalm, Peter, 24, 297
Kean, John, 341
Peter, 214, 217
Kearney, Ann, 45
John, 45
Michael, 267
R., 339
Keenon, Catherine, 51
Mary, 51
Peggy, 51
Peter (Col.), 49, 51, 321
Keirstede, Blandina, 332
Keith's (Washington's Headqts.), 119
Kelly, Elijah, 240
Kelsal, Admiral Norton, 130
Kelshall, Suffolk Co., England, 32
Kemble, Margaret, 255
Mavrocordato, 254
Peter, 34, 35, 45-47, 254, 333
Peter 2nd, 255
Richard, 254
Richard, 2nd, 254
Sampson Gideon, 255
Samuel, 45-47, 255, 256, 338
Stephen (Brig. Gen.), 114, 120, 163, 115, 255, 266, 268
William, 254
Kemp, Bishop of Maryland, 278, 282
Kemper, Isaac, 35
Kent, James, 215, 217, 218
Stephen, 10
Kershon, Joshua, 44
Ketettas, Catherine, 342
Keyworth, John, 52, 358, 361
Kierstede, Jacobus, 276, 343
Maria, 276, 343
King Charles 2nd, 10
King's Bridge, 117
Kingston, 16, 215, 296, 297
Kinsey, James, 111, 315
Kirkpatrick, Andrew, 44, 61, 131, 163, 254, 333, 351, 362
J. B., 240, 201
Judge, 261
Littleton, 58, 60, 166, 167, 200, 240, 223, 227, 324

Miss, 181
Mr., 128
Mrs., 180
Widow, 227
Kill Von Kull, 64
Klady, Jacob, 358, 361
Knight, Eliza, 338
Knyphausen, General, 124
Kocks (Cox), Hannah, 348
Kollock, Shepard, 194
Koster, Benjamin, 360
Kuyper, Hendrick, 139

Labadist's Colony, 293
Labagh, Peter, 142
Lafavor, Martha, 363
Lafayette, General, 130, 157, 237, 260, 270
Laforge, David, 35
Laight, Domine (see Leydt)
Lake, Nicholas, 29, 35
Lamb, John, 103
Lamberton, 212, 213, 215
Lambson, Ebenezer, 35
Lancastrian School, 197, 200, 204, 231
Land Ownership, 354, 365
Landaff, Bishop of, 108
Landing, 33, 121
Bridge, 125, 212, 320
Langfelt, Admiral, 247
Langstaff, Priscilla, 53
Sarah, 53
Langveldt, Mary, 245
Marritje, 245
Langvelt, Jan., 245
(see Longfield)
Lansing, John, Jr., 142
LaRochelle, 47
Launy, Dr. A. S., 228
Laurens (Laurensen), Thomas, 245
Laurense, Ann, 188
Lawrence-Beach Family, 352
Effingham, 337
Isaac, 178, 264, 352
Mrs. Isaac, 282
John, 100, 340
Julia, 264
Mary, 242, 243, 340
Meadows, 215
Mrs., 181
Miss C. A., 181
Rachel Longfield, 247
Ruth, 340
Samuel, 340
Thomas, 12, 21, 22, 24, 242, 245, 247, 267, 294, 340, 354, 355
Thomas, Jr., 340
Lawrence's Brook, 16, 17, 21, 23, 37, 41
Church, 42
Lawrie, Gawen, 12, 13, 212, 292
Lawson, William, 271
Leacraft, Mary, 336
Leal, Mrs., 252
Leaming & Spicer, 203
Lee, 150
David, 28, 35
Gen. Charles, 111, 264, 268, 318
Lee's Colony and State, 64
LeFevre, 153
(see Lafavor)
LeForge, Abram, 18
LeGrange, Bernardus, 45-47, 113, 114, 265, 266, 356

INDEX TO NAMES AND PLACES 379

Isaac, 47, 266
Christian, 266
Family, 266
Jacobus, 47, 266
James B., 266
James W., 266
Johannes De, 47, 266
Johannes, Jr., 266
Omy De, 47, 266
Legislator (steamboat), 178, 179
Leisler troubles, 32, 256, 295
Lenox, Robert, 285
Leonard, Capt. Samuel, 55, 336, 365
  Sarah, 55, 297, 336
  Thomas, 110
Leroy & Bayard, 56
  Herman, 58
Leslie, William, 49, 53
Letson, Clark, 205
  Johnson, 239
  Joseph, 85
  & Strong, 60
  William, 44
Leupp (Lupp), Family, 52
  Henry, 44, 49, 360
  Charles M., 262
  John H., 262
  Mary, 262
  Mr., 210
  William, 49
  William H., 200, 240
Lewis, Hope, 347
  Phœbe, 347
Leydt, John, 139
Lewis, Gov. Morgan, 275, 278, 342
Libraries, 137, 181, 219
Lincoln, General, 123, 304
  School, 209
Lindsey, Rev. Benjamin, 141
Linlithgow, Earl of, 273
Lispenard, Leonard, 100
Little, Mr., 235, 224
  William, 227
Livingston, Family, 272, 273, 274, 275, 276, 277, 338, 341
  & Fulton, 177-8
  J. R., 177, 178, 276, 342, 343, 365
  Miss, 181
  P. Van Brug, 364
  Philip, 100, 101
  Robert Cambridge, 148, 274, 275
  Robert J., 59, 177, 276, 365, 340, 341
  Robert R., 177, 178, 100, 101, 275
  Sarah, 268, 276, 338, 342
  & Stevens, 85
  Susan, 338
  Walter, 47, 48, 258, 274
  Gov. William, 40, 103, 108, 111, 116, 118, 125, 190, 342
Lloyd, John, 113
  Robert, 100
Lockermans, Maria, 333
Locomotives and first Railroads, 220
London, 11
Long Branch (steamboat), 179
Long, Samuel, M. D., 346
  William, 230
Longfield, Anne, 340
  Catherine Cox, 340
  Cornelius, 12, 17, 18, 20-25, 41, 243, 244, 245, 246, 247, 248, 295, 340, 354
  Family, 244

Henry, 27, 34, 35, 246, 247, 340
Mary, 340
Rachel (Lawrence), 247, 340
  (see Langvelt, etc.)
Long Island, 34
Longstreet, Aaron, 83
Loockerman, 245
Lord Berkeley, 10
  Carteret, 10
  Stirling School, 209
Loree, Dr. Ephraim, 44, 361
Lott, Abraham, 112, 284, 319
  Catherine, 334
  Colonel, 127
  Capt. Jeromus, 127
  Gertrude, 257, 284
  Peter, 334
  Ralf P., 361
Lotteries, 33, 45-47, 56, 76, 285, 314
Lovelace, Gov. Francis, 87
  Gov. John, 88
Lovett, Mrs., 230
Low Family, 338
  Cornelius, 363
  H. B., 172
  James B., 51
  John, 92, 339
  Peter, 181, 339
  & Voorhees, 156
Lowe, Widow, 231
Lucas, Nicholas, 212, 292
  Roelof, 42
Lunatics (First expense), 201
Lupardus, Cornelia, 352
  Mecklemus, 364
  R., 361
Lupp (see Leupp)
Lyell, Rev. T., 352
Lyle, Andrew, 271, 272, 358
  Brook, 41, 18
  Elizabeth, 272
  Family, 270
  John, 35, 44, 111, 270-272, 206, 207, 326, 315, 358
  John, Jr., 44, 271
  John 2nd, 44, 271
  John 3rd, 271
  John N., 272
  Martha, 271
  Mary, 271, 272
  Moses, 44, 271
  Robert, 270, 271, 272, 231, 327
  Samuel, 271, 272
Lynch, Thomas, 100, 101
Lyne, James, 35, 45

Mackay, E. G., 149
Mackness, Thos., 362
Mackphaedrix, Catharine, 276, 343
Maidenhead, 212
Mailler Place, 194
Manalapan, 214
Manley, Mr., 232
  Richard, 228
Manning, Catharine, 346
  William, 113
Mansion House (Bayard's), 138, 254
  (DeGraw's), 59, 62
Manson, Elizabeth, 35
Mante, Thomas, 96
Manufacturers, 240, 181
Map (1829), 158
Mapletown, 50

INDEX TO NAMES AND PLACES

Margerum, James J., 160, 172
Market, Houses, 25, 30, 37, 42, 156, 196, 199, 204
  Peter, 35
Marriner, Capt. Hiram, 128
  William, 127
Marschalk, John, 337
Marsh, Hugh, 10
Marshall, John, 215
  Thomas, 28, 35, 356
Marsten, Thomas, 56
Martelle, George, 346
Martin, John, 11, 17
  Joshua, 346
  Lieutenant, 124
  Squire, 172
Martin's Dock, 158, 215
Marvel, Andrew, 192
Maryland (Flying Camp), 118
Masterson, Mrs., 207, 327
Mathews, David, 127
Mathers, Thomas, 12
Matson, John, 65
Mavrocordato, 254
Maxwell, General, 123, 301
Mayo, A. W., 204
Mayors of New Brunswick, 26, 40, 143, 239, 240
McChesney, James, 149
  J. R., 198
McClelland, Professor, 223, 226
McCrellis, 239
McCurdy Place, 194, 269
McDougall, Alexander, 103, 109
  General, 192
McDowell, 150, 214
  John T., 149, 151, 152, 215, 217
McEvers, James, 102
McGregor Clan, 31
McIlvain, Joseph, 219
McKays, Mrs., 227
McKeag, 208, 328
McKean, Thomas, 100, 101
McKeath, William, 356
McKnight, Mr., 296
  William, 179
McLaughlin, James, 230
McLaury, D., 359
McMechin, Mr., 231
McRoe, Duncan J., 206
McWhorter, Rev. Dr., 280
Mechanics' Bank of N. Y., 164
Medical Soc. of N. J., 38, 257
Meeker, David, 216
Meghee, William, 67
Mellet (see Mollet), 354
Melyn, Cornelis, 250
Mercer, Colonel, 92
  William, M. D., 45-47, 52, 258, 364
Mercereau, David, 167, 227
Merchant, Alexander, 330
Merchant's Association, 144
Merritt, W. H., 359
Merrill, Richard, 364
Mersereau, David, 151
  John, 79-81
  Joshua, 75
  Maria Corson, 75
Mersural, John, 111, 318
Mesier, Abram, 77
  Widow, 83
Methodist Church, 53, 206, 207, 224, 227
Meyer, Christopher, 364, 123

Meyers, Benjamin, 197, 226
  John, 44
  Mary, 44
Mew, Richard, 11
Mickaelson, Elias, 248
Middlebrook, 121, 125, 302
Middlebush, 225
Middlesex Battalion Minutemen, 113
  County 15, 17, 18, 20, 43
  2nd Regiment Militia Foot, 112, 113
  Troop Horse, 252
  County, Great Britain, 255
Middletown Harbour, 76, 289
  Point, 76
  Township, 15
  Village, 23, 294
Mile Run, 16, 27-41
Milford, 26
Military Organization, 176
Milledoler, P. H., 154, 239
Miller, Paul, 27, 31, 33-35, 48, 251, 337
  Robert, 171
Miller's Tavern, 31, 48, 297
Miller's Run, 41
Mills, W. J., 93
Millstone, 124, 125, 213, 214, 225
  Bridge, 121
  River, 17, 27, 213, 293
Mine Run, 30
Minesincks, 292
Minnisink Path, 23, 24
  Island, 23
Minturn, Robert, 324
Minutes of Council, 18
Miry Run, 212
Mischianza, 115
Mix, Hannah, 280
Molinaer, Ary, 265
Moll, John, 241
Molleson, F., 178
Mollet, John Patterson, 354
  Theodore, 35
Mollison, George P., 59
  Ruth, 346
Moncrief, Major, 127
Money (Hard and Paper), 145, 160
Monmouth County, 15, 56, 120
Montaynes, H. Q., 109
Montcalm, 92
Montgomeree, Gov. John, 28
Montgomery, Richard, Gen'l, 275, 232, 342
Montieth, Rev. Walter, 144
Moon, James, 65, 67
Moor, Alexander, 27, 35
  Michael, 28, 35
Moore, Abigail, 337
  Charles, 100
  Colonel, 69
  Matthew, 186
  Mrs., 231
  Samuel (Sheriff), 16
  Stephen, 204, 230
Moores, Mary, 339
  Matthew, 345
Moravians, 54, 298
Morgan, Charles, 167
  Emeline, 339
Morgan's Riflemen, 124
Morris, Anne, 130, 267
  Arabella, 267
  Capt., 267

INDEX TO NAMES AND PLACES 381

Catharine, 267
Colonel Lewis, 32, 256, 266, 267
Elizabeth, 130, 260, 267
Euphemia, 267
Family, 266
Gov. Lewis, 46, 49, 51, 130, 251, 267
Gouveneur, 267
Isabella, 267
John, 267
Judge, 261
Lewis, Jr., 340
Margaret, 267
Mary (Molly), 266, 269, 340
Matthew, 267
Mrs. (Actress), 78
Poily, 52
Richard and family, 266, 267
Robert, 49, 51, 131, 267, 356, 360, 361
Robert Hunter, 51, 91, 267
Sarah, 267
Staats, L., 267
Morristown, 284
Mortimer, Benjamin, 228
Morton, John, 100
Joseph, 229
Moschel, George, 73
Mosengail, Capt., 302
Mott. Gershom, 103
Moutton, John, 346
Mount Holly, 76
Mount Hope (steamboat), 180
Mouse and Mountain (steamboat), 85, 178
Mulford, Samuel, 18
Mundy, Samuel, 324
Matilda, 346
Phineas, 359
Munn, Aaron, 84
Machine Shop, 240
Murdock, James, 316
William, 100
Murphy, John, 84
William, 35
Murray, John, 316
Myer, B., 223
Christopher, 173, 364
Theodore, 232

Nafey, Garret, 228
John, 232
Mr., 227
(see Nefie)
Nanfan, 31
Napoleon Co., 179
Nassau in Piscataway, 242
Hall, 299
National Iron Works, 240
Navesink, 18
Naylor, Benjamin, 359
Neale, Thomas, 87
Nefie, Ann, 128
Neinwerd on Rhine, 262
Neilson, A. S., 200, 323
Abraham, 286
Campus, 141
Catharine S., 351
Col. John, 44, 52, 61, 113, 122, 125, 128, 141, 143, 144, 148, 157, 159, 269, 270, 287, 203, 282, 284, 285, 286, 318, 319
Mrs. Col., 284
Dr. John, 283, 353, 348
James, 16, 27, 28, 34, 35, 37, 40, 89, 111, 120, 239, 269, 271, 283, 284, 286, 318
James (2nd), 141, 164, 165, 176, 210, 214, 215, 216, 217, 218, 219, 221, 286, 353, 352, 357, 358, 359
James (2nd), Mrs., Miss, 181
James (3rd), 23, 131, 148, 286, 358
James (3rd), Mrs., 181
John (steamboat), 180, 217
& Miller, 60
William, 48, 275, 316, 340
Nelson, William, 191, 193
Nemcawix, Count, 341
Neversink, 20
Nevill, John, 14
Mary, 23, 262, 360
Samuel, 14, 191, 262
Sarah, 14
Nevill's Laws, 191
Nevius, J. M., 363
James S., 167
James W., 239
Judge, 154
Martin, 138
Newark, 11, 15, 20, 26, 34, 118, 294
Banking & Ins. Co., 163
Charter (1736), 26
Lime and Cement Co., 60
Powles Hook Post Road, 77
Township Charter (1714), 15, 26
Trinity Church, 314
New Barbadoes, 15
New Blazing Star, 75
Newbold, Michael, 179
New Brunswick, 16, 17, 19, 23, 26, 212, 214, 285, 27, 33, 34, 43, 44, 297, 300, 360
a Borrower, 157
Advertiser (1792), 194
Artillery Co., 157, 176, 270
Boundaries, 17, 16, 27, 143, 146
British in, 120, 125
Charters (see City Charters)
City Officers, 27, 143
Court House, 29, 319
Copper Mine, 303
Ferry Rights, 32
Finances, 195, 198
Fountain Co. (1801), 158
Fredonian (1811), 194
Garrison Town, 111
Gazette and Weekly Monitor, 194
Guardian (1793), 194, 210, 212
Jail Lot, 205
Library (1792), 137, 210
(1796), Union Co., 137
(1820), 210
Y. M. C. A. (1868), 210
Free Cir. (1883), 181, 210
Public (1892), 182, 210
Map, 158
Names (1750), 34
N. B., S. & Canal Transpt. Co., 179
N. B. S. Ferry Co. (1815), 178
Night School, 206
Numbering Houses, 157
Ordinances, 28
Paving (1739), 29
Paving (1803), 198
Regiment, 26th at, 113
Regiment, 29th at, 113
Rubber Co., 240
School Co. (1784), 144, 254, 203, 206, 207

INDEX TO NAMES AND PLACES

School District No. 1, 204, 205
Seal, 27
Soc. Encourage Mfgrs., 181
Team & Stb. Co. (1814), 178
Times, 194, 214, 223
Toll Bridge, 285
Wards North, South (1739-63), 37, 40, 158
Wards Three (1784), 158
  Four (1801), 158
  Six (1829), 158, 198
Washington in, 115, 116, 120
Water Co., 357, 360
New Castle, 212
New Coffee House, 209
Newcomb, Silas, 110, 317
Newell, J. H., 60, 227
  J. W., 173
Newell's Pottery, 224
New England, 24
New Gottenburgh, 294
New Hampshire Money, 161
New Jersey Bank for Savings, 176
  College for Women, 131, 261, 287
  College of, 252
  Early Travellers, 288
  Gazette (1777), 194
  Journal (1779), 194
  Journal, Elizabeth (1784), 194
  Medical Society, 38, 257
  Past and Present, 95
  Railroad Co., 58, 59, 180
  Rubber Shoe Co., 240
  St. Agri. Exp. Sta., 135
  Turnpike, 286
New Philadelphia (steamboat), 180
New Piscataqua, 19
New York, 26, 34, 45, 113
  Gazette, 46
  to Philadelphia (Road), 24, 297
Newspaper Lists, 190, 191, 194
Newton, Mr., 56, 57
Nicholas, Capt., 24
Nicholls, Richard, 31, 265
  Mary, 265
Nichols, Thaddeus, 216, 218
Nicholson, Gov. of Va., 295
Nicoll, Governor, 9-12, 288
  Matthias, 243
Niles' Register, 85, 101
Nine-Mile Run, 37
Noe, John, 314
Norfolk & N. B. Hosiery Co., 240
North Branch, 43
North Brunswick Township, 204, 205
North (South) Hampton, Pa., 43
Norwood, Andrew, 35
Novelty Rubber Co., 240

Oake (Oakey, Oaky), (see Ouke)
O'Brien, Daniel, 69, 70, 72
  James, 228
O'Bryant, Daniel, 70-71
Ogden, Aaron, 315
  Abram, 59
  Catherine, 188
  Colonel, 177
  & Gibbon, 177
  John, 10
  Nathaniel, 35
  Rev. Uzal, 280
  Robert, 100
  Samuel, 267
Ogilby, Rev. J. D., 138, 239, 350
Old Bridge School Dist., 205
Olden, David, 43
  James, 16
Olive Branch (steamboat), 85, 178
Oliver, Mr., 102
  Mary, 335
O'Neil, Thos., 359
Onion (see Inian)
Onderdonk & Letson, 240
  Peter, 347
  Peter C., 173, 240, 201
Oppie's Cove, 213
Oram, D., 230
Orchard, T., 231
Ormiston, John, 14, 268
  Rachel (Sonmans), 14
Osgood, Samuel, 90
Osterland & Keyser, 354, 360
Otis, James, 100, 101
  D. C., 357
Ouke, Abraham, 35, 38, 44, 139, 253
  Jacob, 18, 27, 34, 38, 42, 253
  Mary, 38, 253
  Mayor, 40
  William, 16, 27, 29-30, 34, 35, 37, 38, 111, 139, 160, 239, 251, 252, 253, 258, 271, 315, 356
Outcalt, Henry, 324
  John B., 60
  John, 359
  Judge, 229
  Widow, 231
Overfield, Conrad, 363
Oyster Bay, 289

Page, John L., 204
Palmer, Capt. John, 295
Paper Money (City of N. B.), 160
  Proclamation, Etc., 161
Parker, Benjamin, 144
  Capt. 92, 344
  Capt. Elisha, 186, 344
  Catherine, 189
  Charles, 215, 216, 217, 218
  Colonel (6th Va.), 121
  Colonel John (1721), 17
  Cortlandt, 189
  Edward, 187, 189
  Elender, 51
  Elisha, 186, 187, 189, 344
  Elizabeth, 51, 186, 188, 189, 344
  Family, 186, 344
  Gertrude, 188, 189
  H. G., 174
  James, 51, 61, 90, 99, 186-189, 191, 256, 219, 220, 344, 363
  James & Co., 190
  James Eugene, 193
  Jane Ballareau, 193
  Janet, 51, 188, 189, 344
  Joanna, 186
  John, 49, 51, 186 186-189, 344
  Lewis, 189, 344
  Lewis, Jr., 187
  Margaret, 189
  Maria, 181, 188
  Mary, 186, 189, 193, 344
  Mrs. Mary (Ballareau), 193
  Mr., 149, 150
  Nathaniel, 73
  Penelope, 189
  Robert, 186
  Samuel, 186, 189, 191, 344

INDEX TO NAMES AND PLACES 383

Samuel Eugene, 193
Samuel F., 193, 344
Sarah, 186, 188, 189, 344
Thomas, 186, 344
Rev. Thomas, 186
Ursula, 187, 189, 344
William, 188
Parsippany, Parsonage, 314
Parquarry Flats, 292
Partition (East & West Jersey), 243, 16
Partridge, Oliver, 100
Passaic, 117, 118; (Ferry), 64
Paterson, 61
 Block, 18
 Compilation of Laws by, 143
 Euphemia, 130
 Richard, 259
 Gov. William, 44, 56, 61, 130, 144, 259, 260, 316, 361; family, 212, 359
 William B., 59, 138, 324
Patten, Louisa Ayres, 272
Patterson, E. M., 240, 201
 John, 275
Patton, Abraham, 123
 James, 123
Paul, John, 44
Pavonia (Ferry), 64
Peacock, Mrs., 18
 William, 49, 53
Pearl St., N. Y. 1665, 245
Pearse, Capt. Vincent, 267
Peck, Benjamin, 31
 Christina, 31, 337
 Hannah, 31
 Slip, N. Y., 31
Peithesophian Soc. of Queens, 239
Penn. & N. J. Stb. Ferry Co., 179
Penn, William, 11, 87, 249, 212, 292, 295
Pennington, 360, 119
Pennypack, 66
Penny Savings, 181
Pennytown, 119
People's Bank, 164, 173
Pepperel, Sir Wm., 96
Perkins, John, 29, 35
 W. H., Jr., 270
Perrine, Henry, 198
 Matthew, 359
Perry, Mr., 234
Perth, James, Earl of, 12
Perth Amboy, 10, 15, 19, 27, 31, 62, 297
 records at, 318
Peterse, Leffert, 352
Peterson, George, 179
Pettit, Charles, 318
Petty's Island, 315
Phelan, James, 160, 163
 John, 163, 178
Phelps, Rev. Dr., 28, 359
Phenix, J. Philip, 60
Philadelphia, 24, 112
 & N. B. Stage Line, 68
 & Trenton Railroad, 159
Philipse, Adolph, 32, 277
 Anatie, 255
 Frederick, 32, 255
Phillips, Elijah, 44, 363
 Mr., 150
 William, 363
Phœnix (steamboat), 85, 156, 177
Piatt, Capt. Daniel, 111, 317

Pichon, Louis Andre, 270
Picket, Sarah, 230
Pierce, Daniel, 11
 Joshua, 10
Pierson, David Lawrence, 95
 Waller, 350
Pieter, Peritje, 245
Pike, John, 10
 Thomas, 345
Pine Tree Hill, 131
Piscataqua River, 243
Picataway 10, 11, 15, 16, 19, 20, 24, 26, 30, 45, 54, 225, 293, 294, 297
 Deputies, 20
 Population (1683), 16
 Town, 15, 22
 Episcopal Church, 233
Piscopeck Creek, 24
Pitlochie, Scotland, 294
Pitt, Samuel, 35
Pittenger, Elizabeth, 35
Pluckemin, 303
Plum, John, 44, 57, 144
 Mrs., 228
 William, 320
Plumsted, Clement, 11
Pochon, Stephen, 270
Polhemus, Capt. John, 111, 317
 Daniel, 225
Pool, Dr. H. B., 204, 205
 John, 44, 144, 164, 338, 352
 John A., M. D., 176
 Michael, 53
 Mary, 338, 352
 Peter N., 167
Population (1747), 34
Post-Masters, 48, 90, 170, 189, 190
Post-Office, 167, 170
Post-Roads, 17, 27, 68, 77
Potter, Col. Cuthbert, 295, 299
 John, 164, 217, 219, 220, 221, 351
 Rachel, 351
 Samuel, 53
Potter's Field, 355
Potts, Abraham, 360
Powers, Dr., 54
Powles (Paulus) Hook, 64, 77, 84
 Bank (1804), 163
Pratt, Henry, 87
Preparatory School, 38
Presbyterian Church, Bound Brook, 43
 Meeting House, 356
 New Brunswick, 205, 285, 43, 44, 54
Preston, Colonel, 122
 Samuel, 292
Price, Benjamin, 35, 46, 258
 Mary (alias Evans), 139
Pridmore, Benjamin, 17, 18, 72, 365
 John, 35
Priestly, John, 44
Prigmore, John, 71
Princeton 16, 20, 24, 31, 42, 46, 62, 113, 213, 225, 118, 297, 301, 304
Printing Offices, 190
Prison Ships, 115
Probasco, John, 363, 364
 Peter, 61
Proclamation Money, 161
Proprietary Rights, 51
Proprietors, 11-13, 15, 22, 26, 34
 Dividends, 13, 14
Province of N. J. Lottery, 314

INDEX TO NAMES AND PLACES

Provincial Congress, 113, 116, 259
Provost, A. P., 204
   Mr., 231, 232
Public Schools, 156
   Library, 181
Pucklehammer, Horn & French, 41
Punkhill, 122
Purdus, Farmer, 228
Putnam, General, 286

Quackenbos, Adriense, 36
   Jacobus, 34
Queen Anne, 145
Queens, Campus, 189
   College, 33, 38, 148, 256, 281, 355
   Commencement, 140, 141
   Suspended, 140
   Trustees, 139, 282
Quibbletown (New Market), 121, 122, 124, 125
Quick. John P., 229

Radcliff, Mr., 84
Rae. Joseph, Jr., 16
Rahway (Bridgetown), 302
Railroads, 1st, 53, 84, 160
Ramsey, Andrew, 71
Rand, John, 265
Randolph, A. F., 171
   David F., 170, 171, 200, 240
   Francis F., 224, 229
   Isaac F., 75
   James F., 167, 215
   Joel, 233
   Mr., 57
   Rachel, 231, 232
   Reuben, 75
   Samuel F., 152
   Stelle, 57
   W. F., 170
Rappelyea, James, 358
   Jerome, Jr., 176
Raritan, Church (1778), 43
   Court House (1784), 22
   Kill, 294
   Landing, 33, 121, 125, 314
   North Branch of, 16
   River, 10, 12, 17, 21, 22, 24, 41, 122, 212, 225
   River Dam, 41, 158
   Somerville (1801), 43, 46
   Steamboat (1808), 177
   Steamboat (1815), 85, 177
   Steamboat (1840), 180
Ratoon, 352
   William, 137
Rawlins, Edward, 100
Ray, John, 317
Read, Andrew, 90
   Joseph, 90
Reade, Anne, 343
Reason, William, 36
Redford's Ferry, 63, 64
Reed, Hon. George, 282
   James, 36
   John, 16
   Rev. Israel, 44
   Willis, 49, 53
Reeside, James, 159
Reid, John, 11
Reid's Map, 13
Reigert, Charlotte Christiana, 279
Reimer, Louis, 197
Remsen, Peter, 216, 217
Retaliation (steamboat), 178

Reynolds, John, 35
Rezeau (Reseau), John, 71
   Miss Mary, 36
Rhea, Mr., 297
Rhinebeck, 276
Richards, John, 71
   Joseph, 69, 70, 72, 74
   William, 78
Richmond, Catharine, 338
   Dr., 228
   Frederick, 150, 176, 239, 323, 324
   George, 165, 175
   Henry, 60, 173, 228
   Jacob, 151
   James, 44, 144, 164, 356-7-8-9, 360
   Miss, 181
   N. C., 229
   Walter M., 324
   William, 44
Rickey, Lambert, 215
Ridley, Matthew, 338, 342
Riggs, Ambrose, 11
Riley, John, 36
   Patrick, 48, 49, 363
Ringo, John, 106
Ringold, Thomas, 100
Rittenhouse, David, 116
Roberts, E. F., 364
Robins, Daniel, 186, 345
Robinson, Beverly, 188
   Joseph, 44
   Peter, 154, 168
Robison, John, 295
Rocky Brook, 37
   Hill, 46, 298, 303
Rodney, Caesar, 100, 101
Roelofse, Willempsie, 352
Rogers, Clarissa, 228
   Joseph K., 215
   Moses (Capt.), 180
Rolf, Isaiah, 60, 231
   Mr., 231
Rolph, Hannah, 186, 344
Romaine, Jeremiah, 142
Romeyne, James Van Campen. 142
Ross, Alexander, M. D., 50, 337, 365
   Coal Yard Alley, 18
   Elias, 325
   Hall, 50, 130, 266
   James, 234
   Miles, 173
   Moses, 357
Rouse, Eliza, 137
   Rev. Peter P., 137, 350
Rowett, Mrs., 230
Rowland, David, 100
Rowley's Mill, 213
Royce, John, 36
Rubber Factory, 34
Rubsaamen, Mr., 302
Rudyard, Thomas, 11
Ruggles, Timothy, 100
Runk, William T., 171
Runyon, Anne, 346
   Asa, 172
   Family, 345
   Mahlon, 171, 174, 346
   Peter P., 154, 345
   Reuben, 29, 35, 36, 272, 346, 356, 357, 358, 360, 361
   Reune, 110, 272, 315, 345
   Vincent, 272, 345
Russel, Mr., 57
   Robert M., 179

INDEX TO NAMES AND PLACES 385

Rutgers College, 355, 357, 358
 (see Queens)
Rutherford, John, 214
 A. J., 359
Rutledge, John, 100, 101
Ruisen, Jacob, 342
Ryall, Joseph, 256
Ryder (Rider), Andrew, 210
 John, 358
 William, 44, 82
Ryder's Lane, 23, 358
Rynders, Aernout, 245
 Barent, 341
Ryno, James, 149
 Mrs., 207, 327

Sabbath Day Point, 92
 Laws, 156
Sacunk, 12
Saevan, Svens, 298
Salaries in Revolution, 316
Samptown, 121
Sanderson, H., 228
Sandy Hook Lighthouse, 212, 315
Saraghtoge, 276
Satick, Altie, 324
Savage, John, 159
Savannah, 53
 (steamboat), 180
Say, Thomas, 360
Sayre, Daniel, 347
Schenck, H. H., 169, 170
 John, 16
 Judge Peter, 139
 Mayor A. V., 198, 240, 201, 228
 T. E. (Cashier), 174
Schenck's Reach, 213
Schirmer, Gustave, 184
Schlatter, Charles L., 159
Schoepf, Dr. Johann D., 133, 161, 201
Scholfield, Jonathan, 82
School Board, 206
 Committee (1784), 144
 House, Church St., 144
 History, 54, 203
 Master, 41
 Public (1812), 199
Schools, Cost of, 207-209
 First Act as to, 20
 Lancastrian, 197, 203
 New Brunswick, 205
 Sabbath, 181
 Township, 205
Schooner, 53
Schuchardt, Frederick, 357
Schureman, Family, 347
 Jacob, 203, 347
 Jacobus, 41, 347
 James, 111, 141, 145-6, 148, 157, 159, 164, 199, 318, 347, 355, 361-2
 John, 111, 143, 148, 268, 315, 347, 361, 362
 Lieut. James, 111, 348
 Mayor, 159, 348
 William Williamson, 348
Schuyler, Abraham, 34, 36, 55, 111, 257, 315, 348, 361
 Abraham (Mayor), 257
 Abraham, Jr., 257, 348
 Alida, 273
 Anne, 274
 Arent, 256, 349
 Arentje, 257

Catharine, 352
Col. John, 48, 92, 257, 258, 275, 300, 349
Col. Peter, 91-93, 96, 189, 257, 273, 274, 300, 349
Cornelia, 258, 275, 341
Cornelis, 48
David Pieterse, 257, 348
Derrick, 27, 257, 348
Dirck, 29, 34, 36, 257, 354
Family, 256, 348
George L., 59
General, 268
Gertrude, 257, 258, 274, 349
Jacobus, 34, 36
Margaret, 258, 273, 341
Margarite, 273, 343
Mary, 274
Philip, 258, 273, 349
Pieter P., 343
"Scotch" John, 71
Scots, Mary, Queen, 273
Scot's Model, 24
Scott, Anna Cornelia, 350
 Anna Johnson, 137, 350
 Austin, 19, 182
 Charles Smith, 138
 Cornelia de Deimar, 138, 350
 Col. John, 39, 255
 Colonel, 122
 Eliza, 137
 Genealogy, 349
 General, 117
 George, 294
 Hannah, 137, 181, 210, 349
 Jane, 137, 349
 John, 136
 John Morris, 103
 Joseph Griffith, 138, 350
 Joseph Warren, 58, 136-7, 163, 239, 211, 363
 Lavinia Agnes, 138, 350
 Mary Dickenson, 137, 350
 Moses, 44, 56, 59, 112-3, 136, 144, 164, 318, 361, 362
 Moses Warren, 138, 350, 352
 Upham, 294
Scudder, William, 113
Scull, Nicholas, 292
Sea Horse (steamboat), 177
Seaman, Jennie, 336
Sears, Isaac, 103
Sebring, Roelof, 42
Second Mountain, 16
 River, 117, 300, 303, 314
Selyn, Henrycus, 245
Seminary Hill, 130
 Theological, 130
Settlers (First), 133
Shack, Capt., 128
Shannon's Hist., N. Y., 247
Sharlock, Oliver, 151
Shaw, John C., 56
Sheepshanks, William, 179
Shepardy, Mr., 226
Shippen, Ann, 342
Ships, Beula, 316
 Blue Mountain Valley, 318
 Edward, 102
 Philip, 11
 Providence, 247
Shirley, General, 93, 96
Shrewsbury, 15, 23, 76, 110, 294
 Church, 314
 & N. J. Stb. Ferry Co., 179

INDEX TO NAMES AND PLACES

Sidi, Scheick, 298
Silcocks (Sillcocks), Gabriel, 44
  Henry, 225
  Isaac, 232
  James, 225
  Tunis, 225, 232
Simcoe's Raid (1779), 22, 125
Simpson & Co., 178
  John N., 164, 176, 181, 214, 215, 217, 340, 359
Sinclair, Sir John, 299
Sinzendorf, Count, 298
Six-Mile Run, 41, 43, 225
  Court House, 22
Skillman, Abraham, 80
Skinner, Cortlandt, 38, 92
  Gertrude, 188
  Lieut. John, 92
  Susannah, 337
  William (Capt.), 92
  William (Rev.), 31, 32, 249, 334
Skippetauken, 213
Slaughter, E., 20
Slaves, 28
Slight (Sleight), John, 111, 315
  Matthew, 358
  Peter, 36, 270, 358
Sloan, Jeremiah, 221
Sloops, Betsy, 284
  Brunswick, 17, 319
  Favorite, 285
  James, 284
  Jersey, 284
  Phœbe, 61
  Polly, 284
  Two Brothers, 61
Sluyter, Elizabeth, 332
  Peter, 241, 293
Smith, Aaron, 232
  Amy, 230
  Charles, 175, 239, 231
  Charles, M. D., 58, 209, 226, 350, 355, 361
  Digby, 364
  Eleanor, 364
  Fitz Randolph, M. D., 59, 159, 175, 200, 239, 240, 350, 364
  Franklin, 364
  Hatfield, 364
  Hugh, 360
  Isaac, 230
  James, 230
  Jasper, 197
  John, 10, 11, 356
  John, Jr., 44
  Mary, 350
  Miles C., 167, 176, 239, 324, 363, 364
  Miss S., 181
  Moses, 324
  Mrs. Dr., 180
  Oscola, 364
  Rhoda, 336
  Richard, 111, 316
  Samuel Harrison, 254
  Solomon, 65, 67
  William, 276
  William, Jr., 103
Smith's History of New Jersey, 191
Smock, Leandert, 17, 18, 357
Smokers Hook, 293
Smyrna (1704), 254
Smyth, John, 16
Smythe, Andrew, 188
Snelling, Joseph, 12

Soc. Propagation Gospel in Foreign Parts, 192, 334
Sofield, Jeremiah, 234
Solem (Sollem), Cornelius, 68
  Mort, 36
  Tise, 36
Somerset County, 31, 43, 49, 121
  Lines, 15-17, 20, 38
  Court House, 22
  Sheriffs, 139
  Treasurer, 16
Somerville, 16, 22
Sonman (Sonmans), Arent, 12-14
  Bathsheba. 14
  Johanna, 14
  Peter, 14, 22, 268
  Peter (2nd), 14
  Rachel, 14
Sonman's Hill, 221
Sons of Columbus, 51
  of Liberty, 97, 103, 105, 283
  of St. Tammany, 109
South Amboy, 15, 63
South Branch of Raritan, 80
South, Daniel, 36
  River, 12, 16, 17, 21, 27, 214, 293
  River Bridge, 126
South Hampton, Pa., 43
Southern Colonies, 24
Spader, Peter, 149, 168, 171, 172
Spanktown (Rahway), 121
Spencer, Colonel, 121
Sperling, Abraham, 333
Spotswood, Col. Alexander, 88
Spratt, John, 341
Springfield, 117, 121
Squabbletown, 122
Squier, Ludlow, 347
  Zadoc, 280
St. Augustine, Fla., 93
St. John's Church, Elizabeth, 314
St. Jones and Duck Creek, 248
St. Mary Le Bone, England, 255
St. Nicholas (steamboat), 180
St. Peter's Church, 207, 327
Staats, Catriena, 348
  Frederick, 173
  Joanna, 129, 259
  Peter, 358
  Tryntie, 267
Stage Wagon and Coach, 62
  Travel, 61-85
State Bank, 160
  Charter N. B. (1784), 196
Staten Island, 74, 110, 250
Staunton, Francis, 216, 218
Steamboats (Early), 84, 178, 179, 304
Steele, Rev. Dr., 42
Stelle, Benjamin D., 59, 170, 171, 325
  Christina, 346
  Clarkson, 230
  Edward T., 149-152
  Eugenia, 336
  Gabriel, 65
  Pontius, 67
  Peter R., 323
  Rachel, 336
Stephens, General, 116
Stephenson, J. H., Jr., 142
Stevens, Capt. Campbell, 93
  Edwin, 247
  General, 123

INDEX TO NAMES AND PLACES 387

& J. R. Livingston, 178
James, 247
John, 36, 93, 156, 177, 28, 247, 314
Mary, 342
Rachel Cox, 247
Party, 220
Richard, 128, 362
Robert, 177, 247
Robert L., 221
Stevenson, E. L., 347
Stewart, Col. Charles, 133, 302, 363
 John, 230
 Mary Johnson, 133
 Matty, 133
 Otis D., 230, 232
Still House Run, 41
Stillwell, James, 229
 Richard, 356
Stilwell, Ann, 33, 334
Stirling, Lord, 93, 111, 116, 316, 318
Stites, Elizabeth, 189
Stockton, Major R. V., 122
 Mr., 296
 R. F., 220, 221
 Richard, 40, 108, 247, 252, 259, 216, 217, 218, 219, 286
 Robert (Sheriff), 139, 256, 362
 Samuel, 247
Stone, Charles Henry, 134
 Daniel, 60
 Street, N. Y., 244
Stony Brook, 212, 213, 215
Stoothoff, 231
 Mrs., 231
Stoudinger (steamboat), 177, 180
Stout, Augustus T., 171
 Col. Joseph, 192
 Fitz Randolph, 346
 George H., 224, 230, 324
 John W., 200, 239, 210, 231, 357
 Josiah, 239, 324
 Levi, 226
 Ralph, 227
Stranraer, 272
Streets (New Brunswick), Albany, 16, 18, 24, 25, 34, 39, 52, 223, 284
 Barrack, 19, 44, 52, 320
 Bayard, 54, 224, 226, 320
 Burnet, 17, 18, 23, 25, 224, 229
 Broad, 18
 Brewet (John), 113
 Church, 17, 18, 19, 25, 207, 223
 Church Alley, 19
 Clifton Ave., 12, 23
 Council Refused to Mend, 198
 Drift, 15, 19
 French, 16, 18, 25, 34, 56
 George, 12, 19, 52, 53, 224, 227, 320
 George's Road, 18, 21, 24, 37
 Guilden, 207
 Hale, 207, 208
 Hamilton, 207
 John (formerly Brewer), 113
 King (see Neilson), 53
 Liberty, 43, 224, 227
 Little Burnet, 18, 21, 29, 283
 Livingston Ave., 12, 21, 25, 50, 51, 320
 Maiden Lane, 320
 Neilson, 19, 43, 52, 53, 198-9, 224, 228, 320
 New, 18, 50, 224, 228
 Nichol Ave., 23, 51
 Oppression (see Schureman), 131, 261
 Paterson, 44, 224
 Peace, 17, 18, 25, 30, 49
 Prince (see Bayard), 19, 198
 Queen (see Neilson), 261, 320
 Raritan Ave., Highland Park, 24
 Remsen Ave., 23
 Richmond (formerly Court), 19
 Ross' Coal Yard Alley, 18
 Ryder's Lane, 23
 Schureman (formerly Dutch Church), 42, 162, 224, 230, 261
 Somerset, 52, 53
 Turnpike, 225
 Water, 49, 258
 White, 19
 Worked by Citizens till 1803, 198
Strong, Theodore, 239
 Thomas J., 229
Striker, James, 362
Stryker, Antje De Riemer, 347
 Peter, 36
Stuart, Major, 126
Stubbs, Rev. Dr. Alfred, 283
Stuyvesant, Anna, 253, 332
 Peter, 86, 253, 332
Sugar House Prison, 348
Sullivan, General, 126
 Army of, 126
Sumner, Increase, 115
Sunday School, 181
Sutphen, John D., 359
Sutton, Henry, 53, 233
 Jacob, 53
 Joseph, 49, 53
 Priscilla, 53
 Richard, 344
 Sarah, 53
Suydam, Abraham, 167, 194, 239, 355
 & Graham, 194
 Charles, 39, 51
 H., 363
 Hendrick Reycke, 335
 Jac., 226
 Jacob, 336
 Jacob Hendrick, 335
 Jane, 333
 Joseph, 225
 Leitie, 335
 V. M. W., 174
Sven, Saeven, 228
Swift, James, 210
Symmes, John Cleves, 338, 342
Symonds, William, 36
Sythoff's Mill, 213

Taite, Elizabeth, 255
Takanij, 294
Talmage, Thomas, 44
Tannery, 41
Tappan, Chris., 293
Tarff, Edward, 290
Taverns:
 Basking Ridge (Mrs. White), 264
 Bergen Point (Abraham Van Tile), 74
 Blazing Star (John Masherew), 79
 Burlington (Jonathan Thomas), 71, 90

Burlington Road (Dr. Brown), 64
Cranbury (John Pridmore), 35, 72
Elizabethtown Point (William Douglass), 75; (Heard's), 297; (John Watson's), 74, 75; (Dr. Wynant's), 83; (Sybrandt's "Roebuck"), 77, 78
Inian's Ferry (John Inian), 62; (Henry Greenland), 21, 24, 62, 243
Kingston ("Black Lion"), 55, 297
New Blazing Star (Jacob Fitz Randolph), 75; (Joshua Mesereau), 75
New Brunswick (Cornelius Longfield), 23; (Ann Balding's), 61; (Paul Miller's "Admiral Vernon"), 31, 48, 297; ("White Hall"), 52, 56, 62, 93, 270, 269, 268, 255, 252, 116, 115, 112, 90; (William Ouke), 39; ("Indian Queen"), 53, 55, 56, 62, 83, 135, 146, 176, 269, 270; ("City Hotel"), 58, 85, 139, 157, 217, 270 (B. D. Stelle), 59, 169; (Col. Peter Keenon), 51, 321; (De-Graw's "Mansion House"), 59, 62; (Nehemiah Vernon), 49, 52; (William Marriner), 128; (John Keyworth—Steamboat Hotel), 52; (Mrs. Vanderbelt's "Bellona"), 85; (Bennets—Queen Street, 334; (Farmer's & Mechanic's), 170; (Brook Farmar's "Red Lion"), 31, 48; (Voorhees), 112, 116
New Brunswick Ferry (John DeGrove), 82
New York (Abraham Bockey), 74; ("City Arms"), 103; (Scotch John's), 71
Perth Amboy (Obediah Aires), 74
Philadelphia ("Crooked Billet"), 63; ("Cross Keys"), 81, 82; ("Death of the Fox"), 73; ("Golden Ball" John Barnhill), 77; ("Indian Queen"), 81; ("Queen's Head"), 70; ("Sign of the Bunch of Grapes"), 80
Powles Hook (Michael Cornelisse), 77
Princeton (Jacob Hyer's "Hudibras"), 79
Redford's Ferry (Daniel O'Bryant), 70, 71; (Gabriel Stelle), 65; (John Cluck), 70, 71
Savannah, Ga. (Fondee's), 109
South Branch of Raritan (Obediah Taylor), 80
Staten Island (Isaac Dole), 74; (Mrs. Ducket), 74
Trenton (J. G. Bergen), 82; (Nathaniel Parker), 73; (John Wollend), 63; (Andrew Ramsey), 71; (Thomas Hooton), 66
Trenton Ferry (George Moschel), 73
Woodbridge (Heard's), 297
Tax, 30, 197
Appeal, 197

Taylor, A. F., 240
A. R., 53, 146, 176, 200, 270
Benjamin, 359, 360
Family, 351
Grist and Saw Mill, 263
John, 44, 111, 128, 229, 258, 318, 319
John A., 46
Mary, 51
Mayor, 157
Mills, 262, 263
Mrs. Dr., 181
Obediah, 80
Richard, 351
Team & Steamboat Co., 178, 214
Temple, John, 247
Thomas, 247
Ten Brook (Ten Broeck), Catherine, 343
Christina, 341
Cornelius, 269
Gertruy, 348
Johannis, 33
William, 44
Ten Eick, Andrew, 326
Peter, 347
Tunis, 347
Ten Eyke, Peter, 358
Ten-Mile Run, 41
Tennent, Gilbert, 43, 249
Mr., 296
William, 249, 252
William, Jr., 249
Terhune, Albert, 347
Antje Eve, 347
G. W., 239
John, 37
Letson &, 239, 218
Teunison's Lane, 21
Thanksgiving Day, 19
Thistle (steamboat), 178, 270
Thomas, Gabriel, 296
Isaiah, 192
Jonathan, 71, 73
Theodore, 184
Thomson, Archibald, 36, 347
John, 27, 74, 75
John R., 219
Thong, Walter, 274, 341
Mary, 341
Thorne, Thomas, 343
Three-Mile Run, 41, 43
Tibbets, Elisha, 159, 217
Ticonderoga, 92
Tilghman, Edward, 100, 101, 105
Tingle, John, 36
Tinicum, 294
Titsworth, Judge Abraham D., 169
Toll Bridge, 285
Tomson, John, 36
Tories on Long Island, 111
Tornado, 223
Tothill, Jeremiah, 12
Totten, Levi, 283
Town Hall, 200
Town Meeting, 200
Townley, Col. Richard, 295
Townshend, Charles, 96
Townships, 15
Travel (Primitive), 63, 84
Treat, Robert, 26
Trembly, Peter, 347
Susannah, 347
Trenton & N. B. Turnpike, 84, 161, 254

INDEX TO NAMES AND PLACES 389

Trenton, 19, 24, 27, 62, 112, 118, 212,215,223
  Banking Co., 221
  Charter (1746), 26
  Church (1751), 314
  Gazette, 194
Trinity Church, N. Y. City, 31, 115
Troops, 1st Revolutionary, 111, 317
Trotten, Rebecca, 335
Troy Farms, 284
Tunison, Judge John, 22
  Widow, 228
Tunnison, C. W., 360
Turcks, Jacobus, 30
Turkey Parsonage, 314
Turner, Robert, 12
Turnpike, Bordentown & Burlington, 84
  Jersey City & Hackensack, 84
  N. B. & Newark, 84
  Trenton & N. B., 84, 158
Tuttle, Col. Joseph, 92
Tuttle's Federal Stage, 83
Twinning & Johnson, 83
Two Brothers (sloop), 61

Underdonk, H., 363
Union Academy (1829), 204
  Library Co. (1796), 137, 209
  Library Constitution, 211
United States Lotteries (1777), 315
  Magazine (1777), 194
  Stock, 161
Upland (now Chester), 294
Upper Road, 62
Upsala University, 299
Urquhart, Frank J., 95

Vaeder, Engette, 266
Vail, 153
  D. W., 200, 239, 240, 227
  Edward, 165, 168
Van Allen, Dirck, 36
Van Arsdale, Richard, 232
  Widow, 224, 232
Van Arsdalen, 320
  Dirck, 18, 36
Van Bael, Rachel, 332
Van Berg, Dinah, 338
Van Beuren, 36
Van Brug, Catherine, 341
Van Burgh, Madam, 293
Van Cleave, Aaron, 29, 36
  Benjamin, 36
Van Cleaves, 18
Van Corlear, Arent, 36
Van Cortlandt, Annie, 274
  Cornelia, 48, 258, 275
  Gertrude, 258
  Margaret, 254, 333
  Pierre, 278, 343
Van Court, Anise, 346
Van Couwenhoven, Garret Woefertse, 352
  Maritje, 352
Vandam, Rip, 266
Vanderbilt, Cornelius, 75, 85, 164, 178, 270, 357
  Catalyntee, 275, 341
  Denice, 357
  Hendrick, 36
  Jeremiah, 34, 36
  Lena, 355
Vanderhoof, P. P., 228
Vanderveer, Matthew, 336

Van Der Voort, Catrina, 352
Van Deventer, John, 57
Van Dike, F., 361, 362
  Henry Charles, 70, 315
  J. H., 141
Van Ditmarsen, Douwe, 335
  Douwe Jansen, 334
  Jan Jansen, 334
  John, 335
  Peter, 335
Van Doorn, Miss, 231
Van Doorne, Mrs., 231
Van Doren, Jane, 336
  Mill, 213
Van Duersen, A. S., 232
  Dr., 229
  Hendrick, 16, 36, 37, 48
  Staats, 148, 159, 199, 218, 229, 357
  William, 143, 157, 270
Van Dyck, Francis, 36
  Isaac, 37
  John, 27, 36
  Nicholas, 18, 30, 36
Van Dyke, Dr. Frederick, 166
  Frederick, 166
  James C., 166, 239, 324
  John, 154, 168, 171, 200, 240, 201
  Lydia, 166
  Major, 157, 270
Van Emburgh, John, 44, 143
  Major, 128, 284
  Vickers & Taylor, 49
Van Harlingen, Rev., 139
  Edward, 354
  Elizabeth, 336
  Johannes, 48
  John, 53, 351, 361
Van Horn, Ann, 55, 278, 364
  Col. Philip, 92, 125
  Cornelius, 55, 256, 278, 337, 343
  David, 278, 337, 364
  Gerrit, 343
  Gerrit Augustus, 278
  House, 125
  Mary, 50
Van Langvelt, Cornelius, 242, 244-246, 294
  Merritje, Jan, 245
Van Liew, Dennis & Ida, 43, 355
  Elizabeth, 352
  Henry, 150, 151
  Jacques, 354
  Mrs., 227
  Widow, 231
Van Marter, Eyke, 333
Van Metern, Jan, 139
Van Norden, J., Jr., 44
  Jesynthe, 30, 36
  John, 36
  Mr., 210
  Peter, 36
Van Nortwick, C. H., 357
Van Nostrand, Rulef, 232
  Widow, 228
Van Nuis, Jacobus, 36, 111, 120, 215
  James, Jr., 171
  John, 23, 197, 239, 240
  Lyle, 201, 239, 240
Van Nuys, Jan, 43
  Janse Ouckersee, 38, 253
  John, 25, 26, 28, 36, 38, 253-255
Van Orden, John, 18
Van Pelt, Maria, 333

INDEX TO NAMES AND PLACES

Van Rensselaer, Rev. Nicholas, 341, 373
  Johannes, 343
Van Schayck, Annie, 274
  Engeltie, 274
Van Sickle, Ferdinand, 357
  G., 357
Van Syckle, 228
  Mrs., 231
Van Tile, Abraham, 74
Van Tine, Abraham, 356
  Sarah, 340
Van Tuyl & Varrick, 75
  Otto, 75
Van Vecten, Derrick (Dirck), 36, 48, 139
Van Vecten's Bridge, 125
Van Voorhees (Voorhees), A. O., 164, 165
  Abraham, 173
  Altie, 348
  Ann, 353
  B. M. (Adjutant), 157, 231
  & Brower, 328
  & Brown, 208
  Capt. John (Military), 353
  Capt. John (Sea), 112, 283, 285, 286, 319
  Catherine, 283
  Court, 18, 27, 34, 36, 356 (see Koert)
  David, 165. 217
  Eleanor, 347
  Ellen V. D., 338
  Elizabeth, 334
  Family, 257
  Garret G., 175
  Ira C., 165, 166, 173
  Israel H., 175
  Jacob, 44
  Jan, 355, 356
  Johanna, 362
  Johannes, 356, 357
  John, 18, 23, 84, 111, 198, 257, 315, 348, 358, 363
  Ensign John, 111, 112
  John J., 210, 318
  John, Jr., 356
  John M., 357
  John P., 355
  Koert, 355, 356
  Lieut., 269
  & Low, 156
  Lucas, 34, 36, 353, 356, 395
  Lucas (Upon-the-Hill), 36
  Lucresy, 353
  Luke, 356
  Maria, 347
  Martin M., 357
  Martymus, 356
  Mina J., 126
  Minne, 27, 34, 36, 356
  Minne Lucasse, 353
  Misses, 231
  Mr., 112
  Myndert, 112, 116, 318
  Peter, 198, 348, 357
  Capt. Peter, 126, 353
  & Randolph, 235
  Richard, 224, 229, 230
  Roeloff, 355, 356
  Sarah, 340
  Stephen Coerte, 352
  Widow, 116, 261, 262
Van Vorst, Cornelius, 77, 84

Van Wickle, Ann, 264, 352
  Captain, 180
  Evart, 352
Van Wyckelyn, Evart, 351
Varick, Mr., 84
Varleth, Jane, 253, 333
  Julia, 333
  Nicholas, 253, 333
Varrick, Van Tuyle &, 75
Vaughn, General, 119, 122
Vedder, Isaac, 336
Vernon, Nehemiah, 49, 52, 355, 359, 361
VerPlanck, Catalyntie, 347
  G., 362
Vetch, Alida, 278, 343
  Gov. Samuel, 278
Vickers, Joseph, 48, 49, 50, 52, 358, 360
  Lucia, 262, 360
  Mary, 49, 50, 360
  Sarah, 50
  Thomas L., 49, 50
Voorhees (see Van Voorhees)
Vredenburgh, John, 210
  Peter, 36, 361, 362
  Petrus, 347, 361
  Widow, 230
Vreeland, Enoch, 17, 18, 19, 22, 25, 26, 41, 248, 249, 253

Wades, Robert, 291
Waldron, John, 173, 362
  Machine Shop, 239
Waldy, Henry, 87
Wales, Rev. Mr., 296
Walker, Samuel, 153
  Sarah, 49
  Theodore, 16
Wall, Elizabeth, 336
  Garret D., 215, 219
Wallace, Joshua M., 281
  Sarah, 359
  William, 362
Waller, William, 74
Walmseys, Fred., 33
  William, 36
Walton, Mary, 267
Ward, Gov. Samuel (of R. I.), 100
  Henry, 100
  Hermanus, 362
Wardell, Eliakim, 290
Wards by second Charter, 37
  Census of, 198
  Six, 158
Warne, Marinus Willet, 52
  Thomas, 12
Willet, 49, 52
Warner, Edward, 212
Warren, Gen. Joseph, 137
  Mary Hude, 338
Wase, James, 212
Washington, Gen. George, 46, 115, 118, 119, 122, 124, 133, 257, 259, 268, 281, 285, 319, 320
  Mrs., 248
  Rock, 121
Washington's Headquarters, 116, 119, 124, 284
Water Street, 25, 30, 49
Watkins, Hezekiah, 192
Watson, John, 74
  Luke, 10
Watt, Robert, 198
Wayne, General, 124

INDEX TO NAMES AND PLACES

Webb, Abraham, 71
  Moses F., 169
Webster, Daniel, 218, 219
  Robert, 346
Weekly Monitor, 194
Wells, James, 71, 72
  Rev. Ransford, 339
  Thomas L., 264, 352
West, William, 11
Westminster, 47
Weston, Hercules, 359
Weston's Mill Pond, 23
  School, No. 12, 205
Wetherbee, John, 346
Wetherill, Ann, 361
  Colonel, 319
  George, 16, 37
  John, 36, 93, 111, 316, 360, 364, 365
  Vincent, 360
Weyman, 190, 192
Whaling, 127
Wheeler, Mr., 295
White, Anthony, 23, 34, 48, 49, 129, 259, 260, 267, 359, 363
  Anthony Walton, 130, 260, 359
  Bishop, 282
  Canvas, 214, 215, 217, 219, 221
  Euphemia, 130, 259, 359
  Family, 129
  House Farm, 130
  Hugh, 358
  Isabella, 130, 359
  Joanna, 130, 254, 359
  Johanna, 332
  John, 128
  Leonard, 129
  Mary, 240
  Mr. & Co., 295
  Mrs., 51
  Samuel, 100
Whitefield, Mr., 43, 249
Whitehall Slip, N. Y., 70, 71
Whitehead, W. A., 189
Whitlock, Cornelius, 229
  Sarah, 340
Whitwell, Lucie C., 189
Wicks, John, 197
Wiggery, John, 71
Wilber, 355
Wilcox, Moses, 357, 358, 360
  Thomas, 11
Wilcox's Lane, 23
Wiley, John, 356
Wilkes, Charles, 363
Wilkins, Rev. Isaac, 267
Willemse, Laurens, 42
Willets, Frances, 336
  Isaac, 267
  Thomas, 336
Willett, Marinus, 103
Williams, Elizabeth, 29, 36
  Joseph, 53
  Mr., 231
Williamson, D. D., 199, 352
  Eleanor, 348
  Family, 353
  General, 118
  Garret, 353
  Gov. Isaac H., 270
  Helena, 45
  John, 51
  Laurens, 42
  Lawrence, 18, 27, 30, 34, 36
  Mrs., 181
  Nicholas, 335, 352, 353
  William, 27, 34, 36, 353
Willis, John, 82
Willocks, George, 14
  William, 256
Willson, William, 68
Wilson, George, 228
  Hendrick, 132
  James Grant, 248
  Robert, 133
Winant, Dr., 83
Windfalls, 17
Witherspoon, Dr. John, 161
Wolland, John, 63
Women's College, 131, 357
Wood, Alice, 347
  Edward, 154, 165, 175, 347
  George, 216, 218
  James, 216
  Rev. William, 45
Woodbridge, 10, 11, 15, 19, 20, 26, 34, 121, 293, 294
  Population of, 16
Woodbury, Isaac B., 185
Woodhull, Dr. John, 56, 214
Woods, Daniel, 179
Woodsworth, R. N., 173
Worthington, John, 59
Wright, Benjamin, 214
  E. B., 206, 326
  Engineer, 215
  Joseph, 14
  Joshua, 159
  & Ormiston, 14
  Samuel G., 221
  Savage, 347
  Thomas, 36
Wrights, William, 240
Wurtz, (Canal Commissioner), 214
Wyckoff, Anti, 352
  J. P., 225
  Jacob, 228
  John V. M., 171
  Nathaniel, 215
  Nicholas, 150, 231
  P. M., 205, 325
  Peter, 197, 240, 263, 355
  Peter N., 60, 200
  Peter P., 359
Wylee, John, 36
Wylly, Alexander, 100
Wyser, Jacob, 36

Yale College, 190
Yeates, Joseph, 66
York, Duke of, 250
  Road, 80
Young & Grummond, 83
  William, 44
Y. M. C. A. (1858), 210, 240

Zabriskie, James C., 167, 239
  Peter, 139
Zenger, John Peter, 98

www.ingramcontent.com/pod-product-compliance
Lightning Source LLC
Chambersburg PA
CBHW072130220426
43664CB00013B/2199